MOON HANDBOOKS®

COASTAL OREGON

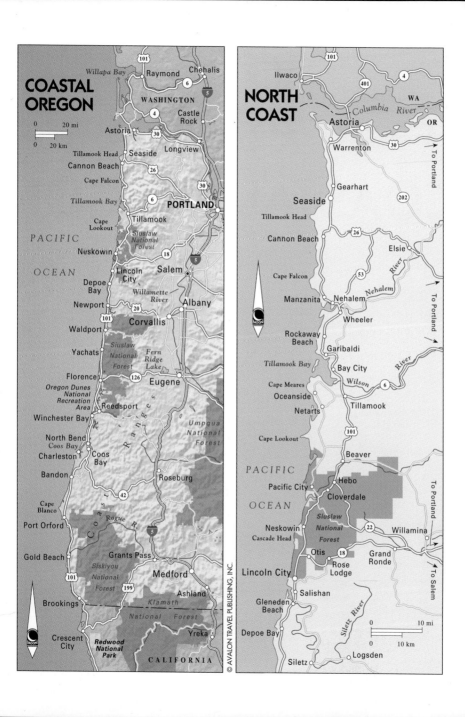

COASTAL OREGON

NORTH COAST

© AVALON TRAVEL PUBLISHING, INC.

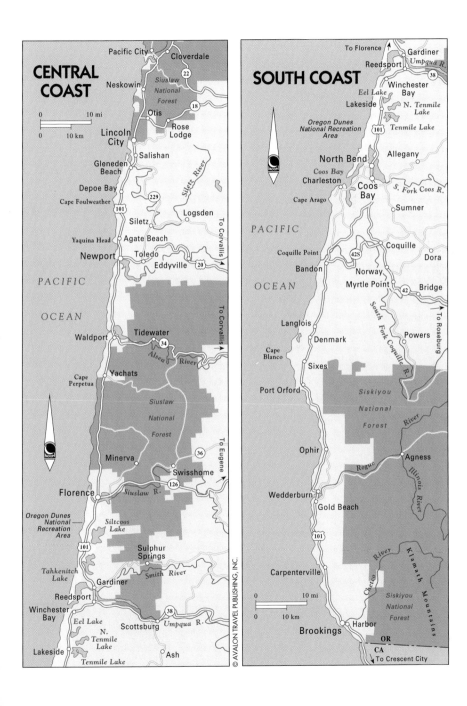

CENTRAL COAST

SOUTH COAST

Pacific City
Cloverdale
22
Neskowin
Siuslaw National Forest
18
Otis
Rose Lodge
Lincoln City
Salishan
Gleneden Beach
Depoe Bay
Cape Foulweather
101
229
Siletz River
Siletz
Logsden
Yaquina Head
Agate Beach
Newport
Toledo
Eddyville
20
To Corvallis

PACIFIC

OCEAN

Waldport
Tidewater
34
Alsea River
Cape Perpetua
Yachats
To Corvallis

Siuslaw National Forest

Minerva
36
Swisshome
126
To Eugene
Florence
Siuslaw R.

Oregon Dunes National Recreation Area
Siltcoos Lake
101
Sulphur Springs
Tahkenitch Lake
Gardiner
Smith River
Reedsport
Winchester Bay
38
Eel Lake
N. Tenmile Lake
Scottsburg
Umpqua R.
Lakeside
Tenmile Lake
Ash

To Florence
Gardiner
Reedsport
Umpqua R.
38
Winchester Bay
Eel Lake
Lakeside
N. Tenmile Lake
Oregon Dunes National Recreation Area
101
Tenmile Lake
North Bend
Allegany
Coos Bay
Charleston
Coos Bay
S. Fork Coos R.
Cape Arago
Sumner

PACIFIC

Coquille
Coquille Point
42S
Dora
Bandon
Norway
OCEAN
Myrtle Point
42
Bridge

Langlois
Denmark
Powers
South Fork Coquille R.
To Roseburg
Cape Blanco
Sixes

Siskiyou National Forest
Port Orford
River
Ophir
Rogue
Agness
Wedderburn
Illinois River
Gold Beach
101
Carpenterville
Chetco River
Klamath Mountains
Siskiyou National Forest
Brookings
Harbor
OR
CA
To Crescent City

0   10 mi
0   10 km

© AVALON TRAVEL PUBLISHING, INC.

MOON HANDBOOKS®
COASTAL OREGON

FIRST EDITION

ELIZABETH & MARK MORRIS

AVALON
TRAVEL

MAPS

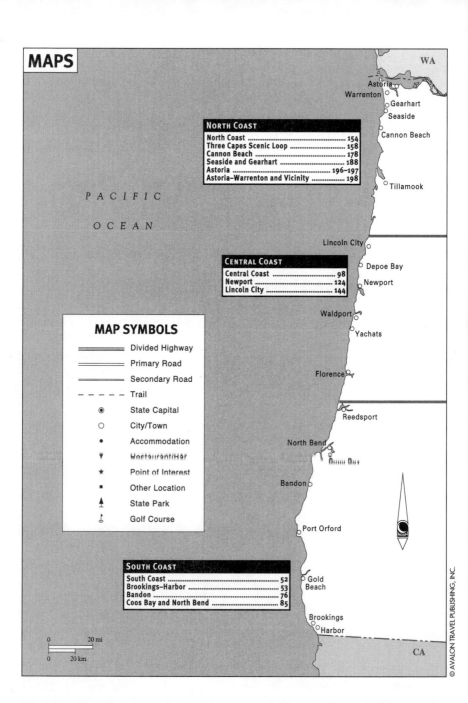

WA

PACIFIC

OCEAN

NORTH COAST

North Coast 154
Three Capes Scenic Loop 158
Cannon Beach 178
Seaside and Gearhart 188
Astoria 196–197
Astoria–Warrenton and Vicinity 198

CENTRAL COAST

Central Coast 98
Newport 124
Lincoln City 144

MAP SYMBOLS

══════════	Divided Highway
════════	Primary Road
────────	Secondary Road
– – – – –	Trail
◉	State Capital
○	City/Town
•	Accommodation
▼	Restaurant/Bar
★	Point of Interest
■	Other Location
▲	State Park
⚲	Golf Course

Astoria
Warrenton
Gearhart
Seaside
Cannon Beach
Tillamook
Lincoln City
Depoe Bay
Newport
Waldport
Yachats
Florence
Reedsport
North Bend
Coos Bay
Bandon
Port Orford

SOUTH COAST

South Coast 52
Brookings–Harbor 53
Bandon 76
Coos Bay and North Bend 85

Gold
Beach
Brookings
Harbor

CA

0   20 mi
0   20 km

Contents

Introduction 1

The meeting of land and sea is nowhere so dramatic as along the 360-mile stretch from the mouth of the Columbia River to the redwood forests at the California border. Linked by an unbroken scenic highway, each part of the Oregon coast possesses a distinct regional flavor that has attracted visitors for centuries—to explore, to enjoy, to escape.

The Land **2;** Flora and Fauna **7;** History **16**

On the Road 20

Need a hand in your quest for the perfect day hike, scenic driving tour, seaside village, or secret spot to land a chinook salmon for tonight's dinner? All the details for planning your coastal getaway are here.

Recreation **21;** Accommodations and Food **34;** Information and Services **39;**
Health and Safety **42;** Transportation **45**

South Coast **50**

Far from the populous interior valleys, the southern region amply rewards travelers with the fairest weather on the coast. Cast a line into one of a half dozen wild rivers, book a tee time at the famed Bandon Dunes, and investigate the rocky garden of sea stacks and islets that host countless flocks of pelagic birds.

BROOKINGS-HARBOR AND VICINITY 51
GOLD BEACH AND VICINITY 62
PORT ORFORD AND VICINITY 70
BANDON AND VICINITY 75
THE BAY AREA: CHARLESTON, COOS BAY, NORTH BEND 84

Central Coast **96**

The wide-ranging contrasts of the central coast satisfy all kinds of adventurers: If you're a hiker or horseback rider, head south to the 32,000-acre Oregon Dunes National Recreation Area; if you're a sportfisher eager to tackle a brawny Umpqua River sturgeon, try Winchester Bay; and if you're a history buff, catch a glimpse of the bygone riverboat era in Florence's restored Old Town.

REEDSPORT/WINCHESTER BAY AND VICINITY 97
FLORENCE AND VICINITY 103
YACHATS AND VICINITY 113
WALDPORT AND VICINITY 120
NEWPORT AND VICINITY 123
DEPOE BAY AND VICINITY 137
LINCOLN CITY AND VICINITY 143

North Coast  153

Cyclists and motorists will find plenty of open road along the lush north coast. The Three Capes Scenic Loop wends its way from Pacific City, where commercial fishing dories launch into the surf, to the spectacular viewpoints and bird-watching at Capes Lookout and Meares. And don't forget to stop in Tillamook for your cheese fix!

NESKOWIN AND CASCADE HEAD 155

THREE CAPES SCENIC LOOP 157
    Cape Kiwanda; Pacific City; Cape Lookout; Cape Meares; Netarts;
    Oceanside; Cape Meares Scenic Viewpoint

TILLAMOOK AND THE TILLAMOOK BAY AREA 164
    Bay City; Garibaldi; Rockaway Beach

NEHALEM BAY AREA 171
    Wheeler; Nehalem; Manzanita and Vicinity

CANNON BEACH AND VICINITY 177

SEASIDE AND GEARHART 187

ASTORIA AND VICINITY 195

Resources 217

SUGGESTED READING 218

INTERNET RESOURCES 220

INDEX 222

ABOUT THE AUTHORS
Elizabeth and Mark Morris

© MARK MORRIS

Mark and Elizabeth Morris first became involved in travel writing while working as editors at Moon Publications, when the original Handbook series was produced in two crowded rooms of the publisher's Northern California office. In those days, the text was set an agonizing 13 picas at a time on a clunky old Linotronic typesetter, and laying out a guidebook called for more hot wax than a beauty salon needs in a month.

Mark made the transition from travel editor to writer with his first book, *Odyssey Illustrated Guide to Ireland.* Elizabeth took up the post of managing editor at Moon, and worked for a time in Hong Kong at Moon's former affiliate, China Guides.

Mark continued to pursue his passion for coastal destinations by writing the first edition of *Moon Handbooks Atlantic Canada.* Their love of the Pacific Northwest led Elizabeth and Mark to settle in Portland and begin their extensive explorations of the region. Together, they wrote the first edition of *Oregon Coast Best Places.*

In the early years of the Internet boom, the pair caught the attention of a little Seattle-based company called Microsoft Corp. Mark was hired to manage travel-content development for what would become Expedia.com, a leading online travel website, while Elizabeth became managing editor for Microsoft's popular mapping and route-planning products. Thrilling as 70-hour work weeks and commuting in Seattle traffic were, after seven years Elizabeth and Mark left the software giant to return to the less hectic life of full-time travel writing.

Having come full circle, Elizabeth and Mark are delighted to be back exploring the Oregon coast, now accompanied by two small but highly opinionated passengers in car seats, on a quest to discover the chunkiest bowl of chowder, the coziest bed-and-breakfast, and the most perfect beach.

They sincerely hope the search never ends.

For Fiona and Eamon,
who can finally go to the beach now that this book is done.

Introduction

The Oregon coast is one of those blessed corners of the earth where you come upon fresh scenes of wonder at every turn. In few other places is the meeting of land and sea so dramatic and beautiful as along this 360-mile stretch from the mouth of the Columbia River to the redwood forests at the California border. Here at the far western skirt of the continent, nature has found an expansive stage on which to act out the full range of its varied and ceaseless dramas, from the microcosm of a tidepool to the ferocious storms that make first landfall here, walloping the headlands and beaches with their full might.

The visitor here can find as intense a solitude as he or she might desire, in company of only the mewing seabirds, and experience firsthand why residents refer to this coast as The Edge. The comforts of civilization and human company are close by in an inviting string of towns and villages, each with its own character and charms, from the resurgent Victorian hospitality of Astoria to the family-friendly resort attractions of Seaside, and the understated sophistication of Cannon Beach to the hard-working fishing harbor of Newport.

Although part of a seamless whole, sharing a common shoreline and linked by an unbroken

Newport harbor

© MARK MORRIS

scenic highway, each part of the coast possesses a distinct regional flavor and allure that have attracted visitors for centuries—to explore, to exploit, to enjoy, to escape. Feeling far from everything, the south coast is a world apart, a landscape of mountains cloaked by dense evergreen forest, parting to reveal wild rivers and black-sand beaches punctuated with dramatic rock formations. Much of the central coast is Dune Country, an otherworldly sandscape dotted with lakes and bisected by broad, lazy estuaries. In the north—journey's end for Lewis and Clark—steep headlands break up wide, sandy beaches, extending to the state's far northwestern tip at the mouth of the Columbia River.

The Land

The Oregon coast we know today encompasses nearly 400 miles of beaches, rainforest, dunes, high-rise headlands, rocky seastacks and islands, and tidal pools showcasing marine worlds in miniature. The narrow coastal plateau is hemmed in by the Klamath Mountains in the state's southern quarter and by the Coast Range beginning near Coos Bay in the north, which together form a palisade between the sea and the state's interior. Neither range is particularly high; the tallest peaks in each of these cordilleras barely top 4,000 feet. More than a dozen major rivers and scores of smaller streams cut through these mountain barriers to the sea. The valleys that the rivers follow through the mountains are the same routes traversed now by the east-west highways that link the coast with the rest of the state.

Tectonics

Timeless as it may appear to the modern observer, the Oregon coast hasn't always been where or as we see it today. Titanic forces shaped—and continue to affect—this coastal region and indeed the entire Pacific Northwest. The giant tectonic plates that make up the earth's crust slide under one another as they collide. In Pacific Northwest coastal regions, this takes place when the Juan de Fuca plate's marine layer is subducted, or pushed under, the continental North American plate. The stress of this collision heaved up the Klamath Mountains some 225 million years ago, and created the Coast Range 20–50 million years ago. This subduction is ongoing, and the resulting geologic pressure that builds from it is released periodically is earthquakes, large and small.

With virtually every part of the state possessing seismic potential that hasn't been released in many years, the pressure along the fault lines is increasing. In 1990, scientists unearthed discontinuities in rock strata and tree rings on the north Oregon coast, indicating that Tillamook County has experienced major tremors every several hundred years. They estimate that the next one could come within our lifetimes and be of significant magnitude. In coastal areas, one of the greatest dangers associated with earthquakes is the possibility of **tsunamis,** popularly (but incorrectly) known as tidal waves.

The ocean waves produced by seismic activity can be enormous and devastating. Ever since a tsunami unleashed by Alaska's Good Friday quake in 1964 (measured at 14.2 feet high at the mouth of the Umpqua River) resulted in four casualties in Beverly Beach and more than $1 million in damage, local authorities have made seismic preparedness a priority.

Along the coast today, warning sirens stand ready. Visitors will also see blue evacuation signs pointing the way to higher ground and escape routes, acknowledging the imminent danger of a 30-foot wave that could strike within minutes of an offshore temblor.

Ice and Fire

At the height of the most recent major glaciation, sea level of the world's oceans was some 300–500 feet lower than it is now. North America and Asia were connected by a land bridge across the Bering Strait. The Oregon seashore lay miles west of where it is now, and the Columbia Gorge extended out past present-day Astoria.

As the glaciers melted, the sea rose. When that glacial epoch's final meltdown 12,000 years ago unleashed water dammed up by thick ice, great rivers were spawned and existing channels were enlarged. A particularly large inundation was the Missoula Flood, which began with an ice dam breaking up in present-day Montana. Before it subsided, it carved out the contours of what are now the Columbia River Gorge and the Willamette Valley. Other glacial floodwaters found their outlet westward to the sea, flushing out silt-ridden estuaries in the process. Pacific wave action eventually washed this debris back up onto the land, creating beaches and sand dunes.

Like the rest of the state, the Oregon coast also shows off distinct remnants of Oregon's volcanic past. The offshore waters are scattered with 1,477 volcanic islets. These rocky outcrops, as well as many of the headlands that separate the beaches, are made of erosion-resistant basalt, an extremely durable igneous material that has endured long after wind and waves have eroded away the softer surrounding earth.

The Beach: Contours and Character

For most Oregon visitors who travel west of the Coast Range, life is a beach. Despite Pacific temperatures cold enough to render swimming an at-your-own-risk activity, the cliffside ocean vistas, wildlife, beachcombing, and other attractions make the coast the state's number-one regional destination.

With rare exceptions, all beaches in Oregon below mean high tide are owned by the public. This is thanks largely to Governor Oswald West, who in 1913 pushed through legislation defining Oregon's ocean beaches as public highways (which they in fact were before real roads were built) and thus off-limits to private encroachment. Later, Oregon's Beach Bills of 1967 and 1972 were written to further guarantee public access to the state's gem of a coastline. In recent years, however, certain sections of this publicly owned paradise have increasingly become exclusive bailiwicks of the wealthy, with gated communities cutting off access to the beaches.

Black sand, high in iron and other metals, is common on the coast, particularly south of

SPRING CLEANING ON THE OREGON COAST

Each year in early April, thousands of volunteers converge on the Oregon coast for a day of picking up litter on the beaches. This one-day event makes a big difference: In spring 2003, 4,300 volunteers hauled off more than 30 tons of trash—cans, plastic bottles, glass, tires, you name it—from Oregon's beaches. Since the nation's first beach cleanup was held in Oregon in 1984, annual beach cleanups have spread to every state and to more than 100 countries around the world.

Oregon's annual Beach Cleanup, coordinated by the Oregon Parks and Recreation Department and a nonprofit organization called SOLV, is a great way to show you care for the coast. To get involved, look for details at the SOLV website (www.solv.org), or call them at 800/333-SOLV.

Coos Bay. There was also enough gold in the black sands to spur a flurry of gold-mining activity on the south coast 140 years ago. Scientists have known for decades of the placer deposits of heavy minerals washed ashore on prehistoric beaches thousands of years ago when ocean levels were much lower. These beach sands now lie submerged. These days, mining companies are eyeing the continental shelf off the south coast for possible exploitation of ilmenite, magnetite, chromite, zircon, garnet, gold, and platinum. Despite a study indicating a significant presence of precious metals in the sands offshore from the Rogue River and Cape Blanco, incipient prospecting ventures were abandoned.

Speaking of sand, the central Oregon coast has about 32,000 acres of shimmering white **dunes,** the largest oceanfront collection in North America and the highest in the world. Some hills top out at more than 500 feet high. Oregon's Sahara is located along a 40-mile stretch between Coos Bay and Florence. Buffeted by winds, the dunes are continually on the move; in some places, highways are in danger of being engulfed by the shifting sands.

CLIMATE

Oregon's location equidistant from the equator and the North Pole subjects the state to weather from both tropical and polar air flows. This makes for a pattern of changeability in which calm often alternates with storm. Although it's difficult to predict daily weather patterns in western Oregon, there are definite seasonal climatic shifts here. In winter, arctic and tropical air masses collide over the Pacific, producing much of the state's rain. During summer, the clashes are much less frequent. At that time, Oregon weather is most affected by Pacific Ocean temperatures and air pressure differences between inland and coastal areas.

Oregon's coastal weather can best be summed up as wet and mild. As the weather chart for selected towns shows (see sidebar), the coast as a whole receives roughly 70 inches of rain yearly on average. Most of that falls from late fall to mid-spring, whereas May through September are generally fairly dry.

Lincoln City and vicinity tend to record the

COASTAL WEATHER

City	Jan.	Feb.	Mar.	Apr.	May	June	July	Aug.	Sept.	Oct.	Nov.	Dec.	*A.A.R.
Astoria													
Hi (°F)	48	51	53	56	60	64	67	68	68	61	53	48	
Lo (°F)	37	38	39	41	45	50	53	53	50	44	40	37	
Rain (inches)	9.6	7.9	7.4	4.9	3.3	2.6	1.2	1.2	2.6	5.6	10.5	10.4	67.2
Brookings													
Hi (°F)	55	56	58	60	63	67	68	68	68	65	58	55	
Lo (°F)	42	42	42	44	47	50	52	53	51	48	45	41	
Rain (inches)	11.3	10.1	9.6	5.7	3.6	1.8	0.5	1	1.9	5.2	10.6	12	73.3
Cannon Beach													
Hi (°F)	52	54	56	58	62	65	68	69	70	64	56	52	
Lo (°F)	38	39	40	42	46	50	53	53	50	46	42	38	
Rain (inches)	10.3	9.6	8.4	5.7	3.9	3	1.6	1.3	3	6.1	11.4	11.3	75.6
Coos Bay													
Hi (°F)	53	55	55	57	61	64	67	68	67	63	57	53	
Lo (°F)	39	41	41	43	47	50	53	53	50	46	43	39	
Rain (inches)	9.5	8.1	7.9	5.2	3.4	1.7	0.5	0.9	1.7	4.6	10.4	10.4	64.3
Florence													
Hi (°F)	51	54	56	59	63	67	69	70	70	63	55	50	
Lo (°F)	36	38	39	41	44	48	50	51	49	45	41	37	
Rain (inches)	10.8	9.3	9	5.2	3.8	2.5	0.9	1.1	2.3	5.3	10.8	12	73

highest amounts of rain, with nearly 100 inches per year, while towns both north and south are generally less wet by comparison. Coastbound travelers should bear in mind that inland from the coastal plateau, the Coast and Klamath ranges receive substantially more precipitation because as moisture-laden westerlies blow in from the Pacific, they slam into the mountain slopes and are pushed upward. As the clouds climb higher, they drop their moisture in the form of rain or snow because rising air cools, and cooler air can't hold as much moisture as warm air. As a conse-quence, precipitation averages 150 inches over the coastal mountains (in the winter of 1996–1997, Laurel Mountain, in the Coast Range near Lincoln City, was drenched with 204 inches, Oregon's record). Anyone driving through the Coast Range sees evidence of the siege mentality that sets in with each winter monsoon season. Giant satellite-TV dishes and stacks of covered firewood are common lawn ornaments here in the rainiest part of the state.

The moderating influence of the Pacific Ocean gives the coastal region an unusually mild climate

													* Average Annual Rainfall
City	Jan.	Feb.	Mar.	Apr.	May	June	July	Aug.	Sept.	Oct.	Nov.	Dec.	*A.A.R.
Gold Beach													
Hi (°F)	55	56	57	59	62	65	68	69	68	65	58	55	
Lo (°F)	41	41	42	43	46	49	51	52	51	47	43	41	
Rain (inches)	11.7	11	10.7	6.5	3.9	1.9	0.5	1.1	2.2	5	11.8	13.3	85.6
Lincoln City													
Hi (°F)	47	51	55	58	62	66	70	72	70	62	52	47	
Lo (°F)	37	38	39	41	44	48	51	51	49	45	40	37	
Rain (inches)	14.1	11.8	10.8	7.2	5.6	3.7	1.7	1.7	3.8	7.6	14.6	15.8	98.4
Newport													
Hi (°F)	51	54	55	57	60	63	65	66	65	61	55	51	
Lo (°F)	39	39	40	41	45	48	51	51	49	45	42	39	
Rain (inches)	10.3	8.7	7.7	4.9	3.7	2.7	1	1	2.4	5.1	10.7	11.4	69.6
Port Orford													
Hi (°F)	53	55	55	57	61	64	67	68	68	63	57	53	
Lo (°F)	39	41	41	43	46	50	53	53	51	47	43	40	
Rain (inches)	11.4	9.6	9.7	5.8	3.9	2.1	0.6	1.2	2	4.9	10.9	12.2	74.3
Tillamook													
Hi (°F)	50	53	54	57	60	64	67	68	69	62	54	50	
Lo (°F)	36	37	37	39	43	47	50	50	47	42	39	36	
Rain (inches)	13.1	10.8	10	6.8	4.8	3.4	1.6	1.4	3.7	7.2	13.7	14	90.5

for a state so far north. Coastal temperatures are fairly constant throughout the year, and extremes are rare. With infrequent freezes and rarely recorded snowfall, Old Man Winter definitely pulls his punches here. In fact, Coos Bay, for example, is often touted as having one of the mildest (in terms of absence of extremes) year-round climates in the United States. Even in winter, daytime highs along the coast tend to reach the mid-50s Fahrenheit, and nighttime lows generally drop into the 40s. Spring, summer, and fall see highs in the 60s and into the 70s, with overnight lows staying in the mid-40s to mid-50s. Summer highs above 90°F are unusual, although the mercury in south coast locations such as Brookings and Bandon has topped 100°F on rare occasions. Midwinter and spring dry spells with 60°-plus temperatures commonly occur.

Any time of year, the coast can be fairly breezy; particularly in winter and spring, you may encounter proper gales scouring the beach. Although that can make for terrific kite-flying, picnics aren't quite so much fun at those times. In winter, the winds typically blow from the south and southwest, whereas the gentler summer winds usually come from the northeast.

When to Go

In general, count on good traveling weather mid-April through mid-September, with a preponderance of daytime highs in the 60s. Within this period, there might be enough cloudy days to dismay travelers who are accustomed to simmering California beaches, but storm-watching is an acquired taste that makes the Oregon coast attractive when the weather turns nasty. An added plus is that when summertime inversions drive temperatures above 100°F east of the Coast Range, the heat draws cooler maritime air to the shore. The mountains often lock in these welcome fronts, although they can also cause coastal fog and overcast conditions to linger. Nonetheless, respite from the characteristic morning fog banks in summer is often only minutes away upriver along one of the many tidal estuaries. As a general rule, September is the most reliable month for clear coastal weather.

Here's a little tip for those looking to take advantage of midwinter lulls in the gray wetness that hangs over much of western Oregon. Should you be inland during a rainy spell, keep an eye on satellite photos on TV or in the paper. By the time a major storm reaches the interior, there is often a respite between fronts at the coast. By anticipating the approach of a "blue hole," you can time your visit to coincide with the arrival of clear weather, short-lived as it may be.

Finally, newcomers to the region at any time of year should know that the icy temperatures of the coastal waters (as low as 40–45°F) make the beaches more valued for beachcombing than for swimming. Even in the hottest days of summer, water temperature doesn't exceed 62°F, and hypothermia is an ever-present danger that sometimes kills. Ironically, 20–30 miles offshore, the warming effects of the Kuroshio current, bringing up water from the equatorial region of the western Pacific Ocean, create subtropical conditions.

All of this information, however, is of course subject to contradiction without warning by Mother Nature. When planning your coast getaway, it's helpful to remember the local adage: "Little boys who tell lies grow up to be Oregon weathermen."

Flora and Fauna

FLORA

The state of Oregon has long been associated in the public mind with such sobriquets as the Emerald Empire and the Chlorophyll Commonwealth. Although giant conifers and a profuse understory of greenery do in fact predominate, this ecosystem represents only the most visible part of the Oregon coast's bountiful botany. In addition to Brookings' Azalea Festival and Florence's Rhododendron Festival, coast-bound travelers come to take in such horticultural highlights as the insect-eating Darlingtonia plant, Oregon myrtle trees, and some remaining stands of ancient old-growth forest. Serious botanists might search out the pine mushroom, exclusive to the Oregon dunes and Japan, or probe the Kalmiopsis Wilderness near the south coast, habitat to many rare plants.

Skunk cabbage, with its bright yellow hood and enormous, paddle-shaped leaves, is a common sight in wet areas along the coast in spring.

Coos Bay marks the boundary between the Mediterranean beach floras found south of California and the subarctic species growing north from there into Washington and British Columbia.

Trees

Sandwiched between the mountains and the sea, the mixed-conifer ecosystem of western Oregon's wet lowlands, comprising primarily fir, western hemlock, Sitka spruce, and cedar, is the most productive belt of evergreens in the world. The conifers are broken up by pockets of alder, oak, vine maple, bigleaf maple, and myrtle trees. With its dense understory of rhododendron, thimbleberry, salmonberry, blackberry, and salal interspersed among the ferns and mosses that carpet the forest floor, this woodland carries up to 1,000 tons of plant matter per hectare and sometimes more. Because of the construction industry's penchant for Douglas fir *(Pseudotsuga menziesii),* which they replant assiduously, this tree predominates.

Oregon schoolchildren first learn to distinguish between fir, spruce, and hemlock by a mnemonic device: The needles of a fir are flat, flexible, and friendly. Spruce needles are square, stiff, and will stick you. Hemlock needles have a hammocklike configuration, and the crown of the tree is curved like it's tipping its hat. *Trees to Know in Oregon,* published by the Oregon State University Extension Service in Corvallis, is an excellent aid to tree identification, as well as a compendium of useful facts.

Oregon myrtles *(Umbellularia californica),* the only tree in its genus, is native only to the Holy Land, southern Oregon, and northern California (where it's more commonly known as California laurel or California bay). The hard, yellowish wood of the aromatic myrtle tree is so dense that when green it sinks in water. It is prized by woodworkers and especially woodturners for its distinctive coloring and grain. The value of myrtlewood, in fact, reached a peak during the Depression, when North Bend issued myrtlewood

INTRODUCTION

© MARK MORRIS

In early spring, trilliums bloom in shaded forest groves.

script, in the form of coins ranging from $.50 to $10, after the only bank in town failed.

Among these coastal forests, several extraordinary individual trees have managed to survive the ax and chainsaw, and the region boasts such record specimens as the 329-foot-high, 11.5-foot-diameter Doerner fir in the Coast Range outside Coquille, rated the nation's largest Douglas fir by the American Forestry Association based on height, diameter, and crown size. The world's biggest Sitka spruce grows off U.S. 26 near Cannon Beach, and the world's largest Monterey cypress is found in Brookings.

Dune, Beach, and Bog

Apart from the spectacular springtime fireworks of rhododendron and azalea blossoms, the Oregon coast doesn't show off its **wildflowers** as boldly as other parts of the state, such as Steens Mountain, the Cascades, and the Wallowas. The flowering plants of beach, dunes, and headlands tend to be more subtle, but are nevertheless varied and worth seeking out. Among some of the species found only along the Oregon coast are beach bursage, yellow sand verbena, beach evening-primrose, seashore bluegrass, dune tansy,

and silvery phacelia. The best time for wildflowers is usually June and July. An excellent guide for those interested in coastal wildflowers is *Introduction to Shore Wildflowers of California, Oregon, and Washington,* published by the University of California Press.

Many coastal travelers will notice **European beachgrass** (*Ammophila arenaria*) covering the sand wherever they go. Originally planted in the 1930s to inhibit dune growth, the thick, rapidly spreading grass worked too well, solidifying into a ridge behind the shoreline, blocking the wind-blown sand from replenishing the rest of the beach and suppressing native plants. Populations of formerly common natives such as beach morning-glory, yellow abronia, gray beach pea, and American dune-grass are now much diminished. The now-endangered pink sand verbena—once abundant along the coast from British Columbia to northern California—is now restricted to a few locations along the central and southern Oregon coast. Herbicides, burning, and tilling have been employed in recent years to remove European beachgrass and restore the dune ecosystem to a more natural state, but progress against the pernicious weed is slow and difficult.

Freshwater wetlands and bogs, created where water is trapped by the sprawling sand dunes along the central coast, provide habitats for some unusual species. Best known among these is the cobra lily (*Darlingtonia californica*), which can be viewed up close at Darlingtonia State Natural Site just north of Florence. Also called Darlingtonia or pitcher plant, this carnivorous bog dweller survives on hapless insects lured into a specialized chamber, where they are trapped and digested. For more information, see Darlingtonia Wayside in the Florence and Vicinity section of the Central Coast chapter.

Coastal salt marshes, occurring in the upper intertidal zones of coastal bays and estuaries, have been dramatically reduced because of land reclamation projects such as drainage, diking, and other human disturbances. The halophytes (salt-loving plants) that thrive in this specialized environment include pickleweed, saltgrass, fleshy jaumea, salt marsh dodder, arrow-grass, sand spurrey, and seaside plantain. For an excellent introduction to this complex ecosystem, visit the South Slough National Estuarine Research Reserve, south of Coos Bay (see the Bay Area section of the South Coast chapter). Bandon Marsh National Wildlife Refuge (see Bandon and Vicinity in the South Coast chapter) protects the largest remaining tract of salt marsh within the Coquille River estuary. Major habitats include undisturbed saltmarsh, mudflat, and Sitka spruce and alder riparian communities, which provide resting and feeding areas for migratory waterfowl, shore and wading birds, and raptors.

Mushrooms

Autumn is the season for those who covet chanterelle, matsutake, and morel mushrooms, particularly from the first rains until the onset of frosts. The Coast Range from September to November is the prime picking area for chanterelles—a fluted orange or yellow mushroom in the tall second-growth Douglas fir forests. If you plan to sell what you find, you need to purchase a permit from the National Forest Service for a nominal fee. Of course, you should be absolutely certain of any wild mushroom's identity before you eat it.

In recent years, fungus fever reached epidemic proportions, largely because of a matsutake mushroom shortage in Japan, where it is prized for medicinal and spiritual qualities and enjoyed as a soup garnish. In the mid-1990s, for example, matsutakes fetched up to $500 per pound in Japan, a price that precipitated violence in northern Klamath County forests and other areas that were saturated with pickers during the fall harvest. This mycological harvest, along with the cutting of ferns (maidenhair ferns command an especially high price from florists), beargrass, and other ornamental greenery, helps many residents of forest communities make ends meet.

FAUNA

The animal kingdom is well represented by a great diversity and abundance of creatures along the coast, in the air, on the land, under the water, and in between. Opportunities for wildlife viewing abound all along the coast, but standout areas

include the state's six coastal national wildlife refuges: Oregon Islands, Cape Meares, and Three Arch Rocks protect important habitat for seabirds, seals, and sea lions among coastal rocks, reefs, islands, and several headland areas, while Nestucca Bay, Siletz Bay, and Bandon Marsh national wildlife refuges preserve estuarine habitats of saltmarsh, wetlands, and woods rich in waterfowl, raptors, fish, and other fauna. *The Audubon Guide to the National Wildlife Refuges: Alaska and the Northwest* is an excellent reference book to have along on your explorations.

Tidepools

For most visitors, the most fascinating coastal ecosystems in Oregon are the rocky tidepools. These Technicolor windows offer an up-close look at one of the richest—and harshest—environments, the intertidal zone, where pummeling surf, unflinching sun, and the cycle of tides demand tenacity and special adaptation of its inhabitants.

Marine biologists subdivide this natural blender where surf meets bedrock into three main habitat layers, based on their position relative to tide levels. The **high intertidal zone,** inundated only during the highest tides, is home to creatures that can either move, such as crabs, or are well adapted to tolerate daily desiccation, such as acorn barnacles, finger limpets, chitons, and green algae. The turbulent **mid-intertidal zone** is covered and uncovered by the tides, usually twice each day. In the upper portion of this zone, California mussels and goose barnacles may thickly blanket the rocks, while ochre sea stars and green sea anemones are common lower down, along with sea lettuce, sea palms, snails, sponges, and whelks. Below that, the **low intertidal zone** is only exposed during the lowest tides. Because it is covered by water most of the time, this zone has the greatest diversity of organisms in the tidal area. Residents include many of the organisms found in the higher zones, as well as sculpins, abalone, and purple sea urchins.

Standout destinations for exploring tidepools include Cape Arago, Cape Perpetua, the Marine Gardens at Devil's Punchbowl, and beaches south and north of Gold Beach—among many other

Green anemones are common inhabitants of Northwest tidepools, like this one near Yachats.

spots. Tidepool explorers should be mindful that, although the plants and animals in the tidepools are well adapted to withstand the elements, they and their ecosystem are fragile, and they're sensitive to human interference. Avoid stepping on mussels, anemones, and barnacles, and take nothing from the tidepools. In the Oregon Islands National Wildlife Refuge and other specially protected areas, removal or harassment of any living organism may be treated as a misdemeanor punishable by fines.

Birds

One of the most immediately noticeable forms of wildlife at the coast are the birds of sea, shore, and estuary. The abundance and variety of species you may encounter are a large part of the reason that Oregon is rapidly gaining a reputation as one of the best bird-watching states. Seasonal variance in populations is often dramatic, so timing is important.

The **Oregon Islands National Wildlife Refuge,** which comprises all the 1,400-plus offshore islands, reefs, and rocks from Tillamook Head to the California border, is a haven for the largest concentration of nesting seabirds along the west coast of the United States, thanks to the abundance of protected nesting habitat. During the April–August breeding season, seabirds that can be seen here include common murres, pigeon guillemots, rare tufted puffins, Brandt's and pelagic cormorants, and black oystercatchers, along with the ubiquitous western gulls. June to October, you may spy brown pelicans skimming the waves. Aleutian Canada geese use Table and Haystack rocks during March and early April.

In terms of sheer numbers and variety, the coast's mudflats at low tide and the tidal estuaries also make excellent bird-watching environments. Species to look for on the flats and shorelines include Pacific golden plovers, pectoral, and

Baird's sandpipers. The **western snowy plover,** listed as threatened under the Endangered Species Act, gets special protection at the state's nine nesting sites in Curry, Coos, Douglas, and Lane counties. The small shorebird, which resembles a sandpiper, nests on open sandy beaches above the high-tide line and is sensitive to disturbance from human foot traffic, vehicles, and unleashed dogs. During the nesting season, mid-March–mid-September, coast visitors may encounter areas posted or roped off to protect snowy plover nests.

Resident and migratory birds commonly spotted on the estuaries and lakes of the coast include common loon, western and horned grebes, great blue heron, American widgeon, greater scaup, common goldeneye, bufflehead, and red-breasted merganser.

> *The abundance and variety of species you may encounter are a large part of the reason that Oregon is rapidly gaining a reputation as one of the best bird-watching states.*

Seals, Sea Lions, and Otters

Pacific harbor seals, California sea lions, and Steller sea lions are frequently sighted in Oregon waters. California sea lions are the animals you might have seen in circuses. These 1,000-pound mammals are characterized by their large size and small earflaps, which seals lack. Unlike seals, they can point their rear flippers forward to give them better mobility on land. Without the dense underfur that covers seals, sea lions tend to prefer warmer waters.

Steller sea lions can be seen at the Sea Lion Caves (see Florence and Vicinity in the Central Coast chapter). They also breed on reefs off Gold Beach and Port Orford. They are the largest sea lion species, with males sometimes weighing more than a ton. Their coats tend to be more gray than the black-coated California sea lion's. They also differ from their California counterparts in that they're comfortable in colder water.

Look for Pacific harbor seals in bays and estuaries up and down the coast, sometimes miles inland. They're nonmigratory, have no earflaps, and can be distinguished from sea lions because they're much smaller (150–300 pounds) and

have mottled fur that ranges in color from pale cream to rusty brown.

Another marine mammal that was once common on the Oregon coast, and along the entire Pacific coast from Japan to Mexico, is the **sea otter.** Two centuries of ruthless hunting by Russian, European, and American fur traders, though, nearly eradicated the species entirely. By the time Oregon's last known sea otter was killed, in 1906, the otters had disappeared from British Columbia to central California. Today, the only sea otters living in Oregon are those in the Oregon Zoo and the Oregon Coast Aquarium, but an organization called the Elakha Alliance is working to restore wild otters to their natural habitat. You can learn about and support their important work at www.ecotrust.org/community/elakha.html.

Gray Whales

Few sights along the Oregon coast (or any coast, for that matter) elicit more excitement than that of a surfacing whale. The most common large whale seen from shore along the west coast of North America is the gray whale (*Eschrichtius robustus*). These behemoths can reach 45 feet in length and weigh 35 tons. The sight of a mammal as big as a Greyhound bus breaking water has a way of emptying the mind of mundane concerns. Wreathed in seaweed and sporting barnacles and other parasites on its back, a California gray whale might look more like the hull of an old ship were it not for its expressive eyes.

After decades of hunting had brought them to the brink of extinction, gray whales gained full protection in 1946 by the International Whaling Commission. In the ensuing years, the population has recovered dramatically. When the gray was delisted from the Endangered Species List in 1994, the population was estimated at 23,000, which is thought to be close to the pre-whaling population. Gray whales continue to enjoy protection worldwide, apart from a quota of 176 whales harvested each year along the Siberian coast.

Some gray whales are found off the Oregon coast all year, including an estimated 200–400 during summer, although they're most visible and numerous when migrating populations pass through Oregon waters on their way south December–February and northward from early March–April. This annual journey from the rich feeding grounds of the Bering and Chukchi seas of Alaska to the calving grounds of Mexico amounts to some 10,000 miles, the longest migration of any mammal.

Grays feed primarily on bottom-dwelling, shrimp-like amphipods, scooping up huge mouthfuls from which they filter out water and sediment through the fringe of baleen inside their mouths. After fattening up in the rich waters of the arctic during the summer and fall, gray whales begin their migration south. In early December, pregnant females are the first to begin showing up along the Oregon coast, followed by mature adults of both sexes and then by juveniles. Their numbers peak usually during the first week of January, when as many as 30 per hour may pass a given point. By mid-February, most of the whales will have moved on toward their breeding and calving lagoons on the west coast of Baja California.

From early March–April, the juveniles, adult males, and females without calves begin returning northward past the Oregon coast. Mothers and their new calves are the last to leave Mexico and move more slowly, passing Oregon from late April–June. During the spring migration, the whales may pass within just a few hundred yards of coastal headlands, making this a particularly exciting time for whale-watching from many vantage points along the coast. Researchers speculate that gray whales stay close to shore as a way to help them navigate.

For more details on how, when, and where to observe these magnificent creatures, see the Recreation section of the On the Road chapter.

Land Mammals

Many of the most frequently sighted animals in coastal Oregon are small scavengers, which are frequently encountered in woodsier campgrounds, parks, and picnic areas: raccoons, skunks, Townsend's chipmunks, Douglas squirrels, and opossums.

Black-tailed deer are commonly spotted in woods and meadows all along the coast, and a herd of their larger cousins, the majestic Roosevelt elk, can be seen at the Dean Creek Elk Viewing Area near Reedsport.

On streams and brooks, observant hikers may spot the handiwork of **beavers**—lodges and dams built of branches and twigs—if not the camera-shy builders themselves. The state's animal mascot is widespread, most commonly sighted in second-growth forests near marshes after sunset. Fall is a good time to spot beavers as they gather food for winter.

Although **black bears** proliferate in remote mountain forests of Oregon (the state's Department of Fish and Wildlife estimates that 14,000–19,000 black bears roam the western Cascades and the Coast Range), chances are slim that you'll sight one. Black bears shy away from people except when provoked by the scent of food, when cornered or surprised, or upon human intrusion into territory near their cubs.

A little-known oddity of the coast, from southern British Columbia to northern California, is the **mountain beaver** *(Aplodontia rufa),* known locally as "boomers." This most primitive species of living rodents is not actually a beaver but resembles (and is roughly the size of) a grayish-brown guinea pig. Although the animal was first reported by Lewis and Clark, and it's still fairly populous, most people have never heard of the boomer, let alone seen one. They thrive in dense understory vegetation such as coniferous forests and coastal scrub. These herbivores eat all types of succulent vegetation, including plants that are often inedible to other species such as nettle, bracken fern, and salal. Their predilection for Douglas fir seedlings has made them the scourge of the timber industry.

Another rodent common along the coast is the **nutria,** introduced to Oregon in the 1930s from South America to be farmed for its fur (and meat). After numerous escapes, this furry pest established a niche in the woodlands of the Coast Range. About two feet long and similar in appearance to a true beaver (minus the

© MARK MORRIS

the banana slug, ubiquitous denizen of the forest floor

flat tail), voracious nutrias damage many crop plants in Oregon. Furthermore, they may cause erosion by digging into streambeds or the levees that protect lowlands from floods. Currently, a year-round open season encourages hunting and trapping of this varmint to reduce its numbers.

Other Land Creatures

You won't have to look for long in the coast woodlands or underbrush before you encounter Oregon's best-known invertebrates—**banana slugs**—and lots of them. In few places on earth do these snails-out-of-shells grow as large and in such numbers. The reason is western Oregon's climate: moister than mist but drier than drizzle. This balance and calcium-poor soil enables the native banana slug and the more common European black slug to thrive while being the bane of Oregon gardeners. When these 3- to 10-inch squirts of slime are not eating plants, you'll see them moving along at a snail's pace on some sidewalk or forest trail. The eight species of non-native slugs that have established themselves in the Northwest tend to prey on crops and gardens. Native species generally confine themselves to forests and eat indigenous plants.

Another distinctive but rarely sighted resident of coastal forests is the **Pacific giant salamander** (*Dicamptodon tenebrus*), the largest terrestrial salamander found in the United States and Canada. This stout, mottled brown or blackish amphibian can reach lengths of 13–14 inches from nose to tail. They may be found around cold streams and mountain lakes in damp forests and around stagnant pools in the Kalmiopsis. They have been known to climb in shrubs and small trees. Among the few salamanders capable of vocalizing, Pacific giants may produce a sharp, low-pitched doglike yelp when agitated. Their powerful jaws can inflict a painful bite and make them a formidable predator of just about anything they can catch, including insects, slugs, snails, frogs, snakes, and rodents.

SALMON AND STEELHEAD SPECIES

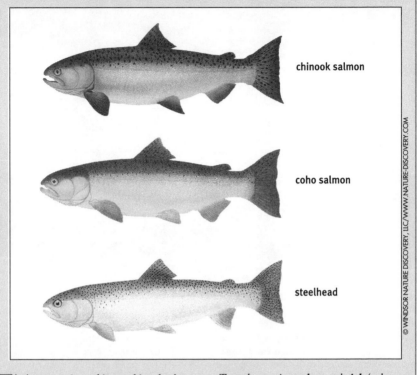

chinook salmon

coho salmon

steelhead

© WINDSOR NATURE DISCOVERY, LLC/WWW.NATURE-DISCOVERY.COM

The largest species are **king** or **chinook** salmon, sometimes weighing in at more than 80 pounds and touted as the best-tasting salmon. **Coho** or **silver** salmon are known as fiercely fighting fish among anglers, despite a weight around 10–20 pounds. In 1994, the El Niño warming current inhibited coho reproduction enough to bring about a total ban on harvesting this species. That turned around after 2000, when a cautious sportfishing season was reopened in Oregon.

Chum salmon (known derogatorily as "dog salmon" because Canadian and Alaskan native people thought them worthy only of being fed to their dog teams) are found only in the Miami and Kilchis rivers, near Tillamook.

Two other species, **sockeye** and **pink** (or humpback) salmon, are not caught south of Washington waters, but you may see them sold in Oregon stores.

Steelhead are sea-run rainbow trout averaging 5–20 pounds whose life cycle generally resembles that of salmon—with the exception that steelhead generally survive after spawning and may live to spawn multiple times. Runs of steelhead, often heavily supplemented by hatchery-raised fish, are found in rivers and streams up and down the coast. They provide great if challenging sport angling but are not harvested commercially.

Salmon and Steelhead

In recent decades, dwindling Pacific salmon and steelhead stocks have prompted restrictions on commercial and recreational fishing in order to restore threatened and endangered species throughout the Northwest. The following paragraphs envision a time when conservation measures have helped restore better health to this ecosystem. Encouraging signs of progress have been seen in the last couple of years, with some rebounding runs, but the jury is certainly still out on the long-term prognosis for many anadromous fish populations. For more information about fish populations and fishing restrictions, visit the Oregon Department of Fish and Wildlife's website (www.dfw.state.or.us).

Spring and fall are prime times to savor the splendor (as well as the flavor) of the Pacific salmon. During these seasons, some of Oregon's rivers and streams become choked with spawning fish returning to the site of their conception, where they mate and die. As with the eruptions of Old Faithful geyser and the return of the swallows to Capistrano, this poignant dance of death affords a look at one of Mother Nature's time clocks.

The salmon's life cycle begins and ends in a freshwater stream. After an upriver journey from the sea of sometimes hundreds of miles, the spawning female deposits 3,000–7,000 eggs in hollows (called redds) she has scooped out of the coarse sand or gravel, where the male fertilizes them. These adult salmon die soon after mating, and their bodies then deteriorate to become part of the food chain for young fish.

Within three to four months, the eggs hatch into alevin, tiny immature fish with their yolk sac still attached. As the alevin exhaust the nutrients in their yolk sac, they enter the fry stage and begin to resemble very small salmon. The length they remain as fry differs among various species. Chinook fry, for example, immediately start heading for salt water, whereas coho or silver salmon will remain in their home stream for one to three years before moving downstream.

The salmon are in the smolt stage when they start to enter salt water. The five- to seven-inch smolts will spend some time in the estuary area of the river or stream, while they feed and adjust to the salt water.

When it finally enters the ocean, the salmon is considered an adult. Each species varies in the number of years it remains away from its natal stream, foraging sometimes thousands of miles throughout the Pacific. Chinook can spend as many as seven years away from its nesting (and ultimately its resting) place; most other species remain in the salt for two to four years. Theories about how the salmon's miraculous homing instinct works range from electromagnetic impulses in the earth to celestial objects, but one thing has been established with certainty—"the nose knows." When salmon's olfactory orifices were stuffed with cotton and petroleum jelly, they were unable to find their spawning streams. The current belief is that young salmon imprint the odor of their birth stream, enabling them to find their way home years later.

The salmon's traditional predators such as the sea lion, squawfish, harbor seal, black bear, Caspian tern, and herring gull pale in comparison to the threats posed by modern civilization. Everything from pesticides to sewage to nuclear waste has polluted Oregon waters, and until recent mitigation efforts were enacted, dams and hydroelectric turbines threatened to block Oregon's all-important Columbia River spawning route.

History

The First Peoples

No one knows when the first inhabitants took up residence on the Oregon coast, but ongoing research periodically turns up ever-older evidence. In 2002, archaeologists began excavating a site at Indian Sands, in Samuel H. Boardman State Park north of Brookings, which yielded artifacts dating back more 12,000 years, making it the oldest known site of human activity yet found on the coast. Prior to that discovery, the dig site at Tahkenitch Landing, in the Oregon Dunes near Gardiner, had been the earliest known coastal habitation, dated at 9000–8630 B.C. It seems likely that further digs will uncover even older human artifacts, though scientists speculate that the oldest sites lie underwater, dating to a time when sea level was significantly lower.

A popular theory concerning the origins of Native Americans maintains that their ancestors came over from Asia on a land-ice bridge spanning what is now the Bering Strait. Along with archaeological evidence, shipwrecks of Asian craft on the Pacific Coast also support the theory that Native Americans had Eastern Hemisphere contact. This contention has been further substantiated by facial features and dental patterns common to both peoples, as well as isolated correspondences in ritual, music, and dialect.

Despite common ancestry, the tribes on the rain-soaked coast and in the Willamette Valley lived quite differently from those on the drier eastern flank of the Cascade Mountains. Tribes west of the Cascades enjoyed abundant salmon, shellfish, berries, and game. Great broad rivers facilitated travel, and thick stands of the finest softwood timber in the world ensured that there was never a dearth of building materials. A mild climate with plentiful food and resources allowed the wet-siders the leisure time to evolve a startlingly complex culture. This was perhaps best evidenced in their artistic endeavors, theatrical pursuits, and ceremonial gatherings such as the traditional potlatch, where the divesting of one's material wealth was seen as a status symbol. Dentalium and abalone shells, woodpecker feathers, obsidian blades, and hides were especially coveted. Later on, Hudson's Bay blankets were added to this list.

After contact with traders, Chinook—a patois of Indian tongues with some French and English thrown in—became the common language among the diverse tribes that gathered in the Columbia Gorge during the summer solstice. At these powwows, the coast and valley dwellers came into contact with their poorer cousins east of the Cascades.

By the time the white explorers and settlers came here, Indian culture was a patchwork of languages and cultural traits as diverse as the topography. Most native coastal communities typically included a dozen or more small bands linked by a common dialect. These bands or villages consisted of perhaps an extended family in one or two houses or a larger grouping under a headman. The linguistic and lifestyle divisions between native communities were reinforced by mountains, an ocean too rough for canoes, and other geographic barriers.

Early Explorers

In 1542, the Spanish explorer Juan Rodríguez Cabrillo sailed into what are now southern Oregon waters. Although partisans in California may dispute it, there's tantalizingly compelling evidence that the English privateer Francis Drake spent the summer of 1579 at Whale Cove (see Depoe Bay and Vicinity in the Central Coast chapter) and named the land New Albion, claiming it in the name of Queen Elizabeth. Other voyagers of note included Spain's Vizcaíno and de Alguilar (1603) and Don Bruno de Heceta (1775), and England's James Cook and John Meares during the late 1770s, as well as George Vancouver (1792). Robert Gray's 1792 voyage 13 miles up the Columbia River estuary was the first American incursion into the area. A succession of Spanish, English, American, and Russian explorers followed in search of whales, sea otter and beaver pelts, and hides for the tallow trade.

COURTESY OF INDEPENDENCE NATIONAL HISTORIC PARK

William Clark and Meriwether Lewis

A major impetus for exploring this coast was the quest for the Northwest Passage—a sea route connecting the Pacific with the Atlantic. Although the Northwest Passage turned out to be a myth, the fur trade became a basis of commerce and contention between European, Asian, and eventually American governments. The pattern was repeated inland when the English beaver brigades eventually moved down from Canada to set up headquarters on the Columbia near present-day Portland.

Dispatched by President Thomas Jefferson to explore the lands of the Louisiana Purchase and beyond, the first American overland excursion into Oregon was made by the Corps of Discovery, which crossed the continent 1804–1806. Led by Meriwether Lewis and William Clark, the expedition trekked to the mouth of the Columbia in fall 1805, and spent a wet and miserable winter camped south of the river and explored as far south as Cannon Beach (see Fort Clatsop in the Astoria and Vicinity section of the North Coast chapter for more details). Lewis and Clark's trailblazing dramatically accelerated interest in the Oregon Territory, and by 1811 John Jacob Astor's Pacific Fur Company had established the settlement of Astoria, just north of their campsite.

Rogue River Wars

In the 1850s, a short-lived gold-mining boom in the Rogue River Valley and south coast beaches drew settlers to southern Oregon. Another gold rush, however, had the greatest implications for development of the region. In 1849, the influx of prospectors into California's Sierra Nevada occasioned a housing boom in San Francisco, port of entry to the goldfields. The demand for Coast Range timber and foodstuffs from Oregon's inland agricultural valleys caused downriver Pacific ports such as Astoria and Newport to flourish. As a result, the coastline of California's friendly neighbor to the north was able to develop the necessary economic base for it to prosper and endure.

Like the tragic story played out all across the continent, however, the coming of white settlers to Oregon meant the usurpation of tribal homelands, exposure to European diseases such as smallpox and diphtheria, and the passing of a way of life. Violent conflicts ensued on a large

White Star Packing Company label, Astoria, 1885

scale with the influx of settlers and government land giveaways, and the mining activity in southern Oregon and on the coast incited the Rogue Indian Wars, when the native peoples along the south coast began to fight back. The conflict lasted for six years, during which more than 2,000 Indians died.

The hostilities compelled the federal government to send in troops and to eventually set up treaties with Oregon's first inhabitants. In the aftermath of the Rogue Indian Wars in the 1850s, the Chetco, Coquille, Coos, Umpqua, Siuslaw, Alsea, Yaquina, Nestucca, and Tillamook peoples were grouped together with the Rogue River tribes and forced to live on the 1.1-million-acre Siletz Reservation, which reached from Cape Lookout in Tillamook County to near the mouth of the Umpqua River. The culture and heritage of many indigenous peoples were lost forever. More tragic than the watering down of cultural distinctiveness was the huge mortality rate resulting from natives being forcibly removed to the reservation. Of the approximately 3,240 natives moved to the reservation in 1857, disease, starvation, and exposure would reduce their number to 1,015 in 1880; by 1900, only 430 coastal Indians survived on the reservation.

Over the years, whatever wealth the Siletz tribes had left was stripped as a result of the United States not honoring a multitude of treaties. The final indignity came in 1951 with the termination of the Siletz Reservation. The divestiture of tribal status meant the loss of health services, educational support, tax exemptions, and other benefits. Predictably, this last in a long line of forced transitions brought about alcoholism and despair in many native peoples. In 1977, Senator Mark Hatfield and Congressman Les AuCoin helped push a bill through Congress for tribal restoration. This has resulted in the tribe getting the wherewithal to flourish economically in everything from logging and construction projects to gaming establishments. The latter endeavor has been accompanied by an interest in the old ways and a renewed sense of pride in native identity.

Industry, Exploitation, and Development

The exploitation of Oregon's fishing resources has been an enduring aspect of life in the region for thousands of years. Salmon has always been the most valued species, from prehistory up to modern times. Native Americans on both sides of the Cascades depended on it, and commercial anglers have viewed it as a mainstay for more than a century. Canning technology and fishing methods first perfected in Alaska made their way to Oregon in the 1860s, in time to meet the demands of emerging domestic and foreign markets. Canneries crowded the shores of the Columbia at Astoria and all of the other major rivers down the coast and exported thousands of tons of fish yearly until the dwindling supplies finally closed them down.

Logging of coastal and inland forests supplied the sawmills that were established at every port, supplying the building booms of the Northwest and beyond. A brisk coastal trade developed, as steamships plied Oregon ports on busy routes between San Francisco and Seattle. Before roads were finally built through the coastal ranges, transportation between coastal communities and the inland valleys was by river, and sternwheelers moved goods and passengers up and down the Siletz, Yaquina, Umpqua, and other navigable rivers. Popular tourist areas developed in Newport, Seaside, and other towns.

In the latter half of the 19th century, rail lines began to connect the coast to the interior, but it took the development of reliable roads to bring the coast out of its isolation. In 1919, Oregon voters approved construction of a north-south coastal route, first called the Roosevelt Military Highway and later the Oregon Coast Highway. The road was completed in 1932, and the last of a dozen magnificent bridges, designed by Oregon's master bridgebuilder Conde McCullough, were finished in 1936, finally opening up the entire coast to auto travel.

On the Road

Coastal Oregon boasts an ideal mix of recreational, cultural, and relaxation opportunities, in a natural setting as pleasing to the senses as any in the world.

A favorite getaway for most Oregonians—not to mention growing multitudes from neighboring states and farther afield—it's a destination whose popularity seems to grow steadily with everyone: vacationing families looking for a safe and satisfying vacation, spring-breakers blowing off steam, couples seeking a romantic weekend away from the routine, RV-driving retirees summering in a cooler clime.

Fortunately, after more than a century as a holiday destination, the coast still retains the charms that made it so popular in the first place. Thanks largely to progressive legislation that makes the beaches public property, most of the Oregon coast remains refreshingly undeveloped, and may it forever stay that way.

In summer, and on weekends and holidays, hotels, campgrounds, and restaurants can fill up fast. You'll probably want to do some advance planning. But keep in mind that the coast isn't just for summer anymore. Increasingly, it's becoming a year-round destination, inviting visitors

Cape Creek Bridge

to come enjoy what some euphemistically call the storm-watching season—when the warm-weather crowds are long gone, beaches are deserted, and prices at most lodgings drop to very attractive rates.

Whenever you choose to go, this chapter, along with the individual destination sections, should give you the tools you need to plan ahead, avoid disappointment, and enjoy the experience you seek.

Recreation

The outdoor appeal of the Oregon coast is unmatched, and the beaches are only the beginning. Hikes through ancient rainforests, excellent fishing for salmon and steelhead, crabbing and clamming in bays and estuaries, white-water jet-boat rides, hiking and cycle-touring, surfing, whale-watching, birding, and more are all on the agenda. Following is an overview of recreational opportunities along the coast; you'll find may additional suggestions and details in individual destination chapters.

BEACHCOMBING

Among the first things a newcomer to the Oregon coast notices are the huge piles of driftwood on the beach. Closer inspection usually reveals other treasures. Beachcombers particularly value agates and Japanese glass fishing floats. The volume and variety of flotsam and jetsam here come courtesy of the region's unique geography. Much of the driftwood, for instance, originates from logging operations located upriver on the many waterways that empty into the Pacific. In addition, storms, floods, rockslides, and erosion uproot many trees that eventually wash up on shore. In addition to driftwood and floats, shells, coral, sand dollars, starfish, and other seaborne trophies can be best culled from the intertidal zone on south coast beaches. Although you may not always come across a perfectly polished agate or a message in a bottle, you'll probably find beachcombing on the Oregon coast to be its own reward.

Japanese fishing floats are swept into Oregon waters when the Kuroshio current crosses the Pacific and takes a southerly turn. These balls of green and blue glass sometimes require more than a decade to reach the Oregon coast after

You never know what you'll find.

© MARK MORRIS

ON THE ROAD

breaking free from fishnets thousands of miles across the sea. Although glass floats are rather rare these days, having largely been replaced by plastic and foam, March is the best time to look for them, especially after two-day storms from the northwest, west-southwest, or due west. December–April is the best season to find agates, jaspers, petrified wood, and a variety of fossils. At that time, the gravel bars covered by sand in summer are exposed.

On the southern coast, the Coos Bay sandspit, Bandon's beachfront, the beaches on the western side of Humbug Mountain, and the isolated shorelines of Boardman State Park are choice treasure-hunting spots. Ten Mile Creek south of

ON THE ROAD

Yachats and Agate Beach north of Newport are the central coast's best places to look. The more settled and accessible north coast has slimmer pickings because of the larger population of resident beachcombers and the higher visitor influx; the best beachcombing is on the Nehalem, the Netarts, and the Nestucca sandspits.

Consult a **tide chart** any time you anticipate an extended beachcombing excursion (or any other activity on or near the sea). Half a dozen people perish here yearly from being washed off a beach, jetty, or outcropping. Local newspapers usually include tide predictions, and tide charts are usually available from visitors centers, chambers of commerce, and shops. Online, you can get free tide charts for three dozen coastal locations at www.saltwatertides.com. It's also wise to anticipate weather changes, so bring layers.

WHALE-WATCHING

Whale-watching charters of various kinds are offered along the coast from December into the early spring. By land or by sea, early morning hours are best because winds can whip up whitecaps later in the day, obscuring the signs of surfacing whales. Remember to bring your binoculars and sunglasses. If you go by boat, dress warmly, take precautions against seasickness, and expect to get wet if you go out on deck.

You don't need to be on a boat or plane to successfully whale-watch, however. Coastal headlands and beaches provide excellent vantage points (some of the best sites are listed in the following section) from which to spy the gray whales on their 10,000-mile round-trip between Baja and the Arctic, the longest migratory movement by land or sea of any mammal. It's possible to spot whales here year-round because several hundred have taken up permanent or semi-permanent residence in Oregon waters, but whales are far more numerous (and your chances of sighting them far better) during their twice-yearly migrations. The southward migration along the

Although you may not always come across a perfectly polished agate or a message in a bottle, you'll probably find beachcombing on the Oregon coast to be its own reward.

Oregon coast lasts until early February, although their numbers usually peak around the last week in December. Whales migrating northward can be sighted off Oregon March–May, with numbers usually peaking in late March.

By Land

Just about any coastal location with a view of the sea holds the potential for a whale sighting, but some spots are definitely better than others. Offshore reefs supporting the proliferation of amphipods, the food of the gray whale, are conducive to sightings. Combine the latter with a promontory such as Cape Perpetua or Yaquina Head and you increase your chances even more.

Whale Watching Spoken Here (http://whalespoken.org) is an organization of enthusiastic, trained volunteers who staff 28 prime whale-watching sites in Oregon (plus one in northern California and one in southern Washington) during key weeks of the gray whale migrations. In coordination with the Oregon Parks and Recreation Department, these folks provide information and assist in spotting whales 10 A.M.–1 P.M., December 26–Janurary 2 and through the week of spring break in late March. Get more information from their website.

These sites, marked by Whale Watching Spoken Here signs during Whale Watch Weeks, are among the best vantage points any time of year. From north to south, with their nearest town, they are:

• Ecola State Park
• Neahkahnie Mountain Historic Marker Turnout (Cannon Beach)
• Cape Meares State Scenic Viewpoint (Three Capes Loop)
• Cape Lookout State Park (Three Capes Loop)
• Inn at Spanish Head (Lincoln City)
• Boiler Bay State Scenic Viewpoint (Depoe Bay)
• Depoe Bay Sea Wall

- Rocky Creek State Scenic Viewpoint (Depoe Bay)
- Cape Foulweather (Depoe Bay)
- Devil's Punchbowl State Natural Area (Otter Rock)
- Yaquina Head Lighthouse (Newport)
- Don A. Davis City Kiosk (Nye Beach, Newport)
- Yaquina Bay State Recreation Site (Newport)
- Seal Rock State Recreation Site
- Yachats State Park
- Devil's Churn Viewpoint (Yachats)
- Cape Perpetua Overlook (Yachats)
- Cape Perpetua Interpretive Center (Yachats)
- Cook's Chasm Turnout (Yachats)
- Sea Lion Caves Turnout (north of Florence)
- Umpqua Lighthouse (Winchester)
- Shore Acres State Park (Charleston)
- Face Rock Wayside State Scenic Viewpoint (Bandon)
- Cape Blanco Lighthouse
- Battle Rock Wayfinding Point (Port Orford)
- Cape Sebastian
- Cape Ferrelo
- Harris Beach State Park (Brookings)

By Sea

Depoe Bay and Newport are the centers for whale-watching, attracting the majority of the state's whale-watching visitors. Other major ports are Charleston, Winchester, and Garibaldi, but you'll find whale-watching charters operating out of just about all the ports along the coast. Rates range $15–50 per person for a two- to three-hour tour. See each destination for specific charter companies and details.

BICYCLING

In the wake of the oil shocks of the 1970s, the Oregon legislature allocated 1 percent of the state highways budget to encourage energy-saving bicycling by developing bike lanes and special parks and campgrounds with bicycle and foot access specifically in mind.

Although not for everybody, biking part or all of the Oregon coast is the surest way to get on intimate terms with this spectacular region. Be-

fore going, get a free copy of **The Oregon Coast Bike Route Map** from the Department of Transportation (Salem, OR 97310, www.odot.state .or.us) or from coastal information centers and chambers of commerce. This brochure features strip maps of the route, noting services from Astoria to the California border. With information on campsites, hostels, bike-repair facilities, elevation changes, temperatures, and wind speed, this pamphlet does everything but map the ruts in the road. Because the prevailing winds in summer are from the northwest, most people cycle south on U.S. 101 to take advantage of a steady tailwind. You'll also be riding on the ocean side of the road with better views, easier access to turnouts, and generally wider bike lanes and shoulders. The entire 370-mile (or 380 miles, including the optional Three Capes Loop) trip involves nearly 16,000 feet of elevation change. Most cyclists cover the distance in 6–8 days, pedaling an average of 50–65 miles daily.

On Oregon's roads and highways, bicyclists have the right of way, which means that cars and trucks are not supposed to run you off the road. Most drivers will give you a wide berth and slow down if necessary in tight spots, but remember that there are also motorists whose concepts of etiquette vis-à-vis bikers were formulated elsewhere. Play it safe: Always wear a helmet and bright or reflective clothing, keep as close to the shoulder of the road as you safely can, and use a light if you must ride at night.

Cycle Tours

Several companies offer preplanned group bicycle trips, with everything from the bicycle to the meals and lodging included. For example, **Scenic Cycling Adventures** (800/413-8432, www .scenic-cycling.com) offers an eight-day Astoria–Crescent City trip and a loop trip combining the south coast with the Cascades. **Bicycle Adventures** (206/786-0989 or 800/443-6060, www.bicycleadventures.com) offers several coast packages at a cost of roughly $200 per day. **Hidden Trails** (604/323-1141 or 888/9-TRAILS, www.bcranches.com/outdoor/bike/index.htm) offers a fully supported, 10-day tour for about $2,500.

HIKING

Opportunities for hiking abound on the coast, from short loops suitable for just about anyone to the magnificent Coast Trail running the entire length of the coast, and a myriad of choices in between. Wherever you choose your outing, here are some suggestions to help keep the environment as natural as possible:

•Stay on the trails so you do not increase the rate of erosion or destroy such fragile vegetation as dune and wetland wildflowers.

•Use established campsites, and avoid digging tent trenches or cutting vegetation.

•In wilderness areas, camp several hundred feet from water sources. Bring a tool to dig a latrine, and make it at least six inches deep.

•If you pack it in, pack it out. Leave nothing but footprints.

•Avoid feeding wild animals so you don't inhibit their natural instinct to fend for themselves.

The Oregon Coast Trail

For 362 miles, from the Columbia River to the California border, the Oregon Coast Trail hugs the beaches and headlands, leading hikers into intimate contact with some of the most beautiful landscapes anywhere. Most of the trail runs through public lands, although some portions traverse easements on private parcels, and the trail follows the highway and city streets in several places. The only coastal long-distance treks separated from U.S. 101 are the 30 miles between Seaside and Manzanita and Bandon and Port Orford. A free trail map and directory are available from the Oregon state parks information center (800/551-6949, www.oregonstateparks.org). This pamphlet makes it clear where the trail crosses open beaches, forested headlands, the shoulder of the Coast Highway, and even city streets in some towns. Be sure to bring water, particularly on northerly sections of the trail, because much of the trek here is on beachfront away from a potable supply.

FISHING

Since the first people arrived on these shores 12,000 years or more ago, Oregon's rich coastal waters have provided sustenance and sport. The king of fish here, economically as well as recreationally speaking, is the salmon. The once-abundant fish was a self-replenishing gold mine that enriched the state and fueled the development of coastal towns like Astoria and Gold Beach.

In the modern era, Oregon salmon fisheries grew into a megabusiness, until stocks dramati-

Informative displays at popular fishing spots help anglers differentiate between coho and chinook salmon.

cally declined in the 1990s. The many factors are complex and fraught with political tension. In the early days, fish wheels and nets depleted rivers once so choked with spawning fish that a pioneer pitchfork stuck haphazardly into the water would often yield a salmon. Dam construction and pollution joined overfishing to further reduce the catch. Watersheds have been compromised by clearcuts, which increases erosion that clogs spawning streams with silt and mud and reduces shaded riparian environments for the coldwater-loving salmon. Cattle grazing has also affected spawning areas with collapsed stream banks and polluted water.

Despite the habitat degradation and other pressures, hope is being restored by the resurgence of salmon and steelhead populations in Oregon waters since the year 2000. In 1997, returning Oregon coastal coho salmon numbered an alarmingly low 22,000 fish, which triggered a listing as threatened under the Endangered Species Act. Commercial and sport fishing for coho were shut down. Five years later, 268,000 cohos returned, and a tentative fishery was reopened, which was expanded again in 2003. The resurgence has been attributed to the return of colder water and upwelling of nutrients, after an absence of several decades. Naysayers point out that most of the returning fish are from hatcheries, with negative implications for the long-term health of the species.

Nevertheless, in recent years, sportfishers have enjoyed some of the best seasons in memory, and the near future, at least, looks promising. Runs of spring and fall chinook, coho, and steelhead draw thousands of anglers to the coast each year to enjoy some of the best fishing this side of Alaska. Fleets of charter boats operate out of all the navigable ports on the coast, and there are countless opportunities for do-it-yourselfers from boats, banks, jetties, and piers.

Past salmon shortfalls have spawned alternative ocean fisheries. Bottom fishing for black ling cod and rockfish, together with the harvest of such long-ignored species as hake, whiting, and pollock, have increased in proportion to the decline of salmon, flounder, albacore tuna, smelt, and halibut. Growing out of the pollock fishery

has been the development of a successful surimi (artificial crab) industry supplying Asian and U.S. markets. Be that as it may, the aggressive harvest of the 55 species of rockfish that are marketed as red snapper brought about catch limits in 2000, giving another signal that fisheries are in transition.

Where and When to Go

Salmon are targeted offshore, as well as in fresh water. The Coastal Fishing chart (see sidebar) indicates when runs of anadromous fish (i.e., species that spend parts of their life cycles in both fresh water and at sea) are expected in various coastal bays and rivers. The chart does not indicate legal fishing seasons; for up-to-date information on exactly where, when, and how you can fish—which is subject to frequent change—get a copy of the **Oregon Department of Fish and Wildlife**'s regulations (2501 SW 1st Ave., Portland, OR 97207, 503/872-5268, www.dfw.state.or.us), available at sporting goods stores and many other outlets; better yet, check their website for the most current information.

In addition to chinook and coho salmon and steelhead in scores of coastal rivers, the Kilchis and Miami rivers near Tillamook see Oregon's only runs of chum salmon, in autumn; this is a catch-and-release fishery only. Another catch-and-release-only species is wild sea-run cutthroat trout, which return to the Alsea River and Yaquina Bay, among other waterways, in summer. Sturgeon are popular gamefish (weighing into the hundreds of pounds) in the larger rivers, particularly the Columbia and the Umpqua.

Bottom-fishing for rockfish and other species is pretty much a year-round activity—depending on the weather. Warm ocean currents bring albacore tuna in August and September, and halibut are usually available in summer, although the season is variable and is set yearly by the Pacific Fishery Management Council.

Charters and Guides

Major charter-fishing centers on the coast include Astoria, Hammond, Warrenton, Garibaldi, Depoe Bay, Newport, Winchester Bay, Charleston, Gold Beach, Bandon, and Brookings. Charter rates vary

COASTAL FISH RUNS

Please note that these dates indicate when fish are expected, *not* necessarily legal fishing seasons. Check with the Department of Fish and Wildlife (www.dfw.state.or.us) for current seasons and restrictions.

Waterway	Jan.	Feb.	Mar.	Apr.	May	June	July	Aug.	Sept.	Oct.	Nov.	Dec.
Alsea River and Bay												
Fall chinook									X	X	X	
Winter steelhead	X	X	X								X	X
Sea-run cutthroat trout								X	X	X		
Fall chinook										X	X	X
Winter steelhead	X	X	X									X
Columbia River (lower)												
Spring chinook	X	X	X	X	X							
Summer chinook						X	X					
Fall chinook								X	X	X		
Summer steelhead					X	X	X	X	X			
Sturgeon	X	X	X	X	X	X	X					
Coho								X	X	X	X	X
Coos River												
Fall chinook								X	X	X	X	X
Coho									X	X	X	
Coquille River									X	X	X	X
Fall chinook									X	X	X	X
Winter steelhead	X	X	X								X	X
Elk River												
Fall chinook										X	X	X
Winter steelhead	X	X	X									

continued on next page

ON THE ROAD

	Jan	Feb	Mar	Apr	May	Jun	Jul	Aug	Sep	Oct	Nov	Dec
Kilchis River												
Fall chinook								X	X	X	X	X
Winter steelhead	X	X	X								X	X
Chum salmon										X	X	
Miami River												
Fall chinook								X	X	X	X	X
Winter steelhead	X	X	X								X	
Chum salmon										X	X	
Necanicum River												
Fall chinook									X	X	X	X
Winter steelhead	X	X	X							X	X	X
Nehalem River and Bay												
Summer chinook					X	X	X	X				
Fall chinook								X	X	X	X	X
Sturgeon	X	X	X	X	X	X	X	X	X	X	X	X
Coho									X	X	X	
Nestucca River												
Spring chinook				X	X	X	X	X				
Fall chinook									X	X	X	X
Rogue River												
Spring chinook			X	X	X	X	X	X				
Fall chinook								X	X	X	X	X
Coho								X	X	X	X	X
Summer steelhead				X	X	X	X	X	X	X	X	X
Winter steelhead	X	X	X									X

COASTAL FISH RUNS (CONT'D)

Waterway	Jan.	Feb.	Mar.	Apr.	May	June	July	Aug.	Sept.	Oct.	Nov.	Dec.
Siletz River												
Fall chinook								X	X	X	X	X
Steelhead	X	X	X			X	X	X	X	X	X	X
Siuslaw River												
Fall chinook								X	X	X	X	X
Winter steelhead	X	X	X			X	X	X	X	X	X	X
Tillamook Bay												
Spring chinook				X	X	X	X					
Fall chinook								X	X	X	X	X
Sturgeon	X	X	X	X	X	X	X	X	X	X	X	X
Coho								X	X	X		
Umpqua River												
Spring chinook			X	X	X	X	X					
Fall chinook								X	X	X	X	X
Coho								X	X	X	X	X
Shad					X	X	X					
Sturgeon	X	X	X			X	X					
Yaquina Bay												
Fall chinook									X	X	X	
Sea-run cutthroat trout								X	X	X		

Data adapted from the Oregon Department of Fish and Wildlife a bit, but typical prices up and down the coast are $55–60 for a half day (5–6 hours) of bottom fishing, $100 for a full day; $100 for an eight-hour salmon outing; $175 for 12 hours of tuna fishing; $150 for a 12-hour halibut charter. Guide and charter services are listed in each destination chapter. Chambers of commerce in each town can also provide extensive listings.

Crabbing and Clamming

Egalitarian ventures that require a minimum of gear and no license, crabbing and clamming are popular ways to land a delicious meal. The Oregon Department of Fish and Wildlife's *Sport Fishing Regulations* booklet has details, or check their website (www.dfw.state.or.us) for more information.

Crabbing just requires a trap, ring, or pot, and some bait (veteran crabbers recommend raw poultry—chicken or turkey backs and necks). Opinions vary about the best time to crab, but many agree that an incoming tide yields the best catches. Just drop your trap in a likely spot, with a tethered float marking the spot, and haul it up 15–30 minutes later—hopefully full of legal-sized male Dungeness crabs. A handy item to have is a crab caliper, a gauge that measures the minimum-sized crabs you can keep. Bait shops and marinas can instruct you on how to catch dinner. Boats and crab pots are usually available to rent at these places. If boats are unavailable, many harbors have public piers. Some of the best crabbing spots are the estuaries of the Coos, Siuslaw, Yaquina, Tillamook, Netarts, and Nehalem rivers. Bays and estuaries are open for Dungeness year-round; the ocean is open year-round except August 15–November 30.

A spade or small pitchfork—and a bucket to carry away your take—are all you need to dig clams on beaches and mudflats. Large gaper clams, cockles, soft-shells, and little-necks are the most common clams found in tidewater areas, while prized razor clams are found on north coast beaches. With the exception of the summer closure for razor clams north of Tillamook Head, the season on shellfish is year-round in Oregon. Low tides, particularly morning minus tides during spring and summer, are the best times for clamming. Mussels are also available for harvest

from rocky intertidal areas. Note that all oyster beds are privately owned. Check the *Sport Fishing Regulations* for catch limits, and before harvesting always inquire locally or contact the Recreational Shellfish Hot Line (503/986-4728) to get current information on shellfish toxins and quarantines.

USER FEES AND PASSES

In recent years, numerous state and federal parks, national recreation areas, trails, picnic areas, and other facilities have begun charging day-use fees, which are separate from overnight camping fees (the exception to this is camping at rustic campsites in national forests, which is covered by the Northwest Forest Pass). At sites that charge fees, the day-use fee is currently $3

© MARK MORRIS

The Oregon Parks and Recreation Department operates more than 80 sites along the coast.

per vehicle at state parks, $5 per vehicle at federal sites. Proposals to expand the number of sites charging fees were defeated in 2003. Visitors can pay for day use at individual sites, or if you're planning to visit several coastal parks or hike the trails on federal lands, you can save money by purchasing one of the passes described as follows.

Oregon Pacific Coast Passport

The best deal if you plan to visit many state and federal sites, this pass covers entrance, day-use, and vehicle parking fees at all state and federal fee sites along the entire Oregon portion of U.S. 101. It does not cover the cost of camping at state parks, which is a separate fee. This pass was created to alleviate some of the confusion caused

by having to buy different passes at the various federal (Forest Service, National Park Service, Bureau of Land Management or BLM) and state (Oregon Parks and Recreation Department) fee sites along the U.S. 101 corridor.

As of 2003, more than 15 coastal sites managed by the National Park Service, U.S. Forest Service, BLM, and Oregon state parks are covered by the passport, including Fort Stevens State Park, Ecola State Park, Nehalem Bay State Park, Cape Lookout State Park, Fogarty Creek State Recreation Area, Heceta Head Lighthouse Viewpoint, Honeyman State Park, Shore Acres State Park, Fort Clatsop National Memorial, Oregon Dunes National Recreation Area, Sutton Recreation Area, Cape Perpetua Scenic Area, Sand Lake Recreation Area, Marys Peak Recreation

LEWIS AND CLARK BICENTENNIAL EVENTS

While you may have missed the National Lewis and Clark Bicentennial Kickoff Event at Monticello in Charlottesville, Virginia, in January 2003, it's not too late to participate in celebrating the Corps of Discovery's final destination: the Pacific Coast.

Among 15 bicentennial "Signature Events" scheduled across the country through September 2006, "Destination: The Pacific" commemorates the four months Lewis and Clark spent near the mouth of the Columbia River in southwestern Washington and northwestern Oregon.

As this book goes to press in 2004, plans are still evolving for commemorative events along the coast, to take place from November 2005 through March 2006. An organization called **Destination: The Pacific** (P.O. Box 2005, Astoria, OR 97103, www.destinationthepacific.com) is working with other local groups to stage events in Cannon Beach, Oregon, to Long Beach, Washington, and is updating its website as events and dates are finalized.

Oregon-Washington Kickoff Events

The focus of Destination: The Pacific events is a week of activities that commemorate the Arrival, the Vote, the Crossing, and the Wintering

Over of the Lewis and Clark Expedition on the shores of the Pacific "Ocian," as Captain William Clark called it in his journal. The Signature Event takes place November 23–27, 2005, kicking off four months of activities concluding at the end of March 2006, when a special departure celebration will take place.

The Signature Event is scheduled to include a reenactment of the arrival of the Corps at Station Camp, Chinook, Washington, and at Fort Clatsop, south of Astoria.

Also during the Signature Event week, live theater will be ongoing at several venues. A country-dance featuring traditional music and a gala at Astoria's historic Liberty Theater to honor the cultures of the Chinook and Clatsop tribes will top off the week. The Clatsop County Fairgrounds will host an exposition, with crafts, food, entertainment, and activities for all ages.

Among the many events to follow are the opening of new trails, including the Fort-to-Sea trail from Fort Clatsop to Sunset Beach in Oregon and the Lewis and Clark Discovery Trail between Ilwaco and Long Beach in Washington; the official dedication of monuments, such as the Maya Lin Confluence piece at Fort Canby State Park, Ilwaco, Washington; boat excursions on the Columbia

Area, Drift Creek Falls Trail, Yaquina Head Outstanding Natural Area, and Hebo Lake.

Two basic passports are available, depending on customer needs and preferences. An **Annual Passport,** valid for the calendar year, is $35. A **Five-Day Passport** is $10. Passports may be purchased at welcome centers, ranger stations, national forest headquarters, national memorials, and State Park offices. Call 800/551-6949 to purchase by credit card or for directions to a convenient location.

State Park Passes
Another option, valid only at Oregon state parks, is to buy a one-year ($25) or two-year ($40) pass. They're available from state park offices, by phone (800/551-6949), and from G.I. Joe's stores and other vendors. See the Oregon State Parks website (www.oregonstateparks.org/dayuse_permit.php) for more details and a complete list of vendors.

Northwest Forest Pass
In response to major reductions in timber harvests and cutbacks in federal money, a revenue shortfall has made it hard to keep up trails and campgrounds at a time when the region's population has put more demand on these facilities. The Northwest Forest Pass ($30, valid for one year) is a vehicle-parking pass for the use of many improved trailheads, picnic areas, boat launches, and interpretive sites in the national forests of Oregon and Washington. Funds generated from pass sales go directly to maintaining and improving the trails, land, and facilities. You will

COURTESY OF THE OREGON TOURISM COMMISSION

Fort Clatsop reconstruction, built in 1955

River to view the route of the Expedition's crossing; and a rededication of Fort Clatsop. Check the website for specific venues, dates, and times, which are subject to change.

Exhibits and Interpretations
At Fort Clatsop, along the Washington Discovery Trail, at the Salt Works in Seaside, and along the Lewis and Clark National Historic Trail to the ocean, volunteers will don period clothing and personae to act out historically accurate interpretations of members of the Corps of Discovery. The Journey's End National Art Exhibit will show art featuring Lewis and Clark–related themes. Check their website (www.jsend.org) for locations and information.

The National Park Service's live traveling exhibit, "Corps II," will re-create the journey of Lewis and Clark by retracing the original historic trail on the dates chronicled in the journals, 200 years later. This exhibit will make its debut in Oregon in November 2005–March 2006. Refer to the NPS website (www.nps.gov/focl) for exact Corps II sites and dates.

Take the Train
For a special treat, ride the Lewis & Clark Explorer Train from Portland along the Oregon shore of the lower Columbia River to Astoria. The train takes passengers close to several historic sites visited by the expedition and includes passage through nature reserves and over river trestles. Portland Western is operating the train, but tickets and reservations are available from Amtrak (800/USA-RAIL or 800/872-7245, www.amtrak.com) and through travel agents selling Amtrak tickets. See the Astoria and Vicinity section of the North Coast chapter for additional details.

ON THE ROAD

see Northwest Forest Pass Required signs posted at participating sites. Passes are available at kiosks or dispensed by machine. Passes are also available at many local vendors (such as G.I. Joe's, park stores, and chambers of commerce), as well as by phone (800/270-7504). You can also order them online at www.fs.fed.us/r6/feedemo. You can also check this website to find out if a pass is required before you head out.

In contrast to the old fee system, these passes are good all over the Northwest, eliminating the necessity to purchase a separate pass with each entrance to another national forest. This pass covers most national park and Forest Service sites in Oregon and Washington but is not valid

for campground fees (with the exception of rustic campsites), concessioner-operated sites, and Sno-Parks.

Golden Passport Program

Get additional details or purchase these passes from the National Forest Foundation (877/465-2727, www.natlforests.org).

EVENTS AND ENTERTAINMENT

It seems there's some kind of festival or other event happening just about every week somewhere on the coast. Celebrations revolving around cultural or historical heritage, food and

ANNUAL EVENTS

January

Crustacean Classics	Lincoln City

February

Newport Seafood and Wine Festival	Newport
Oregon Dixieland Jubilee	Seaside
Fisher Poets Gathering	Astoria

March

Beachcomber's Festival	Brookings
Dune Mushers Mail Run	North Bend, Florence
Original Yachats Arts and Crafts Fair	Yachats

April

Depoe Bay Classic Wooden Boat Show, Crab Feed, and Ducky Derby	Depoe Bay
Puffin Kite Festival	Cannon Beach
Crab and Seafood Festival	Astoria

May

Loyalty Days and Sea Fair	Newport
Crafts on the Coast	Yachats

Azalea Festival	Brookings
Wild Rivers Coast Seafood, Art, and Wine Festival	Gold Beach
Wine and Seafood Festival	Bandon
Sandcastle Contest	Bandon
Rhododendron Festival	Florence
Fleet of Flowers	Depoe Bay
Spring Kite Festival	Lincoln City
Kite Festival	Rockaway Beach

June

Chainsaw Sculpture Championships	Reedsport
Jetboat Races	Gold Beach
Pistol River Wave Bash National Windsurfing Competition	Gold Beach
Ernest Bloch Music Festival	Newport
Cascade Head Chamber Music Festival	Lincoln City
Dairy Festival	Tillamook
Sandcastle Day	Cannon Beach
Scandinavian Midsummer Festival	Astoria

wine, crafts, kites, sandcastles, windsurfing, the arts—you name it, and there's probably a festival dedicated to it—and more sprout up every year. Most, of course, are concentrated during summer, when the choices can be overwhelming. In the Events chart (see sidebar), we've highlighted our choices for the biggest, best, and most unusual. Each is detailed in its respective destination chapter. This list is far from exhaustive; chambers of commerce in each town can fill you in on the full gamut.

Through 2006, events commemorating the bicentennial of the Lewis and Clark Expedition's 1805–1806 stay in Oregon are scheduled in Astoria and elsewhere in Clatsop County, as well as southwestern Washington; see the sidebar "Lewis and Clark Bicentennial Events" for more information.

SHOPPING

The lack of sales tax in Oregon is a boon to visitors. They can revel in the shopping opportunities on the coast, which include a profusion of shops selling local art, collectibles and antiques, handmade items, as well as the requisite T-shirts and trinkets.

If it's mall-type shopping you live for, the Seaside Factory outlet center (1111 N. Roosevelt Dr., www.seasideoutlet.com) has 30 big-name

July

Fourth of July celebrations	everywhere
Lincoln County Fair and Rodeo	Newport
Southern Oregon Kite Festival	Brookings
Oregon Coast Music Festival	Coos Bay, North Bend, Charleston, Bandon
Smelt Fry	Yachats
Yachats Music Festival	Yachats
Dory Festival	Pacific City
Curry County Fair and Rodeo	Gold Beach
Haystack Summer Program in the Arts	Cannon Beach

August

Sandcastle Building Contest	Lincoln City
Tillamook County Fair	Tillamook
Blackberry Arts Festival	Coos Bay
Prefontaine Memorial Run	Coos Bay
Astoria Regatta Week	Astoria
Arts and Crafts Fair	Rockaway Beach

September

Cranberry Festival	Bandon
Tsalila	Reedsport
Chowder, Brews, and Blues	Florence
Depoe Bay Salmon Bake	Depoe Bay
Fall Kite Festival	Lincoln City
Roadster Show	Seaside
Seaside Sand Sculpture and Beach Festival	Seaside

October

Yachats Village Mushroom Fest	Yachats
Celtic Music Festival	Yachats
Silver Salmon Celebration	Astoria

November

Stormy Weather Arts Festival	Cannon Beach

December

Holiday Lights and Open House	Shore Acres State Park, Charleston
Festival of Lights	Bandon
Nature's Coastal Holiday Light Show	Brookings

manufacturers with designer labels and national brands. With products (of all quality levels) at about 20–50 percent below regular retail price, the center is also home to one of the best wine shops on the Oregon Coast, featuring more than 850 labels, plus 309 imported and domestic beers. Lincoln City is home to another outlet mall, Factory Stores at Lincoln City (1500 SE East Devil's Lake Rd., www.shoplincolncity.com), with similar offerings.

For unique arts and crafts, the coastal resort areas are overflowing with the work of local and nationally known potters, woodworkers, painters, jewelers, and glass artisans. These homemade items often go for quite a bit less than would be charged in out-of-state markets for work of com-

parable quality. While these arts cottage industries don't have the bottom line of timber and agriculture, they are one of the more visible and appreciated forms of economic activity.

Seasonally, farm stands, farmer's markets, and U-pick options dot the routes to the coast. Oregon berries (so quick to ripen that their unparalleled sweetness is more likely to be appreciated in jams and ice cream than in the supermarket) and other indigenous treats can be bought direct from the farmer here. Oregon coast stores also purvey locally made food products, which make excellent gifts. You'll come across shops full of Oregon jams, smoked fish, hazelnuts, wines, cheese, sweets, and similar products.

Accommodations and Food

ACCOMMODATIONS

Coastal accommodations run the gamut from campgrounds and humble fishing lodges to bona fide five-star resorts. In between are a kaleidoscopic range including condominiums rented as guest rooms, bed-and-breakfasts, vacation rentals, a lighthouse keeper's quarters, yurts, a paddlewheeler, and a plethora of conventional motels.

Regardless of the lodging, you'll generally pay a bit more for direct access to the beach or for an ocean view. If you're willing to walk a block or two, or settle for a view of mountains or forests, you'll probably save a few dollars.

Finally, keep in mind that a hotel reservation at many lodgings *does not* guarantee exactly what you reserved. Regardless of how far in advance you reserve or even if you gave them your credit card number, all you are really guaranteed is a room. Especially during peak season, this may translate to the whole family piling onto a king-size bed for a dubious night's rest, sleeping in a foul-smelling smoker's den, or perhaps bedding down in a dingy closet-sized cell instead of the suite you requested. Nonsmoking rooms, bed configuration, and preferred room styles are often given out to

confirmed-reservation guests on a first-come, first-serve basis. To avoid problems, clarify exactly your room and the check-in time when you make the reservation, and schedule an early check-in time (most hotels have midafternoon vacancies available) that may be followed up by an afternoon activity.

Although there's no sales tax in Oregon (yet), note that you will find local lodging taxes—ranging 8–12 percent, depending on the locale—added to your bill.

Cutting Costs

Prices up and down the coast peak during summer, a flexible term that generally means Memorial Day to Labor Day. In summer, as well as during spring break, many destinations may fill up, and you'll need to reserve well in advance if you don't want to sleep in your car. Many lodgings drop their rates a bit during spring and fall shoulder seasons. In winter, euphemistically called the storm-watching season, room rates can drop still further, sometimes approaching 50 percent less, with special weekend-getaway packages quite common. This can be a wonderful time for a stay at the coast, when the crowds are long gone and the sea and sky are at their most dramatic. When making a reservation, it pays to ask (or check the lodging's website) about specials and discounts.

The cost-conscious traveler should also keep in mind that there is no shortage of large condos and vacation homes that rent out to large parties who can split costs. We have also recommended a few budget motels that feature cable TV and other basics and are usually conveniently located and cheap.

Bed-and-Breakfasts

This European-style lodging provides a homey alternative to the typical motel room. The Oregon coast leads the country in bed-and-breakfast establishments per capita, but the idea seems to be catching on elsewhere. And why not? Whether they offer a glass of sherry by a crackling fire to warm up beachgoers or a huge picture window on a Pacific storm, these retreats can impart that extra-special personal touch to the best the coast has to offer.

If an early-1900s Victorian or an old farmhouse doesn't give a bed-and-breakfast an extra measure of warmth, the camaraderie of the guests

and the host family usually will. Most bed-and-breakfasts restrict kids, pets, and smoking in deference to what are often close quarters. Private baths are also sometimes in short supply. Offsetting any potential intrusions on privacy is an included full or continental breakfast, sometimes in bed. In Oregon, it has become customary to see homemade jams and breads, as well as a complimentary glass of local wine for a nightcap.

Vacation Rentals

B&Bs can add to a romantic weekend on the coast, but these establishments don't make sense all the time for everyone. This book also lists property rental agencies and realty companies in certain locations whose properties afford more privacy. Deals are plentiful, thanks to the volume of vacation homes that often sit idle or can accommodate large enough parties to offset a high nightly rate.

Campgrounds and RVs

Oregon lodging prices are, for the most part, significantly lower than those of neighboring

Yurts, wood-floored circular tents, are an increasingly popular option for overnighters at several state parks.

California and Washington. Nonetheless, coastal resort areas can put a strain on the pocketbook. Fortunately, state park and national forest campgrounds proliferate in these areas, offering low-cost overnight lodgings in attractive settings. As if by design, the highest percentage of Oregon's 200 state parks surround the high-ticket areas, with sites usually priced around $12–20 per night. Most of these have restrooms, showers, fire rings, piped water, and other basic amenities. National Forest campgrounds usually cost less but offer more primitive facilities; many of them are chosen for their proximity to swimming holes and/or scenic appeal.

If creature comforts are a priority, privately owned RV parks and campgrounds are often equipped with every amenity you can ask for, from laundry facilities to game rooms to cable hookups.

Camping in State Parks

Despite charging the highest camping fees in the West, the coast's state parks are still the most heavily used (per state park acre) in the country—a tribute to their excellence.

Regarding the cost of campgrounds, there's good news and bad news. The bad news is fees at state park campgrounds have gone up in the past few years. The good news is they are not expected to go up much more. Park rates are also subject to change, and some of the less developed, more off-the-beaten-path parks don't even charge a fee. But for those that do, prices average at about the following rates May 1–September 30: electrical hookup sites $21; tent sites $17; primitive/overflow sites $9; hiker/biker sites $4–6; yurts $29–42. During the discounted Discovery Season, October 1–April 30, prices average as follows: electrical hookup sites $17; tent sites $13; hiker/biker sites $4; yurts $27–42. The extra vehicle charge during any season is $7.

One of the newest additions to the coastal camping scene is the yurt, which has started to appear at many campgrounds. Yurts are canvas-walled, wood-floored, and equipped with fold-up beds, heaters, and lamps; they sleep five people.

Half of Oregon's state park campgrounds accept campsite reservations, but the other half are first-come, first served. The state has a central information phone, 800/551-6949, and a reservation line, 800/452-5687. (Go to www.oregonstateparks.org to look up specific rates or to get information.) You can also make reservations for any of these options online with a Visa or MasterCard through ReserveAmerica (800/452-5687, www.reserveamerica.com). Reservations may be made from two days up to 11 months in advance. In addition to the campsite fee, which ranges $7–21 per night, a $6 processing fee is charged. Reservations can also be faxed at 503/378-6308. During winter, hours are Monday–Friday 8 A.M.–5 P.M. The rest of the year, hours are Monday–Friday 8 A.M.–9 P.M., Saturday 8 A.M.–5 P.M.

If you need to **cancel your reservation** three days or more before your scheduled arrival, call Reservations Northwest (800/452-5687 statewide, 503/731-3411 in Portland). Two or fewer days before your trip, call the park directly to cancel your reservation. Phone numbers for all parks are found on each individual park's website (www.oregonstateparks.org). Cancellation service fees and requirements for special facilities, such as yurts and cabins, may vary. Your $6 reservation fee is nonrefundable, and a $3 cancellation fee will be charged if you cancel in the last two days. If you reserve through ReserveAmerica, the cancellation policy differs; see their website for details.

Camping in National Forests

The U.S. Forest Service maintains campsites, trails, and day-use areas in both the Siuslaw and Siskiyou national forests. The Siuslaw National Forest encompasses more than 630,000 acres and is situated within the Oregon Coast Range. It's one of only two national forests located in the lower 48 to include beachfront. The Siskiyou National Forest is located in the Klamath Mountains and the coast ranges of southwestern Oregon, with a small segment of the forest extending into northern California and the Siskiyous. It includes 1,163,484 acres within its boundaries, 69,234 acres of which are owned or privately managed by other agencies. Within the boundaries of these two national forests, there are hundreds of choices. Refer to the Forest Service website (www.fs.fed.us.gov/recreation) or one of the specific destination chapters in this guide for listings.

Campsites generally include a table, a fire grate, and a tent or trailer space. Electric hookups are not available, although most campgrounds have water and vault or flush toilets. Most overnight sites require a user fee. You may camp a maximum of 14 days out of every 30 in the forest. Fees are $10–15 for campsites; $5–7 for an extra vehicle. Campsites can be reserved online with a Visa or MasterCard through ReserveAmerica (800/452-5687, www.reserveamerica.com).

It's important to note that National Forest passholders who plan to use specialized facilities (such as camping, trailhead, parking, boat launch, ramps, swimming sites, etc.) in the national forest still have to pay for an overnight campsite. (See User Fees and Passes in the Recreation section for details on day-use passes for national forests.)

RVs

The Oregon coast is a summer haven for RVers, with activities in each coastal town designed to appeal to this perennial visitor. RV sites in private parks and state parks are abundant but can fill up as early as April with travelers fleeing the hot winds of the California desert for the balmy climes of the coast. (Coastal Oregon receives abundant rainfall, mostly between October and April.) Many RV grounds are open year-round, but some are seasonal, responding to the level of visitors.

Along the coast, many service stations, truck stops, campgrounds, and RV parks provide RV sanitary dump stations. Local chambers of commerce and visitors centers can provide information on activities for seniors, RV-friendly sites, and other services.

FOOD AND DRINK

Visiting gourmets can tell you why many people will happily drive two hours from Portland for a meal at any number of coastal restaurants: In-

MO'S FISH SHANTY

In 1946, Mohava Niemi started up her first humble fish shanty on the Newport bayfront. Locals extolled her tasty and reasonably priced seafood, especially the clam chowder. Knowledge became more widespread during the filming of *Never Give an Inch,* starring Paul Newman and Henry Fonda. Restaurant scenes from this movie (based on Ken Kesey's *Sometimes a Great Notion*) were filmed here, and the stars soon became restaurant devotees. Over the years, other luminaries ranging from Robert Kennedy to Bruce Springsteen joined the club. Soon outlets at Coos Bay, Florence, Lincoln City, Otter Rock, and Cannon Beach opened up, along with an annex to handle the overflow in Newport. Menus are pretty much standard in each restaurant, with fresh fish, clam chowder, and burgers as the main bills of fare. Long benches around the kind of tables you'd find in a logging camp cookhouse impart an air of informality to what has become an institution on the Oregon coast.

ventive chefs, fully exploiting the freshest regional ingredients—wild chanterelles, fiddlehead ferns, marionberries, locally made cheeses, Oregon wines, and, of course, seafood—mean that limited notions of clam chowder and greasy fish and chips are long out of date. Not that there aren't plenty of eateries along the coast where everything but your salad—if you can get one—has been battered and deep-fried. It's just that now there are plenty of exciting alternatives. The coast seems to attract restaurateurs who want to dispel the old myths about the region being a culinary backwater, and here they can start with unbeatable raw materials to work their craft on, especially when it comes to seafood. The fish, oysters, crab, and clams here are as fresh as they can be. At many restaurants, it's a very short trip from the boat to the plate, with a short detour through the kitchen.

Not so long ago, coffee on the coast meant a thin, vengeful, and bitter brew that tasted like bilgewater. How things have changed! Now, it seems as if every bait shop and gas station has a neon Espresso sign glowing warmly in its window, and latte addicts no longer have to suffer through withdrawals as they drive U.S. 101.

Tipping

Tipping for food service is customary but discretionary. As elsewhere in Oregon, the suggested rate of recompense for acceptable service is 15 percent. Diners in larger parties (usually six or more) may find that a restaurant enforces a mandatory tipping policy as part of the bill.

Coastal Cuisine

What will newcomers to the Oregon coast notice most on their plates? The coast boasts such delicacies as Dungeness crab, razor clams, Yaquina Bay oysters, and bay shrimp, as well as world-famous salmon.

Let's start with the bay shrimp as an appetizer. Although a hasty visual appraisal of an Oregon shrimp cocktail might prompt an unfavorable comparison to the larger Gulf prawns, these savory morsels prove that good things come in small packages. Expect them to be in season during August. Another coveted crustacean is the Dungeness crab. West Coast chefs haven't yet mastered the succulence of Maryland-style crabcakes, but the Dungeness tastes richer in a cocktail than the less meaty Atlantic blue crab. The firm texture of Dungeness in peak season (March or October) has been compared to that of Maine lobster.

Speaking of which, those used to *Homarus americanus* from the East Coast will be disappointed by the oversized crayfish passed off as lobster on some menus. Freshwater crawdads here are another distant cousin. Among nonambulatory shellfish, Oregon's Yaquina Bay oysters are considered gourmet fare. If you want them fresh, avoid the summer months and wait until the weather is cooler. Razor clams are another indigenous shellfish—an acquired taste for many. Once you get past their rubbery consistency, however, you might enjoy this local favorite. Local mussels and albacore tuna near the end of July are also worth a try.

When it comes to fresh fish, you'll notice a variance in price based on how the salmon was caught. Troll-caught salmon (usually chinook and coho in Oregon) are landed in the ocean by hook and line, one at a time. This method permits better handling than netted salmon, which are caught in large groups as they come upriver from the ocean to spawn. Thus, you'll pay more for troll salmon, but you can taste the difference. Currently, as efforts are undertaken to restore the species in the Northwest, most grocery-store salmon and some in restaurants come from Alaska or fish farms in Chile. There are limited stocks of Oregon-caught salmon available, however, and it pays to be sensitive to nuances of harvest and preparation.

Spring chinook salmon (Apr.–May) from the Rogue River estuary seems to be a can't-miss item for almost everyone. Although red snapper would normally also merit such an assessment, this is not always the case in Oregon, largely because of a case of mistaken identity. In contrast to the red snapper found on Southern and Eastern menus, this Pacific version is a bottomfish. The brown widow rockfish and dozens of other bottomfish species that receive the "red snapper" designation out here have a similar consistency but a fishier taste than their East Coast counterpart.

Despite the many delicacies available on the Oregon coast, it *is* still possible to have a bad meal in the region. In fact, the quality of the cuisine in some smaller towns is a source of self-deprecating humor for the locals. As many Yankees will tell you, there is no shortage of bland New England–style clam chowder on the Oregon coast. And some of the freshest fish can be had at even the most basic chowder house along the coast, although it may be fried to a crisp.

Still, it's easy to dine well at an affordable price; in fact, you'd be hard-pressed to spend more than $20 on a dinner entrée in most coastal towns. Because the region abounds in places with genuine ambience and home cooking at a good value, fast-food listings are kept to a minimum in this book. Budget travelers might want to shop at local markets or bring their own.

The restaurant recommendations in this book were made with the traveler in mind who would prefer to have some cash left over at the end of a meal to take advantage of a raft trip or a museum. At the same time, we recognize that one of the most pleasurable ways to get to know a locale is at the dinner table. Thus, justifiable splurges occasionally supplant dollar-value orientation, especially when the locale lends itself to gourmet dining.

Alcohol
As more and more wineries and wine outlets are popping up along the coast, a glass of an Oregon Pinot Gris makes a perfect complement to any seafood meal.

Please note Oregon's liquor laws: Liquor is sold by the bottle in state liquor stores, which are open Monday through Saturday. Beer and wine are also sold in grocery stores and retail outlets. Liquor is sold by the drink in licensed establishments 7 A.M.–2:30 A.M. The minimum drinking age throughout the state is 21.

Information and Services

INFORMATION
Visitor Information and Maps
The **Oregon Coast Visitors Association** (137 NE 1st St., P.O. Box 74, Newport, OR 97365, 541/574-2679 or 888/OCVA-101, www .visittheoregoncoast.com) is a good clearinghouse of information for the entire coast, including events listings, weather, and links to all coastal chambers of commerce. The best sources of detailed, current information for the coast are the individual chambers of commerce in each town. Most do an excellent job of helping travelers with their questions, and all now have websites. See the Coastal Chambers of Commerce and Visitor Information chart (in sidebar) for contact information. They provide free maps of their towns and regions.

The **Oregon Tourism Commission** (775 Summer St. NE, Salem, OR 97310, 800/547-7842, www.traveloregon.com) is another good resource, producing several useful free maps and pamphlets on the coast and offering extensive listings of lodgings and activities.

Other useful contacts are the **Oregon Parks and Recreation Department** (1115 Commercial St. NE, Salem, OR 97301, 503/378-6305 or 800/551-6949, www.prd.state.or.us), the **U.S. Bureau of Land Management** (333 SW 1st Ave., Portland, OR 97204, 503/808-6002, www.or.blm.gov), and the **U.S. Forest Service** (333 SW 1st Ave., Portland, OR 503/808-2971, www.fs.fed.us/r6/). All offer free information and maps on the specific recreation areas and preserves under their respective auspices.

For members only, **AAA Oregon/Idaho** (600 SW Market St., Portland, OR 97201, 503/222-6734 or 800/452-1643, www.aaaoregon.com) provides free, high-quality, detailed maps of each coastal county. Their Oregon Coast Tour Map is particularly good.

The Oregon and Washington coasts are served by the **U.S. Coast Guard** 13th District. Their Public Information Site (www.piersystem.com/ external/index.cfm?cid=21) has useful information on boating and water safety.

Travelers with Disabilities
The following numbers will serve outdoors enthusiasts who have disabilities, with specific information on their many options in Oregon: the U.S. Forest Service (503/872-2750) provides information on the Golden Access Passport and on specific accessibility features of each area; those visiting areas managed by the Bureau of Land Management (503/375-5646) can also use the Golden Access Passport; the U.S. Fish and Wildlife Service (503/231-6214) can answer site-specific questions about accessibility; and the Oregon Department of Fish and Wildlife (503/872-5263) puts out a useful guide, called *Access Oregon*, which lists accessible recreation areas.

Publications
For big-city publications, both the Portland *Oregonian* and the *Eugene Register Guard* are available on the coast.

Even though regional monthlies such as *Northwest Travel* and *Sunset* magazines do not have a strictly Oregon focus, there are usually

COASTAL CHAMBERS OF COMMERCE AND VISITORS CENTERS

Oregon Coast Visitors Center
137 NE 1st St.
P.O. Box 74
Newport, OR 97365
541/574-2679 or 888/628-2101
www.visittheoregoncoast.com

Astoria-Warrenton Area Chamber
111 West Marine Dr.
P.O. Box 176
Astoria, OR 97103
503/325-6311 or 800/875-6807
www.oldoregon.com

Bandon Chamber of Commerce
300 Second St.
P.O. Box 1515
Bandon, OR 97411
541/347-9616
www.bandon.com

Bay Area Chamber of Commerce
50 E. Central
P.O. Box 210
Coos Bay, OR 97420
541/269-0215 or 800/824-8486
www.oregonsbayareachamber.com

Brookings/Harbor Chamber of Commerce
16330 Lower Harbor Rd.
P.O. Box 940
Brookings, OR 97415
800/535-9469
www.brookingsor.com

Cannon Beach Chamber of Commerce
2nd and Spruce
P.O. Box 64
Cannon Beach, OR 97110
503/644-0123
www.cannonbeach.org

Depoe Bay Chamber of Commerce
70 NE Hwy. 101
P.O. Box 21
Depoe Bay, OR 97341
541/765-2889 or 877/485-8348
www.stateoforegon.com/depoe_bay/chamber/

Florence Area Chamber of Commerce
270 Hwy. 101
P.O. Box 26000
Florence, OR 97439
541/997-3128 or 800/524-4864
www.florencechamber.com

Garibaldi Chamber of Commerce
605 Garibaldi Ave.
P.O. Box 915
Garibaldi, OR 97118
503/322-0301
www.garibaldioregon.com

Gold Beach Promotion Committee
29279 Ellensburg Ave.
Gold Beach, OR 97444
541/247-7526 or 800/525-2334
www.goldbeach.org

several destination pieces about the state in each edition. Sold throughout the state, *Oregon Coast* magazine (P.O. Box 18000, Florence, OR 97439-1030) is an excellent bimonthly about life on Oregon's western edge.

The alternative newspaper *Hipfish,* published in Astoria, is one of the liveliest community-based monthlies in the state. Frequent coverage of environmental issues is interspersed with cultural listings, reviews, and commen-tary. It's distributed free at selected locales on the coast.

MONEY AND COMMUNICATION
Money

Oregon has no state sales tax, although that could change in the future. For now, it makes purchases at the coast all the more attractive, partic-

Greater Newport Chamber of Commerce
555 SW Coast Hwy.
Newport, OR 97365
800/262-7844
www.newportchamber.org

Lincoln City Chamber of Commerce
801 SW Hwy. 101, #1
P.O. Box 787
Lincoln City, OR 97367
541/994-8378 or 800/452-2151
www.oregoncoast.org

Nehalem Bay Area Chamber of Commerce
8th and Tohl St.
P.O. Box 159
Nehalem, OR 97131
503/368-5100 or 877/368-5100
www.nehalembaychamber.com

Port Orford Chamber of Commerce
Battle Rock Park, Hwy. 101 S.
P.O. Box 637
Port Orford, OR 97465
541/332-8055
www.portorfordoregon.com

Reedsport/Winchester Bay Chamber of Commerce
805 Hwy. Ave.
P.O. Box 11
Reedsport, OR 97467
541/271-3495 or 800/247-2155
www.reedsportcc.org

Rockaway Beach Chamber of Commerce
103 1st St.
P.O. Box 198
Rockaway Beach, OR 97136
800/331-5928
www.rockawaybeach.net

Seaside Oregon Visitor Bureau
989 Broadway
Seaside, OR 97138
503/738-6391 or 888/306-2326
www.seasidechamber.com

Tillamook Chamber of Commerce
3705 Hwy. 101 N.
Tillamook, OR 97141
503/842-7525
www.tillamookchamber.org

Waldport Chamber of Commerce
620 NW Spring St.
P.O. Box 669
Waldport, OR 97394
541/563-2133
www.pioneer.net/~waldport

Yachats Area Chamber of Commerce
241 Hwy. 101
P.O. Box 728
Yachats, OR 97498
541/547-3530 or 800/929-0477
www.yachats.org

ularly to out-of-state visitors. Major credit cards are widely accepted at shops, lodgings, restaurants, and other establishments, but not everywhere. Acceptability of personal checks varies; it's worth asking beforehand. Traveler's checks in U.S. currency, issued by major firms such as American Express, are generally accepted with official picture ID.

The larger towns on the coast have at least one bank with an automated teller machine (ATM), and these are noted in individual desti-

nation chapters. Many of the coast's small towns and villages, however, have no banking services. Larger grocery stores, such as Fred Meyer, Safeway, Ray's, and Clark's, with numerous coastal locations, usually have an ATM.

Mail

Most post offices open around 7–9 A.M. and close around 5–6 P.M. Sometimes drugstores or card shops have a postal substation open on weekends and holidays when the government operations are closed. If it happens to be Sunday and the post office is closed, you can also get stamps from grocery stores and hotels, with little or no markup. Oregon also has many FedEx, UPS, and other private shipping companies operating across the state to complement government services.

Telephone

Coastal Oregon has two area codes: **503** for Astoria to Lincoln City and **541** for the rest of the coast. Note that you must dial the area code, even for local calls. For long-distance calls within the state, dial 1 before the correct area code and then the seven-digit telephone number. For directory assistance, dial 1, followed by the appropriate area code for the locale you are searching, and then 555-1212.

Cell phone users should be aware that service in some coastal areas and in the coast ranges can be spotty, particularly along the south coast. As of 2004, users may find that they cannot get service south of about Port Orford.

Internet Access

The Oregon coast isn't the most thoroughly wired corner of the world, but that's changing fast, and you shouldn't have too much trouble getting logged on. Some options are noted in individual destination chapters. Many larger hotels and motels now offer Internet access, as do most libraries. Internet cafés, providing access by the hour, seem to come and go; see specific destination chapters for details.

Health and Safety

EMERGENCY SERVICES AND HEALTHCARE

Throughout Oregon, dial **911** for medical, police, or fire emergencies. You may always dial 0 to get the operator. In this book, look for contact information on additional local services in each destination's Information and Services section.

There are hospital facilities in Brookings, Bandon, Coos Bay, Florence, Newport, Seaside, and Astoria with 24-hour emergency rooms. See each destination chapter for details.

Oregon's larger cities maintain switchboard referral services, as well as hospital-sponsored free advice lines. Remember that medical costs are high here, as in the rest of the United States. Emergency-room care is the most expensive.

COASTAL HAZARDS

Whether you're merely admiring its natural beauty or braving its waves, the Oregon coast holds potential dangers. Children are especially at risk because they can be easily distracted by tide pools and sandcastle construction, and they may not be aware of tidal changes, changing weather, or other natural dangers. For both

adults and children, a little common sense goes a long way.

Hypothermia

The cold temperatures of Oregon's coastal waters (as low as 40–45°F) make swimming and other water sports potentially dangerous any time of year. Even in the hottest days of summer, sea temperature doesn't exceed 62°F. Hypothermia—a condition that sets in when the core temperature of the body drops to 95°F or below—is a danger visitors should be aware of. Hikers and others engaging in outdoor activities away from the water can be at risk as well, particularly when the weather is cool and windy.

One of the first signs of hypothermia is a diminished ability to think and act rationally. Speech can become slurred, and uncontrollable shivering usually takes place. Stumbling, memory lapses, and drowsiness also tend to characterize those afflicted. Unless the body temperature can be raised several degrees by a knowledgeable helper, cardiac arrhythmia and/or arrest may occur. A wet human body loses heat 23 times faster than a dry one, so getting out of the water and being sheltered from the wind and rain in a dry, warm environment is essential for survival.

WARNING

FOR YOUR SAFETY BE AWARE OF OCEAN SHORE HAZARDS

Unusually high (Sneaker) waves

Incoming tides isolate rocks from shore

Deep water & strong outgoing currents

Overhanging cliffs & falling rocks

High waves sweep over rocks & jetties

Drift logs roll in surf

High steep cliffs

TSUNAMI HAZARD ZONE

IN CASE OF EARTHQUAKE, GO TO HIGH GROUND OR INLAND

NO LIFEGUARD

For additional information call (503)378-6305 Oregon Parks and Recreation Department

© MARK MORRIS

Have fun, but be careful out there.

This might mean placing the victim into a pre-warmed sleeping bag, which can be prepared by having another person strip and climb into the bag with the endangered person. Ideally, a groundcloth should be used to insulate the sleeping bag from cold surface temperatures. Internal heat can be generated by feeding the victim high-carbohydrate snacks and hot liquids. Placing wrapped heated objects against the victim's body is also a good way to restore body heat. Be careful, however, not to raise body heat too quickly, which could also cause cardiac problems. If body temperature doesn't drop below 90°F, chances for complete recovery are good; with body temperatures between 80–90°F, victims are more likely to suffer some sort of lasting damage. Most victims won't survive a body temperature below 80°F.

Measures you can take to prevent hypothermia include avoiding the cold water of the Pacific, eating a nutritious diet, avoiding overexertion followed by exposure to wet and cold, and dressing warmly in layers of wool and polypropylene. Wool insulates even when wet, and because polypro wicks moisture away from your skin, it makes a good first layer. Gore-Tex and its counterparts, such as Helly-Tech or other new breathable fabrics, make for more comfortable raingear than nylon because they don't become cumbersome and hot. Finally, wear a hat: More radiated heat leaves from the head than from any other part of the body.

Why Not to Swim

Hypothermia aside, casual waders and swimmers alike are at risk of being swept off by riptides or undertows, which occurs when one layer of water flows against the direction of the surface water. These powerful, usually localized, currents can be found just about any place along the coast and would be a challenge even to swimmers of Olympic ability. What every swimmer must know is that when caught in a riptide, one should swim with or across the current, not against it, which will only exhaust you; rather, try to swim parallel to shore, edging closer and closer to shore until it's possible to come in or call for help.

Floating debris is another concern for swimmers and waders. Storms can churn up inland riverbanks, yielding huge floating logs, which are then carried into shore along the backs of waves. These heavy objects can slam into swimmers or pin them down, so give these potential killers a wide berth.

Boating

Life jackets or vests are strongly advised for anyone aboard a watercraft. In 2003, a tragic fishing accident on Tillamook Bay yielded stark proof that life vests save lives. A 35-foot charter boat capsized while crossing the bar in rough conditions. Eleven people—none wearing life vests—were lost. In addition to keeping a person afloat and face-up, whether or not he or she can swim, the vests provide some insulation from the frigid water, thus decreasing the risk of hypothermia and injury.

State law requires that all children age 12 and younger must wear a Coast Guard–approved personal flotation device (PFD)/life vest while on an open deck or cockpit of sailboats, motorized and nonmotorized vessels (such as canoes, kayaks, rafts). Life vests are also a smart idea for small children any time they're near the water.

Dangerous Terrain

Part of the appeal of the coast is its rugged terrain and raw natural state—two features that can also make it a dangerous place to explore. High cliffs, undesignated trails, rocky out-croppings, tidepools, and pocket beaches often lure intrepid hikers who are bent on getting that perfect view or photo opportunity. These are the same folks who are rescued from clifftops, stranded by a changing tide, or worse. In other words, stay on designated paths, avoid unfenced cliff edges, check your tide tables, and follow signage. The worst damage is often done to the environment, when hikers trample a native species habitat or disturb organisms living in tidal areas. Please stay on paths and avoid climbing on rocks that may be home to living things.

Part of the appeal of the coast is its rugged terrain and raw natural state—two features that can also make it a dangerous place to explore.

Sneaker Waves

Many a visitor to Oregon's coast have been the victim of the potentially deadly "sneaker wave." Not as uncommon as one might imagine, these treacherous out-of-nowhere waves have a habit of cropping up when you least expect them. Most prevalent during the stormiest times of the year, sneaker waves are powerful enough to knock an angler from his or her perch or sweep an unsuspecting beachcomber out to sea. Unfortunately, small children are most vulnerable, so constant supervision is a must.

Even the unexpected large breaker can have the same effect as the rogue wave. So, be mindful of the everyday risks of strolling the beach or admiring the vista. Pocket beaches rimmed with cliffs are especially hazardous, as are rocky areas. A flat, gradually sloping sand beach is usually safer, but not without some risk.

Tsunamis

Many people think that tsunami is a Japanese term for "tidal wave." Not so. Tsunami is a Japan-ese term for "harbor wave." But a tsunami is not just one wave; it is a series of waves that are the direct result of seismic activity, such as earthquakes or marine quakes. A tsunami may begin in the middle of the ocean as a two-foot wave heading for shore at several hundred miles per hour—by this definition, it may sound like a great opportunity to put your surfing skills to the test—but once it reaches land or harbor, it can strike with devastating force.

As a tsunami draws closer to the shore, driven by the force of the quake, it takes in preceding waters and builds into a series of waves traveling as fast as 500 miles per hour and reaching as high as 100 feet. Waves of this size would submerge whole towns; smaller ones would cause major property damage and threaten the lives of those in its path.

Along the coast, you will see blue-and-white tsunami evacuation signs, which warn locals and visitors of impending danger and direct them to higher, safer ground. Visitors should also be aware

Signs up and down the coast point the way to safer ground in the event of a tsunami warning.

of the global alarm system, which sounds off when tsunami danger is high. To be fully prepared, one must be attuned to any news of seismic activity in the area or in the Pacific Rim.

Also note that any dramatic change in water levels (which are not part of the normal tidal activity) may be nature's own early warning that a tsunami may be minutes away.

Transportation

BY AIR

Of the dozen airports on the coast, only North Bend Municipal Airport enjoys regularly scheduled commercial service. **Horizon Air** (800/547-9308, www.horizonair.com), the commuter-league farm club of Alaska Airlines, connects Seattle and Portland with directs flights to and from North Bend. Flights to and from other Horizon destinations (in Alaska, Washington, California, Idaho, and beyond) are routed through these hubs. Horizon operates commuter prop planes with 10–40 seats. If you are sensitive to loud noises and pressure change, you may want to ask for earplugs when you check in for your boarding pass.

Newport Municipal Airport, North Bend, and other coastal and inland airports (including Eugene, Medford, Portland, Corvallis, and Grants Pass) are also served by **Sky Taxi** (866/759-8298, www.skytaxi.com), a charter service that flies twin-prop Cessnas for up to five passengers.

BY BUS
Getting There
Greyhound sold off many of its coastal routes in the early 1990s, making for a patchwork quilt of mass-transit providers on the western edge of the state. Add a dearth of city buses and only two airports serving Oregon's shoreline, and you can understand why it's especially difficult to see this area if you're not traveling by car. In most coastal towns, a local supermarket or convenience store usually acts as the bus stop.

Greyhound (800/229-9424, www.greyhound .com) does still operate a coast route twice daily between Portland and Brookings (and on to San Francisco), via Lincoln City and points in between.

For the north coast, **Amtrak Thruway Motorcoach Service** buses (800/USA-RAIL or 800/872-7245, www.tickets.amtrak.com) run a daily coastal loop: Astoria-Warrenton-Gearhart-Seaside-Cannon Beach Portland's Union Station and Astoria. **Pierce-Pacific Stage Line** (503/717-1651 in Seaside, 503/436-2523) operates a similar route daily (except Christmas day and Thanksgiving) that also takes in Kelso, Washington.

To get to and from the central coast, **Valley Retriever** (541/265-2253) buses connect Newport with Corvallis Monday–Saturday.

Getting Around
Local north coast service in Clatsop County is provided by the Sunset Empire Transportation District, better known as **The Bus** (503/861-RIDE or 800/776-6406, www.ridethebus.org), which provides reasonably frequent transportation around Astoria and along the coast from Warrenton (including Fort Stevens State Park and Fort Clatsop) to Cannon Beach. Operates Monday–Saturday.

On weekdays, **Lincoln County Transit** (541/265-4900, www.co.lincoln.or.us/transit) runs buses four times daily between Lincoln City and Yachats, with numerous stops en route. On the south coast, **Coastal Express** buses (541/469-6822) run up and down the south coast between North Bend and Brookings, weekdays only.

You'll find additional details on local bus transport in respective destination chapters.

BY TRAIN

In 2003, Amtrak initiated train service between Portland and Astoria for the first time in living memory, with the **Lewis & Clark Explorer.** From late May to early September, the excursion train

ON THE ROAD

ON THE ROAD

DRIVING DISTANCES

All distances are given in miles.

	Astoria	Seaside	Tillamook	Lincoln City	Newport	Florence	Reedsport	Coos Bay	Bandon	Gold Beach	Brookings
Astoria	X	16	64	111	136	186	207	234	257	312	341
Seaside	16	X	48	95	120	170	191	218	241	296	325
Tillamook	64	48	X	47	72	122	143	170	193	248	277
Lincoln City	111	95	47	X	25	75	96	123	146	201	230
Newport	136	120	72	25	X	50	71	98	121	176	205
Florence	186	170	122	75	50	X	21	48	71	126	155
Reedsport	207	191	143	96	71	21	X	27	50	105	134
Coos Bay	234	218	170	123	98	48	27	X	23	78	107
Bandon	257	241	193	146	121	71	50	23	X	55	84
Gold Beach	312	296	248	201	176	126	105	78	55	X	29
Brookings	341	325	277	230	205	155	134	107	84	29	X
Portland	96	80	78	89	114	164	185	212	235	290	319
Salem	131	115	75	58	83	122	143	170	193	248	277
Albany	154	138	93	76	66	99	120	147	170	225	254
Eugene	191	175	130	113	95	61	82	109	132	177	206
Roseburg	260	244	203	168	143	93	72	87	87	142	169
Grants Pass	331	315	275	237	212	162	141	142	142	129	100

departs Linnton Station in Northwest Portland (get there by bus from downtown's Union Station at 7:30) Friday–Monday at 7:50 A.M., follows the scenic route along the Columbia on the water-level Burlington Northern tracks, and arrives at Astoria's old train depot on 20th Street off Marine Drive at 11:50 A.M. The train departs Astoria at 4:50 P.M., arriving in Portland at 8:50 P.M. One-way tickets are $24 general, $20 seniors. Contact Amtrak (800/USA-RAIL or 800/872-7245, www.tickets.amtrak.com) for reservations and more details. As part of the Lewis and Clark Bicentennial, this special train is slated to run summers through 2005, although Oregon's budget woes could change those plans.

BY CAR

Ever since the "Daddy Train" linking Portland to Seaside shut down in the 1930s, the automobile has been the vehicle of choice for getting to and around the coast.

Routes to the Coast

From the I-5 corridor, where most of the state's population is concentrated, 10 main routes will get you to the coast. Most are two-lane state highways for all or part of the journey through rural hinterlands and the coastal mountains.

From Portland, **U.S. 30** runs north through St. Helen's and follows the bottomlands along the south bank of the Columbia River to Astoria, 98 miles to the northwest. If you're coming down from the north on I-5, cross the Columbia from Longview, Washington, to Rainier, Oregon, and continue west on U.S. 30 from there.

Busy **U.S. 26** runs west, then angles northwest, from Portland, through agricultural Washington County and then into the woods of the Clatsop State Forest before joining U.S. 101 between Cannon Beach and Seaside. About 25 miles west of Portland, **ORE 6** branches off from U.S. 26 and follows a roller-coaster course alongside the Wilson River to Tillamook.

A third route from Portland starts with **ORE 99W** and a dozen maddening stop-and-go miles through the strip development of Tigard. After Newburg you emerge into a lovely countryside of

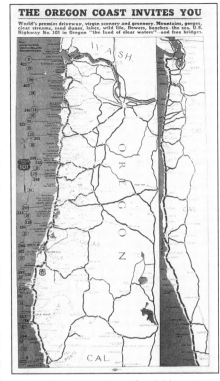

"Land of Clear Waters" and free bridges: A 1940s tourist map beckons visitors to drive U.S. 101.

vineyards and hazelnut orchards around Dundee. Pick up **ORE 18** for the second half of the trip, which runs past Oregon's number-one attraction, the Spirit Mountain Casino in Grande Ronde, before you hit the Coast Highway just north of Lincoln City and another Indian-owned casino, Chinook Winds. Note that the casinos attract more than three million visitors per year, which helps make ORE 18 one of the most dangerous roads to drive in the state.

From Salem, **ORE 22** runs 26 miles to the west and connects with ORE 18 about midway to the coast.

Farther south, **U.S. 20** curves down from Albany through Corvallis and on to Philomath. From there you can continue 46 miles to Newport or veer southwest on **ORE 34** for a winding 59 miles through a remote section of the Siuslaw National Forest to Waldport.

ORE 126, from Eugene to Florence, is one of the more direct routes, zipping through the flatlands and foothills before throwing you a few curves on the way to the burg of Mapleton, and then hugging the Siuslaw River the last dozen miles.

Near Curtin, south of Cottage Grove, leave I-5 for a brief detour on ORE 99 before catching **ORE 38.** This scenic two-lane road—Oregon's "foremost motorcycle road," according to Harley-Davidson—follows the valley of the mighty Umpqua River to Reedsport, about a 57-mile trip. If you're coming from the south on I-5, cut off onto **ORE 138** at Sutherlin to save some miles on this route.

ORE 42 shadows the Coquille River through farm country for much of its course from Roseburg to Coos Bay. Recent improvements to this highway make it possible to get there in less than two hours, but it's a longish 87 miles. Motorists should still be aware that this thoroughfare carries more truck traffic than any other interior-to-coast road in Oregon. But weekenders will encounter few trucks and light traffic to impede the enjoyment of the waysides, wineries, and historic buildings. If the southern coast is your destination, branch off on **ORE 42S** at Coquille; from there it's 17 miles to Bandon.

South of Roseburg, if you're partial to pavement, there's no good direct route to the coast. The only option is **U.S. 199** from Grants Pass, skirting the remote eastern edge of the Kalmiopsis Wilderness before dropping into northern California. The highway runs through the awesome giants of Redwoods National Park before hitting the Coast Highway near Crescent City. From there, it's 22 miles north up to Brookings. All told, count on about two hours to travel this roundabout, albeit beautiful, 100-mile route.

Driving U.S. 101, The Oregon Coast Highway

The Main Street of the Oregon coast, this 363-mile National Scenic Byway was recently designated an "All-American Road," one of 20 in the country selected for their archaeological, cultural, historic, natural, recreational, and scenic qualities.

As such, it's a route to be savored, not hurried through—and that's just as well, because sustained high-speed travel is not among the highway's many qualities. Maximum posted speed on U.S. 101 is 55 miles per hour; actual average speed is usually around 50 mph or less. Along the way, several beach loops and inland routes are often less traveled and offer some outstanding scenery in their own right.

The Oregon Coast Highway is a route to be savored, not hurried through.

U.S. 101 is a two-lane road most of the way, with occasional passing lanes and four lanes along the main drags of the larger coastal cities. You can count on heavy traffic during summer and holidays, and chances are you'll spend at least a little time getting to know the rear end of a slow-moving log truck or a lumbering Winnebago. Relax. Be prepared to modify your schedule to accommodate inevitable slowdowns and enjoy the breathtaking scenery surrounding the road.

The automobile may be the first transportation choice for most visitors to the coast, but it's not the only vehicle on the road. Especially in summer, be mindful of bicyclists sharing the shoulder. Hills and dips, tight turns, and foliage can often obscure them from view until the last moment. And always beware of cars whose drivers are paying more attention to the view than to the road. Another consideration for drivers is the fact that the road signs found throughout the state are sometimes less than explicit. Whether it's a turn signpost 50 yards after the fact or directional markers hidden by shrubbery, Oregon seems to have more than its share of unwanted surprises for motorists.

In winter, heavy rain and wind are possible dangers, and you may encounter thick fog just about any time of year.

The Oregon Department of Transportation advises on **road conditions** by phone (800/977-ODOT in Oregon, 503/588-2941 out of state) and via their TripCheck website (www.tripcheck.com).

Fuel

Gas is readily available on the Coast Highway, but motorists heading to the coast via some of the 10 main routes through the coast ranges should be aware that there are long stretches without a drop, so be sure to fill up beforehand. Out-of-state visitors will soon learn that Oregon is one of the few states that does not allow motorists to pump their own gas. This, combined with the gas tax levied to help pay for Oregon's roads, helps give the state some of the highest gas prices in the country.

Car Rentals

Car rentals are not unheard of on the coast, but most visitors arrive driving their own. Renting a car is pain-free, as long as you plan ahead and have a credit card. The rental chains (Avis, Alamo, Budget, Dollar, National, and Thrifty) have outlets in the main population centers and airports (such as Portland, Medford, and Eugene). Astoria has the most car rental agencies on the coast, but still far fewer than in larger cities elsewhere. For other locations, check the individual destination chapters in this guide or log on to www.american-car.net/car-rental/OR for a statewide directory of car rental agencies.

You can flip through the Yellow Pages and try to save some bucks with an independent operator, but consider that the larger chains have more service centers set up to assist you in case you break down in a backwater. Although it costs a bit more, it's always wise to buy the car rental insurance. Members of AAA can call 503/222-6734 to receive guidebooks, maps, and tow, repair, and insurance services applicable to car rental.

ON THE ROAD

South Coast

Stretching from the California border to the Coos Bay Area, much of the region is a long way from the population centers of Oregon's interior valleys, but the south coast amply rewards visitors who make the effort to get here. The foothills of the Klamath Mountains tumble down the narrow coastal plain and fall off in precipitous headlands at the ocean's edge. Inshore, the waters are a rocky garden of sea stacks and islets that are home to uncounted flocks of pelagic birds. With half a dozen wild rivers slicing through the mountains to the sea, the south coast is famed for its outstanding salmon fishing, especially on charters from the harbors Gold Beach, Bandon, and Brookings.

In addition, blessed with the fairest weather on the Oregon coast, the southern region generally gets the most sunshine, least rain, and warmest temperatures—attributes that are as appealing to visitors as to retirees and other transplants.

Scenic highlights of the south coast include the gorgeous scenery of Boardman and Harris Beach

Harris Beach, Brookings

State Parks, the weather-beaten bluffs and formal gardens farther north at Cape Arago and Shore Acres state parks, and just about every inch of the drive between Brookings and Port Orford.

In addition to fishing, recreational opportunities are seemingly endless: A pair of outstanding courses draws golfers to Bandon (*Golf* magazine hailed Bandon Dunes as one of the country's top three courses) and Brookings (where the Chetco River, full of spawning salmon, winds through the links of Salmon Run Golf Course), some of the coast's top windsurfing is near Cape Sebastian, and popular jetboat tours run up the Rogue River from Gold Beach.

Brookings-Harbor and Vicinity

If you cross the California–Oregon state border on U.S. 101 in late spring or early summer, the welcome mat of blooming Easter lilies often lines the way into the southern Oregon coast's gateway city of Brookings (population 5,725) and its unincorporated bigger neighbor, Harbor (population 8,775). While the lilies may not carpet these roadsides so extravagantly during the rest of the year, the coast-bound traveler can still look forward to being greeted by mild temperatures and colorful bouquets, even in winter. Enough 60–70°F days occur during January and February in this south coast "banana belt" town that more than 50 species of flowering plants thrive here—along with retirees, sportsmen, and beachcombers. With two gorgeous state parks virtually part of the city and world-class salmon and steelhead fishing nearby, only the lavish winter rainfall that averages more than 73 inches per year can cool the ardor of local outdoors enthusiasts.

Brookings and the adjacent town of Harbor sit on a coastal plain overlooking the Pacific six miles north of the California border, split by U.S. 101 (Chetco Avenue) and the Chetco River. Flowing out of the Klamath Mountains east of town, the Chetco drains part of the nearby **Siskiyou National Forest** and the **Kalmiopsis Wilderness,** extensive tracts encompassing some of the wildest country in the Lower 48 and renowned for their rare flowers and trees. This area enjoys strict federal protection, safeguarding the northernmost stand of giant redwoods and the coveted Port Orford cedar (whose strong but pliable lumber can fetch $10,000 and up for a single tree). The Kalmiopsis Wilderness is named for a unique shrub, the *Kalmiopsis leachiana,* one of the oldest members of the heath family (Ericaceae) that grows nowhere else on earth.

But you don't have to trek miles into the backcountry to enjoy the natural beauty of Brookings and its vicinity. Just make your way past the main drag to **Samuel Boardman State Park** north of town, where 11 of the most scenic miles of the Oregon coast await. Or head down to the harbor to embark on a boating expedition, amid some of the safest offshore navigation conditions in the region. In short, Brookings is the perfect place to launch an adventure by land or by sea.

HISTORY

What is now the shopping hub of rural Curry County started out as a factory town for the Brookings Box Company in 1913. Owner J. L. Brookings hired the architect Bernard Maybeck (famous for designing the Palace of Fine Arts in San Francisco) to lay out the streets and design housing and community buildings for his mill workers. Maybeck drew up extensive plans for what was to be a model company town, but most of them were never realized, and his central vision was eventually gutted when the state highway was laid through, rather than around, the town. Examples of Maybeck's craftsmanship can still be seen around Brookings, notably in the 1917 Craftsman-style residence (now the South Coast Inn B&B) he drew up for lumber baron William Ward.

In the years that followed, the lumber industry was augmented with fishing, horticulture, and tourism. Omitting, for the moment, the possibilities that the offshore waters here were visited by Juan Cabrillo (in 1542) and the English explorer

SOUTH COAST

PACIFIC

OCEAN

© AVALON TRAVEL PUBLISHING, INC.

Sir Francis Drake (in 1579), the local event with the greatest historical significance was the Japanese aerial bombing in 1942. On September 9 of that year, a Japanese incendiary bomb scorched the treetops of Mt. Emily, southeast of town, in one of only two documented wartime air bombing missions against the U.S. mainland (the other occurred three weeks later, near Port Orford). The resulting fires were quickly dowsed by the damp conditions, and no significant harm was done.

Ironically, this episode had two positive outgrowths of enduring significance. First, it sounded the death knell for a secessionist movement by southern Oregonians and northern Californians. During the 1930s, these people wanted to break off from the Union to set up the self-sufficient agrarian state of Jefferson. Second, the bombing encouraged the local lily industry to expand in an effort to make up for the cutoff of Japanese flowers. Today, the area produces 90 percent of the world's Easter lily crop.

Twenty years after the bomb attack, the Japanese pilot Nobuo Fujita accepted an invitation to return to Brookings during the town's Azalea Festival. He brought with him the 400-year-old samurai sword he had carried on his missions during the war, and presented it to the people of Brookings as a token of reconciliation. It still hangs on display in the Brookings city library. Fujita returned again in 1992, as the guest of honor for the opening of a new Forest Service trail to the bomb site, on the 50th anniversary of the attack. At age 80, he hiked the new trail and planted a redwood seedling in the bomb crater as a token of peace.

Since the late 1980s, Brookings' greatest growth industry has been as a haven for retirees, and that population has been booming in recent years.

SIGHTS

Camellias bloom at Christmas, and the flowering plums add color the next month. Daffodils, grown commercially on the coastal plain south of Brookings, bloom in late January and into February. Magnolia shrubs, some early azaleas, and rhododendrons also bloom in late winter.

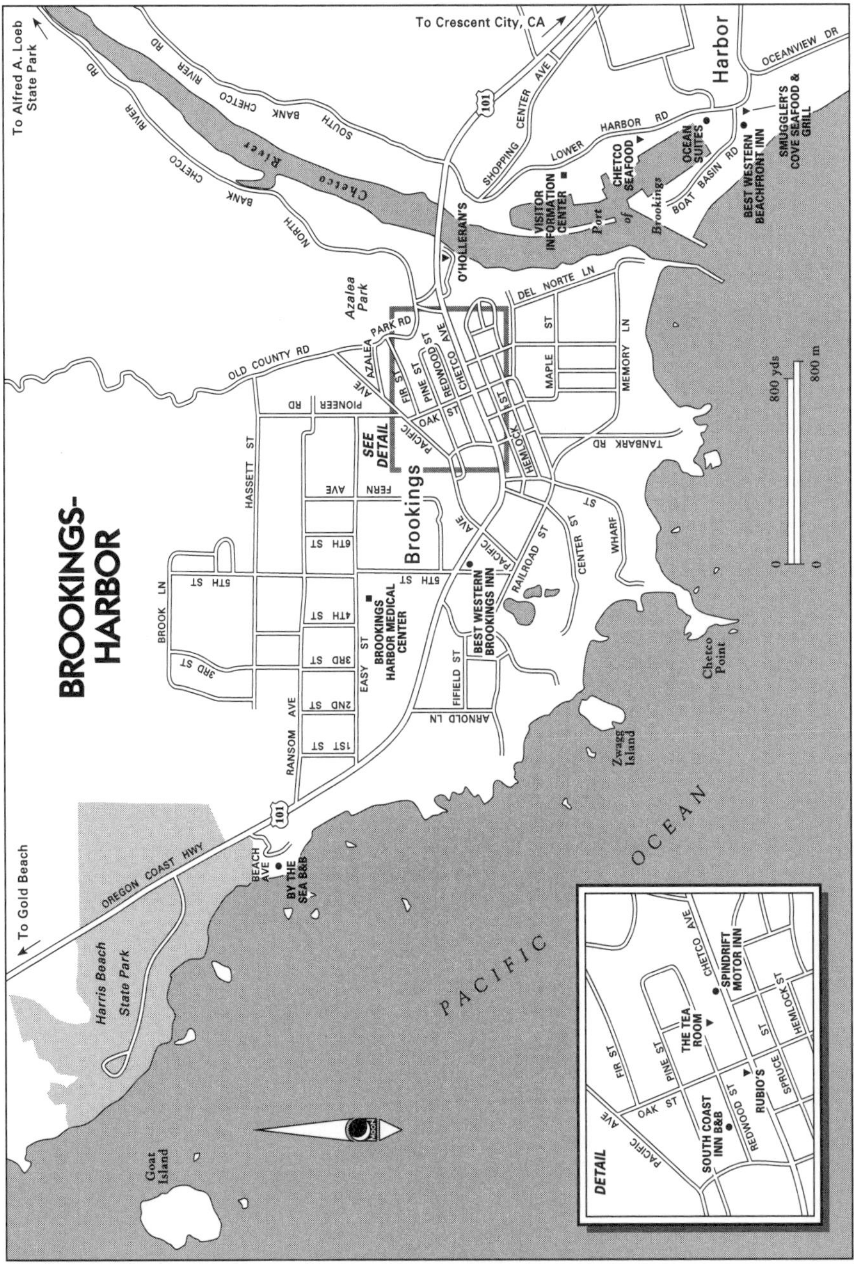

To Crescent City, CA

Harbor

OCEANVIEW DR

To Alfred A. Loeb
State Park

SHOPPING CENTER AVE

LOWER HARBOR RD

SOUTH BANK CHETCO RIVER RD

NORTH BANK CHETCO RIVER RD

Chetco River

CHETCO SEAFOOD

OCEAN SUITES

SMUGGLER'S COVE SEAFOOD & GRILL

BEST WESTERN BEACHFRONT INN

VISITOR INFORMATION CENTER

Port of Brookings

BOAT BASIN RD

O'HOLLERAN'S

DEL NORTE LN

Azalea Park

AZALEA PARK RD

OLD COUNTY RD

PIONEER RD

MAPLE ST

MEMORY LN

800 yds

800 m

FIR ST
PINE ST
REDWOOD AVE
CHETCO AVE

OAK ST

PACIFIC ST

HEMLOCK ST

TANBARK RD

SEE DETAIL

Brookings

HASSETT ST

FERN AVE

ST

WHARF ST

CENTER ST

RAILROAD ST

PACIFIC AVE

BROOK LN

6TH ST

5TH ST

4TH ST

3RD ST

Chetco Point

BROOKINGS-HARBOR

BROOKINGS HARBOR MEDICAL CENTER

BEST WESTERN BROOKINGS INN

5TH ST

EASY ST

FIFIELD ST

ARNOLD LN

RANSOM AVE

1ST ST
2ND ST
3RD ST

101

Zwagg Island

BEACH AVE

BY THE SEA B&B

OREGON COAST HWY

To Gold Beach

Harris Beach State Park

PACIFIC OCEAN

Goat Island

SOUTH COAST

N

DETAIL

PACIFIC AVE

FIR ST
PINE ST
OAK ST
REDWOOD ST
SPRUCE ST
HEMLOCK ST

CHETCO AVE

SPINDRIFT MOTOR INN

THE TEA ROOM

RUBIO'S

SOUTH COAST INN B&B

© AVALON TRAVEL PUBLISHING, INC.

Chetco Valley Historical Society Museum

The Chetco Valley Historical Society Museum (5461 Museum Rd., Brookings, 541/469-6651, 9 A.M.–5 P.M. Fri.–Sun. Nov.–mid-May, 2–6 P.M. Tues.–Sat. and noon–6 P.M. Sun. the rest of the year, $3 donation suggested), in the red-and-white Blake House, sits on a hill overlooking U.S. 101 two miles south of the Chetco River. The structure dates to 1857 and was used as a stagecoach waystation and trading post before Lincoln was president.

Even if you are not one for museums, several exhibits here stand apart from the traditional collections of pioneer wedding dresses, Indian baskets, and spinning wheels. These include a small trunk that came around Cape Horn in 1706 and an Indian dugout canoe. Should these fail to inspire, a mysterious iron casting of a woman's face might do the trick, especially in light of the speculation that this relic was left by an early undocumented landing on the Oregon coast, perhaps by Sir Francis Drake. Drake has been commonly suggested because of the mask's likeness to Queen Elizabeth.

Oregon's largest Monterey cypress tree is located on the hill near the museum. The 99-foot-tall

tree has a trunk circumference of more than 27 feet and has been home to a pair of owls for years.

Carpenterville Road

The current roadbed of U.S. 101 was laid in southern Oregon in 1961. The previous coastal route still exists along Carpenterville Road, which can be picked up near Harris Beach (inquire at the State Welcome Center located nearby). It comes out near the Pistol River, where it descends in a series of switchbacks. Its highest point is 1,700 feet above sea level at Burnt Hill. Views of the Siskiyous to the east and the Pacific panoramas to the west make the sometimes rough road worth the effort. In very clear weather, it's possible to look back toward the southeast at Mt. Shasta between the ridge lines. This route is best appreciated going south.

Harris Beach State Park

You're driving north along the first dozen miles of scenic U.S. 101 in Oregon, but instead of stopping to take out the camera, you're asking yourself, "So, where's the Oregon coast?" It's easy to have second thoughts after a half-hour drive through the "Twilight Zone" of small-town America, with only a few fleeting glimpses of

© MARK MORRIS

the rock gardens of Harris Beach State Park

the ocean. And then, at the northern limits of Brookings, across from the State Information Center on U.S. 101, you find your lost picture postcard at Harris Beach State Park. One look at the 24 miles of rock and tide visible from the parking-lot promontory should quell any misgivings.

Harris Beach was named after the Scottish pioneer George Harris, who settled here in the late 1880s to raise sheep and cattle. Besides stunning views, this state park offers many incoming travelers from California their first chance to actually walk on the beach in Oregon. You can begin directly west of the park's campground, where a sandy beach strewn with boulders often becomes flooded with intertidal life and driftwood. The early morning hours, as the waves crash through a small tunnel in a massive rock onto the shoreline, are the best time to look for sponges, umbrella crabs, solitary corals, and starfish.

Offshore, Bird Island (also called Goat Island) is the largest island along the Oregon coast and the state's largest seabird rookery. This outpost of Oregon Islands National Wildlife Sanctuary dispatches squadrons of cormorants, pelicans, tufted puffins, and other waterfowl who divebomb the incoming waves for food. In addition to beachcombing, you can picnic at tables above the parking lot, loll about in the shallow waters of nearby Harris Creek, or cast the surf for perch.

Mill Beach is the southernmost part of the Harris Beach area. Locals prefer the beach access from downtown, which is easy to miss. To get there, drive toward the ocean on Center Street in downtown Brookings, make a right at the plywood mill, and stop next to a small ballpark. An unimproved road leads to a hillock from which trails take you down to a beach full of driftwood. Residents say that Japanese fishing floats occasionally roll up onto the beach after a storm.

Samuel H. Boardman State Scenic Corridor

The stretch of highway from Brookings to Port Orford is known as the "fabulous 50 miles." Some consider the section of coastline just north of Brookings to be the most scenic in Oregon— and one of the most dramatic meetings of rock and tide in the world. The offshore rock formations and winding roadbed hundreds of feet above the surf invite comparison to Europe's Amalfi Drive. This sobriquet is perhaps most apt in the first dozen miles north of Brookings, encompassed by Samuel Boardman State Scenic Corridor. You'll want to have plenty of film and a loose schedule when you make this drive, because you'll find it hard not to pull over again and again, as each photo opportunity seems to outdazzle the last. Of the 11 named viewpoints that have been cut into the highway's shoulder here, the following are especially recommended (all viewpoints are marked by signs on the west side of U.S. 101 and are listed in order of appearance).

House Rock was the site of a World War II air-raid sentry tower that sits hundreds of feet above whitecaps pounding the rock-strewn beaches. To the north, you'll see one of the highest cliffs on the coast, Cape Sebastian. A steep, circuitous trail lined with salal (a tart blueberry) goes down to the water. The path begins behind the Samuel Boardman monument on the west end of the parking lot. The sign to the highest viewpoint in Boardman Park is easy to miss, but look for the turnout that precedes House Rock, called Cape Ferrelo (for Cabrillo's navigator, who sailed up much of the West Coast in 1543).

Thomas Creek Bridge, the highest bridge in Oregon (345 feet above the water) as well as the highest north of San Francisco, has been used as a silent star in many TV commercials. A parking lot at the south end of the bridge marks a trailhead down. Do not take the path you see closest to the bridge because it's too steep. At the south end of the lot, the true trail eventually leads down to a view of the bridge on one side and miles of coast on the other. The offshore rock formations here are especially interesting. From here some hikers access the Indian Sands Trail, ending up in pine-rimmed dunes and a sandstone bluff high above the sea.

Two miles down the highway, the **Natural Bridges Cove** sign seems to front just a forested parking lot. However, the paved walkway at the south end of the lot leads to a spectacular overlook. Below, several rock archways frame an azure cove. This feature was created by the collapse of the entrance and exit of a sea cave. A steep, winding trail through giant ferns and towering Sitka spruce and Douglas fir takes you down for a closer look. Thimbleberries (a sweet but seedy raspberry) are sometimes plentiful. Here, as in similar forests on the south coast, it's important to stay on the trail. The rainforest-like biome is exceptionally fragile, and the soil erodes easily when the delicate vegetation is damaged.

Natural Bridges' counterpart is near the north end of Boardman Park. A short walk down the hillside trail leads you to the **Arch Rocks** viewpoint to see an immense boomerang-shaped basalt archway about one-quarter mile offshore. This site has picnic tables within view of the monolith.

Alfred A. Loeb State Park

Eight miles northeast of Brookings on North Bank Chetco River Road along the Chetco River, Loeb State Park preserves 320 acres of old-growth myrtlewood, the state's largest grove. Many of the aromatic trees here are well more than 200 years old. The park is open mid-April to late October.

The quarter-mile Riverview Trail passes numerous big trees to connect Loeb Park with the **Redwood Nature Trail.** This trail winds 1.2 miles through the northernmost stands of naturally occurring *Sequoia sempervirens.* This is Oregon's largest redwood grove and contains the state's largest specimens. Within the grove are several trees more than 500 years old, measuring 5–8 feet in diameter, towering more than 300 feet above the forest floor. One tree here has a 33-foot girth and is estimated to exceed 800 years in age. When the south coast is foggy and cold on summer mornings, it's often warm and dry in upriver locations such as this one.

The Kalmiopsis Wilderness

The lure of untrammeled wilderness attracts intrepid hikers to the Kalmiopsis, despite the summer's blazing heat and winter's torrential rains. In addition to enjoying the isolation of Oregon's largest (179,655 acres) and probably least-visited wilderness, they come to take in the pink

rhododendron-like blooms of *Kalmiopsis leachiana* (in June) and other rare flowers. The area is also home to such economically valued species as Port Orford cedar and *Cannabis sativa.* The illicit weed is the leading cash crop in the state, and its vigilant protection by growers should inspire extra care for those hiking here during the late fall harvest season. The potential for violence associated with the lucrative mushroom harvest here also mandates a measure of caution.

In any case, the Forest Service prohibits plant collection *of any kind* to preserve the region's special botanical populations. These include the insect-eating Darlingtonia plant and the Brewer's weeping spruce. The forest canopy is composed largely of the more common Douglas fir, canyon live oak, madrone, and chinquapin. Stark peaks top this red-rock forest, whose understory is choked with blueberry, manzanita, and dense chaparral.

Many of this wilderness's rare species survived the glacial epoch because the glaciers from that era left the area untouched. This, combined with the fact that the area was an ancient offshore island, has enabled the region's singular ecosystem to maintain its integrity through the millennia. You'd think that federal protection, remoteness, and climatic extremes would ensure a sanguine outlook for this ice-age forest, but an active debate still rages over the validity of some logging claims.

In summer 2002, the so-called **Biscuit Fire** raged out of control for weeks, ravaging nearly half a million acres of southwestern Oregon, engulfing most of the Siskiyou National Forest and virtually all of the Kalmiopsis Wilderness. This inferno, the nation's largest wildfire of 2002 and the biggest in Oregon for more than a century, destroyed extensive habitat of the endangered northern spotted owl, whose population U.S. Forest Service biologists predict may drop by 20 percent. It will likely be decades before the forest returns to normal. The good news, however, is that flora of the region is well adapted to periodic fires; many of the old-growth trees survived the blaze, and within a few months green sprouts and new growth of many species were reappearing amid the ashes.

Even if you don't have the slightest intention of hiking the Kalmiopsis, the scenic drive through the **Chetco Valley** is worth it. From Brookings, turn off U.S. 101 at the north end of the Chetco River Bridge, follow County Roads 784 and 1376 along the Chetco River for six miles, and then turn right and follow County Road 1909 to its end. Driving distance from Brookings is 31 miles. Here, a one-mile trail leads to **Vulcan Lake** at the foot of Vulcan Peak, the major jumping-off point for trails into the wilderness. Hikers should watch out for the three shiny leaves of poison oak, as well as for rattlesnakes, which are numerous here. Black bears also populate the area, but their lack of contact with humans makes them more shy than their Cascade counterparts.

Here's what to expect on the way to Vulcan Lake: County Road 1909 takes off up the mountains past Pollywog Butte and Red Mountain Prairie. The open patches in the Douglas fir reveal a kaleidoscope of Pacific Ocean views and panoramas of the Chetco Valley and the Big Craggies. For the botanist in search of rare plants, however, the real show is on the trail. No matter how expert you might consider yourself, bring along a good plant guide to help you identify the many exotic species here. On the final leg of the hike, sadler oak, manzanita, Jeffrey pine, white pine, and azalea precede the sharp descent to the lake. Despite steep spots, the walk from County Road 1909 to Vulcan Lake is not difficult.

If you backtrack from the lake to Spur 260 on the trail, you can make the steep ascent over talus slopes and brush to Vulcan Peak. At the top, from an old lookout, a view of Kalmiopsis treetops and the coast awaits. Before going, check with the Forest Service in Brookings to see if the road to Vulcan Lake trailhead is open, because weather-related closures occasionally occur.

If you've always romanticized about mountain fire lookout stations but have never seen an operating one, visit the **Quail Prairie Lookout,** 17 air miles northeast of Brookings. This is one of the few remaining outposts still staffed each summer during the fire season. Because negotiating the Forest Service roads just west of the Kalmiopsis Wilderness can be tricky, get exact directions to 3,000-foot Quail Prairie Mountain from the Chetco Ranger Station in Brookings (541/469-2196). You can also find out about renting a night in several out-of-operation fire lookouts in the area.

RECREATION

Fishing

Fishing on the Chetco was once one of southern Oregon's best-kept secrets, but word has gotten out about the river's October run of huge chinook and its superlative influx of winter steelhead. If river traffic becomes too heavy, the late-summer ocean salmon season out of Brookings may be the best in the Northwest. Boatless anglers can try their luck at the public fishing pier at the harbor and on the south jetty at the mouth of the Chetco. Chinook season generally runs mid-May to mid-September, but that's subject to change, so check the regulations.

Various salmon ($75 for 5–6 hours), tuna ($125 for 12 hours), and bottom-fishing ($60 for 5–6 hours) trips can be arranged through **Sporthaven Marina** (16374 Lower Harbor Rd., 541/469-3301). In addition to fishing charters, **Tidewind Sportfishing** (16368 Lower Harbor Rd., 541/469-0337) offers whale-watching excursions in season.

Golf

All the press about Bandon Dunes has obscured the development of another great course, **Salmon Run Golf and Wilderness Preserve** (99040 South Bank Chetco River Rd., 541/469-4888, green fees $45 for 9 holes, $60 for 18 holes, $15 for executive 9, all prices include cart). This beautiful new 18-hole public links—not far from the Kalmiopsis Wilderness—was designed with environmentally sensitive imperatives, so numerous wildlife sightings may be enjoyed here long into the future. Whether it's the chance to see salmon (usually after the first rains in November) and steelhead spawning (January), black bears, elk, and wild turkeys, or just the opportunity to play a first-rate course, golfers shouldn't overlook this one. Beginner and intermediate players may find the executive

9 ideal. This par-34 course within a course is located on the back nine holes and measures 1,310 yards. Your Oregon coastal golf pilgrimage can begin here, then hit Bandon Dunes, Sandpines (Florence), and Salishan (near Lincoln City).

Other

Wilderness Canyon Adventures (541/247-6924 or 888/517-1613, www.wilderness-canyon-ex.com) is an outfitter focusing on southwestern Oregon and offering a variety of guided trips in the region, including kayak trips on the Chetco (part-day up to three-day excursions) and backpacking and horsepacking trips in the Kalmiopsis Wilderness.

For some fun in the sun, cruise down Easy Street, east off U.S. 101, to Bud Cross City Park for some tennis or a dip in the outdoor pool.

EVENTS

The **Beachcomber's Festival** (800/535-9469), held in late March at the Azalea Middle School, features exhibits, demonstrations, and slide shows, as well as an art competition for the best works wrought from indigenous materials such as driftwood, agates, and other beachcomber treasures. To get there, follow Pacific Avenue east of the highway.

The **Azalea Festival** is an unforgettable floral fantasia that takes place each Memorial Day weekend. Among the activities are a parade, flower display, crafts fair, five-kilometer run, seafood luncheon, and beef barbecue. Much of the activity revolves around Azalea Park. This Works Progress Administration (WPA)–built enclave features 20-foot-high azaleas (several hundred years old) and hand-hewn myrtlewood picnic tables. Wild cherry and crabapple blooms, wild strawberry blossoms, and purple and red violets round out the bouquet. Butterflies, bees, and birds all seem to concur with locals that this array

Fishing on the Chetco was once one of southern Oregon's best-kept secrets, but word has gotten out about the river's October run of huge chinook and its superlative influx of winter steelhead.

smells sweetest around graduation time in mid-June. To get there, take Pacific Avenue east of the highway, and turn onto Azalea Park Road.

Like several other Oregon coast towns, Brookings puts its windy weather to good use, with its annual **Southern Oregon Kite Festival** (541/469-2218), held over two days in mid-July. Individuals and teams display their aerial skills at the port of Brookings-Harbor.

Azalea Park is also home to **Nature's Coastal Holiday Light Show** in December, with more than 75,000 lights. The city park is located on the south end of town. The Brookings-Harbor Garden Club and Chamber of Commerce offer garden tours of this park and other gardens. Call the chamber (541/469-3181) for more information on tours and garden-related events.

ACCOMMODATIONS

Motels

If you're weary from your journey to Oregon from California and want to stop in at the first motel you see, try one of the **Harbor Inn Motel's** (15991 U.S. 101 S., 541/469-3194 or 800/469-8444, $50–89) 30 units. Small pets are allowed.

With 35 units and reasonable prices, the **Spindrift Motor Inn** (1215 Chetco Ave., 541/469-5345 or 800/292-1171, $39–79) is a good dollar value. Soundproofed walls blunt traffic noise from U.S. 101, and there are ocean views you'd expect to find at higher-priced lodgings.

Hotels

Up a rung in the price range, the **Best Western Brookings Inn** (1143 U.S. 101, 541/469-2173 or 800/822-9087, $69–110), may be about a mile from the ocean, but it's family-friendly with a pool and whirlpool tub, a comfy myrtlewood-panelled lounge, and a very good on-site restaurant. No pets are allowed.

For the full oceanfront experience, head south to the town of Harbor. Here, **Best Western**

Beachfront Inn (16008 Boat Basin Rd., Harbor, 541/469-7779 or 800/468-4081, $79–165) offers a window on a colorful port. All units feature private decks, microwaves, and refrigerators. Kitchenettes, as well as suites with oceanview hot tubs and an indoor pool, are offered here. Rates differ depending on the season and the room configuration.

The **Pacific Sunset Inn** (1144 Chetco Ave., 541/469-2141 or 800/469-2141) has 40 units right downtown. Rates are $30–85. With just eight units, **Ocean Suites** (16045 Lower Harbor Rd., 541/469-4004) has rooms by the week for $365 or $59 and up for a night. Each comes equipped with full kitchens and living room. No pets are allowed.

Bed-and-Breakfasts

A coastal gem one block north of the highway, the **South Coast Inn B&B** (516 Redwood St., Brookings, 541/469-5557 or 800/525-9273, www.scoastinn.com, $99–139) is a 1917 Craftsman building and was once the home of lumber baron William Ward. Designed by famed architect Bernard Maybeck and situated in the heart of old Brookings just blocks away from the beach and shopping, this 4,000-square-foot B&B offers three rooms and a guest cottage that also has a kitchen. All rooms have VCR/TVs (and access to the inn's video library), private bath, and other amenities. An indoor spa with a sauna and hot tub and an included breakfast featuring a health-conscious menu are additional enticements to book space early. Ask the innkeepers about other Maybeck structures in town, as well as the bicycle/walking treks they conduct June–October.

Surrounded by water on three sides, the **Chetco River Inn** (21202 High Prairie Rd., 541/251-0087 or 800/327-2688, www .chetcoriverinn, $125–145), is also an intimate alternative. Eighteen miles inland from the coast, the inn lies at the end of a half-hour drive to the periphery of the Kalmiopsis; it makes you feel as if you're in your own private forest. Its location near prime fishing river frontage makes this place especially popular during steelhead season on the Chetco. Many swimming holes are close by,

and the absence of city lights makes for good stargazing. In addition to an included gourmet breakfast, picnic lunches and dinners are available upon request. The welcome mat here is laid out in the form of thick Oriental carpets on floors of green and black marble. Tasteful antiques also decorate this reasonably priced first-class lodging. Rooms include a full country breakfast, with all the coffee, tea, and cookies you can eat. The five rooms plus cottage can easily accommodate up to 14 people in separate beds, or six couples. Children are welcome; cottages are suggested for their comfort. Smoking is limited to outdoors only. No pets are allowed.

For a B&B with an ocean view, **By the Sea B&B** (1545 Beach Ave., 541/469-4692 or 877/469-4692, www.brookingsbythesea.com, $98–150) offers a choice of two rooms or the lodge room, featuring fishing and hunting decor. A full breakfast is served upstairs in the dining room. Enjoy breakfast and breathtaking ocean views from the stained-glass–topped windows. The house is filled with antiques and the smell of homemade bread. A deluxe continental breakfast is also available, with seasonal fruits and homemade breads, if you prefer to eat in private. On the upper veranda, a spa and a wood-burning fire pot is available for guest use.

For vacation home rentals, **3PM Vacation Rentals** (611 Spruce St., 541/469-6456) and **Premier Properties Brokerage & Property Management** (1025 Chetco Ave., Ste. 3, 541/469-7400 or 800/221-8175) can provide you with a list of available homes from which to choose. Call for the list, availability, and prices.

Campgrounds

Campers should pick up literature on fishing and a **Siskiyou National Forest** map at the ranger station in town. In addition to printed matter about Siskiyou and Kalmiopsis trails for hikers, the rangers can tell you where to find some good fishing holes on the nearby Chetco River, noted for its good fall salmon runs and winter steelhead.

Harris Beach State Park (1655 U.S. 101, 541/469-2021 or 800/452-5687), two miles north of town, is open all year, but reservations are definitely necessary from Memorial Day through Labor Day. With a total of 155 spaces ($15–17), there are 149 paved sites (50 electricity only, 36 full), some with shade, six yurts, and a special camping area for hikers and bicyclists. Picnic tables and fire grills are provided. Flush toilets, electricity, piped-in water, sewer hookups, sanitary service, showers, firewood, laundry, and a playground are available. Whale-watching is particularly good here in January and May on this piece of beach peppered with basalt outcroppings.

The 320-acre **Alfred A. Loeb State Park** (541/469-2021, sites $12–16 depending on season, cabins $35 year-round) is nine miles northeast of Brookings on North Bank Chetco River Road. The park is open mid-April to late October, but camping is allowed only during summer; no reservations are necessary. There are 53 sites with electrical hookups for trailers/motor homes (50 feet maximum), a special campground for bicyclists and hikers, and some cabins. Electricity, piped water, and picnic tables are provided; flush toilets and firewood are available. The campground is located in a fragrant, secluded myrtlewood grove on the east bank of the Chetco River. From here, the Riverview Trail takes hikers to the Siskiyou National Forest's Redwood Nature Trail, where nature lovers will marvel at 800-year-old redwood beauties.

Beyond Loeb State Park is the more primitive **Little Redwood Campground,** which can't be beat for the price. To get there, go one-half mile south of Brookings on U.S. 101 to County Road 784, then go northeast for seven miles. At Forest Service Road 376, turn northeast and drive six miles to the campground. Contact **Chetco Ranger District** (P.O. Box 730, Brookings 97415, 541/469-2196) for information. There are several fee and no-fee sites; call for rates and availability. Some have picnic tables and grills, pit toilets, and available firewood. Although it lacks showers and other amenities, Little Redwood is located on the main access route to the Kalmiopsis Wilderness, 20 miles away, and is a good spot for fishing during the winter steelhead run. Other Forest Service properties include Winchuck, Packer's Cabin, Ludlum House, and a few fire lookouts.

FOOD

Brookings has a profusion of family-friendly restaurants that serve large portions at a good dollar value with enough creativity to suit the most finicky eater.

Mexican and Seafood

At the north end of town in a small building that gives the appearance of a drive-in is **Rubio's** (1136 Chetco Ave., 541/469-4919, 11 A.M.–9 P.M. daily), one of the better and inexpensive Mexican places along U.S. 101. This will be apparent upon tasting the house salsa and the chiles rellenos. The house specialty, Seafood à la Rubio, throws together prawns, lingcod, and scallops in a butter, garlic, wine, and jalapeño sauce. Fish tacos, tamales, and margaritas here are also recommended. Rubio's can be spotted on the east side of the highway across from the Flying Gull. Just look for a low-slung wooden building painted yellow with red trim.

For a rare oceanview dining experience in Brookings, try **Smuggler's Cove Seafood & Grill** (16011 Boat Basin Rd., 541/469-6006), serving prime rib and seafood.

Another seafood option is **Chetco Seafood** (16182 Lower Harbor Rd., Harbor, 541/469-9251), which has reasonably priced fresh fish, plus chips in beer batter as good as any on the coast. Or, **Flying Gull Restaurant** (next to the Best Western, 541/469-5700) has a huge menu with one of the largest seafood selections on the coast, plus certified Black Angus steaks.

Casual Fare

Home of Wild River Brewing, **Wild River Pizza** (16279 U.S. 101, Harbor, 541/469-7454) has a menu similar to its outlet in Cave Junction, highlighting crispy crust pizza, salad, and microbrews. Look for it on the east side of the highway about one mile south of the Brookings Harbor Bridge at the four-way stoplight. While the food is good and inexpensive, this large restaurant tends to fill up with families enjoying the video games and pool tables on weekends. In other words, go elsewhere for an intimate Saturday night dinner.

For prime rib in a low-key lounge atmosphere, head to **O'Holleran's** (1210 Chetco Ave., 541/469-9907, 5–10 P.M. daily).

For lighter fare for those heading out to explore, try **The Tea Room** (434 Redwood St., #4, 541/469-7240) for sandwiches, soups, salads, and baked goods; fill your to-go mugs with a nice cuppa the hot stuff.

INFORMATION AND SERVICES
Visitor Information

Before you continue north on the country's longest (361 miles) designated scenic highway, U.S. 101, stop off and talk to the friendly folks at the **Oregon Welcome Center** just north of town (1650 U.S. 101, Brookings 97415, 541/469-4117, 9 A.M.–5 P.M. Mon.–Sat. mid-Apr.–Oct.). The facility has brochures covering the coast and the rest of the state. For additional information pertinent to Brookings and environs, the **Brookings-Harbor Chamber of Commerce** (16330 Lower Harbor Rd., Brookings 97415, 541/469-3181 or 800/535-9469, www.brookingsor.com) is located down at the harbor.

Recreational information, including forest and trail maps, is available at the **Chetco Ranger Station** (539 Chetco Ave., Brookings 97415, 541/412-6000, 7:30 A.M.–4:30 P.M. Mon.–Fri., closed holidays). The station's advisories include information on the Siskiyou National Forest and the Kalmiopsis Wilderness. Inquire here about mushroom-picking.

Wondering about **offshore weather conditions?** The Coast Guard hotline (541/469-2242) has the answers.

Services

Brookings-Harbor Medical Center (585 5th St., 541/469-7401) is the largest medical facility on this southern stretch of coast. The **post office** (711 Spruce St., Brookings 97415, 800/275-8777) is downtown, one block south of U.S. 101. For laundry, the **Old Wash House** (corner of Shopping Center Ave. and Grodendorst Lane, 541/469-3975) is clean and convenient.

For banking and walk-up ATM, try **Evergreen Federal** (850 Chetco Ave.).

Transportation

Greyhound (601 Railroad Ave., 541/469-3326) stops twice daily at the corner of Tanbark Road and Railroad Avenue. The fare to Portland is about $40. Curry County's **Coastal Express** buses (in Brookings, call 541/469-6822) run up and down the south coast weekdays only between North Bend and the California border, including local service in Brookings.

Gold Beach and Vicinity

Despite the name Gold Beach, the real riches here are silver, and they swim up the Rogue River in great numbers every year. This town is one part of the coast where the action is definitely away from the ocean. To lure people from Oregon's superlative ocean shores, the Rogue estuary has been bestowed with many blessings. First, the gold-laden black sands were mined in the 1850s and '60s. While this short-lived boom era gave Gold Beach its name, the arrival of Robert Hume, later known as the Salmon King of the Rogue, had greater historical significance. By the turn of the 20th century, Hume's canneries were shipping some 16,000 cases of salmon per year and established the river's image as a leading salmon and steelhead stream. This reputation was later enhanced by outdoorsman Zane Grey in his *Rogue River Feud* and other writings. Over the years, Herbert Hoover, Winston Churchill, Ginger Rogers (who had a home on the Rogue), Clark Gable, Jack London, George Bush, and Jimmy Carter, among other notables, have come here to try their luck. During the last several decades, white-water rafting and jetboat tours focusing on the abundant wildlife, scenic beauty, and fascinating lore of the region have hooked other sectors of the traveling public.

Today, Gold Beach is a town of about 2,100 and the Curry County seat. Besides serving as the south coast tourism hub, a pulp mill and commercial ocean fishing industry make up the local economy here. The seasonal nature of many local businesses creates serious wintertime unemployment. This fact, combined with torrential rains, drastically reduces the population of Gold Beach from Thanksgiving until spring. Thereafter, the wildflowers and warm weather transform this town into a vacation mecca.

At the north end of town, just before the road gives way to Conde McCullough's elegant Patterson Bridge, the harbor comes into view on the left, full of salmon trawlers, jetboats, pelicans, and seals bobbing up and down. Across the bridge is **Wedderburn,** a baby sister to Gold Beach. Named for the Scottish birthplace of

Robert Hume, its major claim to fame is as the home port of the Mailboat, which has been the mail carrier to upriver residents on the Rogue since 1895.

SIGHTS

Museums

At the **Curry County Historical Museum** (920 S. Ellensburg, Gold Beach, 541/247-6113, 1–5 P.M. Mon.–Sun. May 15–Sept. 30, noon–4 P.M. Fri.–Sat. Oct. 11–May 15, free), the local historical society has assembled a small collection of exhibits on Indian and pioneer life, mining in the region's golden age, logging, fishing, and agriculture. It's located at the county fairgrounds at the south edge of town. Particularly interesting are a realistic reconstruction of a miner's cabin, vintage photos, and Indian petroglyphs.

In the harbor area on the west side of U.S. 101, Jerry's Jetboats has assembled the best regional museum on the south coast, the **Rogue River Museum** (541/247-4571, 8 A.M.–9 P.M. in summer, until 6 P.M. the rest of the year, free). Centuries of natural and human history are depicted here. In addition to geologic history, photos of pioneer families, arrowheads and other native artifacts, and a taxidermic collage of local critters will round out your introduction to the Rogue Valley. Jerry's river tour clientele will find that perspectives from the museum on the local salmon industry in the 1920s and early river travel are expanded upon in their jetboat guide's commentary. Museum photos of early river runs—hauling freight, passengers, and mail—also can impart a sense of history to your trip upriver or up the road.

Cape Sebastian

Seven miles south of Gold Beach is Cape Sebastian. This spectacular windswept headland was named by Sebastián Vizcaíno, who plied offshore waters here for Spain in 1602 along with Manuel d'Alguilar. At least 700 feet above

Myers Creek Beach, south of Cape Sebastian

the sea, Cape Sebastian is the highest south coast overlook reachable by paved public road. On a clear day, visibility extends 43 miles north to Humbug Mountain and 50 miles south to California. This is one of the best perches along the south coast for whale-watching. A trail zigzags through beautiful springtime wildflowers down the south side of the cape for about two miles until it reaches the sea. In April and May, Pacific paintbrush, Douglas iris, orchids, and snow queen usher you along. In addition, Cape Sebastian supports a population of large-headed goldfields, a summer-blooming daisylike yellow flower found only in coastal Curry County.

In 1942, a caretaker here heard Japanese voices drifting across the water through the fog. When the mist lifted he looked down from Cape Sebastian trail to see a surfaced submarine. This sighting, together with the Japanese bombing at Brookings and the incendiary balloon spotted over Cape Blanco, sent shock waves up the south coast. But the potential threat remained just that, and local anxiety eventually subsided.

Beaches

The driftwood-strewn strand of **South Beach,** just south of Gold Beach's harbor, is convenient but only so-so. You'll find more exciting stretches both north and south of town. Tidepoolers might want to stop at the visitors center before heading out and ask for the "Tidepools Are Alive" brochure, with tips and species descriptions. Two miles south, there's easy access to a nice beach and some tidepooling at tiny **Buena Vista State Park,** at the mouth of Hunter Creek. Seven miles south of Gold Beach, there's more tidepooling amid the camera-friendly basalt seastacks at beautiful **Myers Creek Beach,** part of Pistol River State Park south of Cape Sebastian. The south side of Cape Sebastian and **Pistol River State Park,** a couple of miles farther south, are the best places on the Oregon coast where windsurfers can enjoy wave sailing. The beaches around Pistol River are also productive areas for finding razor clams.

Bailey Beach, north of town between the Rogue River jetty and Otter Point, is another popular spot for razor clamming, and **Nesika**

Beach, seven miles from Gold Beach, is another good tidepooling destination.

Scenic Drives

From U.S. 101, two miles south of town, you can pick up Hunter's Creek Road, which loops north through the forest, finally following the course of the Rogue back into Gold Beach along Jerry's Flat Road. The three-hour drive follows Hunter's Creek inland for several miles. The route goes past interpretive markers explaining "our national forest, land of many uses" and is mapped out in a free pamphlet available at the Gold Beach Ranger Station. This map shows locations of several picnic areas and campgrounds.

Other roads less traveled include the old coast highway, which you can pick up near Pistol River and Brookings; the Shasta Costa Road paralleling the Rogue from Gold Beach to Galice; and an unpaved road into the Rogue Wilderness from Agness (a town upriver on the Rogue) to Powers. Despite most of these routes being paved (except the last one), they are all narrow, winding, and not suitable for trailers or motor homes. Maps and directions to these back roads can be obtained from the Gold Beach Ranger Station.

RECREATION

Jetboat Trips

The best way to take in the mighty Rogue is on a jetboat ride from Gold Beach harbor. Several different companies run this trip, and they all provide comparable service and prices. It's an exciting and interesting look at the varied flora and fauna along the estuary, as well as the changing moods of the river. Most of the estimated 50,000 people per year who do the Rogue in this way take the 64-mile round-trip cruise. This and the more adventurous 104-mile cruise include a stop for a sumptuous lunch at one of several secluded fishing lodges upriver. The pilots/commentators usually have grown up on the river, and their evocations of the diverse ecosystems and Indian and gold-mining history add greatly to your enjoyment. Bears, otters, seals, and beavers may be sighted en route, and anglers may hold up a big keeper to show off. Ospreys, snowy egrets, ea-

gles, mergansers, and kingfishers are also seen with regularity in this stopover for migratory waterfowl.

In the first part of the journey, idyllic riverside retreats dot the hillsides, breaking up stands of fir and hemlock. Myrtle, madrone, and impressive springtime wildflower groupings also vary the landscape. Both the 64- and 104-mile trips focus on the section of the Rogue protected by the government as a Wild and Scenic River. Only the longer trips take you into the pristine Rogue Wilderness, an area that motor launches from Grants Pass do not reach either. The 13 miles of this wilderness you see from the boat have canyon walls rising 1,500 feet above you. Geologists say that this part of the Klamaths is composed of ancient islands and sea floor that collided with North America. To deal with the rapids upstream, smaller, faster boats are used that skim over the boulders with just six inches of water between hull and rock surface.

The season runs May 1–October 15. Remember that chill and fog near the mouth of the estuary usually give way to much warmer conditions upstream. These tour outfits have wool blankets and complimentary hot beverages available on cold days. Also keep in mind that the upriver lodges can be booked for overnight stays, and your trip may be resumed the following day. The following suppliers offer 64- and 104-mile trips; rates range $30–75 ($12–35 for children) for these itineraries (meals included in the cost of the 104-mile trip). Each has other specific offerings available—inquire for more information.

Just south of the Rogue River Bridge, west of U.S. 101 on Harbor Way, is **Jerry's Rogue River Jetboats** (P.O. Box 1011, Gold Beach 97444, 541/247-4571 or 800/451-3645, www.roguejets.com). This heavily patronized company runs trips May–October. Jerry's is noted for personable, well-informed guides. If you forgot to bring a hat to buffer the winds at the mouth of the Rogue, stop in at Jerry's gift shop. While you're there, check out the local jams and critically acclaimed fish prints by local artist Don Jensen.

Rogue River Mailboats (P.O. Box 1165, Gold Beach, 541/247-7033 or 800/458-3511, www.mailboat.com), is located one-quarter mile upstream from the north end of the Rogue River bridge. Besides human cargo, this boat also carries sacks of U.S. mail, ensuring a warm welcome in upriver locations.

Fishing

Fishing is a mighty big deal in Gold Beach, which has one of the highest concentrations of professional guides in the state. There's something to fish for just about year-round here, but salmon and steelhead are the top quarry. When the spring chinook pour in (Apr.–June), anglers will need to book guided trips well in advance to get a shot at them. Catches peak in May. Summer steelhead and fall-run chinook usually arrive July–September, and then it's hatchery-bred coho September (sometimes as early as Aug.) through November. In December, the first of the winter steelhead make their appearance and continue into March.

The **Rogue Outdoor Store** (560 N. Ellensburg Ave., Gold Beach, 541/247-7142) is well stocked with fishing, camping, and other gear, and can advise on where, when, and what to fish. Typical rates for guides on salmon trips here are $150–200 per person. Contact the Gold Beach Visitor Center (see Information and Services section) or the Curry Guide Association (800/775-0886) for a list of more than two dozen licensed guides.

Some well-established guides include: Darrell Allen (541/247-2082); Denny Hughson (541/247-2684 or 503/819-1607); Steve Beyerlin (541/247-4138 or 800/348-4138, www.fishoregon.com) for both conventional and fly fishing; Shaun Carpenter (541/247-2049) for conventional and fly fishing; Helen Burns (541/247-2441 or 541/290-8402, www.helensguideservice.com), one of the few women in a male-dominated club; Ron Smith (541/247-6046 or 800/501-6391); and John Ward (541/247-2866 or 290-2281).

> *The best way to take in the mighty Rogue is on a jetboat ride from Gold Beach harbor. It's an exciting and interesting look at the varied flora and fauna along the estuary, as well as the changing moods of the river.*

Hiking and Horseback Riding

The 40-mile **Rogue River Trail** offers lodge-to-lodge hiking, which means you need little more in your pack than the essentials. The lodges here are comfortably rustic, serve homestyle food in copious portions, and run $150–200 for a double room. They are also comfortably spaced, so extended hiking is seldom a necessity. Call **Rogue Quest** (888/517-1614) if you would like a guide (about $80 per day).

Before you go, check with the Gold Beach Ranger Station on trail conditions and specific directions to the trailhead. Pick up the western end of the trail 35 miles east of Gold Beach, about one-half mile from Foster Bar, a popular boat landing. Park there and walk east and north on the paved road until you see signs on the left marking the Rogue River Trail. Go in spring before the hot weather and enjoy yellow Siskiyou iris and fragrant wild azaleas. The trail ends at Graves Creek, 27 miles northwest of Grants Pass. Be careful of rattlesnakes on the trail.

Hawk's Rest Ranch at Siskiyou West Day Lodge (94667 N. Bank Pistol River Rd., Pistol River 97444, 541/247-6423, www.siskiyouwest.com) offers horseback riding on the beach near the scenic Pistol River, riding lessons, a petting zoo, and other family-oriented attractions.

Golf

Cedar Bend Golf Course (P.O. Box 1234, Gold Beach 97444, 541/247-6911, green fees $13 for 9 holes, $18 for 18 holes) is located in nearby Ophir. Eleven miles north of Gold Beach, pick up Ophir Road off U.S. 101. Follow it to Squaw Valley Road, turn right at the Old Ophir Store, and continue until you see the links. Woods line the fairways, and a winding creek offers a challenge on each of the nine holes.

Other Activities

Gold Beach Adventures (Box 636, Gold Beach, 541/247-9420 or 888/301-6480, www.goldbeachadventures.com), headquartered in the

A-frame at the Port of Gold Beach, is an all-purpose outfitter that arranges trips and rents equipment for a variety of activities: kayaking and canoeing, rafting, cycling, crabbing, and even gold panning, as well as fishing charters, jetboat tours, and horseback riding.

ENTERTAINMENT AND EVENTS

The **Wild Rivers Coast Seafood, Art, and Wine Festival** is a two-day event that celebrates wine, fine dining, and arts and crafts of the southern Oregon coast, in mid-May at the Event Center on the Beach (29392 Ellensburg Ave., 541/247-4541).

People line the river for the annual **jetboat races,** which take place in mid-June. Contact Jot's Resort (800/367-5687) or the chamber of commerce for further information.

In late July or early August, the **Curry County Fair and Rodeo** takes place at the Event Center on the Beach. Highlights include Oregon's largest flower show and a lamb barbecue.

The **Pistol River Wave Bash National Windsurfing Competition** brings four days of competitive riding to Pistol River State Park each June. For details, contact the Gold Beach Visitor Center (541/247-7526 or 800/525-2334).

Since 1982, the Pistol River Concert Association (541/247-2848, www.pistolriver.com) has produced a top-notch **concert series,** encompassing bluegrass, folk, jazz, classical, and blues at the Pistol River Friendship Hall. Past and present performers are a who's who of acoustic music, including Greg Brown, Mike Seeger, Peggy Seeger, Kevin Burke, Norman and Nancy Blake, Peter Rowan, and Tony Rice, to name a few. To get there from Gold Beach, take U.S. 101 10 miles south, to the second Pistol River exit (Pistol River/Carpenterville) and take the first right. The Pistol River Friendship Hall is approximately one-half mile on the right.

ACCOMMODATIONS

As in most coastal towns, there is no shortage of places to stay along the main drag, Ellensburg Street (a.k.a. U.S. 101). In fact, Gold Beach offers the largest number and widest range of accommodations on the south coast, with intimate lodges overlooking the Rogue as popular as the oceanfront motels. A discount of 20 percent or more on rooms is usually available during winter here, when 80–90 inches of rain can fall.

Motels

The cheapest place in town is probably the **Oregon Trail Lodge** (550 N. Ellensburg Ave., 541/247-6030). For about $25–60, you get no-frills accommodation close to the harbor. Beware that the paper-thin walls may put you on more intimate terms with your next-door neighbor than you really want to be.

Formerly the River Bridge Inn and now a **Motel 6** (1010 Jerry's Flat Rd., 541/247-4533 or 800/759-4533, $50–80) this inn/motel has modern, comfy riverview rooms. Kitchenettes are available, as are spa suites.

Ireland's Rustic Lodges (29330 Ellensburg Ave., 541/247-7718, www.irelandsrusticlodges .com, lodge units $50–80, houses $95–105) was started by two women who used to bring meals to the cabins. Although this is no longer the case, the touch of home has not been lost. Many of the rooms have fireplaces, knotty-pine interiors, and distinctive decor. Best of all, the grounds are lovingly landscaped with pine trees, flowers, and ocean views. A sandy beach is a short stroll to the west. There are 33 motel lodge units (some with kitchens), seven old but well-kept log cabins (recommended) that sleep up to five, and houses that sleep as many as 11. Ireland's also has an RV park close to the lodge.

Hotels

Located on the Rogue River's north bank, **Jot's Resort** (94360 Wedderburn Loop, Wedderburn, 541/247-6676 or 800/FOR-JOTS, www.jotsresort .com, $75–300) can host a full vacation in one compound featuring pool and spa, sports shop, private dock, rental boats, and a restaurant across the street. The rooms here are at a premium in summer, when the motorcoach tours come through, leaving other travelers with the less desirable rooms. There are numerous room styles—

from standard-view rooms to riverfront condos big enough for six people—and a wide range of prices, so it's best to call for current rates and specials. The Rod 'n' Reel across the street features evening entertainment with low-stakes blackjack, a country music duo, and a big-band dance on weekends.

Tu Tu' Tun Resort (96530 N. Bank Rogue River Rd., 541/247-6664 or 800/864-6357, www.tututun.com, $85–290 with lower rates in winter) emphasizes the tranquility reinforced by the absence of TV in the rooms (except in the suites and houses). Although there is a TV in the cedar-planked lodge, most guests prefer to take in the river view through the floor-to-ceiling windows or enjoy a good book from the lodge's library in front of the massive river rock fireplace. As you sit on your patio overlooking the water along with two nearby resident bald eagles, only the sounds of an occasional passing boat may intrude upon your Rogue River reverie. The lodge is located seven miles up the Rogue River from Gold Beach.

A heated pool and other recreational facilities, the lodge's beautifully appointed interiors, and delicious meals served family style are other appeals of this acclaimed retreat. Meals are available on an inclusive Modified American Plan, which includes hors d'oeuvres, a gourmet four-course dinner, and a bountiful breakfast buffet (for about $50 per person).

The cuisine here is worth special mention. Whether it's blackberry muffins and house-cured pepper bacon at breakfast or a mesquite-grilled pork loin doused in Hood River apple juice for dinner, gustatory highlights abound. The dining room is open May–October only. In the off-season, guests are served a continental breakfast only.

Spring is the best time to be here because much of the traveling public is still at home and the wildflowers are in their glory. Pink rhododendrons, native to Oregon, blossom at the edge of the forest in May. From early summer to late fall, a huge dahlia garden at the lodge is in bloom. Although autumn is also beautiful, business meetings in September and October necessitate that bookings be made well in advance for stays after Labor Day.

Set atop a bluff over the Pacific north of town, **The Inn at Nesika Beach** (33026 Nesika Rd., 541/247-6434, $130–165 with a discount for two or more nights) is a three-story neo-Victorian B&B with mind-stopping views, featherbeds, and spas in each of its four rooms. A wraparound porch and an enclosed oceanfront deck also highlight the setting. Breakfast is an event here, served in an elegant dining room facing the ocean. The inn does not accept credit cards or children.

Bed-and-Breakfast

For B&B-goers, the **Rogue Reef Inn** (30530 Old Coast Rd., 877/234-7333, www.roguereef .com, $85–95, no credit cards accepted) is just one mile north of the Rogue River and directly overlooking the Rogue Reef and Northwest Rocks. In this contemporary home with four guest rooms (each with private bath), guests walk out onto the three-mile stretch of beach, which partially intersects the Oregon Trail. The inn is the first home north of the Rogue River north jetty.

Upriver Lodges

Several lodges on the Rogue—some accessible only by boat or via hiking trails—lure visitors deep into the interior. Jetboat trips can drop you off for an overnight or longer stay. Advance reservations are essential.

Accessible by road or jetboat 32 miles inland from the coast, the **Cougar Lane Lodge** (04219 Agness Rd., 541/247-7233, $45–65) was established in 1949 on the east shore of the Rogue. Spend the night in one of the simple lodge rooms, or come for the day to fish (licenses and tackle available at the Cougar Lane store). Dine at the lodge restaurant, overlooking the Rogue, which serves standard American breakfast, lunch, and dinner every day. From here, hike the Rogue or Illinois trails. The Agness RV Park is nearby for overnight camping.

Also accessible by road and boat, the **Lucas Pioneer Ranch & Fishing Lodge** (03904 Cougar Lane, 541/247-7443, $45–80) is also 32 miles east of Gold Beach. Cabins here come equipped with cooking and noncooking options. Lunch and dinner are served daily in the lodge—chicken, biscuits, garden vegetables. Reservations are required.

The more remote **Half Moon Bar Lodge** (Box 455, Gold Beach 97444, 541/247-6968 or 888/291-8268, www.halfmoonbarlodge.com, $110 per adult, $55 per child under 11) is located in a wild and secluded piece of wilderness, once the site of Native American encampments. Choose from three private cabins or stay in the rustic lodge, which houses a sauna, dining room, and bar. Nightly lodge rates include two meals, which are served family-style and include fresh seasonal garden veggies and fruits. Tour boats take visits 52 miles upriver; you can raft down with a white-water guide or fish for steelhead. To get there, hike in 11 miles from Foster Bar along the Rogue River Trail or five miles from Bear Camp near Agness. The lodge can also accommodate small planes on its private airstrip. Call to make arrangements.

Only accessible by helicopter, jetboat, foot, or float, the **Paradise Lodge** (541/247-6504 or 800/525-2161, www.go-oregon.com) attracts nature enthusiasts interested in the wildest experience. Only the meals are scheduled here, where you can take an ecotour, enjoy a sauna, raft or jetboat the rapids, see some of the Rogue's history at the nearby Rogue River Museum, or check out some of the old mining sites. A huge on-site garden provides ingredients for home-cooked meals. Rates are $107 per adult (includes three meals) and $77 for children ages 4–11. Jetboat round-trip rates are $95 per adult and $50 per child.

Campgrounds

Campsites east of town along the Rogue and off U.S. 101 en route to Port Orford provide wonderful spots to bed down for the night. Those taking the road along the Rogue should be alert for oncoming log trucks, raft transport vehicles, and other wide-body vehicles.

Foster Bar Campground (Siskiyou National Forest, Gold Beach Ranger Station, P.O. Box 548, 1225 S. Ellensburg Ave., 541/247-6651, $5) is located 30 miles east of Gold Beach on the south bank of the Rogue. Take Jerry's Flat Road east for 30 miles to the turnoff for Agness. Turn right on Illahe Agness Road and drive

three miles to camp. Recently transformed from primitive to developed, campsites here now come equipped with drinking water, toilets, handicapped-accessible facilities, picnic tables, fire rings, and a boat ramp. Sites are available on a first-come, first-served basis. The campground is generally open March–October, but may vary depending on the weather. This is a popular spot from which to embark on an eight-mile inner tube ride to Agness. It's also where rafters pull out, so the parking lot may be jam-packed. The rapids are dangerous—wear a life jacket. You are also within walking distance of the trailhead of the Rogue River Trail (see the Recreation section).

Lobster Creek Campground (contact the Forest Service, 541/247-3600, $5) is nine miles East of Gold Beach via Forest Service Road 33. This campground is open year-round and has three tent sites, three trailer sites, one group site, picnic tables, fishing, and flush toilets—but no drinking water. Ask the Forest Service for directions to the Schrader old-growth trail nearby. It is a gentle one-mile walk through a rare and majestic ecosystem that is under siege in other forests throughout the state. Also nearby is the world's largest myrtle tree.

Honeybear Campground and RV Resort (P.O. Box 97, 34161 Ophir Rd., Ophir 97464, 541/247-2765 or 800/822-4444, www.honeybearrv.com, $15–25, open year-round) is nine miles north of Gold Beach on U.S. 101, then two miles north on Ophir Road, but could just as well be in the Black Forest. The owners have built a large rathskeller with a dance floor. Six nights a week during the summer, there are dances here with traditional German music. Check out their version of October Fest. Locals praise the Honeybear's on-site delicatessen for its homemade German sausage. There are 20 tent and RV sites, picnic tables, flush toilets, hot showers, firewood, a launderette, and ocean views.

FOOD

You can't eat scenery, but Gold Beach restaurants charge you for it anyway. Still, this is one place where the oceanfront and riverside views are often worth it. Then, too, there's always the option of cheaper restaurants away from port. Spring chinook salmon, blackberry pie, and other indigenous specialties taste good anywhere.

Standard American

Grant's Pancake House (29790 U.S. 101, 541/247-7208) is the breakfast place of choice from the Rogue estuary to California. Omelets, pancakes, waffles, and corned beef hash often make lunch (in the same price range) an afterthought. Nonetheless, locals consider the Thursday clam steaks lunch special (breaded East Coast sea clams in a spicy homemade sauce) one of the town's culinary highlights. Open for breakfast and lunch.

Spada's (29174 Ellensburg Ave., 541/247-7732, daily 11 A.M.–9:30 P.M.) is one of the few "Chinese" restaurants on the coast. The menu is a mixed bag, however, including many American favorites such as pizza, seafood, and chicken-fried steak.

Steak and Seafood

The Nor'Wester (10 Harbor Way, 541/247-2333, daily for dinner only) is located at the port of Gold Beach, so sometimes you get to watch boats unloading your dinner. Not surprisingly, the menu is dominated by seafood, although the waitstaff tout the New Zealand lamb chops. What is surprising are such occasional culinary flourishes as chinook salmon broiled under a flame, then covered with a glaze of sake, cayenne, ginger, and soy. Dinner prices top out above $40 for steak and lobster, but most entrées are in the $18 range. There are also lighter, less expensive dinner options.

Chives Oceanfront Dining and Lounge (29212 U.S. 101, 541/247-4121, www.chives .net, open daily for lunch and dinner, closed Jan., $15–25) is the kind of upscale restaurant one might encounter in Marin County but at Oregon prices. (They share a driveway with Gold Beach Resort.) While the menu rotates seasonally, imagine steamer clams in white wine and garlic butter broth or marinated and grilled lamb loin chops with risotto to get an idea of the offerings here. Sophisticated salads and creative sandwiches

are also in ample evidence at lunch, where shrimp bisque is a nice way to get started. Dinner entrées include king salmon fillet, and the bread pudding with a Jack Daniels sauce is recommended for dessert. Reservations are a good idea.

If you're in the mood for a tasty martini after dining at Chives, or if you're just looking for simpler fare, head next door to the **South Beach Bar** (541/247-4121) for salads, burgers, and onion rings.

Locals recommend the **Port Hole Café** (29975 Harbor Way, 541/247-7411, daily 6 A.M.–9 P.M.), in the Cannery building at the port with bay and river views, for hearty portions of fish and chips, chowder, and homemade pies at decent prices.

Seafood lovers will find some hard choices at **The Chowderhead Restaurant** (29430 Ellensburg Ave., 541/247-0588, open for lunch and dinner only), which serves the full range of seafood, plus steaks, soups, and sandwiches.

INFORMATION AND SERVICES

Visitor Information

The **Gold Beach Visitor Center** (29279 Ellensburg Ave., Gold Beach 97444, 541/247-7526 or 800/525-2334, www.goldbeach.org, 9 A.M.–5 P.M. Mon.–Fri., 10 A.M.–4 P.M. Sat.–Sun.) has an excellent and informative website, and they'll send you a good, comprehensive information folder upon request. **Goldbeach.net** is an independently run website that's also packed with detailed tourist information.

The **Gold Beach Ranger District** (29279 Ellensburg Ave., Gold Beach, 541/247-3600, 7:30 A.M.–5 P.M. Mon.–Fri.) offers a free packet on camping and recreation in the district.

Services

The **post office** (Gold Beach 97444, 541/247-7610) is at the port on Harbor Way. A modern building houses the **public library** (29775 Colvin St., 541/247-7246, 10 A.M.–8 P.M. Mon.–Thurs., 10 A.M.–6 P.M. Fri.–Sat.), one block east of the highway in the north end of town. Comfy armchairs here would make this a good alternative to the Greyhound waiting room, across the street. **Stonsell's Coin-Op Laundry** is located on U.S. 101 near 8th Street.

   Curry General Hospital (220 E. 4th, Gold Beach, 541/247-6621) is the only hospital in the county. It coordinates the "Mercy Flight," an air-taxi service to Medford, in case there are any cases it can't handle.

   For your banking and walk-up teller needs, go to the **First Interstate Bank of Oregon** (365 S. Ellensburg Ave.).

Transportation

Curry County's **Coastal Express** buses (in Gold Beach, call 541/247-7506) run up and down the south coast weekdays only between North Bend and the California border, including local service in Gold Beach. The **Greyhound station** (29770 Colvin St., 541/247-7246) is one block east of the highway in the north end of town.

Port Orford and Vicinity

In 1850, the U.S. Congress passed the Oregon Donation Land Act, allowing white settlers to file claims on Indian land in western Oregon. This was news, of course, to the Indian nations of the region, who had not been consulted on the decision. William Tichenor, captain of the steamship *Gull,* hoping to exploit the new act, had ambitions to establish an outpost on the coast at what's now Port Orford. When Tichenor observed the hostility of the Quatomah band of Tututni Indians in the tidewater, he put nine men ashore on an immense rock promontory fronting the beach because of its suitability as a defensive position. The Indians besieged the rock for two weeks before the whites escaped under cover of night. Tichenor returned with a well-armed party of 70 men and succeeded in founding his settlement.

   From this inauspicious beginning, "Awferd," as the locals call it, established itself as the first townsite on the south coast. Shortly thereafter, the town became the site of the first fort established on the coast during the Rogue Indian Wars. This conflict started when gold miners and settlers came into Indian lands. As a result of the clashes, hundreds of local natives were rounded up and sent to the Siletz Reservation near Lincoln City in 1856.

   Besides the tragic Indian conflicts, Port Orford has other claims to fame. It is the most westerly incorporated city in the contiguous United States. What's more, *Forbes* magazine has dubbed Port Orford the "sleeper" of the Oregon coast, ready to be awakened because of its "knockout"

view. Impressive potential, however, has not yet translated into any great prosperity for the region. Commercial fishing and cedar logging were once the leading revenue producers. In recent years, tourism and many eclectic cottage industries have sprung up to supplement the boom/bust, resource-based economy. The outskirts of Port Orford host such diverse undertakings as an escargot-breeding farm, llama and sheep ranches, a goat-milk dairy, and commercial berry growers, as well as plots of land devoted to Christmas trees and exotic herbs. Offshore, divers harvest kelp for use as a food supplement and sea urchins to supply the Japanese with a popular aphrodisiac and seafood delicacy. In town, the stunning scenery and low rents probably have played a role in the development of a passel of galleries here, evidencing a nascent artist colony.

SIGHTS

Port Orford has an ocean view from downtown that is arguably the most scenic of any city on the coast. A waterfront stroll lets you appreciate the cliffs and offshore sea stacks, as well as the unique sight of commercial fishing boats being hoisted by large cranes into and out of the harbor. With only a short jetty on its north side, Port Orford's harbor, the only open-water port in Oregon, is unprotected from southerly swells, so boats can't be safely moored on the water. When not in use, the fleet rest on wheeled, trailer-like dollies near the foot of the pier.

Battle Rock Park

As you come into town on U.S. 101, it's hard to ignore enormous Battle Rock on the shoreline, the site of the 1851 conflict between the local Indians and the first landing party of white settlers. If you can make your way through the driftwood and blackberry bushes surrounding its base, you can climb the short trail to the top for a heightened perspective on the rockbound coast that parallels the town. You'll also notice the east-west orientation of the harbor. Once you get to the top of the rock, don't think that the battle is necessarily over. Bracing winds often chill you, and high tides can sometimes render this huge coastal extension an island. The rock is also the focus of a **Fourth of July Jubilee Celebration,** which reenacts the historic battle.

Port Orford Heads State Park

Another shoreline scene worth taking in, featuring a striking panorama from north to south, is located up W. 9th Street at what the locals call "The Heads," Port Orford Heads State Park. If you go down the cement trail to the tip of the blustery headland, you look south to the mouth of Port Orford's harbor. To the north, many small rocks fill the water, along with boats trolling for salmon or checking crab pots. On clear days visibility extends from Cape Blanco to Humbug Mountain.

Also located here is the historic **Port Orford Lifeboat Station** (541/332-0521), built by the Coast Guard in 1934 to provide rescue service to the southern Oregon coast. After it was decommissioned in 1970, the officer's quarters, the pleasingly proportioned crew barracks, and other outbuildings were converted to a **museum** (open 10 A.M.–3:30 P.M. Thurs.–Mon. Apr.–Oct.) depicting the work of the station. A trail leads down to Nellie's Cove, site of the former boathouse and launch ramp.

Humbug Mountain

Some people will tell you that 1,756-foot-high Humbug Mountain, six miles south of Port Orford on U.S. 101, is the highest mountain rising directly off the Oregon shoreline. Because the criteria for such a distinction varies as much as the tides, let's just say it's a special place. There's more than one version of how the peak, formerly called Sugarloaf Mountain, got its name. According to one version, gold miners who were drawn here in the 1850s by tales of gold in the black sands nearby soon discovered that the rumored riches proved to be just "humbug." Perhaps more reliable is the Indian legend that says that if the top of the mountain can be seen, the weather will be good.

Once the site of Native American vision quests, today Humbug Mountain's shadow falls upon an Eden-like state park campground surrounded by myrtles, alders, and maples. Just north is a breezy black-sand beach. A three-mile trail to the top of Humbug rewards hardy hikers with impressive vistas to the south of Nesika Beach and a chance to see wild rhododendrons 20–25 feet high. Rising above the rhodies and giant ferns are bigleaf maple, Port Orford cedar, and Douglas and grand firs. Access the trail from the campground or from a trailhead parking area off the highway near the south end of the park. In addition, the **Oregon Coast Trail,** which follows the beach south from Battle Rock, traverses the mountain, and leads down its south side to the beach at Rocky Point.

Prehistoric Gardens

What can we say about this unique roadside attraction, featuring a 25-foot-tall, Formica-green *Tyrannosaurus rex* standing beside the parking lot? Is it kitsch, or is it educational? You decide. In any case, if you've got children in the car, unless they're sleeping or blindfolded, you're probably going to have to pull over. Prehistoric Gardens (36848 U.S. 101, Port Orford 97465, 541/332-4463 or 877/332-4463, 9 A.M.–dusk daily spring–fall, call for winter hours, $7 adults, $6 ages 11–17 and 65-plus, $5 children 3–10), about 10 miles south of Port Orford, is the creation of E. V. Nelson, a sculptor and self-taught paleontologist who began fabricating life-size dinosaurs here back in 1953 and placing them amid the lush rainforest on the backside of Humbug Mountain. Paths lead through the ferns, trees, and undergrowth to a towering brontosaurus, triceratops, and 20 other ferro-concrete

© MARK MORRIS

You can't miss the Prehistoric Gardens on the backside of Humbug Mountain.

replicas, painted in a dazzling palette of Fiestaware colors.

Cape Blanco State Park, Hughes House

Four miles north of Port Orford, west of U.S. 101, is Cape Blanco, whose remote appendages give you the feeling of being at the edge of the continent—as indeed you are, here at the westernmost point in Oregon. From the vantage of Cape Blanco, dark mountains rise behind you and the eaves of the forest overhang tidewater. Below, driftwood and 100-foot-long bull kelp on slivers of black-sand beach fan out from both sides of this earthy red bluff. Somehow, the Spaniards who sailed past it in 1603 viewed the cape as having a *blanco* (white) color. It's been theorized that perhaps they were referring to the fossilized shells on the front of the cliff.

With its exposed location, Cape Blanco really takes it on the chin from Pacific storms. The vegetation along the five-mile state park road down to the beach attests to the severity of winter storms in the area. Gales of 100-mph winds (the record winds were clocked at 184 mph) and horizontal sheets of rain have given some of the usually massive Sitka spruces the appearance of bonsai trees. An understory of salmonberry and bracken fern help evoke the look of a southeast Alaska forest.

Atop the weathered headland is Oregon's oldest, most westerly, and highest lighthouse in continuous use. Built in 1870, the beacon stands 256 feet above sea level and can be seen some 23 nautical miles out at sea. **Cape Blanco Lighthouse** (541/332-2207, tours 10 A.M.–3 P.M. Thurs.–Mon. Apr.–Oct., $3 donation requested) also holds the distinction of having Oregon's first female lighthouse keeper, Mabel E. Bretherton, who assumed her duties in 1903. Tours of the facility include the chance to climb the 64 spiraling steps to the top; this is the only operational lighthouses in the state that allows visitors into the lantern room, to view the working Fresnel lens.

Over the years, several shipwrecks have occurred on the reefs near Cape Blanco, including the *J. A. Chanslor,* an oil tanker that collided with the offshore rocks in 1919, with a loss of 36 lives.

Near Cape Blanco on a side road along the Sixes River is the **Hughes House** (541/332-0248, 10 A.M.–3 P.M. Thurs.–Mon. Apr.–Oct.), a restored Victorian home built in 1898 for rancher and county commissioner Patrick Hughes. Owned and operated today by the state of Oregon, the house serves as a museum and repository of antique furnishings. In addition to the regular season, it's also open during the winter holiday season, when punch and cookies are often served on the weekend before Christmas.

Grassy Knob Wilderness

The Grassy Knob Wilderness encompasses 17,200 acres of steep, rugged terrain and protects rare stands of Port Orford cedar. The wood of this majestic, fragrant tree is light, strong, and durable. Its use in planes during World War II and in Japanese construction has also made it highly valued, but a fatal root fungus spread by logging trucks accounts for its rarity and astronomically high price. During World War II, Japanese submarines used Cape Blanco Lighthouse as an orientation mark to aim planes loaded with incendiary bombs at the Coast Range. The Japanese hoped to ignite forest fires that would destroy the region's Port Orford cedar trees, which were used to construct airplanes then. Because of the perennial dampness, the results were negligible. A short (.8 mile) but moderately difficult trail leads to the summit of Grassy Knob. To get there, follow U.S. 101 north of Port Orford about four miles, go east on County Road 196 to Forest Service Road 5105, which ends at the trailhead. For more information, contact the Siskiyou National Forest, Powers Ranger District (Powers, OR 97466, 541/439-3011).

RECREATION

Beachcombing for agates and fishing floats on nearby beaches and searching for the lost Port Orford meteorite in the surrounding foothills typify the adventures available in the area. The meteorite was found in the 1860s by a government geologist, who estimated its weight at 22,000 tons. Unfortunately, he was unable to relocate the meteorite when he returned for another look.

In the northwest of town, drive west of the highway on 14th or 18th streets to 90-acre **Garrison Lake** for boating, water-skiing, and fishing for stocked rainbow and cutthroat trout. **Buffington Memorial City Park,** at the end of 14th Street, has a dock for fishing or swimming, plus playing fields, tennis courts, picnic areas, hiking trails, and a horse arena. One-half mile north of the lake, look for agates on **Paradise Point Beach.**

The **Elk River,** which empties on the south side of Cape Blanco, and the **Sixes River,** which meets the sea north of the cape, are two popular streams for salmon and steelhead fishing. Chinook and steelhead begin to enter both rivers after the first good rains of fall arrive, usually in November. Private lands limit bank access, with the exception of a good stretch of the Sixes that runs through Cape Blanco State Park. The salmon season runs to the end of the year, steelhead through the following March. **Lamm's Guide Service** (541/440-0558, www.umpquafishingguide.com) runs trips on both rivers.

Between Port Orford and Bandon (just south of Langlois) is **Floras Lake,** which is becoming a mecca for coastal windsurfing. For more information, contact Floras Lake Windsurfing School (P.O. Box 1591, Bandon 97411, 541/347-9205). It's 11 miles north of Port Orford, about four miles west of the highway on Floras Lake Loop Road. On the lake is **Boice Cope County Park,** which has basic tent and RV sites and a boat ramp. From Floras Lake north to Bandon, the most desolate beachfront on the coast can be found—ideal for beachcombing. Grasses, dunes, and shore pine usher you the 25 miles back to Bandon, and chances are good you won't see a soul.

ACCOMMODATIONS

Port Orford is the kind of place where a room with a view will not break your budget.

Motels

The **Shoreline Motel** (206 6th St., 541/332-2903, $38–58), across the highway from Battle Rock, has an outstanding view, offers clean rooms, and accommodates pets.

Castaway-by-the-Sea (545 W. 5th St., 541/332-4502, $45–95) features ocean/harbor views from high on a bluff, fireplaces, and housekeeping units, and will allow pets. The rates on the upper-end lodgings go down significantly in the off-season. It's said that Jack London once stayed in an earlier incarnation of this place.

The **Seacrest Motel** (44 U.S. 101 S., 541/332-3040, $57–74) features views of coastal cliffs and a garden from a quiet hillside on the east side of the highway.

Bed-and-Breakfast

Home-by-the-Sea (444 Jackson St., 541/332-2855 or 800/480-2144, www.homebythesea.com, $95–105 d) includes a full breakfast in its rates. The dramatic hillside view of Battle Rock seascape makes for excellent storm-watching here. Wireless Internet access is available.

Campgrounds

Humbug Mountain State Park (541/332-6774), six miles south of Port Orford, features 80 tent sites and 30 sites for trailers and motor homes ($14–16), and wind-protected sites reserved for hikers and bikers ($4). Flush toilets, showers, picnic tables, water, and firewood are available.

Arizona Beach Campground (P.O. Box 621, Gold Beach 97444, 541/332-6491, www .arizonabeachrv.com, $14–20) is a 70-acre campground close to a beach with lots of driftwood. It has 31 tent sites and almost 100 RV spaces. You can camp on the beach, in an adjoining meadow, or back in the woods by a tiny stream. All the amenities are here, 15 miles north of Gold Beach on U.S. 101, but the closely spaced sites lack privacy. Nonetheless, there are few better places for kids because of the creek running though the site and the proximity of the Prehistoric Gardens. It's open all year. Reservations are needed during holidays only.

Cape Blanco State Park (39745 U.S. 101 S., 541/332-6774 info, 800/452-5687 for cabin reservations) can be reached by driving four miles north of Port Orford on U.S. 101, then heading northwest on the park road that continues five miles beyond to the campground. It features 54 tent sites ($16), four cabins ($35), trailer and motor home sites ($16), a horse camp ($14), and hiker/biker sites ($4); picnic tables, water, and showers are available. For horseback riders, there's a seven-mile trail and a huge open riding area; horses are also allowed on the beach. Regular sites are first-come, first-served.

FOOD

In Port Orford, pickings are slim. Vegetarian soup and sandwiches ($3–5) can be enjoyed at **Seaweed Natural Food and Grocery** (832 Ore-gon St., 541/332-3640). More elaborate fare can be had across the street from Battle Rock at **Paula's Bistro** (236 6th St., 541/332-9378, open for dinner only Tues.–Sun., closed Mon.), whose menu of pasta, barbecue, and seafood specials ($12–18) and wild decor show ambition and creativity. It also wins by default in "Awferd's" anemic dining scene. **Bartlett's Café** (831 Oregon St., 541/332-4175) serves familiar American diner fare for breakfast, lunch, and dinner.

Dining choices are pretty basic here after massive restaurant closures in the mid-1990s. You're better off waiting to take advantage of Bandon's or Gold Beach's array of restaurants.

INFORMATION AND SERVICES

Begin your travels here at **Battle Rock Information Center** (541/332-8055), open daily on the west side of U.S. 101. The people here are especially friendly and helpful. Information is also available at www.portorfordoregon.com. The **library** (555 W. 20th St.) is open weekdays 8 A.M.–5 P.M.

The **First Interstate Bank of Oregon** (716 U.S. 101 N.) in Port Orford offers ATM and banking services.

Transportation

Greyhound stops at a convenience store at 914 N. Oregon Street (541/332-3181). Two buses go in each direction up and down the coast daily. Curry County's **Coastal Express** buses (in Port Orford, call 541/332-5771) run up and down the south coast weekdays only between North Bend and the California border, including local service in Port Orford.

Bandon and Vicinity

In contrast to the glitzy tourist trappings of some of the larger coastal towns, Bandon-by-the-Sea (pop. 2,900) is characterized by the style and grace of an earlier era. The glory that was Bandon is alive and well in Old Town, a picturesque collection of shops, galleries, restaurants, and historical memorabilia. The coast highway finally re-encounters the coast at Bandon, after long inland stretches of pastureland and forests to the south and north.

Although logging, fishing, dairy products, and the harvest of cranberries have been the traditional mainstays of the local economy, in the early part of the 20th century Bandon also enjoyed its first tourism boom. In addition to being a summer retreat from the heat of the Willamette Valley, it was a port of call for thousands of San Francisco–Seattle steamship passengers. This era inspired such touristic venues as the Silver Spray dance hall and a natatorium with a saltwater swimming pool. The golden age that began with the advent of large-scale steamship traffic in 1900, however, came to an abrupt end following a devastating fire in 1936, which destroyed most of the town. The blaze was started by the easily ignitable gorse weed, imported from Ireland (as was the town's name) in the mid-1800s. Dramatic descriptions of the townspeople fighting the flames with their backs to the sea earned the incident a citation as one of the top-10 news stories of the year.

The facelift given Old Town decades later, and the subsequent tourist influx, conjured for many the image of the mythical phoenix rising from its ashes to fly again. On the wings of the recovery, Bandon has established itself as a town rooted in the past with its eyes on the future. Today, Bandon is a curious mixture of provincial backwater, destination resort, and new-age artist colony. Backpack-toting travelers from all over the world flock to this town because of its beaches, its cultural and recreational pursuits, and its European-style hostelry. They coexist happily with the large population of retirees, award-winning artisans, and locals who seem to have cornered the market on late-model pickups with gun racks.

SIGHTS

One of the appealing things about Bandon is that most of its attractions are within walking distance of each other. In addition, on the periphery of town is a varied array of things to see and do.

Old Town

Bandon's Old Town, much of which dates from after the 1936 fire, is a half-dozen blocks of shops, cafés, and galleries squeezed in between the harbor and the highway. The renovated waterfront invites relaxed strolling, and crabbers and anglers pull in catches right off the city docks. The small commercial fleet based here pursues salmon and tuna offshore.

Preservation buffs should check out **Masonic Hall** (2nd and Alabama), one of the few buildings to have survived Bandon's 1914 and 1936 blazes. A photo in the historical museum (see next listing) shows the same building and surrounding structures on Alabama Street (then called Atwater) circa 1914. The photo depicts boardwalks leading to a woolen mill, old storefronts, a theater, and the Bandon Popular Hotel and Restaurant, outside which a horse and buggy await. The scene today has changed dramatically, but nonetheless an early-1900s charm still pervades the neighborhood.

Throughout Old Town are artists and artisans pursuing their crafts and selling their wares. **2nd Street Gallery** (210 2nd St., 541/347-4133, 10 A.M.–5:30 P.M. daily) has a little of everything, from functional and art pottery to blown glass to paintings and sculptures. Another shop, the **New Gallery** (155 Baltimore, 541/347-8221), showcases the work of local jewelers and woodworkers. **Winter River Books and Gallery** (170 2nd St., 541/347-4111) has crystals, objets d'art, and a wide-ranging

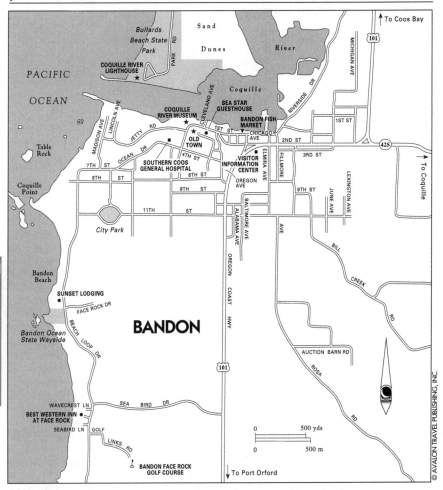

assortment of travel titles, photo essays, fiction, and tapes that makes this the best bookstore on the south coast.

Close by, the **Bandon Driftwood Museum and Art Gallery** (130 Baltimore Ave., 541/347-3719, 9 A.M.–7 P.M. Mon.–Sat., 10 A.M.–6 P.M. Sun. in summer, call for winter hours) shows off an interesting collection of natural sculptures, from gnarly root balls to whole tree trunks. It's housed at the **Big Wheel General Store**, where you'll also find the Fudge Factory (24 flavors of homemade ice cream and butter fudge).

Coquille River Museum

This museum, at the corner of U.S. 101 and Fillmore Street (270 Fillmore St., 541/347-2164, 10 A.M.–4 P.M. Mon.–Sat., 10 A.M.–3 P.M. Sun., closed Sun. in winter, $2 for adults, free for kids), in Bandon's former city hall, traces the history of the Coquille tribe and its forebears. The chronology continues with the steamers and the railroads that brought in white settlers. One room is devoted to Bandon's unofficial standing as the Cranberry Capital of Oregon. Black-and-white blowups showing women stooping over in the bogs to harvest the ripe berries are captioned with such quips as this politically incorrect classic from an overseer: "I had 25 women picking for me, and I knew every one by her fanny." Color photos spanning five decades of Cranberry Festival princesses also adorn the walls.

Another room depicts "Bandon's Resort Years, 1900–1931," when the town was called the Playground of the Pacific. The most compelling exhibits in the museum deal with shipwrecks and the fires of 1914 and 1936.

The Beach Loop

U.S. 101 follows an inland path for more than 50 miles between Coos Bay and Port Orford, but you can leave the highway in Bandon and take the four-mile Beach Loop for a lovely seaside detour south of town. Several access roads lead west from the highway to Beach Loop Drive (County Road 29), each about one-quarter mile from each other. Most people begin the drive by heading west from Old Town on 1st Street along the Coquille. Another popular approach is from 11th Street, which leads to Coquille Point. The south end of the drive runs through the northern portion of **Bandon State Natural Area,** providing parking, beach access, and picnic tables.

Along the fine stretch of beach are rock formations with such evocative names as Table Rock, Elephant Rock, Garden of the Gods, and Cat and Kittens Rocks. The whole grouping of sea stacks, included within the Oregon Islands National Wildlife Refuge, looks like a surrealist chess set cast upon the waters. The most eye-catching of all is **Face Rock,** Bandon's answer to New Hampshire's lately lamented Old Man of the Mountain. This basalt monolith resembles the face of a woman gazing skyward. An Indian legend says that she was a princess frozen by an evil sea spirit. Look for the Face Rock turnout one-quarter mile south of Coquille Point on the Beach Loop.

One-half mile north of Face Rock is the Bandon Face Rock Golf Course, and another mile on is Bandon Beach Riding Stables, which offers beach rides; see the Recreation section for details on both. Despite its scenic and recreational attractions, the beaches south of town can be surprisingly deserted, perhaps because of the long, steep trails up from the water along some parts of the beach. In any case, this dearth of people can make for great beachcombing. Agates, driftwood, and tidepools full of starfish and anemones are commonly encountered here, along with bird-watching opportunities galore. Elephant Rock has a reputation as the Parthenon of puffins, while murres, oystercatchers, and other species proliferate on the other offshore formations.

Bullards Beach State Park

Two miles north of Bandon, bordering the Coquille River estuary and more than four miles of beachfront, Bullards Beach State Park (P.O. Box 25, Bandon 97411, information 541/347-2209 or 800/551-6949, reservations 800/452-5687) is a great place to fish, crab, bike, fly a kite, windsurf, picnic, or overnight in the large, sheltered campground. The beach and lighthouse

THE BIRD MAN OF BANDON

In the 1962 movie *The Birdman of Alcatraz,* Burt Lancaster portrays an embittered convict who lifts his spirits by caring for birds. Dan Deuel is Bandon's bird man, a Vietnam veteran with shattered limbs who takes in injured and abandoned seals, sea lions, raptors, seabirds, and other wild animals brought to him by beachcombers and government agencies. If you are interested in animal rehabilitation, call ahead to schedule a tour of the **Free FlightBird and Marine Mammal Rehabilitation Center** (1185 Portland Ave., Bandon 97411, 541/347-3882). Particularly interesting are several resident owls and A-Shau, a female bald eagle who is permanently grounded. Sometimes there aren't too many critters to look at, because they are released back into the wild after being nurtured back to health, but Dan's wealth of knowledge about his charges is always edifying. This worthy and heroic operation is staffed by volunteers and largely self-sustaining, so donations are a great help.

SOUTH COAST

© MARK MORRIS

Coquille River Lighthouse, Bullards Beach State Park

are reached via a scenic three-mile drive paralleling the Coquille River. Look for jasper and agates amid the heaps of driftwood on the shore. Equestrian trails and horse camping facilities make this a popular destination for riders. The boat ramp gives anglers, kayakers, and canoeists access to the lower Coquille River and Bandon Marsh National Wildlife Refuge (see the Recreation section).

The riverside road going out to the Coquille's north jetty takes you through the dunes to the picturesque **Coquille River Lighthouse,** a squat tower with adjacent octagonal quarters. The last lighthouse built on the Oregon coast, it was completed in 1896, then was abandoned in 1939 when the Coast Guard installed an automated light across the river. After years of neglect, the structure was restored in the late 1970s and is now open throughout the year. Etchings of ships that made it across Bandon's treacherous bar—and some that didn't—greet you as you enter. Volunteers are on duty April–October to staff the gift shop and show you around.

West Coast Game Park

Seven miles south of Bandon is the West Coast Game Park (46914 U.S. 101 S., 541/347-3106, 9 A.M.–7 P.M. daily June 15–Sept. 1, 9 A.M.–5 P.M. the rest of the year, $11 ages 13 and up, $10 seniors, $8 ages 7–12, $5 ages 2–6), the self-proclaimed "largest wild-animal petting park in the country." There are 450 animals, represented by 75 different species, including tiger cubs, chimps, camels, zebras, bison, and snow leopards. Along with these exotics you'll also encounter such indigenous species as elk, bears, raccoons, and cougars. Visitors may be surprised to see a lion and tiger caged together, or a fox and a raccoon sharing the same nursery. The park tries raising different species together and often finds that animals can live harmoniously with their natural enemies. Free-roaming animals include deer, peacock, pygmy goats, and llamas. An elk refuge is another popular area of the park. Even if you're not with a child, the opportunity to pet a pup, a cub, or a kit can bring out the kid in you. The park is open year-round, but call during winter because of restricted hours of operation.

RECREATION
Bandon Marsh National Wildlife Refuge

Bird-watchers flock to the Bandon Marsh National Wildlife Refuge (541/347-3683), especially in the fall, to take in what may be the prime birding site on the coast. The extensive mudflats attract flocks of shorebirds, including red phalaropes, black-bellied plovers, long-billed curlews, and dunlins, as well as such strays from Asia as Mongolian plovers.

Bandon Marsh lies a short paddle across the river from the state park, or via Riverside Drive, which runs from Bandon to U.S. 101 on the south side of the Coquille River bridge. The refuge protects more than 700 precious acres of the Coquille estuary's remaining saltmarsh habitat, along the southeastern side of the river. Migrating waterfowl, bald eagles, California brown pelicans, and other birds feast on the rich food sources here. The refuge and its elevated observation deck are open daily from sunrise to sunset.

Fishing

The Coquille River runs 30 miles from its Siskiyou headwaters before meandering leisurely through Bandon. The north and south jetties are popular spots for perch and rockfish, while the city docks right in Old Town yield catches of perch and crab April–October and smelt July–September. The spring chinook run pales in comparison to those in the Rogue and Chetco to the south, but the fall run of chinook (beginning Sept.–Oct.) and coho (Oct.–Nov.) are strong and productive. Steelhead usually arrive in November, and the run gathers steam January–February. A boat is necessary for the best steelhead and salmon water, but bank anglers can fish the mouth of Ferry Creek, just off Riverside Drive in Bandon. Fishing guides and gear can be arranged through the **Bandon Bait Shop** (1st and Alabama, 541/347-3905), across from the boat basin. The shop also rents crab rings and other gear and can point you to productive spots for catching Dungeness crab.

Just off the south end of Beach Loop Drive, 30-acre **Bradley Lake,** protected from ocean winds by high dunes, offers good trout fishing

and a boat ramp. Trophy rainbows averaging five pounds, reared at the Bandon Fish Hatchery east of town, are stocked here each spring.

Golf

Dubbed "Pebble Beach North," **Bandon Dunes Golf Resort** (57744 Round Lake Dr., Bandon 97411, 541/347-4380 or 888/345-6008, www .bandondunesgolf.com) was hailed by *Golf Digest* as the number-one new course in 1999 and named the third-best course in the United States by *Golf* magazine for its seven holes by the Pacific and unobstructed ocean views from all 18. A second 18-hole course, **Pacific Dunes,** opened here in 2001, and a third course is on the drawing board for the future. To preserve the natural surroundings along the ocean bluffs, this Scottish links course doesn't allow carts (the only missing amenity here), so you'll have to hire a caddy or schlep your own bag. A luxurious resort (see the Accommodations section) with Pacific views from a sand dune and a restaurant are also here for those who come to worship in the south coast's Sistine Chapel of golf. It's one mile north of the Coquille River. Green fees for either course, June–September, are $160 for hotel guests and

© MARK MORRIS

They're readily available in Bandon Harbor.

$200 for nonguests; call for rates the rest of the year. The caddie fee is $35 per bag.

Duffers and other mortals may choose instead to tread the equally scenic seaside links two miles south of town at **Bandon Face Rock Golf Course** (3235 Beach Loop Rd., Bandon 97411, 541/347-3818, green fees $10 for 9 holes, $16 for 18 holes).

Other Activities

On the waterfront in Old Town, **Adventure Kayak** (315 1st. St., 541/347-3480, daily 10 A.M.–5 P.M. in summer) rents kayaks (from $10 per hour), teaches classes on a variety of kayak techniques, and offers guided sea-kayak tours of the lower Coquille ecosystem (and farther afield) with a naturalist from $35 for a two- to three-hour paddle.

Bandon Beach Riding Stables (2640 Beach Loop, 541/347-3423) is four miles south of Face Rock on the Beach Loop. Several beach rides are offered daily, plus sunset rides in the summer. Prices range $30–40 for a 1.5- to 2-hour ride. Reservations are advised. Open year-round.

EVENTS

The annual **Wine and Seafood Festival** happens every Memorial Day weekend, at the Community Center in City Park off 11th Street West in Bandon. The event is free and includes live music, horse-drawn buggy rides, arts-and-crafts booths, and wine tasting. Contact the chamber of commerce (541/347-9619) for details. The same weekend, competitors in the **Sandcastle Contest** create amazing sculptures out of sand, water, and imagination. This takes place on the beach off Beach Loop Drive at Seabird Lane. Construction starts at 9 A.M.; judging is at 1 P.M. Call the chamber for more information.

A fish fry, kayak and driftboat races, parade, and classic car and motorcycle show are highlights of Bandon's **Fourth of July** celebration; at dusk, fireworks are launched across the Coquille to burst above the river.

The biggest weekend of the year for Bandonians comes the second weekend in September, when the **Cranberry Festival** (541/347-9616) brings everyone together in Old Town for a parade, crafts fair, tours of a cranberry farm, and the Bandon High Cranberry Bowl—in which the local footballers take on traditional rival Coquille High.

During the late November to early January holiday season, the merchants of Old Town and anglers deck their stores and boats with twinkling lights in the traditional **Festival of Lights.** Particularly striking is the Coquille River Lighthouse, lit up across the water like a Christmas tree.

ACCOMMODATIONS

The expression "You can't go wrong" applies for price, view, cleanliness, and whatever else you're looking for in this town. Bandon bills itself as America's Storm-Watching Capital, and special packages are often available October–March.

Motels

A favorite place to stay is the older-but-refurbished **Windermere Motel** (3250 Beach Loop, 541/347-3710, $68–145). Baby-boomers can relive their childhood beach getaways in cedarwood efficiencies or two-story condolike units, situated on a bluff above a windswept beach. Sunset views and a two-mile walk to town along one of Oregon's most scenic beachfronts can structure a contemplative stay here. Housekeeping facilities and proximity to restaurants (Lord Bennett's) and the West Coast Game Park also make this an ideal family vacation spot.

Not far away is **Sunset Lodging** (1865 Beach Loop, 541/347-2453 or 800/842-2407, www.sunsetmotel.com, rooms $52–110, cabins $165 and up). With some units built right into the cliff above a scenic beach, the view here is hard to beat. Whether you're looking for rooms with a kitchen, rooms that accommodate pets, or rooms with a fireplace, there's something here for you in a variety of price ranges. A hot tub, indoor pool, on-site laundry, and Lord Bennett's Restaurant across the street also make this place a good choice. Nonetheless, the steep steps down the 80-foot-high bluff to the beach and the popularity of the place might not be to everyone's liking.

CRANBERRIES

From the vantage point of U.S. 101 between Port Orford and 10 miles north of Bandon, you'll notice what appears to be reddish-tinged ground in flood-irrigated fields. If you get close, you'll see cranberries, small evergreens that creep along the ground and send out runners that take root. Along the runners, upright branches 6–8 inches long hold pink flowers and fruits.

These berries are cultivated in bogs to satisfy their tremendous need for water and to protect them against insects and winter cold. Bandon leads Oregon in this crop, with an output ranking third in the nation. Oregon berries are often used in juice production by Ocean Spray because of their deep red pigment and high vitamin C content.

It is possible to arrange a visit to see some of these bogs—the most interesting time is during the late autumn harvest. **Faber Farms** (519 Morrison Rd., 541/347-1166) offers free tours through bogs 10 A.M.–4 P.M. Monday–Saturday from June through mid-November. A sweeter encounter can be found at **Cranberry Sweets** (1st St. and Chicago St., Bandon, 800/527-5748, 9 A.M.–5:30 P.M. daily). Herein are confections ranging from cranberry fudge to cranberry truffles. Sugar fans will be glad it's open seven days a week.

Oregon bogs were producing wild cranberries when Lewis and Clark first traded with the Indians for them in 1805. Shortly thereafter, cultivated bogs were developed in Massachusetts, which like Oregon has acidic soils with lots of organic materials conducive to berry production. By the California gold rush of 1849, East Coast growing and harvesting techniques had transformed Bandon's marshes into commercial cranberry bogs. In the years to come, much of the modern equipment for harvesting these bogs was developed in Bandon. Wet-picking, for instance, is facilitated by the water reel, which is rotated to create eddies on the bog to shake berries off the vines. After they float to the surface, the cranberries are pushed by long booms toward a submerged hopper. They are then transferred by conveyor belt onto trucks. Walking through the bogs without trampling the berries is made possible by fastening wooden platforms with short pegs to the soles of boots.

Without such innovations, Thanksgiving dinner wouldn't be the same. In order to bring the enormous annual volume of cranberries to the dinner table for the holidays, all of these harvesting techniques—as well as processing and packaging technology—are called into play.

The "sleeper" property (for those making a hasty visual appraisal) on the beach loop is **The Best Western Inn at Face Rock** (3225 Beach Loop, 541/347-9441 or 800/638-3092, $80–205, half price in Jan.). Part of this status has to do with the motel's location near the end of the beach loop across the street from Bandon's coastline and near the nine-hole golf course. Many of the modern well-appointed rooms have magnificent ocean views. An indoor pool, fitness room, whirlpool, and restaurant also make this an especially good choice for active travelers. Best of all are some of the sweetest off-season rates on the coast. Some suites have fireplaces, kitchenettes, and private patios. Other rooms have coffeemakers, microwaves, and refrigerators. There's an on-site restaurant and a short path to the beach.

Hotel

For avid golfers, the **Lodge at Bandon Dunes** (57744 Round Lake Dr., 888/345-6008, www .bandondunesgolf.com, rooms and suites $150–900, see Golf for green fees) is a deluxe resort at what is considered one of the country's finest courses. The lodge offers 15 single rooms, four larger single rooms, and two four-bedroom suites. View options vary from the golf course and the ocean to dunes and surrounding woods. The Lodge is five minutes from Bandon, one mile north of the Coquille, and 30 minutes from the North Bend Airport, which is served by daily flights from Portland. Room and suite rates and green fees are seasonal and subject to change.

Bed-and-Breakfast

The Sea Star Guesthouse and Hostel (375 2nd

St., 541/347-9632, www.seastarbandon.com, café 541/347-9694, $70–105) has skylights, a natural wood interior, a wood stove, and a harbor view. Private, couple, and family rooms are available. The latter are more likely found in the four units of the adjoining Sea Star Guesthouse (370 1st St.), where you get the feel of a tasteful motel. Guesthouse suites sleep 2–6, have private baths, cable TV, queen-sized beds, in-room coffee and tea service, and fireplaces. Private rooms for two are a bit cheaper. All units are nonsmoking, and no pets are permitted.

Campgrounds
Bullards Beach State Park (P.O. Box 25, Bandon 97411, information 541/347-2209 or 800/551-6949, reservations 800/452-5687, campsites $16–20, yurts $27) is a wonderful state park in a great location, between the Coquille River and four miles of beach. The park has 190 campsites, 13 yurts, eight horse-camping sites, and hiker/biker spaces. To get there, drive north of town on U.S. 101 for about one mile; just past the bridge on the west side of the highway is the park entrance. The beach is reached via a scenic two-mile drive paralleling the Coquille River. Electricity, picnic tables, and fire grills are provided. You'll also find a store, a café, a laundry room, horse-riding/camping facilities, an inviting sandy beach, summer evening campfire talks Tuesday–Saturday, and hiking trails.

FOOD
Local Delicacies
Bandon's Cheddar Cheese (800/548-8961, 9 A.M.–5:30 P.M. daily), on the east side of U.S. 101 just east of Old Town, was once the second-largest cheese maker in Oregon. The factory, a popular tourist stop known for its huge cheddar bricks, cheese curds, and flavored cheeses, began operation in the early 1900s. Recently purchased by the Tillamook Creamery Association, the location is now an associated retail outlet. There are rumors that Tillamook has plans to create a cheese-making museum on the premises. Visitors can still view the cheese-making video

and sample cheeses. The gift store also sells cheesy knick-knacks.

Five miles south of Bandon, on the east side of U.S. 101, hit the brakes at **Misty Meadows Jams** roadside stand (48053 U.S. 101 S., 541/347-2575, 8 A.M.–6 P.M.) for first-rate jams and jellies, including a variety of products incorporating Bandon cranberries. This family-owned and -operated business has been making delicious concoctions from Oregon-grown fruits since 1970. In addition to preserves, the shop sells olives and fruit-based barbecue sauces, syrups, honey, and salsas.

Steak and Seafood
Bandon Boatworks (275 Lincoln Ave. SW, 541/347-2111) has delicious traditional breakfast/brunch entrées, fresh seafood, and steaks for lunch and dinner. The Boatworks has great views of the Coquille Lighthouse and an intimate lounge with entertainment. The restaurant is closed Mondays and often goes into winter hibernation during January and February, so call for reservations or hours.

Budget diners and smoked fish connoisseurs will appreciate the **Bandon Fish Market** (at the boat basin near the intersection of 1st and Chicago, 541/347-4282). Heartier appetites call for the market's excellent fish and chips (takeout only). A picnic table outside by the harbor is the place to enjoy it all with a trip across the street to **Cranberry Sweets** for dessert.

The moderately priced **Wheelhouse Seafood Grill** (1st and Chicago, 541/347-9331) deep-fries the fish (they also grill and broil) with a beer batter that doesn't mask the taste of the food. Their homemade soup is a specialty (as is the sirloin steak with prawns), especially the Cioppino Rick, using diverse shellfish and bottomfish in a marinara base.

South of downtown, **Lord Bennett's** (1695 Beach Loop Dr., 541/347-FOOD or 541/347-3663) cliffside aerie looks out over the breakers toward Bandon's most dramatic restaurant view. Lunch and dinner do justice to these surroundings with elegantly rendered seafood dishes. Recommended are the bouillabaisse, crab cakes, and the blackened ahi. Jazz on selected evenings in the lounge is another nice touch.

INFORMATION AND SERVICES

The **Bandon Chamber of Commerce** (300 W. 2nd St., Bandon 97411, 541/347-9616, www .bandon.com), in Old Town, distributes a comprehensive guide and a large annotated pictographic map of the town. Ask them about what they call "the best river fishing and crabbing docks on the coast."

Southern Coos General Hospital (640 W. 4th St., 541/347-2426) features an ocean view that in itself is therapeutic, as well as an emergency room and facilities for coronary/respiratory care.

For banking services, the **Security Bank Bandon Branch** (1125 U.S. 101) or the **Bank of America** (1110 Oregon Ave. SW) should be able to accommodate you.

Transportation

The **Greyhound bus** (800/229-9424) stops at the Sea Star Guesthouse (375 2nd St.) at 11:05 A.M. for Portland and at 4:30 A.M. and 4:25 P.M. for San Francisco. North- and southbound **Coastal Express** buses (541/469-6822) run three times daily, weekdays only, between North Bend and Brookings, stopping near the north end of Bandon at Ray's Food Place supermarket.

Heading north, you can escape the tedium of U.S. 101's inland route to Coos Bay by taking the **Seven Devils Road** about three miles north of Bandon. This route runs 13 miles to **Charleston,** a fishing village that sits closer to the ocean than its larger neighbors to the northeast, Coos Bay and North Bend. En route, beaches, state parks, and an estuarine preserve make the drive interesting, although the miles of heavily logged mountainsides you'll pass through are a little depressing.

COURTESY OF THE OREGON STATE ARCHIVES

Conde B. McCullough Bridge, spanning Coos Bay, shortly after its completion in 1936 opened the final stretch of U.S. 101

The Bay Area: Charleston, Coos Bay, North Bend

The towns around the harbor of Coos Bay—Charleston, Coos Bay, and North Bend—refer to themselves collectively as the Bay Area. In contrast to its namesake in California, the Oregon version is not exactly the Athens of the coast. Nonetheless, visitors will be impressed by the area's beautiful beaches, the largest oceanfront dunes in North America, and three wonderfully scenic and historic state parks. Because much of this natural beauty is on the periphery of the industrialized core of the Bay Area, away from U.S. 101, it's easy to miss. All that many motorists see upon entering Coos Bay/North Bend on the Coast Highway are the dockside lumber mills and foreign vessels anchored at the one-time site of the world's largest (and currently, Oregon's second busiest) lumber port.

The little town of Charleston (pop. 700) to the southwest makes few pretensions of being anything other than what it really is—the third-largest commercial fishing port on the Oregon coast. Four processing plants here can or cold-pack tuna, salmon, crab, oysters, shrimp, and other kinds of seafood. The town might occasionally smell of fish, but the few restaurants and lodgings here are good values. Moreover, a post office, a launderette, and a visitors information center are all conveniently crammed together on the main street, the Cape Arago Highway (County Rd. 240), and the town is the gateway to a trio of extraordinary state parks: Sunset Bay, Shore Acres, and Cape Arago.

HISTORY

Radiocarbon testing shows that Indians were living in the Coos Bay area more than 8,500 years ago, thriving on the region's abundant natural resources. Francis Drake took shelter in the South Cove of Cape Arago, to the southwest, in 1579, and Captain James Cook noted the area in his explorations two centuries later. The era of modern settlement, though, really began by accident.

In January 1852, the *Captain Lincoln,* sailing with supplies and reinforcements against hostile Indians at Port Orford, wrecked on the North Spit of Coos Bay. (This would be far from the last wreck on this dangerous stretch of coast. See the "Coos Bay Shipwrecks" sidebar.) The survivors, including 52 soldiers, established Camp Cast-A-Way, utilizing salvaged supplies from the grounded ship. In the several months before their rescue from this remote stretch of then little-known coast, they conducted the first explorations of the bay. News of the area soon reached the attention of the public, and within the year miners began to arrive on south coast beaches, including Whiskey Run, just south of Cape Arago.

In 1854, a settlement called Marshfield developed near the south end of the bay, which would eventually grow into the city of Coos Bay. A couple of miles north, Asa Meade Simpson established one of the first sawmills and shipyards on the bay, exploiting the region's dense and untapped timber wealth and supplying lumber to the gold rush–era housing boom in San Francisco. By the turn of the 20th century, Simpson ships were hauling lumber to 11 nations.

Asa's son, Louis Jerome Simpson, platted and incorporated the new town of North Bend in 1903, and three years later completed a lavish summer house at Shore Acres on Cape Arago. That home burned to the ground in 1921, and the Simpson family later donated a portion of the Cape Arago estate to the state of Oregon, which converted the spectacular property to a state park.

Today, the Bay Area, along with other western Oregon towns dependent on timber, is in transition. A perfect illustration of this is the Mill Casino, opened in the mid-1990s by the Coquille Indian Tribe in North Bend's former Weyerhaeuser mill, which had shut down because of declining timber-industry fortunes. The region's wealth of diversions and what is probably the mildest weather of any major city in Oregon are being promoted to draw tourists and retirees and to recruit new businesses—and it seems to be paying off. In recent years, the Bay Area, Oregon's coastal population hub with

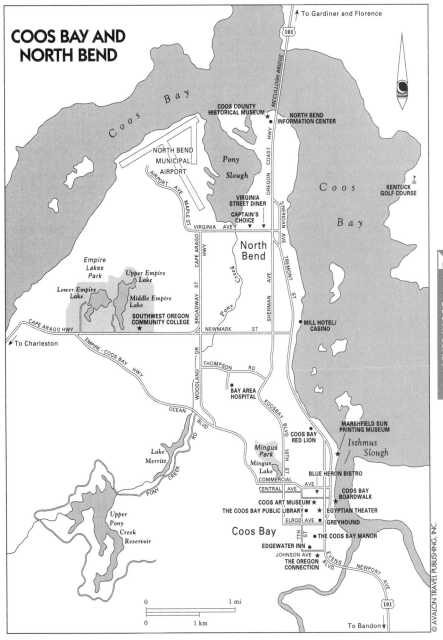

COOS BAY AND NORTH BEND

To Gardiner and Florence

101

McCULLOUGH BRIDGE

Coos Bay

Coos Bay

COOS COUNTY
HISTORICAL MUSEUM ★
NORTH BEND
INFORMATION CENTER

NORTH BEND
MUNICIPAL
AIRPORT

AIRPORT AVE

MAPLE ST

Pony

Slough

Coos

Bay

KENTUCK
GOLF COURSE

VIRGINIA
STREET DINER

CAPTAIN'S
CHOICE

VIRGINIA AVE

CAPE ARAGO HWY

North
Bend

SHERIDAN AVE

TREMONT ST

Empire
Lakes
Park

Upper Empire
Lake

Lower Empire
Lake

Middle Empire
Lake

SOUTHWEST OREGON
COMMUNITY COLLEGE ★

Pony

Creek

BROADWAY ST

SHERMAN AVE

NEWMARK ST

MILL HOTEL/
CASINO

CAPE ARAGO HWY

To Charleston

EMPIRE - COOS BAY HWY

WOODLAND DR

OCEAN

BLVD

RD

THOMPSON RD

BAY AREA
HOSPITAL

KOOSBAY BLVD

MARSHFIELD SUN
PRINTING MUSEUM

Isthmus
Slough

COOS BAY
RED LION

Lake
Merritt

PONY CREEK RD

Mingus
Park

Mingus
Lake

10TH ST

BLUE HERON BISTRO

COMMERCIAL AVE

CENTRAL AVE

COOS ART MUSEUM ★

THE COOS BAY PUBLIC LIBRARY ■

ELROD AVE

COOS BAY
BOARDWALK

★ EGYPTIAN THEATER

GREYHOUND

Upper
Pony
Creek
Reservoir

Coos Bay

7TH ST

● THE COOS BAY MANOR

EDGEWATER INN ●

JOHNSON AVE
THE OREGON
CONNECTION

EVANS BLVD

NEWPORT AVE

101

0   1 mi

0   1 km

To Bandon ▼

SOUTH COAST

© AVALON TRAVEL PUBLISHING, INC.

COOS BAY SHIPWRECKS

The *Captain Lincoln*, whose grounding on the treacherous North Spit of Coos Bay led to settlement of the area, would not be the last ship to meet its end on these dangerous shores. In 1910, the *Czarina* foundered in heavy seas on the bar; 24 people were killed in one of the worst shipwrecks on Oregon's south coast. The *Claremont* and the *Santa Clara* both wrecked on the bar in 1915, and the *Sujameco* grounded on Horsfall Beach in 1929. Although most of the ship was removed during salvage operations, iron projections can still sometimes be seen in the sand at the low tide.

The most recent and infamous shipwreck here, though, was the February 4, 1999 grounding of the 640-foot wood-chip carrier *New Carrissa*, on the North Spit. After the Coast Guard firebombed the freighter in an attempt to burn off the 150,000 gallons of fuel oil on board, the vessel broke into two parts. After weeks of failed attempts, the bow section was finally towed out to sea and sunk in 10,000 feet of water by a Navy torpedo. Most of the stern was finally removed, but a section of it remains mired in the sand on the North Spit, just beyond the surf. During the shipwreck and months of salvage efforts, the hulk leaked some 70,000 gallons of oil, which killed an estimated 2,400 seabirds and destroyed oyster beds. The media circus that sprang up around the site generated a temporary economic boomlet for the region, but the long-term ecological damage is still to be determined.

more than 26,000 people, has seen an increase in dining spots and lodging, as well as boutiques and galleries.

SIGHTS

The Harbor: Milling Around

A good place to take in the bustling bayfront is the **waterfront boardwalk and overlook pier,** U.S. 101 and Anderson Avenue, where you can check out the oceangoing freighters, visit a restored tugboat, and learn of the harbor's history courtesy of interpretive placards. A 400-gallon saltwater aquarium holds fish and other marine life of Coos Bay.

Because of the decline in the supply of lumber and the subsequent mill closures, the Weyerhaeuser and other forest-product facility tours are currently not operating. But this is still the largest coastal harbor between San Francisco and Puget Sound (more than 100 deepwater vessels call here each year), and it's still fun to watch the ships docking and the portside wood-chip piles growing by dozens of feet overnight. Wood chips are Oregon's primary forest-product export. What had been considered surfeit slivers can now be made into a low-grade paper with the addition of chemicals during processing aboard the Japanese factory ships in the harbor. What's left onshore is often enough "hog fuel" to provide sufficient BTUs to heat a mill. Given the return on these chips, locals call these piles the "million-dollar view." Another roadside perspective on the mills is the sight of "log broncs." These short, powerful boats are highly maneuverable. The broncs evoke the "little engine that could" as they move the floating logjams from the millpond to the conveyors into the mill.

The Rendezvous Tour Company (541/267-5661), moored at Coos Bay's Boardwalk, offers bay and dinner cruises.

Coos Art Museum

The Coos Art Museum (235 Anderson Ave., Coos Bay, 541/267-3901, 11 A.M.–5 P.M. TUES.–FRI., 1 p.m.–4 P.M. Sat., free), in downtown Coos Bay, is the Oregon coast's only art museum and features primarily 20th-century and contemporary works by American artists, including pieces by Robert Rauschenberg and Larry Rivers. Etchings, woodcuts, serigraphs, and other prints make up a large part of the permanent collection, which includes several of Janet Turner's richly detailed depictions of birds in natural settings. Other highlights include Kirk Lybecker's photo-realistic watercolors. Don't miss the Prefontaine Room on the second floor of the museum. Photos, trophies, medals, and other memorabilia of this native-son world-class runner illustrate his credo: "I want to make something beautiful when I run."

In addition to the permanent collection, recurring events worth detouring for are the May–June juried show of artists from the western states, and the Maritime Art Exhibit, August–mid-September.

Coos County Historical Museum

The Coos County Historical Museum (1220 Sherman Ave., North Bend 97459, 541/756-6320, www.cooshistory.org, 10 A.M.–4 P.M. Tues.–Sat., $1–2) is located near the south end of the Conde McCullough Bridge, one of several distinctive Depression-era high-wire acts by Oregon's master bridgebuilder. The museum houses more than the usual bric-a-brac from earlier eras, thanks largely to the region's heritage as a shipping center. An early-1900s Regina music box, a piano shipped around Cape Horn, miniature boat models, and a jade Chinese plaque, as well as Coos Indian beadwork and other artifacts, make this collection especially memorable. Outside, old-time logging equipment and a 1920s steam train are also worth a look.

Marshfield Sun Printing Museum

This interesting little museum (1049 N. Front St., 541/269-2775, 1–4 P.M. Tues.–Sat. Memorial Day–Labor Day, free) in Coos Bay features an original press, some 200 cases of type fonts, and other equipment used in publishing the weekly *Sun* newspaper, back when Coos Bay was called Marshfield. Started by Jesse Allen Luse in 1891, at the time it ceased operations in 1944, *The Sun* was the oldest newspaper in Oregon continuously published under one editor.

Sunset Bay State Park

The Cape Arago Highway west of Charleston leads to some of the most dramatic beaches and interesting state parks on the coast. Among the several beaches on the road to Cape Arago, the strand at Sunset Bay State Park (13030 Cape

Arago Hwy., information 541/888-4902, reservations 800/452-5687) is the big attraction because its sheltered shallow cove, encircled by sandstone bluffs, is warm and calm enough for swimming, a rarity in the Pacific Ocean north of Santa Barbara, California. In addition to swimmers, divers, surfers, kayakers, and boaters, many people come here to watch the sunset. Local legend tells that pirates hid out in this well-protected cove.

A four-mile cliffside segment of the Oregon Coast Trail from Sunset Beach south is the best way to appreciate the sea stacks and islands between here and Cape Arago. Good views of Cape Arago Lighthouse across the water can be had along this route. Listen for its unique foghorn. For a shorter hike, follow the signs from the mouth of Big Creek to the viewpoint overlooking Sunset Bay.

Shore Acres State Park

Less than one mile south of Sunset Bay at Shore Acres State Park (541/888-3732), the grandeur of nature is complemented by the hand of man. The park is set on the grounds of lumber magnate and entrepreneur Louis J. Simpson's early-1900s mansion, which began as a summer home in 1906 and grew into a three-story mansion complete with an indoor heated swimming pool and large ballroom. Originally a Christmas present to his wife, Shore Acres became the showplace of the Oregon coast, with formal and Japanese gardens eventually added to the 743-acre estate. After a 1921 fire, a second, larger (two stories high and 224 feet long) incarnation of Simpson's "shack by the beach" was built. Over the following years the building fell into disrepair, and it and the grounds were ceded to the state in 1942. Because of the high cost of upkeep, the mansion had to be razed, but the gardens have been lovingly maintained.

The gardens here are compelling attractions, but the headland's rim is more dramatic. Perched near the edge of the bluff, on the site formerly occupied by the mansion, a glass-enclosed observation shelter makes a perfect vantage point from which to watch for whales or marvel at the crashing waves. When there's a

formal gardens at Shore Acres

storm, the waves really slam into the sandstone reefs and cliffs, hurling up tremendous fountains of spray. It's not uncommon to feel the spray atop the 75-foot promontory. The history of the Simpson family is really the history of the Bay Area, and their story is captioned beneath period photos in the observation gazebo and in the garden in a small enclosure at the west end of the floral displays.

In the seven neatly tended acres of gardens, set back from the sea, the international botanical bounty culled by Simpson clipper ships and schooners is still in its glory, complemented by award-winning roses, rhododendrons, tulips, and azaleas. A restored gardener's cottage with antique furnishings stands at the back of the formal gardens. It's open for special occasions and during the winter holidays. Also in the gardens, note the copper egret sculptures at the pond and the greenhouse for rare plants from warmer climes.

From Thanksgiving through New Year's, during the annual **Holiday Lights and Open House,** the gardens are decorated with 250,000 colored lights and other holiday touches, 4–10 P.M. daily The gardener's cottage opens and serves free refreshments during this time.

If you bear right and follow the pond's contours toward the ocean, you'll come to a trail. Follow it north for cliffside views of the rock-studded shallows below. Southward, the trail goes downhill to a scene of exceptional beauty. From the vantage point of a small beach, you can watch waves crash into rocks with such force that the white spray appears to hang suspended in the air. Exploring tidepools and caves, as well as springtime swimming in a cove formed by winter storms on the south side of the beach, are pursuits for the active traveler here. In summer, thimbleberries and salal growing along the trail down to the beach can provide sustenance for these activities.

Shore Acres is open year-round 8 A.M. until sunset, with a $3 day-use fee charged per vehicle; the Coast Passport is also valid. The gift shop near the entrance to garden usually opens 11 A.M.–4:30 P.M.

Cape Arago State Park

A little more than one mile south of Shore Acres is Cape Arago State Park (800/551-6949), at the end of the Cape Arago Highway. Locals have made much of the fact that this was a possible landing site of the English explorer Sir Francis Drake in 1579, and they put a plaque here commemorating him.

Beachcombers can make their own discoveries in the numerous tidepools, which are some of the best on the coast. The south cove trail runs down to a sandy beach and the better tidepools, while the north cove trail leads to more tidepools, good spots for fishing, and views of the colonies of seals and sea lions at Shell Island, including the most northerly breeding colony of enormous elephant seals. Their huge pups, when just a month old, may already weigh 300–400 pounds. Note that the north trail closes March 1–June 30 to protect seal pups. The picnic tables on the headlands command beautiful ocean panoramas and are superbly placed for whale-watching. The park is free and open for day use only year-round.

South Slough Estuarine Research Reserve

To many people, an estuary is just a place where you get stuck in the mud. More often than not, however, the interface of fresh water and salt water represents one of the richest ecosystems on earth, capable of producing five times more plant material than a cornfield of comparable size, while supporting great numbers of fish, birds, and other wildlife. The South Slough of Coos Bay is the largest such web of life on the Oregon coast. The South Slough Estuarine Reserve Interpretive Center (on Seven Devils Rd., 541/888-5558, www .southsloughestuary.org, 8:30 A.M.–4:30 P.M. daily in summer, weekdays only Sept.–May, free), four miles south of Charleston, will help you coordinate a canoe trip through the estuary and offers guided hikes as well.

The center looks out over several estuarine arms of Coos Bay, the largest harbor between San Francisco Bay and the Columbia River. These vital wetlands nurture a vast web of life, which is detailed by the placards captioning the center's ex-

© MARK MORRIS

hibits. The coastal ecosystem is presented by the "10-minute trail" behind the interpretive center. The various conifers and the understory are clearly labeled along the gently sloping half-mile loop. Branch trails lead down toward the water for an up-close view of the estuary. Down by the slough, you may see elk grazing in marshy meadows and bald eagles circling above, while *Homo sapiens* harvest oysters and shrimp in these waters of life.

Beginning near the visitors center is the easy, three-mile **estuary study trail,** which follows Hidden Creek from the wooded uplands down the valley to a boardwalk that winds through fresh- and saltwater marshes and leads to several wildlife-observations points.

Whiskey Run Beach

Midway between Charleston and Bandon is the quiet beach at Whiskey Run, whose ore-bearing sands spread gold fever down the south coast in the early 1850s. As many as 2,000 miners worked here until a storm washed away the deposit. Other forms of beachcombing at Whiskey Run and on the beaches to the north are still thriving, however. Agate-hunting after a season of winter storms and clamming at low tide make these solitary shorelines ideal places to forget the cares of the world. To get there, turn west from the lightly traveled Seven Devils Road onto

SOUTH COAST

Whiskey Run Road, and drive 1.5 miles to this county park.

Myrtlewood

To see Oregon coast folk art in the making, visit the **Oregon Connection** (1125 S. 1st St., Coos Bay, 541/267-7804), just off U.S. 101 at the south end of Coos Bay. The myrtlewood factory tour shows you how a myrtlewood log gets fashioned into bowls, clocks, tables, and other utensils. No admission is charged for this 25-minute guided run through a working factory. After you're done, the store is a delight, with Oregon gourmet foods and crafts supplementing the quality woodwork.

In 1869, the golden spike marking the completion of the nation's first transcontinental railroad was driven into a highly polished myrtlewood tie. Novelist Jack London was so taken by the beauty of the wood's swirling grain that he ordered an entire suite of furniture. Hudson's Bay trappers used myrtlewood leaves to brew tea as a remedy for chills.

During the Depression, the city of North Bend issued myrtlewood coins after the only bank in town failed. The coins ranged from $.50 to $10 and are still redeemable, although they are worth far more as collector's items.

Five miles north of North Bend, **The Real Oregon Gift** (3955 U.S. 101, 541/756-2220) is another large myrtlewood factory and showroom.

Golden and Silver Falls State Park

Twenty-five miles northeast of Coos Bay in the Coast Range is Golden and Silver Falls State Park (800/551-6949). Two spectacular waterfalls are showcased in this little-known gem of a park. Getting there involves driving east of Coos Bay along the Coos River, crossing to its north bank, and continuing along the Millicoma River through the community of Allegany. To find your way from Coos Bay, look for the Allegany/Eastside exit off U.S. 101. Beyond Allegany, continue up the East Fork of the Millicoma River to its junction with Glenn Creek, which ultimately leads to the park. The narrow, winding gravel roads make this half-hour trip unsuitable for a wide-body vehicle.

You can reach each waterfall by way of two half-mile trails. Both 100-foot cataracts lie about one mile apart, and although both are about the same height, each has a distinct character. For most of the year, Silver Falls is more visually arresting because it flows in a near semicircle around a knob near its top. During or just after the winter rains, however, the thunderous sound of Golden Falls makes it the more awe-inspiring of the two. Along the trails, look for the beautifully delicate maidenhair fern.

RECREATION
Golf

There are two public golf courses in the Bay Area. The **Sunset Bay Golf Course** (11001 Cape Arago Hwy., Charleston 97420, 541/888-9301, weekend green fees $11 for 9 holes, $19 for 18 holes) is a nine-holer close to Sunset Bay State Park that has been described as "one of the most interesting courses anywhere" by *Golf Oregon* magazine. The 18-hole **Kentuck Golf Course** (675 Golf Course Ln., North Bend 97459, 541/756-4464, green fees $16 for 18 holes weekdays, $18 weekends) is across the bay from North Bend along the Kentuck Inlet.

Fishing

In fall 1995, 150,000 spring chinook smolts were released in Coos Bay. In 1997 they returned as mature fish averaging 12–18 pounds, reviving the days of "combat fishing" when hundreds of anglers jostled each other along the bank as they vied for the best fishing spot. These "springers" sometimes exceed 30 pounds and are renowned as an unrivaled dining treat. Also during the last decade, fall chinook and hatchery-reared coho salmon runs have seen healthy increases. Mid-August through November, Isthmus Slough sees a good return of fin-clipped cohos. In saltwater, chinook and coho are found in good numbers within a one- to two-mile radius of the mouth of Coos Bay May–September, although the legal season varies; carefully check the regulations. Remnant striped bass are still occasionally caught in Coos Bay's sloughs and upper tidewater, but their numbers are diminishing.

"To the sea they gave their lives": Fisherman's Memorial in Charleston Harbor

Coos Bay is also one of the premier areas for crabbing and clamming. The Charleston Fishing Pier is a productive spot for crabs, while the best clamming spots are found along the bay side of the North Spit.

Fishing charters, bay cruises, whale-watching, and the like can be arranged through several charter outfits based at the Charleston Boat Basin. **Betty Kay Charters** (541/888-9021 or 800/752-6303, www.bettykaycharters.com) charges typical per-person prices: five hours of rock fishing ($60); five hours of salmon fishing ($80); 12 hours of tuna fishing ($150); 12 hours of halibut fishing ($160); bay cruise, whale-watching, or eco-tours $30. Other operators include **Bob's Sportfishing** (541/888-4241 or 800/628-9633, www.bobssportfishing.com) and **Fishin's The Mission** (541/297-3474, www.fishinsthemission.com).

Mill Casino
Occupying the former bayside site of the Weyerhaeuser mill alongside U.S. 101 in North Bend, the Mill Casino (3201 Tremont Ave., North Bend, 541/756-8800 or 800/953-4800, www.themillcasino.com) is operated by the Coquille tribe. Open 24 hours a day, the casino offers blackjack, lots o' slots, poker, and bingo. A large hotel, lounge, and several restaurants are on-site. Nightly entertainment includes jazz and R&B, while headliners lean toward country performers such as Wynonna Judd and Kenny Rogers.

Bike Rental
GVH Bikes, Inc. (813 S. 5th St., Coos Bay, 541/266-8831) rents a variety of bicycles.

Other Outings
Perhaps the best place to see migratory shorebirds in the Northwest each fall is the Oregon Shorebird Festival on Cape Arago, taking place the second weekend in September. Boat trips out to see albatrosses and other seldom-seen species that frequent the open ocean and excursions to the Bandon Marsh National Refuge and to Coos Bay to see plovers, loons, and a variety of other shorebirds are arranged through the **Cape Arago Audubon Society** (541/267-7208 or 541/756-5688).

Wavecrest Discoveries (P.O. Box 1795, Coos Bay 97420, 541/267-4027, http://wavecrestdiscoveries.com) offers a cornucopia of guided outdoor activities around the Bay Area and beyond, including clamming and tidepooling excursions, sea kayaking, dune and estuary tours, and more.

EVENTS AND ENTERTAINMENT
The **Dune Mushers Mail Run** (541/269-0215) is a noncompetitive endurance dogsled run held annually the first weekend in March. This is the world's longest organized dry-land run for dogsled teams. Small team of three to five dogs, and larger teams of five to 10 dogs, haul mushers on wheeled buggies over 70 miles of dunes from North Bend to Florence. The smaller teams start off from Horsfall Beach on Friday, while the larger teams leave the next morning. En route, spectators have opportunities to watch the teams as they passes through Spinreel Park, Winchester Bay, Gardiner, and Florence's South Jetty area, to

finish up with a parade through Old Town Florence on Sunday. The "mail" carried by the dog teams are commemorative envelopes, which are sold as souvenirs to support the event.

The first event of note in summer is the **Oregon Coast Music Festival** (P.O. Box 663, Coos Bay 97420, 541/267-0938 or 877/897-9350, www.coosnet.com/music, tickets $5–18), which runs for two weeks in mid-July and has been going on for more than 25 years. Coos Bay is the central venue for these south coast classical, jazz, pop, and world music concerts, but Bandon, North Bend, Charleston, and other neighboring burgs host some performances as well.

In late August, the ubiquitous Oregon blackberry is celebrated with the **Blackberry Arts Festival** (541/888-1095 or 888-6572). Food and wine-tasting booths, a juried arts-and-crafts show, and entertainers fill the Coos Bay Mall (Central Avenue in downtown Coos Bay).

In mid-September, perhaps the best-known Bay Area figure, Steve Prefontaine, is honored with a 10-km race and two-mile walk in the annual **Prefontaine Memorial Run** (541/269-1103, www.prefontainerun.com). Prefontaine was a world-class runner whose gutsy style of running and record performances made him a major sports personality until his premature death at 24 years old in 1974. Many top-flight runners pay homage by taking part in the race. Events begin and end at the runner's alma mater, Marshfield High School (4th and Anderson, Coos Bay).

The **Egyptian Theater** (229 S. Broadway, Coos Bay, 541/267-3456) is a movie house with a pharaonic motif that goes back to the 1920s, when many small towns took to emulating the opulence and foreign intrigue of such big-city movie houses as Graumann's Chinese Theater in Hollywood. Four first-run films are usually playing here.

Across the street, the players of the **On Broadway Theater** (226 S. Broadway, 541/269-2501) stage a changing program of live theater throughout the year, ranging from current Broadway hits to relatively unknown scripts to children's entertainment.

ACCOMMODATIONS

Some people take umbrage at the fact that many Bay Area accommodations face industrial sites. Nevertheless, there is no shortage of low-cost places to stay, and noise is seldom a problem.

Charleston

Capt. John's Motel (63360 Kingfisher Dr., 541/888-4041, $44–77) is clean and quiet and has some units with kitchenettes. It's within walking distance of fishing, charter boats, clamming, and dock crabbing. Close by is a special fish/shellfish-cleaning station and, with any luck, your dinner. Staying in Charleston also puts you close to state parks and within easy reach of laundry and postal services, as well as offering temperatures that are warmer than Coos Bay in winter and cooler in summer. The studio rates on the higher end of the price range. Reserve well in advance for July and August; pets are okay.

If you'd rather catch your own dinner, the **Plainview Motel** (91904 Cape Arago Hwy., 541/888-5166 or 800/962-2815, $40 d, $90 for six people) provides guests with crab rings and fishing poles. This smaller motel has 12 pet-friendly units, some with kitchens. Pets cost an extra $5.

Coos Bay

A costlier alternative is the **Coos Bay Red Lion** (1313 N. Bayshore Dr., 541/267-4141 or 800/RED-LION, $65–125). Large rooms with immense beds, thick pile carpets, and everything else in the way of little extras are characteristic of these units. The hotel is also distinguished by having one of the best restaurants in town, a lounge with quality entertainment, and a happy hour with complimentary hors d'oeuvres. Only 10 minutes from the airport via complimentary shuttle, Coos Bay Red Lion is also close to many recreational pursuits.

The **Coos Bay Manor** (955 5th St., 800/269-1224, $80–100, higher prices mean private bath, lower rates in winter) is the kind of place where a fluffy terrycloth robe and bubble bath sustain the first impressions made by the grand, high-ceilinged colonial-style home and eye-popping river views from the B&B's open-air second-floor breakfast balcony. The five spacious rooms here have their own distinct decor, and three have private baths. A full breakfast is provided.

The bayfront **Edgewater Inn** (275 E. Johnson Ave., 541/267-0423 or 800/233-0423, $75–90) has loads of perks. With 82 units, many with views and kitchens, guests can take advantage of the fitness and tanning rooms, indoor pool, spa and sauna, and meeting room. A shuttle is also provided.

North Bend

The Mill Hotel (3201 Tremont Ave., 541/756-8800 or 800/953-4800, www.themillcasino.com, rooms $109–129 and suites $100–207 in summer) is located just south of the Mill Casino along the waterfront in a building that once housed a plywood mill. But rather than a mill-town ambience, this economic development project of the Coquille (pronounced Ko-KWELL in native dialect) tribe expresses its owners' patrimony. The exterior of this three-story hotel is the same cedar that tribe members used to build their plank houses, and the fireplace in the lobby is made of Coquille River rocks. The canoe displayed behind the front desk was carved by tribal members and is part of an interpretive display that tells the story of the Coquilles. Rooms feature views of oceangoing ships and well-appointed furnishings, including Internet access. Look for discount deals throughout the year.

Also popular with the casino crowd is the **Ramada Inn** (1503 Virginia Ave., 541/756-3191 or 800/272-6232, $69–100), just five blocks from U.S. 101. With 96 units and the standard chain hotel amenities, this hotel provides a quiet escape.

Campgrounds

Bastendorff Beach County Park (63379 Bastendorff Beach Rd., Charleston 97420, 541/888-5353) is a conveniently and beautifully located park two miles west of Charleston just off the Cape Arago Highway. It's open for camping year-round, with RV and tent sites ($15–18, less off-season), as well as cabins ($30) and some

hiker/biker sites. Campsites have drinking water, wood stoves, flush toilets, and hot showers (for an extra $2). Fishing, hiking, and a nice stretch of beach are the recreational attractions, plus there's a good playground for toddlers.

Even though the crowds at **Sunset Bay State Park** (13030 Cape Arago Hwy., Coos Bay 97420, 541/888-4902, reservations 800/452-5687) can make it seem like a trailer park in midsummer, the proximity of Oregon's only major swimming beach on the ocean keeps occupants of the 66 tent sites ($12–16) and 65 trailer sites ($16–20) here happy. The eight yurts go for $27, and primitive hiker/biker sites are $4. Facilities include laundry and showers, and a boat launch at the north end of the beach. This site, located three miles southwest of Charleston, is popular with anglers, who can cast into the rocky intertidal area for cabezon and sea bass.

Northwest of the Bay Area—2.5 miles north of the McCullough Bridge—is the Trans-Pacific Parkway, a causeway west across the water leading to Coos Bay's North Spit and the south end of the Oregon Dunes National Recreation Area, with four Siuslaw National Forest campgrounds and expansive dunes that draw off-road vehicle enthusiasts. The main **Horsfall Campground** is popular with crowds of noisy all-terrain vehicles and RVs. For more quiet and privacy, continue another mile on Horsfall Beach Road to **Bluebill Lake.** The 18 tent/RV sites are equipped with picnic tables and bathrooms, and the campground is open all year. Ask the campground hosts about area trails and the nearby oyster farm for the ultimate in campfire fare. Close by, **Horsfall Beach Campground** is located in the dunes next to the beach. OHV (off-highway vehicle) access and beachcombing are popular activities. Showers are available two miles east at Horsfall Campground. One-half mile away, **Wild Mare Horse Camp** has beach and dune access and a dozen primitive campsites, each with a single or double horse corral. Each of these Siuslaw National Forest campgrounds charges $15 nightly year-round. Only Horsfall Campground takes reservations (877/444-6777, www.reserveusa.com) May–September.

FOOD

Oregon's Bay Area has many eateries where your nutritional needs can be met, if not in fine style then at least at the right price. Oddly enough, prime rib is a recurring special in this coastal town. There is no shortage of seafood places along this part of the coast, but you'll find the freshest, cheapest maritime morsels close to where they're caught.

Charleston

The Sea Basket (63502 Kingfisher Rd., 541/888-5711, open daily for breakfast, lunch, and dinner) typifies the good seafood, fast service, and relatively low prices in these parts. Oysters are especially tasty in this restaurant, with noted breeding farms close by. They are also famous for their BIGMAN burgers. The fluorescent glare above the cafeteria-style tables frequented by anglers in work-blackened denims may not count much for atmosphere, but you'll leave satisfied.

The **Portside** (63383 Kingfisher Rd., Charleston Boat Basin, 541/888-5544) close by has won Silver Spoon Awards from the Diners Club the past three years. Fine dining in Charleston might seem a contradiction in terms, but the chance to select your own lobsters and crabs out of a tank, along with the sight of the fleet unloading other dinners just outside the door, would whet the appetite of any gourmet. Reserve ahead for the 30-item Friday night all-you-can-eat seafood buffet at a reasonable price—it's not to be missed. But you may want to pass on the karaoke, depending on your singing prowess.

Just before the Charleston Bridge, the **Fisherman's Grotto** (541/888-3251) serves all-you-can-eat fish 'n' chips seven days a week. Or, if you're an oyster lover, you'll certainly want to visit **Quallman's** (4898 Crown Point Rd., 541/888-3145, 10 A.M.–5:30 P.M.). Just look for the signs on the north side of the Charleston Bridge on the east side of the highway. It has fresh, high-quality oysters for sale. Several other oyster purveyors make this delicacy available at other Bay Area outlets.

Coos Bay

Even though the **Blue Heron Bistro** (110 W. Commercial Ave., 541/267-3933) is located in the heart of downtown Coos Bay, it evokes dining experiences in San Francisco, Portland, or some other place far from this logging port. This impression can come from opening the door to the restaurant or opening the menu. The restaurant's tile floors, newspapers on library-style posts, and international posters adorning the walls are in keeping with a European-influenced bill of fare. The extensive menu's eclectic array ranges from Greek salad to Cajun-style blackened fish and emphasizes the freshest ingredients (nitrite-free German sausage) and a creative interpretation whenever possible. An impressive list of microbrews and imports, as well as Oregon, California, and European wines, will complement whatever dish you order. Best of all, for not much more than you'd pay at Denny's, you can enjoy an oasis of refinement in Timbertown, U.S.A.

The dining room at **Brickstones** at the Coos Bay Red Lion (1313 N. Bayshore Dr., 541/267-4141, ext. 305) offers extra-thick cuts of prime rib and flambé items prepared tableside that are as much a treat to look at as to taste. This restaurant is an "in" place to eat out, so make reservations. The smoked prime rib is recommended. For a "logging camp breakfast," locals recommend the **Timber Inn Restaurant** (1001 N. Bayshore Dr., 541/267-4622), where it's served all day long. Natural-food fans converge at **Coos Head Natural Foods** (1960 Sherman Ave., 541/756-7264), which has the largest selection of certified organic produce and food on the south coast. For a few prime-rib-free dinner options, head over to **Elizabeth's** (274 S. Broadway, 541/266-7708, open for dinner only Mon.–Sat.) near the Egyptian Theatre, which features classic American and French cuisine on most nights, with Thai and Indian dishes on select nights.

North Bend

A prime rib special is usually on the menu at the **Mill Casino** (800/953-4800) on the east side of U.S. 101 in North Bend. The restaurant's windows on Coos Bay make the bargain meal of prime rib, salad, vegetables, dessert, and beverage taste even better. Even if you miss the special, you'll appreciate that the restaurant is open 24 hours. A seafood buffet on Friday and other buffets are featured throughout the week for less than $10.

A 1950s-style diner serving malts, meatloaf, and burgers, plus an all-day breakfast, the **Virginia Street Diner** (1430 Virginia St., 541/756-3475) also provides RVers with easy parking. For sit-down or takeout seafood, the **Captain's Choice** (1210 Virginia Ave., 541/756-0125) serves enormous pots of clam chowder and oyster stew, but has plenty of "steak and [insert your favorite seafood here]" selections for about $10. If you've had enough of the standard coastal fare, try **Yesterday's Café** (1860 Union St., 541/751-0837) for Mediterranean food, including a locally loved lentil soup, in a family-style setting.

INFORMATION AND SERVICES

Information

The **Bay Area Chamber of Commerce** (50 E. Central, Coos Bay 97420, 541/269-0215 or 800/824-8486, www.oregonsbayareachamber.com, open 9 A.M.–7 P.M. Mon.–Fri. and 10 A.M.–4 P.M. weekends June–Aug., 9 A.M.–5 P.M. Mon.–Sat. Sept.–May) is five blocks west of U.S. 101 off Commercial Avenue. Inquire here about tours of the *New Carissa* shipwreck site north of town near Horsfall Dunes.

The **North Bend Information Center** (138 Sherman Ave., North Bend 97459, 541/756-4613) is just south of the McCullough Bridge. It's open 8:30 A.M.–5 P.M. Monday–Friday, 10 A.M.– 3 P.M. on Saturday, and 10 A.M.–4 P.M. on Sunday. From Labor Day to Memorial Day, the center is closed on weekends.

The Coos Bay World is the largest daily paper on the south coast. In May and August, catch their "Let's Go" section on area getaways.

Services

For health care and emergencies, the **Bay Area Hospital** (1775 Thompson Rd., Coos Bay, 541/269-8111), one-half mile west of U.S. 101 via Newmark Street, is the south coast's largest medical facility.

In what's considered a big city on the Oregon coast, you might need the **police** (541/269-8911). The Coos Bay **post office** (4th and Golden, Coos Bay 97420, 541/267-4514) is two blocks west of the highway, just south of city center.

Wash-a-Lot (1921 Virginia Ave., 541/756-5439) is Coos Bay's version of a fast-disappearing American institution—the all-night launderette.

The **Coos Bay Public Library** (525 W. Anderson, 541/267-1101) is open 1–4 P.M. Monday–Thursday, 10 A.M.–5 P.M. Friday, and noon–5 P.M. Saturday. And for ATM or banking needs, the Coos Bay **Bank of America** (245 S. 4th St.) has it all.

Transportation

Recent improvements to ORE 42 make it possible to get to and from Roseburg, 87 miles from Coos Bay, in less than two hours. Motorists should still be aware that this thoroughfare carries more truck traffic than any other interior-to-coast road in Oregon. But weekenders will usually encounter few trucks and light traffic.

The **Greyhound** bus depot (275 N. Broadway, 541/267-4436) has arrivals from Portland and Lincoln City. Two buses also run between Coos Bay and Eugene. If Greyhound doesn't fit into your plans, consider the North Bend Airport (1321-D Airport Way, North Bend 97459) at the north end of town. Horizon Air (800/547-9308) flies between the Bay Area and Portland daily. To get to the airport, follow the signs on the road between Charleston and North Bend.

Public transportation in the Bay Area is limited. **Dial-A-Ride** (541/267-7111) operates on-call daily 8:30 A.M.–4:30 P.M. At press time, the Coos County Area Transit has plans to reinstate regular bus service in North Bend, Coos Bay, and Charleston; call for information. Curry Public Transit's **Coastal Express** buses (541/469-6822) run three times daily, weekdays only, from North Bend and Coos Bay to Brookings, with stops at Bandon, Port Orford, and Gold Beach. The North Bend stop is at the West Pony Village Mall, on Virginia Avenue, while the bus stops in Coos Bay at the Fred Meyer store on U.S. 101.

Central Coast

Oregon's central coast, from Reedsport to Lincoln City, embraces such contrasts that it's difficult to generalize about the region. The southern portion is Dune Country: Hikers, horseback riders, and off-road-vehicle enthusiasts flock to the 32,000-acre national recreation area, a fantastic landscape of dazzling white mountains and jewel lakes stretched along nearly 50 miles of shoreline. The sportfishing fleet at Winchester Bay draws thousands of anglers eager to tackle a brawny Umpqua River salmon or sturgeon, and a short drive away the Dean Creek Elk Viewing Area offers an excellent chance to view wild Roosevelt elk in a natural setting. From Florence's restored Old Town, excursions on an authentic sternwheeler give a taste of the bygone era when riverboats were the primary transport between coastal towns and the Oregon interior.

Farther north, the dunes give way to forested heights, culminating atop vertigo-inducing Cape Perpetua, where the panorama on a clear day can extend 75 miles in each direction. At Sea Lion Caves, a touristy but unique experience between Florence and Yachats, the world's largest sea cave is the only mainland rookery of Steller sea lions in the Lower 48 states. Close by, more film is spent by photographers trying to capture the perfect image of Heceta Head Lighthouse than any other sight along the entire coast.

Heceta Head, north of Florence

© MARK MORRIS

A necklace of small state parks adorns the shore every couple of miles all the way up past Depoe Bay, while inland, the Siuslaw National Forest safeguards several wilderness areas and groves of rare old-growth coastal forest, beckoning hikers to explore the primeval landscapes.

The bustling harbor at Newport is home to the state's largest commercial fishing fleet and second-largest recreational fleet, which runs charters year-round for rockfish and seasonally for salmon, tuna, and halibut. Newport also boasts the state-of-the-art Oregon Coast Aquarium, former residence of Keiko the beloved orca, and the bohemian resort community of Nye Beach, which has been attracting tourists since the 19th century. Just north of town, Yaquina Head Outstanding Natural Area offers excellent vantage points for up-close whale-watching and bird-watching, plus tidepools that are accessible to wheelchair-bound visitors.

The superlatives continue to the north, where Depoe Bay—built around the world's smallest navigable natural harbor—is headquarters for the coast's busiest whale-watching fleet. Lincoln City's dense mix of lodgings and shopping opportunities, combined with its Indian-run casino, generates the coast's worst traffic jams, especially on holidays and weekends. The sprawling town isn't everyone's first choice for a quiet getaway, but it must be doing something right.

Reedsport/Winchester Bay and Vicinity

If you're going fishing or are coming back from a dunes hike, you'll appreciate a hot meal and a clean, low-priced motel room in Reedsport. Otherwise, this town of 5,000 people might seem like a strange mirage of cut-rate motels, taverns, and burger joints in the midst of the Oregon Dunes National Recreation Area.

Jedediah Smith explored this country in 1828, after the Hudson's Bay Company's Peter Skene Ogden theorized that the Umpqua River—the largest river between San Francisco Bay and the Columbia—might be the fabled Northwest Passage. It wasn't, of course, but this river is still one of the great fishing streams of the state. Zane Grey avoided writing about it, lavishing the publicity instead on the Rogue to divert people from his favorite steelhead spots here.

Cargo ships from Scottsburg, a hamlet some 17 miles upriver from Reedsport, supplied San Francisco markets with meat, milk, and produce between 1856 and the early 20th century. In its 1850s heyday, Scottsburg was larger than Portland, with some 5,000 residents, before an 1861 flood destroyed much of the town.

Two miles north of Reedsport, the little burg of Gardiner was created in the wake of a shipwreck. The *Bostonian* (owned by a Mr. Gardiner) was dashed against the rocks at the mouth of the Umpqua in 1856, and from its remnants the first wood-frame structure in this area was built. It was soon joined by other white-painted homes and facilities for a port on the Umpqua. Although this "white city by the sea" declined in importance when the highway elevated Reedsport to regional hub status, the homes still bear the same color scheme from the earlier era.

Three miles southwest of Reedsport, Salmon Harbor Marina in Winchester Bay (pop. 1,000), a busy port for commercial sport fishing at the mouth of the Umpqua, has given the whole area new life in recent years, following hard times precipitated by the decline in timber revenues.

SIGHTS
Umpqua Discovery Center
In Reedsport's Old Town on the south bank of the river, the Umpqua Discovery Center (409 Riverfront Way, 541/271-4816, 9 A.M.–5 P.M. daily June–Sept., 10 A.M.–4 P.M. daily the rest of the year, closed Thanksgiving, Christmas, and New Year's Day, $5 adults, $2.50 kids) interprets the regional human and natural history of this area through multimedia programs, dioramas, scale models, and helpful staff. The boardwalk

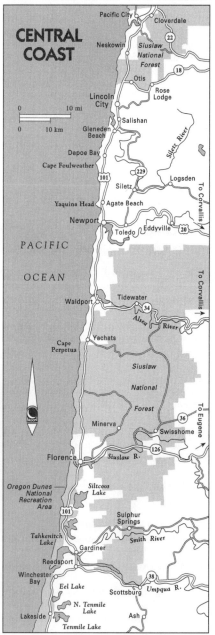

CENTRAL COAST

and observation tower give a good view of the broad lower reaches of the Umpqua. In summer, free Friday evening concerts are staged here, and the center is the site of the September Tsalila festival.

Dean Creek Elk Viewing Area

Three miles east of Reedsport, and stretching three miles along the south side of ORE 38, the Dean Creek Elk Viewing Area provides parking areas and viewing platforms for observing the herd of some 120 wild Roosevelt elk that roam this 1,100-acre preserve. The elk move out of the forest to graze the preserve's marshy pastures, sometimes coming quite close to the highway. Oregon's largest land mammal can reach 1,100 pounds at maturity, and the majestic rack on a fully grown bull can spread three feet across. Early mornings and just before dusk are the most promising times to look for them; during hot weather and storms the elk tend to stay within the cover of the woods.

Umpqua Lighthouse State Park

Less than one mile south of Winchester Bay is Umpqua Lighthouse State Park (460 Lighthouse Rd., Winchester Bay, 541/271-4118). Tours of the red-capped 1894 lighthouse (information and schedules at 541/271-4631, $2) are offered May 1–September 30. At other times, you can get a close look at it from the roadside. Adjacent, in a former Coast Guard building, the **visitors center and museum** (541/271-4631, 10 A.M.–5 P.M. Wed.–Sat. and 1–5 P.M. Sun. May–Sept.) has marine and timber exhibits. Directly opposite the lighthouse, overlooking the mouth of the Umpqua and oceanfront dunes, is a whale-watching platform with a plaque explaining where, when, and, what in the world to look for.

Lake Marie, just south near the camping area, has a swimming beach and is stocked with rainbow trout. A one-mile forest trail around the lake makes for an easy hike. A trail from the campground leads to the highest dunes in the United States (elev. 545 feet), west of Clear Lake.

© AVALON TRAVEL PUBLISHING, INC.

Umpqua River Lighthouse, near Winchester Bay

© MARK MORRIS

RECREATION
Fishing
Winchester Bay and the tidewater reaches of the lower Umpqua River comprise Oregon's top coastal sturgeon fishery and one of the best areas for striped bass, particularly near the mouth of the Smith River, which enters the Umpqua just east of Reedsport. The best action for the Umpqua's spring chinook tends to be inland, below Scottsburg. Fall chinook enter the bay July–September. Other notable fisheries here are the huge runs of shad, which peak May–June, and smallmouth bass offer action upstream from Reedsport. Crabbing and clamming are also popular and productive pastimes in Winchester Bay and the lower reaches of the river. Every year from August 1 to mid-September, tagged crabs are released into the water in and around Winchester Bay, one of them worth a cash prize of $5,000 to whomever catches it.

Charter services operating in the area include **Reel Fishing Trips** (541/271-3850), **Strike Zone Charters** (541/271-9706 or 800/230-5350, www.strikezonecharters.com), **River's End Guide Service** (541/271-3125, www.umpquafishing.com), and **Jerry Jarmain** (541/271-5583 or 800/653-5583, www.umpqua-river-guide.com).

Dune Access
North and south of Reedsport, the most spectacular dunes landscape can be found nine miles south of Reedsport at **Umpqua Dunes,** at North Eel Campground near Lakeside. After you emerge from a quarter-mile hike through coastal evergreen forest, you'll be greeted by dunes 300–400 feet high. It's said that dunes near here can approach 500 feet high and one mile long after a windblown buildup. The views here are most photogenic.

Because a regular trail through the dunes is impossible to maintain, you should only expect to find wooden posts spaced at irregular intervals west of the dunes to guide you to the beach. This trail can also be accessed from the Middle Eel Creek campground. Look for gray posts about 10 feet high with a blue band at the top marking the trail to the beach, a fairly strenuous five-mile round-trip mostly over soft sand. A shorter and easier one-mile loop trail leads through woodlands to the dunes for a quick introduction to this landscape.

Lakeside Area
Ten miles south of Reedsport, the sleepy resort town of **Lakeside** hosted visits from Bob Hope, Bing Crosby, and the Ink Spots, among other luminaries, back in its 1930s and '40s heyday. Today, it's still a popular destination, primarily for its proximity to the sprawling, many-armed Tenmile and North Tenmile Lakes. These large, shallow lakes offer water-skiing and excellent fishing for stocked rainbow trout and warm-water species, including crappie, yellow perch, bluegill, and lunker largemouth bass up to 10 pounds. A quarter-mile channel connects the two lakes, and a county park on Tenmile Lake has a paved boat ramp, fishing docks, sandy swimming beach, and picnic area.

CENTRAL COAST

DUNE COUNTRY: COOS BAY TO FLORENCE

Even though the 47-mile stretch of U.S. 101 between Coos Bay and Florence does not overlook the ocean, your eyes will be drawn constantly westward to the largest and most extensive oceanfront dunes in the world.

How did they come to exist in a coastal topography otherwise dominated by rocky bluffs? A combination of factors created this landscape over the past 12,000 years, but the principal agents are the Coos, Siuslaw, and Umpqua rivers. The sand and sediment transported to the sea by these waterways are deposited by waves on the flat, shallow beaches. Prevailing westerlies move the particulate matter exposed by the tide eastward up to several yards per year. Over the millennia, the dunes have grown huge, with some topping 500 feet.

Constantly on the move, the shifting sands have engulfed ancient forests, a fact occasionally proven by hikers as they stumble upon the top of an exposed snag. The cross section of sandswept woodlands seen from U.S. 101 demonstrates that this inundation is still occurring. Nonetheless, the motorist gets the impression that the trees are winning the battle because the dunes are only intermittently visible from the road.

The Oregon Dunes National Recreation Area (NRA) is home to more than 400 species of flora and fauna, but the only dangerous animal within this ecosystem is possibly the American teenager. This species migrates here during summer vacation to enact puberty rites or assault the dunes

with a variety of all-terrain vehicles. Of the 31,500 acres within the NRA, nearly half are designated open sand and riding trails for off-highway vehicles such as dune buggies.

Getting Oriented

Reedsport and the nearby fishing village of Winchester Bay have carved out identities as refueling and supply depots for excursions into Oregon's Sahara-by-the-Sea. A great place to start your explorations is the **Oregon Dunes NRA Visitor Information Center** (885 U.S. 101, Reedsport 97467, 541/271-3611, www.fs.fed.us/r6/siuslaw), at the junction of the Coast Highway and ORE 38. In addition to the information on hiking, camping, and recreation, the Siuslaw Forest Service personnel are very helpful.

Note that a **$5 day-use fee** is charged per vehicle at most facilities and access points within the NRA. You can purchase an annual pass at the Dunes Visitor Center for $30.

Because the dunes are difficult to see from the highway in many places, the most commonly asked question in the visitors center is "Where are the dunes?" To answer it for everybody, the National Forest Service opened **Oregon Dunes Overlook** just south of Carter Lake, midway between Florence and Reedsport, at the point where the dunes come closest to U.S. 101. In addition to four levels of railing-enclosed platforms connected by wooden walkways, there are trails down to the sand. It's

EVENTS

Every June, over Father's Day weekend, chainsaw sculptors compete for $10,000 in prizes as they transform pieces of raw western red cedar into grizzly bears, giant salmon, and other rustic works of art during the **Chainsaw Sculpture Championships** (800/247-2155) at the Rainbow Plaza Old Town Reedsport.

An interesting annual event is **Tsalila** (800/247-2155). Based on the Coos Indian word for "river" (pronounced sa-LEE-la), this festival features interpretive tours of the Umpqua, alderbaked salmon with squash and corn-on-the-cob

dinners, and a traditional Indian village centered around the waterfront at the Umpqua Discovery Center. Music and other food service appear here on the second weekend in September. There's no charge except dinner prices of $10 for adults and $5 for kids.

ACCOMMODATIONS

Motels

Of the half-dozen motels that sit along U.S. 101 in Reedsport, the **Fir Grove Motel** (2178 Winchester Ave., 541/271-4848, $34–100) is slightly less expensive but comparable in only about one-quarter mile to the dunes and, thereafter, a mile through sand and wetlands to the beach.

You can hike a loop beginning where the sand gives way to willows. Bear right en route to the beach. Once there, walk south 1.5 miles. A wooden post marks where the trail resumes. It then traverses a footbridge going through trees onto sand, completing the loop. If you go in February, this loop has great bird-watching potential. A day-use fee is charged for cars.

Other sites for easy introductions to the dune topography are (from south to north): Spinreel Campground, Umpqua Dunes Trail, Honeyman State Park, and Florence's South Jetty.

Recreation in the Dunes

There are three excellent state parks and a dozen Siuslaw National Forest Campgrounds within the NRA. Although joyriding in noisy dune buggies and other off-road vehicles doesn't lack for devotees, the best way to appreciate the interface of ecosystems is on foot. Dunes exceeding 500 feet in height, wetland breeding grounds for animals and waterfowl, evergreen forests, and deserted beaches can be encountered in a march to the sea. Numerous designated hiking trails, ranging from easy half-mile loops to six-mile round-trips, give visitors a chance to star in their own version of *Lawrence of Arabia* as they moonwalk through this earthbound Sea of Tranquility. The soundtrack can be provided by the 247 species of birds here—along with your heartbeat—as you scale these elephantine anthills. Deserted beaches and secret swimming holes are among the many rewards of the journey.

Before setting out, pick up the *Hiking Trails Recreation Opportunity Guide* from the Oregon Dunes NRA Visitor Center. This and their other publications will correct the superficial impression that the dunes are just a domain for all-terrain vehicles and campgrounds for day hikers.

To ensure a *bon voyage*, it's important to understand this terrain. Carry plenty of water and dress in layers—there are hot spots in dune valleys and ocean breezes at higher elevations. Expect cool summers and wet, mild winters. Although rainfall here can average more than 70 inches per year (with 75 percent of it falling Mar.–Nov.), a string of dry, 50–60°F days in February is not uncommon. Another surprise is summertime morning fog, brought in by hot weather inland. These fogs, together with the inevitable confusion caused by dunes that don't look much different from each other, make a compass necessary. The lack of defined trails also compels such measures as marking your return route in the sand with a stick. Binoculars can help with visual orientation, not to mention bird-watching opportunities galore.

comfort (i.e., clean with no frills) to its counterparts.

Anchor Bay Inn (1821 Winchester Ave., 541/271-2149 or 800/767-1821, $47 and up, ask for discounts) also has clean rooms with one, two, or three beds, family suites, and kitchenettes. For something not so different, try the **Best Budget Inn** (1894 Winchester Ave., 541/271-3686, $45 and up) downtown, which has all the basic amenities. For an even cheaper stay, try the **Economy Inn** (1593 Highway Ave., 541/271-3671 or 800/799-9970, $30 and up).

If you're interested in this area's ultimate getaway-from-it-all alternative, try the **Salbasgeon**

Inn of the Umpqua (45209 ORE 38, Reedsport, 541/271-2025, $65–95) with nicely appointed rooms on the Umpqua and a romantic location near the elk preserve. This moderately-priced lodging should fill the bill. They also have an upscale motel unit managed by Best Western (541/271-4831 or 800/528-1234) in Reedsport's downtown, on U.S. 101. By the way, the name was inspired by the trio of most popular sport-fishing species (i.e., salmon, bass, sturgeon) in the region.

The **Winchester Bay Motel** (4th and Broadway, Winchester Bay, 541/271-4871 or 800/246-1462, www.winbayinn.com, $48–70) puts you next to the water with all of the comfort bases covered. Be sure to reserve ahead of time in fishing season.

Bed-and-Breakfast

A few miles north of Reedsport in Gardiner is another lodging with more character than those along motel row for not significantly more money. The **Gardiner Guest House** (401 Front St., 541/271-4005, $55–75 in peak season) is located in a cute, tranquil, former paper-mill town that sits close by the confluence of the Smith and Umpqua rivers. The 1883 home was built by local bigwig and State Senator Albert Reed, for whom Reedsport was named. The recently remodeled home still has the Victorian feel, without lacking in modern conveniences. If you like to peruse old books by a fire or watch bald eagles from a bay window above the Umpqua River, you'll love this place. Choose between a cheaper room with the facility down the hall and a higher-priced view room with private bath. A large home-cooked breakfast is included in the rate.

Campgrounds

Choices abound in this recreation-rich area. Just south of Winchester Bay is **Umpqua Lighthouse State Park** (460 Lighthouse Rd., Winchester Bay, information 541/271-4118, reservations 800/452-5687). The campground alongside Lake Marie has firewood, flush toilets, showers, picnic tables, electricity, and piped water. The 20 RV sites go for $16–20, 24 tent sites are $12–16, two basic yurts are $27, six deluxe yurts (with shower, small kitchen area, refrigerator, microwave, TV/VCR) are $45–65, and two rustic cabins are $35. The lake offers fishing, boating, and swimming. Trails from here lead to the highest dunes in the United States (elev. 545 feet), west of Clear Lake.

William A. Tugman State Park (information 541/759-3604, reservations 800/452-5687) is eight miles south of Reedsport, in the heart of Dune Country. This larger campground, with 115 sites, has a similar range of creature comforts, price, and recreation. It sits on the west

shore of Eel Lake, east of U.S. 101 across from where the dunes reach their widest extent, two miles to the sea.

Windy Cove Campground (541/271-4138) is a county park with 24 full hookup sites and four other sites with electric service only. Located on the south side of Salmon Harbor Drive, across from the Winchester Bay marina, it has restrooms, picnic tables, grass, and paved site pads. No reservations are accepted. It is legal to drive your OHV (off-highway vehicle) from this campground directly to the dunes, but it is a couple of miles on the pavement.

About nine miles south of Reedsport, set along Eel Creek near Eel Lake and Tenmile Lakes, is **Eel Creek Campground,** a Siuslaw National Forest facility with 51 basic tent and RV sites. Open mid-May through September, reservations (877/444-6777, www.reserveusa.com, $15) are advised. The Umpqua Dunes Trail offers access to the dunes and beach.

Eight miles north of Reedsport, the **Tahkenitch Campground** (reservations 877/444-6777, www.reserveusa.com, open mid-May–Sept., $15) is another Forest Service facility, set among ancient Douglas firs and conveniently located near Tahkenitch and other lakes, dunes, and ocean beaches. A network of trails branch out from here through the dunes, along Tahkenitch, and to the beach.

Another cluster of Siuslaw National Forest campgrounds lies a few miles north; see the Accommodations section in Florence and Vicinity for details.

Winchester Bay's **Discovery Point Resort** (242 Discovery Point Lane, 541/271-3443, www.discoverypointresort.com, campsites $18, cabins $68–98) offers dunes enthusiasts dune access and all-terrain vehicle (ATV) rentals, while providing one- to three-bedroom cabins (sleep up to six) or 60 RV spaces. To get there from Reedsport, head two miles south on U.S. 101 to Winchester Bay, then turn right at Pelican Market onto Salmon Harbor Drive. Go one mile, and you'll see Discovery Point Resort on the left. Reservations are highly recommended.

FOOD

Casual Fare

There is no shortage of basic but decent places to eat here. An example is **Don's Main Street Restaurant** (U.S. 101, Reedsport, 541/271-2032, open daily), whose burgers and soup are good enough to get you to Florence. After a bite of Umpqua ice cream (touted by many to be the best in the state), however, you might stick around until you're hungry again.

The **Schooner Café** (423 Riverfront Way, Reedsport, 541/271-3945), on the boardwalk next door to the Discovery Center, has a pleasant riverside patio with a casual atmosphere for a burger, salad, or sandwich.

Steak and Seafood

Another place that rates a special mention is **The Landing** (345 Riverfront Way, Reedsport, 541/271-3328, open daily), on the Umpqua near the Umpqua Discovery Center. An *Oregon Coast* magazine readers' poll rated the restaurant's steak the best in the region. Their oysters, fresh from Umpqua aquaculture in Winchester Bay, are also top-notch. The steak and seafood special that appears every so often also has a following.

The French country cooking at **Café Français** (U.S. 101 in Winchester Bay, 541/271-9270, open for dinner Wed.–Sun.) stands out among its fried-fish counterparts. Special-ties include lamb chops, baked salmon, escargot (but, of course), and a wine cellar that's stocked with premium vintages. Reservations are suggested.

The early-morning crowd head to the conveniently located **Salmon Harbor Café** (196 Bayfront Loop, Winchester Bay, 541/271-5523, open daily) for homestyle breakfast and lunch fare. Just next door, the friendly staff at the **Sportsmen's Cannery and Smokehouse** (Bayfront Loop, Winchester Bay, 541/271-3293) hosts a seafood barbecue smorgasbord that features the catch of the day, oysters, prawns, and all the trimmings. You can also purchase smoked or canned fish; they'll even smoke your catch for you.

INFORMATION AND SERVICES

The **Oregon Dunes NRA Visitor Information Center** (885 U.S. 101, Reedsport 97467, 541/271-3611, www.fs.fed.us/r6/siuslaw/odnra.htm) and **Reedsport Chamber of Commerce** (541/271-3495 or 800/247-2155, www.reedsportcc.org) share a building at the junction of U.S. 101 and ORE 38. Mid-May through mid-September, it's open weekdays 8 A.M.–4:30 P.M. and weekends 10 A.M.–4 P.M., weekdays only the rest of the year. Ask about guided visits to an archaeological dig site that was inhabited by the Coos Indians until about 3,000 years ago.

Florence and Vicinity

Location, location, location. This tenet of business success also explains the growing appeal of Florence (pop. 7,000) for retirees and vacationers. Many people who could afford to live almost anywhere choose to do so here between the Oregon Dunes NRA and some of the most beautiful headlands on U.S. 101. The fact that Florence is also situated halfway up Oregon's coastal route and little more than an hour's drive from shopping and culture in Eugene has made it a major beachhead of vacation-home development in the region. A mild climate, a modern health-care facility, the award-winning Sandpines Golf Course nearby, and lower housing prices than would be encountered elsewhere in a comparable setting also explain the influx. In recent years, the Florence Events Center has added a cultural dimension to the community calendar.

Florence began shortly after the California gold rush of 1849 put a premium on the lumber and produce shipped out via the Siuslaw River estuary here. Several decades later, the town's name was inspired by a remnant from a

Many of the buildings in Florence's Old Town have been renovated as boutiques and eateries.

French shipwreck that floated ashore, bearing the ship's name, *Florence.* The townspeople either recognized an omen when they saw it or just figured they couldn't come up with anything better.

SIGHTS

If first and last impressions are enduring, Florence is truly blessed. As you enter the city from the south, a graceful bridge over the Siuslaw greets you. Shortly after you leave city limits to the north, U.S. 101 climbs to dizzying heights above the ocean.

The Siuslaw River Bridge is perhaps the most impressive of Conde McCullough's WPA-built spans. The Egyptian obelisks and art deco styling characteristic of other McCullough designs are complemented by the views to the west of the coruscating sand dunes. To the east, the riverside panorama of Florence's Old Town beckons further investigation.

Old Town itself is a tasteful restoration, with all manner of shops and restaurants and an inviting boardwalk along the river. The absence of car traffic is conducive to a pleasant walk after lunch

there. Easy access to beach and dunes is offered by South Jetty Road just south of the Siuslaw River Bridge.

Siuslaw Pioneer Museum

To fill yourself in on the early history of Florence and the Siuslaw River valley, and get some notion of Indian and pioneer life, spend an hour or so at the Siuslaw Pioneer Museum (85294 U.S. 101, Florence, 541/997-7884, 10 A.M.–4 P.M. Tues.–Sun., $2). You'll find it on the south side of the Siuslaw River on the west side of the highway in a converted church. Along with exhibits on early logging and farming, read an account of how the U.S. government double-crossed the Siuslaw tribespeople, who sold their land to the feds and never received the promised recompense.

Jessie M. Honeyman Memorial State Park

Honeyman State Park, three miles south of Florence, also has a spectacular dunescape and then some. Come here in May when the rhododendrons bloom along the short, sinuous road heading to the parking lot. A short walk west of the lot brings you to a 150-foot-high dune overlooking Cleawox Lake. From the top of this dune, look westward across the expanse of sand, marsh, and remnants of forest at the blue Pacific, some two miles away. A $3 day-use fee applies here, or use the Oregon Coast Passport.

Darlingtonia Wayside
Three miles north up the Coast Highway from Florence, in an area noted for dune access and freshwater lakes, is the Darlingtonia Wayside. In a sylvan grove of spruce and alder are a series of wooden platforms that guide you through a bog where carnivorous *Darlingtonia californica* plants thrive. Shaped like a serpent head, the darlingtonia is variously referred to as the cobra orchid, cobra lily, or pitcher plant. The sweet smell the plant produces invites insects to crawl through an opening into a chamber.

Inside, thin transparent "windows" allow light to shine inside the chamber, confusing the bug as to where the exit is. As the insect crawls around in search of an escape, downward-pointing hairs within the enclosure inhibit its movement to freedom. Eventually, the tired-out bug falls to the bottom of the stem, where it is digested. The plant needs the nutrients from the trapped insects to compensate for the lack of sustenance supplied by its small root system. If you still have an appetite after witnessing this carnage, you might want to enjoy lunch at one of the shaded picnic tables here.

Sea Lion Caves
Ten miles north of Florence, you can descend into the world's largest sea cave to observe the only mainland rookery of Steller's sea lions (*Eumetopias jubatus*) in the Lower 48. Sea Lion Caves (91560 U.S. 101, 541/547-3111, 9 A.M.–7 P.M. daily in summer, 9 A.M.–4 P.M. daily in winter except Christmas, $7 adults, $4.50 ages 6–15, free ages 5 and under) is home to a herd that averages 200 individuals of this species, although the numbers change from season to season. These animals occupy the cave during the fall and winter, which are thus the prime visitation times. The Steller sea lions you'll see at those times are cows, yearlings, and immature bulls. In spring and summer, they breed and raise their young on the rock ledges just outside the cave. In addition, California sea lions (*Zalophus californianus*), common all along the Pacific Coast, are found at Sea Lion Caves from late fall to early spring.

Enter Sea Lion Caves through the gift shop on U.S. 101. A steep downhill walk reveals stunning perspectives of the coastal cliffs, as well as several kinds of gulls and cormorants that nest here. The final leg of the descent is facilitated by an elevator that drops an additional 208 feet. After disembarking the lift into the cave, your eyes adjust to the gloomy subterranean light and you'll see the sea lions on the rock shelves amid the surging water inside the enormous cave. Flash photography is forbidden, so bring high-speed film if you wish to take pictures inside. You have a better chance of seeing these animals inside during fall and winter. A set of stairs here leads up to a view of Heceta Head Lighthouse through an opening in the cave.

Steller sea lions were referred to as *lobos marinos* (sea wolves) in early Spanish mariners' accounts of their 16th-century West Coast voyages, and their doglike yelps might explain why. You'll notice several shades of color in the herd, which has to do with the progressive lightening of their coats with age. Males sometimes weigh more than a ton and dominate the scene here with macho posturings to scare off rivals for harems of as many as two dozen cows. Their protection as an endangered species enrages many anglers, who claim that the sea lions take a significant bite out of fishing revenues by preying on salmon. In any case, the sight of these huge sea mammals close-up in the cavernous enclaves of their natural habitat should not be missed—despite an odor not unlike sweat-soaked sneakers.

If you can't observe the animals to your satisfaction in the cave, go one-quarter mile north of the concession entrance to the "rockwork" turnout, where the herd sometimes populate the rocky ledges several hundred feet below. It's also a good place to snap a shot of the picturesque Heceta Head Lighthouse across the cove to the north from the turnout.

Heceta Head Lighthouse is reputedly the most photographed spot on the Oregon coast.

Heceta Head State Scenic Viewpoint and Devil's Elbow

About 11 miles north of Florence, Heceta Head State Scenic Viewpoint is located in a lovely cove at the mouth of Cape Creek, at the base of thousand-foot-high Heceta Head. From here you can get a good look at the graceful arc of Conde McCullough's Cape Creek Bridge, spanning the chasm more than 200 feet above you. Across the cove, photogenic Heceta Head Lighthouse (541/547-3416, open for tours daily 11 A.M.–5 P.M. Mar.–Oct., free), completed in 1894, beams the strongest light on the Oregon coast, from a shelf 205 feet up the rocky headland. An easy half-mile trail leads up from the park's picnic and parking area to the tower. Admission is free, but donations aid restoration work here. A little below the lighthouse is **Heceta House,** where the lighthouse keepers used to live. Today, it's a B&B (see the Accommodations section).

Heceta Head is said to be the most photographed lighthouse in the country; that may be difficult to verify, but it's impossible to quibble with the magnificent sight of the gleaming white tower and outbuildings on the headland, particularly when viewed from a set of highway pullouts just south of the bridge. The vistas from the lighthouse and network of trails on the headland are no less dramatic: See murres, tufted puffins, and other seabirds, as well as sea lions, on the rock islands below, bald eagles soaring overhead, and, in spring, northbound female gray whales and their calves as they pass close to shore. A trail leading to the north side of Heceta Head offers views to Cape Perpetua, 10 miles to the north.

Just south of Heceta Head is a trail down to the beach at adjoining **Devil's Elbow State Park.** Be conscious of tides here if you climb along the rocks adjoining the beach.

RECREATION

Golf

Ocean Dunes Golf Links (3315 Munsel Lake Rd., 541/997-3232) lets you tee off with sand dunes (some more than 60 feet tall) as a backdrop. The manicured 18-hole course has a driving range, a full pro shop, and equipment rentals on-site. For the ultimate in golfing by the dunes, however, try **Sandpines Golf Course** (1050 35th St., 541/997-1940, green fees $48, carts $26), which was voted *Golf Digest*'s number-one new public course in 1993. To get there, go west off U.S. 101 on 35th Street. In May and June, rhododendrons line this drive, which heads into dune country as you move toward the sea. Follow the signs until you see a water tower not far from the pro shop. Sandpines' layout features fairways lined with Douglas fir and beachgrass on gently undulating terrain. Coastal winds that kick up in the morning can figure prominently in your shot selection.

River Cruises

Paddlewheelers along the Siuslaw were part of the two-day Eugene–Florence pilgrimage a century ago. Today you can get a taste of that experience aboard the 65-foot sternwheeler *Westward Ho!* (541/997-9691), which leaves from Florence's Old Town docks for a variety of cruises on the river. In addition to the succession of historic sites along the Siuslaw between Florence and Mapleton detailed in the 11 A.M. hour-long cruise, several other daily half-hour cruises at 1 P.M., 2 P.M., and 3 P.M. feature lunch and "lots of music and cool spirits," respectively. On Friday and Saturday there are dinner cruises. Weekday hour-long cruise fares are $12 for adults and $6 for kids under 12; the dinner excursion is $33 per person.

Horseback Riding

Riding across the dunes into the sunset on a trusty steed sounds like a fantasy, but you can do it, too, thanks to **C&M Stables** (90241 U.S. 101, Florence 97439, 541/997-7540). Rates range $30–45 per person for trips of 1–2 hours (with discounts for larger parties). The stables are open daily. With beach rides, dune trail excursions, and sunset trips, there's something for everybody. Call for specific times and reservations.

Dune Rides

Another option for those who fear to tread is **Sand Dunes Frontier** (83960 U.S. 101, Florence 97439, 541/997-3544). This company

rents vehicles for travel in specially designated areas within the Dunes NRA. Odysseys, small one-person dune buggies, go for $35 per hour plus a $50 deposit. You must be strapped in, with a helmet, stay within the marked territory, and be especially careful going uphill. If you lose power on an incline, it's possible to roll over when turning around to go back down. The 20-person dune buggy rides cost $10 adults, $5 ages 4–11, free ages five and under. A four-seater goes for $45 per hour. Protective goggles are provided, along with a driver. Go in the morning when the sand tends to blow around less.

Siltcoos Lake

Oregon's largest coastal lake, six miles south of Florence, 3,100-acre Siltcoos Lake offers excellent fishing and other recreation. Rainbows are stocked in the spring, and steelhead, salmon (closed to coho fishing), and sea-run cutthroat trout move from the ocean into the lake via the short Siltcoos River in late summer and fall, but the real excitement here is the fishing for warm-water species, which is some of the best in the Northwest. Bluegill, crappie, yellow perch, and brown bullhead action is good through the summer, while fishing for largemouth bass can be good year-round. Access points include several public and private boat ramps on the lake, as well as a wheelchair-accessible fishing pier at Westlake Resort.

In addition, the **Siltcoos River** invites kayakers and canoeists to explore the two-mile stretch between the lake and the sea. Meandering two miles through dunes, forest, and estuary, the Siltcoos is a gentle, Class-I paddle with no white-water or rapids, although a small dam midway must be portaged. Wildlife that you may encounter along the way include mink, raccoons, otters, beaver, and even bears. In the estuary, sea lions and harbor seals are common.

For more information on the Siltcoos area, contact the Oregon Dunes National Recreation Visitor Center (541/271-3611) in Reedsport.

Flightseeing

Seaplane Enterprises (83763. U.S. 101 S, 541/991-0669), based at Lakeshore RV Park about three miles south of Florence, operates scenic seaplane flights in a Piper Tri-Pacer over the coastline, the dunes, and tranquil hidden lakes. Spring whale-watching trips are also offered. Fifteen-minute flights taking off from Woahink Lake start at $20 per person, 30-minute flights over Charleston or Sea Lion Caves are $40 per person, and longer flights are $120 per hour for up to three passengers. The season runs Monday–Saturday from Memorial Day to October 15.

Other Activities

Huckleberry picking is another attraction just outside town. Some prime pickings are found about five miles north of Florence at the Sutton Creek Trail, which begins in the campground with the same name that's just off U.S. 101. During late summer or fall, these berries flourish below the dense canopy of shorepines here. Rhododendrons bloom in profusion mid-May to early June. In addition to these delights, you can hike through the dunes, which are broken up by several freshwater lakes.

EVENTS AND ENTERTAINMENT

Art shows, classical concerts by acclaimed virtuosi (including performances as part of the Ernest Bloch Music Festival—see the Newport and Vicinity section for more details), ballet, theater, and community events can be enjoyed within the warm, welcoming, and spacious **Florence Events Center** (715 Quince St., 541/997-1994 or 888/968-4086, www.eventcenter.org). An onsite gallery displays the works of local artists.

The **Dune Mushers Mail Run,** held the first weekend of March, is the world's longest organized dry-land run for dogsled teams, which mush up the dunes from North Bend. On Sunday, the teams pass through Florence's South Jetty area, to finish up with a parade through Old Town Florence.

During the third weekend of May, Florence celebrates the **Rhododendron Festival,** coinciding with the bloom of these flowers that proliferate in the area. It's a tradition that goes back to 1908, when the festival was started as a way to

draw attention and commerce to the area. A parade, carnival, flower show, 5- and 10-km "Rhody Run," and the crowning of Queen Rhododendra are highlights of the festivities. Today, the event attracts more than 15,000 visitors each year. Contact the chamber of commerce (541/997-3128) for more information.

Fourth of July celebrations include live outdoor music and a barbecue in Old Town, and a fireworks display over the river.

Chowder, Brews, and Blues (541/997-1994, $5–7) in late September is a three-day event honoring several things the community relishes. A coastwide clam chowder contest here is a highlight, along with live music and microbrew tasting at the Florence Events Center.

ACCOMMODATIONS

As just about everywhere else, there are budget motels on the main drag here, but to experience the coast fully, try one of the romantic getaways between Florence and Yachats. There are many romantic B&Bs north of town, covered in detail in the Yachats and Vicinity section.

Vacation Rentals

The properties listed highlight Siuslaw Bay and/or Old Town and will enhance your appreciation of this estuarine environment. Another alternative is renting a house out in the dunes through **Dolphin Property Management** (508 Kingwood St., 541/997-7368). For other rental locations, try **Elson Shields Property Management** (1287 Bay St., 541/997-6235).

Motels

One of the best bargains in town is the **Lighthouse Inn** (155 U.S. 101, 541/997-3221, $35 and up), a Cape Cod–style two-story motel on the highway close to the bridge and convenient to Old Town. With neatly kept rooms in an untouched 1938 lodging, decorated with brica-brac and other homey touches, it may give you the feeling that you're spending the night at your grandmother's house. No in-room kitchens, but a common refrigerator and microwave are available for guest use. Most rooms have a queen- or king-sized bed and sleep two; some are considered suites, with two rooms and a connecting bath, and they sleep up to five guests. Ask about the plushest of all, the honeymoon/anniversary suite.

One block north of Old Town, just across the highway from the Lighthouse Inn, the **Money Saver Motel** (170 U.S. 101 N., 541/997-7131) provides guests with basic, affordable rooms in the same price range.

For a river experience, try the **River House Motel** (1202 Bay St., 541/997-3933, $69–89). Guests pay a bit more for river views.

Hotel
On the south bank of the river, the **Best Western Pier Point Inn** (85625 U.S. 101, 541/997-7191, $60–140 off-season, $129 and up in summer) offers spacious, well-appointed rooms, bay views, sand-dune hiking across the street, and a good restaurant on-site (Lovejoy's fish and chips and selection of English ales and microbrews are worth a stop). There is also a beach house that sleeps six for rent along the Siuslaw River.

Bed-and-Breakfasts
The Edwin K B&B (1155 Bay St., 541/997-8360 or 800/8-EDWINK, $115–125, less in winter) has six units with private bath two blocks from Old Town near the Siuslaw River. River views, period antiques, and multicourse included breakfasts with locally famous soufflés and homebaked breads on fine china have established this gracious 1914 home as Florence's preeminent B&B. Add private baths and whirlpool tubs in some units, a private courtyard and waterfall in back, and the reasonable rates, and you'll understand the need to reserve well in advance.

To sample a piece of coastal history in the heart of Old Town, stay at the **Johnson House** (216 Maple St., 541/997-8000 or 800/768-9488, $75–125), a restored 1890s Victorian furnished with period details throughout, also featuring private bathrooms and a gorgeous flower garden. Touted as the longest established inn on the coast, the Johnson House is close to shops and restaurants, but you'll want to stick around for their breakfast spread.

About three miles east of town, **The Blue Heron Inn** (6563 ORE 126, Florence, 541/997-4091 or 800/997-7780, www.blue-heroninn.com, $65–140) is a good choice for amateur ornithologists. River frontage highlighted by a spotting scope might reveal cormorants, herons, bald eagles, and every so often, a tundra swan. Whirlpool tubs, antiques, and a charming home rich in nooks and crannies make the rates a good value. A full breakfast enthusiastically touted by its guests compounds the impression. A newer media room downstairs entertains guests with rented or inhouse videos.

Nine miles north of Florence, and just a short walk from Heceta Head Lighthouse, is **Heceta Light Station B&B** (92072 U.S. 101, 541/547-3696, www.hecetalighthouse.com, $130–230 d), built in 1893, where the lighthouse keepers used to live. Today, it's a B&B with antique furnishings and vintage photos, which help re-create the lives of the keepers of the flame. Among the three upstairs bedrooms, the Mariner's room commands the finest view and is the only room here with private facilities (the other two share a bathroom down the hall). Vintage photos of early lighthouse keepers add a historical dimension to the experience. The current caretakers maintain a flock of chickens on the grounds, as did the actual lighthouse keepers of yesteryear. Your current hosts keep them as a source of fresh eggs to be used in the seven-course included breakfast. The latter is a glorious several-hour affair replete with such dishes as d'Anjou pear with chevre and Oregon honey and vol-au-vent stuffed with chived eggs and asparagus. The innkeepers are more likely to tell you about resident ghosts here during breakfast than right before bedtime.

Campgrounds
Camping here offers recreational opportunities comparable to those at the Oregon Dunes NRA, with more varied scenery.

Carl G. Washburne State Park (93111 U.S. 101 N., information 541/547-3416, reservations 800/452-5687, open year-round, $16–20, $5 hiker/biker spaces) is popular with Oregonians because of its proximity to beaches, tidepools,

Sea Lion Caves, and elk. The eight tent sites and 58 RV sites have such modern conveniences as showers, laundry, electricity, and piped water. They also have two yurts, which can also be reserved. It's 14 miles north of Florence on U.S. 101 (several miles past Sea Lion Caves), then one mile west on a park road.

In addition, there are nearby forest pathways such as the **Hobbit Trail,** named after the furry-footed characters in J. R. R. Tolkien's works. You'll probably feel like a hobbit when peering up at the high walls woven of roots, peat, and sand that loom above the trail cut deep into the forest floor here. The path winds through dense forest thickets of pine, fir, and rhododendrons down to the beach. Look for the turnout on the right side of the road just over the hill north of the Heceta Head curves on U.S. 101. Ask the park personnel about this and China Creek Trail. You might also ask about a relatively new trail that begins close by that part of U.S. 101 where the Hobbit Trail begins. In three-quarters of an uphill mile, you'll be at Heceta Head Lighthouse.

Three miles south of Florence's McCullough Bridge and on both sides of U.S. 101 is **Honeyman State Park** (84505 U.S. 101 S., information 541/997-3641, reservations 800/452-5687). This exceedingly popular campground gets very crowded in the summer—reservations are a must—but it empties out enough during spring and autumn to make a stay here worthwhile. There are 240 tent sites with the basics, a large number of RV spaces with all the amenities, and many hiker/biker spots as well (more than 400 in total). Ask about canoe rentals to savor the serenity of Cleawox Lake. Fishing, swimming, hiking, and dune buggies are available nearby, so there's always something to do. In spring, pink rhodies line the highway and park roads. Advance reservations are accepted Memorial Day through Labor Day (800/452-5687), and the sites cost $13–21, depending on the season and type.

An ideal place to escape from the summertime coastal crowds is the **North Fork of the Siuslaw** campground. Chances are you'll see mostly locals here—if anybody. From Florence follow ORE 126 about 15 miles to Mapleton and the junction with ORE 36. The latter road

takes you 13 miles to County Route 5070. Then it's a short drive to the riverside campsite (or you can drive the North Fork Siuslaw River Road from Florence for 14.5 miles). The fee is $4 between July and early September. Picnic tables, fire pits, and crawdads are other reasons to come. Contact the Siuslaw National Forest Ranger Station (4480 U.S. 101 N., Florence, 541/902-8526) for more information.

Close by is the **Pawn Old Growth Trail,** a half-mile pathway through several-hundred-year-old, 100-inch-diameter, 275-feet-tall Douglas fir and hemlock. The trailhead, located at the confluence of the North Fork of the Siuslaw and Taylor's Creek, is a good place to see salmon spawning in the fall and observe water ouzels (also called "dippers"). It follows the creek and offers interpretive placards along the way. At one point in the trail visitors walk through fallen Douglas fir logs 260 inches in diameter. Placards explain the science of tree rings. Consult the ranger station in Florence to get exact directions.

By the way, nearby ORE 36 makes an interesting access road back to the Willamette Valley if you're not in a hurry. Its circuitous route passes through Deadwood and ends up in the Junction City area.

FOOD

A famous Zen master once said, "If you can make a cup of tea right, you can do anything." The same aphorism seems to apply to clam chowder in coastal restaurants, if three Florence eateries are any indication.

Steak and Seafood

In Old Town, the local **Mo's** (1436 Bay St., 541/997-2185) is the largest outlet of this famed Oregon chowderhouse, and its fresh fish, fast service, fair prices, and Siuslaw River frontage make it this neighborhood's most popular restaurant. Lunch with a cup of chowder might run $6, and bouillabaisse is the most expensive item on the menu. Even if you don't eat here, you might want to stock up on Mo's clam chowder base packaged to go.

Another award-winning chowder, and also an *Oregon Coast* magazine poll winner, is the creamy clam-filled concoction made by **The Blue Hen** (1675 U.S. 101, 541/997-3907, 7 A.M.–8 P.M. daily, $3–10 breakfast, $5–10 lunch, $7–12 dinner) at the north end of town. Fourteen finely chopped items go into this orange-specked beige soup. However, as the name and the sign out front imply, chicken is the mainstay of this small café operating out of a home on the highway—but don't overlook the berry pies. You may be asked to share your table with the interesting cross-section of travelers drawn to this Oregon coastal hub. You'll enjoy dining on the outdoor deck in summer.

For yet another chowder champ, **Ruby Begonia** (1565 9th St., 541/997-1821, 8 A.M.–9 P.M. daily) has one of the best seafood chowders on the coast, according to *Sunset* magazine. This golden-hued soup has salmon, halibut, prawns, and clams. The tasty homemade pie and the Mexican entrées add another dimension to the Florence dining scene.

The Bridgewater Seafood Restaurant and Oyster Bar (129 Bay St., Old Town, 541/997-9405, $8 lunch, $10–15 dinner) features exotic clam chowder with Indonesian clams, in keeping with a Banana Republic decor, and the only "fine dining" in Old Town. Of course, this also means the highest prices on the waterfront. But to be fair, you're getting what you pay for and then some. The Bridgewater was the recipient of a People's Choice Award for the best clam chowder in town for several years. Fresh fish, often with a Cajun flair, is the star of the menu. A lower-priced option exists on Wednesday, winter through early spring, with the all-you-can-eat seafood dinner buffet.

For a panoramic river view the whole family can enjoy, the **Bay Bridge** (1150 Bay St., 541/997-7168, open daily) has moderately priced steak and seafood, as well as pasta and chicken dishes.

Traveler's Cove (1362 Bay St., 541/997-6845, 9 A.M.–9 P.M.) manages to combine an import shop and gourmet café under the same roof. The café serves good lunches and is worth a stop for the homemade clam chowder and interesting salads and sandwiches. Fresh Dungeness crab makes an appearance here with crab quiche, crab

enchiladas, and "crabby" Caesar salad. Best of all, the patio out back provides riverfront views to enjoy along with your meal. A full bar with flavored margaritas might also enhance your appreciation of the river frontage.

The **International C-Food Market** (1498 Bay St., 541/997-9646) gets good word-of-mouth from locals. This combination restaurant and retail market offers seafood right off the boat. Not only is the freshness of the fish exceptional, but prices are also low. The catch of the day and the smoked salmon pizza are both excellent. In September 2000, the ICM won a coastwide clam chowder competition. Open for lunch and dinner daily.

Scandinavians played a major role in settling the Oregon coast. Enjoy some of this tradition at **Synnove's** (2825 U.S. 101, 541/902-9142, open for lunch and dinner Wed.–Sun.). Be sure to try such Norwegian specialties as light, delicate halibut and salmon cakes and pan-fried sole.

North of town, the **Windward Inn** (3757 U.S. 101, 541/997-8243, open daily) rates a special mention. Long a mainstay of the coastal dining scene, the fresh-cut flowers, skylights, and wood-paneled interior have set the stage for memorable repasts for more than 50 years. Dinners are typified by such creations as fresh mussels broiled on the half shell with Oregon hazelnuts, Oregon peppered bacon, and Tillamook cheddar cheese.

Casual Fare

Another venue that aims to satisfy is the **Firehouse Restaurant** (1263 Bay St., 541/997-2800), serving standard American fare—dinners include choices such as steak, seafood, pasta, and tri-tip. They also have a full bar, which includes a good variety of Northwest microbrews.

The health-conscious crowd head over to **Salmonberry** (812 Quince St., 541/997-3345, open daily) to stock up on organic produce, bulk grains, spices, supplements, and the like.

Coffee and Ice Cream

After dinner, have dessert at either of **BJ's Ice Cream Parlor**'s two locations (2930 U.S. 101 or 1441 Bay St., 541/997-7286, open daily). BJ's churns out hundreds of flavors, with 48 on display any given time, famous all over Oregon. Full fountain service, ice cream cakes, cheesecakes, gourmet frozen yogurt, and pies complement the cones and cups.

Old Town is fortunate to have not one but two excellent coffeehouses that roast their own. **Old Town Coffee Roasters** (125-1/2 Nopal St., 541/997-1786), one block away from the docks, is a friendly place that brews a hearty cup and serves baked goods. Close to the bridge, **Siuslaw River Coffee Roasters** (1240 Bay St., 541/997-3443) draws a convivial crowd to its shop right on the river.

Out-of-Town Dining

Driving east on ORE 126 en route to Eugene from the coast lets you follow the Siuslaw past isolated farms and lush forests topped by clear-cut ridges. Fourteen miles east of Florence, you come to Mapleton. Set at the base of the Coast Range, it's one of the rainiest burgs in the whole state. It also has two restaurants that evoke remembrances of things past. **The Alpha Bit Crafts Café** (10780 ORE 126, Mapleton, 541/268-4311, $3–7) is only a 20-minute drive from Florence, but it exists in a different time and space. Started by a group of 20 or so people who share land in the nearby town of Deadwood, the restaurant serves a varied menu of good ol' American food and vegetarian fare (try the grainburger) at reasonable prices. The preparations frequently include produce grown on Alpha Farm, and the coffee for two bits puts the higher-priced coastal brews to shame. Also don't miss the home-baked cakes and pies, and the December 1991 *Life* magazine article about the creators, available upon request. Finally, the unusual local crafts and fine selection of books make Alpha Bit the cultural center of Mapleton.

A mile or two down ORE 126 from Mapleton is the **Gingerbread Village** (12300 ORE 126, 541/268-4713, open daily except holidays). This is the kind of place your parents might have taken you when you were a kid—you know, a greasy spoon without the grease, serving simple, wholesome meals. While the food here is good enough to get you to Eugene, the gingerbread is unforgettable. Order it warm so the vanilla ice cream on top melts down decadently. Getting this dish to go costs a quarter more, but the "boat" it comes in carries a disproportionately larger serving.

SHOPPING

A nice selection of Oregon food products and crafts is available in Old Town Florence at **Incredible Edible Oregon** (1350 Bay St., 541/997-7018). One place to stop if you're looking for regional titles is next door, at **Old Town Books and Country Gifts** (1340 Bay St., 541/997-6205). The friendly staff here will also gladly direct you to local attractions and answer any questions you might have about the region.

INFORMATION AND SERVICES

The **Florence Area Chamber of Commerce** (270 U.S. 101, Florence 97439, 541/997-3128, www.florencechamber.com, 9 A.M.–5 P.M.), is three blocks north of the Siuslaw River Bridge.

The **Siuslaw National Forest Ranger Station** (4480 U.S. 101 N., Florence, 541/902-8526) is located near the BiMart on Florence's main drag. Tune into radio station **KCST,** at 106.9 FM or 1250 AM, for coastal news, weather, and a whole lotta Paul Harvey.

Peace Harbor Hospital (400 9th St., Florence, 541/997-3128) is open 24 hours, with a dozen specialists and an emergency room. The post office is at 770 Maple Street, Florence 97439, 541/997-2533. Close by the junction of ORE 126 and U.S. 101 is the library.

For a walk-up teller or Internet access, the **Old Town Coffee Company** (125-1/2 Nopal) can meet your needs. Internet use is free with a coffee purchase.

Transportation

The **Greyhound** (541/902-9076) bus stop, at the 37th Street Laundry (1856 37th St., 541/997-5111), sees twice-daily service from two different routes. In addition to two buses coming down from Portland via Lincoln City en route to San Francisco on U.S. 101, there are two buses a day from Eugene.

Yachats and Vicinity

Yachats (pronounced "YAH-hots") is derived from an Alsea Indian word meaning "dark waters at the foot of the mountain." The phrase aptly describes the location of this picturesque resort village of 635 people, clustered on the hillsides and coastal shelf beside the Yachats River mouth in the shadow of Cape Perpetua. Word of mouth has helped to spread the popularity of Yachats as a place for a quiet getaway and a base for enjoying the Cape Perpetua Scenic Area and nearby beaches.

The most notable sight near Yachats, indeed on the whole central coast, is the view from 803-foot-high Cape Perpetua. . . . On a clear day, you can see 39 miles out to sea.

SIGHTS AND RECREATION

Cape Perpetua

The most notable sight near Yachats, indeed on the whole central coast, is the view from 803-foot-high Cape Perpetua. The name derives from Captain Cook's sighting of the promontory on March 7, 1778, St. Perpetua's Day. It's too bad the British explorer didn't make landfall here to enjoy one of the world's preeminent coastal panoramas. Oregon's highest paved public road this close to the shoreline affords 150 miles of north-to-south visibility from the top of the headland. On a clear day, you can see 39 miles out to sea.

Before hiking the 23 miles of foot trails or driving to the top of the cape, stop off at the **Cape Perpetua Visitor Center** (541/547-3289), three miles south of Yachats on the east side of the highway. A picture window framing a bird's-eye view of rockbound coast, along with exhibits on forestry and marine life, begin your orientation to the region here. Cataclysms such as the forest fire of 1846, the monsoons and 138-mph winds unleashed by the 1962 Columbus Day Storm, and 1964 Hurricane Frieda and their effects on the 2,700-acre Cape Perpetua Scenic Area are artfully explained by exhibits here. An excellent 15-minute film about Oregon's intertidal biome will also hold your interest.

Personnel at the desk have maps and pamphlets about such trails as Cook's Ridge, Riggin' Slinger, and Giant Spruce, as well as directions for the auto tour to the summit. In addition, they can point the way to tidepools and berry patches. Two naturalist-guided hikes a day are offered to coastal rainforest and tidepools. The center is open 9 A.M.–5 P.M. from early May to October and opens during peak whale-watching weeks from Christmas to New Year's and in late March. Admission is $3 per car. The Pacific Coast Passport, NW Forest Pass, and Golden Passports are honored here.

The awe-inspiring 1.5 mile **Saint Perpetua Trail** (from the visitors center) to the cape's summit is of moderate difficulty, gaining 600 feet in elevation. En route, placards explain the role of wind, erosion, and fire in forest succession in this mixed-conifer ecosystem.

At the crest of Cape Perpetua, the **Trail of the Whispering Spruce** begins, a quarter-mile loop through the grounds of a former World War II Coast Guard lookout built by the Civilian Conservation Corps in 1933. The southern views from the crest take in the highway and headlands as far as Coos Bay. Halfway along the path, you'll come to a WPA-built rock hut called the West Shelter that makes a lofty perch for whale-watching, one of the best spots on the entire coast. Beyond this ridgetop aerie the curtain of trees parts to reveal fantastic views of the shoreline between Yachats and Cape Foulweather.

The two-mile drive up the cape (where the Whispering Spruce Trailhead can be accessed) is complicated by a not-so-prominent sign on U.S. 101 (milemarker 188.5) indicating the turnoff onto Forest Service Road 55. To begin your auto ascent, drive a hundred yards north on U.S. 101 from the visitors center and look for the steep, winding spur road on the right. As you climb, you'll notice large Sitka spruce trees abutting the road. Halfway up, you'll come to a Y in the road. Take a hard left and follow the road another mile to the top of Cape Perpetua. (If you miss the left turn here and go straight ahead, you'll soon find yourself on a 22-mile loop through the Coast Range to Yachats.) Along the way, 18 placards annotate forest ecology.

Another hike from the visitors center goes down to a blowhole called the spouting horn. This is the Captain Cook Trail, which goes six miles through a dense wind-carved forest and the remains of an old Civilian Conservation Corps camp under U.S. 101 to an ancient lava deposit on the shore. Given enough wave action, water bubbles up through fissures in the basalt. There are also Indian shell middens built up 300–2,000 years ago in the area.

State Parks and Coastal Waysides

In this part of the coast, state parks and viewpoints abound with attractions. There's so much to see here that keeping your eyes on the road in this heavily traveled section becomes a challenge.

One mile north of town, **Smelt Sands State Recreation Site** gives access to tidepools and the three-quarter-mile 804 Trail, which follows the rocky shore to a broad, sandy beach to the north. In Yachats, turn west onto 2nd Street to loop around wave-battered **Yachats State Recreation Area,** overlooking Yachats Bay. The route heads north along the ocean, where it becomes Marine Drive. After going through a residential community, it eventually takes an easterly turn to reconnect with U.S. 101.

On the south bank of the Yachats River is a short but beautiful beach loop off U.S. 101 (going south, look for the sign that says Beach Access). The road runs between the landscaped grounds of beach houses and resorts on one side and the foamy sea on the other. A wide beach, tidepools, and blowholes on the bank by the river's mouth are a special treat.

Devil's Churn, at the base of Cape Perpetua

CENTRAL COAST

Just north of the turnoff for the top of Cape Perpetua (Forest Service Rd. 55) and U.S. 101 is the turnout for **Devil's Churn,** on the west side of the highway. Here, the tides have cut a deep fissure in a basalt embankment on the shore. You can observe the action from a vertigo-inducing overlook high above, or take the easy, switchbacking trail down to the water's edge. While watching the white-water torrents in this foaming cistern, beware of "sneaker waves," particularly if you venture beyond the boundaries of the **Trail of the Restless Waters.** The highlights here are the spouting horns where sea water is funneled between rocks and explodes into spray. All along this stretch of the coast, many trees appear to be leaning away from the ocean as if bent by storms. This illusion is caused by salt-laden westerlies drying out and killing the buds on the exposed side of the tree, leaving growth only on the leeward branches. A $3 day-use fee is collected here.

One mile south, **Neptune State Park** has a beautiful beach and is near the 9,300-acre **Cummin's Creek Wilderness** east of U.S. 101. Just north of Neptune Park, Forest Service Road 1050 leads east to the Cummins Creek Trailhead. One-half mile south, gravelly Forest Service Road 1051 can take you to a point where a moderately difficult 2.5-mile hike leads to Cummin's Ridge Trailhead. This pathway has some of the last remaining coastal old-growth Sitka spruce stands. Get maps and detailed directions for these and other area trails at the Cape Perpetua Visitor Center.

Close by, there's a chance to explore tidepools and sometimes observe harbor seals at **Strawberry Hill.** Scenic shorelines can also be found in the next few miles farther south at **Stonesfield Beach State Recreation Site** and **Muriel O. Ponsler State Scenic Viewpoint,** before you arrive at **Carl G. Washburne State Park.**

Bike Rental

Zuzu's Pedals at Rachel's Roadhouse (U.S. 101 at 4th St.) rents bicycles during summer.

EVENTS

This little village seems to be busy with some festival or other event just about every weekend. For a full schedule, see the Chamber of Commerce website (www.yachats.org/events.html). Following are some highlights:

Spring brings two arts-and-crafts festivals to the Yachats Commons (U.S. 101 and W. 4th St.): In late March, the Chamber-sponsored **Original Yachats Arts and Crafts Fair** (541/547-3530 or 800/929-0477) exhibits the work of some 75 Pacific Northwest artists and artisans. Admission is free. If you miss that one, come back in late May for **Crafts on the Coast** (541/547-4738 or 541/547-4664).

Yachats really pulls out the stops for the **Fourth of July.** Events include the short and silly La De Da Parade at noon, the Yachats Yamboree (food booths, beer gardens, live music), farmers' market, a musical variety show, and a fireworks show on the bay when darkness falls.

During the Yachats **Smelt Fry,** held the second Saturday of July, up to 750 pounds of this sardinelike fish are served on the grounds of Yachats Commons on 4th Street (just follow the signs to this refurbished schoolhouse). Yachats used to be one of the few places in the world blessed with a run of oceangoing smelt, but they have declined drastically because of changing ocean conditions. Nonetheless, the town's traditional "welcome to summer" event has continued thanks to imported Northern California smelt, which augment the local catch. For $8 (or $3 for children 12 and younger), you get all the deep-fried delicately flavored smelt you can eat (or a sausage plate for $5) with side dishes and a beverage. What you're really paying for is a classic small-town festival where you get to rub elbows with a spirited community. More info is available from the chamber of commerce.

The same weekend, the **Yachats Music Festival** takes place several blocks north at the Presbyterian Church (360 W. 7th St., info. at 541/547-3141 or 510/601-6184). Admission is $15 for each performance. The lineup features classical virtuosi and vocalists from the San Francisco Bay Area for evening concerts and a Sunday matinee performance.

A relatively new but popular event here is the **Yachats Village Mushroom Fest** (541/547-3530 or 800/929-0477), held the third weekend in October. Native mushrooms thrive in the temperate rainforests of the Cape Perpetua region, and fall is the season to harvest them. The Yachats event was started by Chef John Ullman, who was inspired by similar festivals in Italy. Activities over the weekend include the Friday-night Yachats Rainforest Fungi Feast, mushroom-cooking demonstrations, guided mushroom walks at Cape Perpetua Visitors Center, and the last farmers' market of the season.

Another exciting recent addition to the Yachats calendar is the annual **Celtic Music Festival,** held in mid-November. It's a full weekend of concerts and workshops provided by local and visiting musicians. For details, contact the Raindogs shop (162 Beach St., 541/547-3000).

ACCOMMODATIONS

Vacation Rentals
Yachats Village Rentals (541/547-3501) has a varied stable of vacation homes ($110–215) for rent. **Horizon Property Management** (205 U.S. 101, P.O. Box 1047, Waldport, OR 97394, 541/563-5151)has a list of oceanfront homes that sleep up to 12.

Motels
At the beginning of the beach loop (on the south bank of the Yachats River and west of U.S. 101) are the **Shamrock Lodgettes** (105 U.S. 101 S., 541/547-3312 or 800/845-5028). Shamrock's beautiful parklike landscape frames a selection of individual log cabins, redwood units, and deluxe rooms. Stone fireplaces, in-room movies, and ocean or bay views all contribute to a relaxed get-away-from-it-all feeling. The sauna and whirlpool tub on the premises also enhance the mellowing-out process, which begins as soon as you set foot here. Reserve early for the much-requested cabins that range $115–150 for two and $131–175 for four, while other motel units average $75–110—a small price for peace of mind. The more expensive rooms in the latter category have whirlpool bathtubs. There is also a health club on the premises with a redwood hot tub and sauna. Ask about midwinter specials. Kids are permitted, and pets are allowed in some units.

A short drive farther south, the modern **Yachats Inn** (331 U.S. 101, 541/547-3456 or 888/270-3456, www.yachatsinn.com, $51–125) is a great place for group retreats or families, with spacious units that are more like well-furnished apartments, all just steps from the beach. The landscaped grounds include an indoor pool, sauna, and teahouse (for large groups, meetings, or parties).

For those looking for a budget place close to the center of town with some of the comforts of home, try **Rock Park Cottages** (431 W. 2nd, 541/547-3214 or 541/343-4382, $60–115), two blocks from the chamber of commerce and adjacent to the Yachats State Park. Consisting of five rustic cottages arranged around a courtyard, Rock Park has to be considered one of the better bargains on the coast. If weather keeps you inside, the wood-paneled walls hold bookshelves with reading matter and board games, and the kitchens are well equipped.

The **Dublin House Motel** (U.S. 101 and 7th St., 866/922-4287, www.dublinhousemotel.com, $45–109) offers large guest rooms and ocean views, each with microwaves, refrigerators, coffee makers, and cable TV; some kitchen units are also available. The indoor heated pool is especially nice in winter.

A little north of the town center, the imposing **Adobe Resort** (155 U.S. 101 N., 541/547-3141 or 800/522-3623, $100–120) overlooks Smelt Sands Beach. If you appreciate all services in one compound, from dining room to gift shop, the Adobe suite ($245) gets the nod. Pets are accepted in some rooms.

But for about the same or less money, the **Fireside Motel's** (U.S. 101, 541/547-3636 or 800/336-3573, $50–130) smallish rooms have more than enough amenities. In addition to ocean views, many of the rooms also have such extras as refrigerators and fireplaces. The Fireside also allows pets. Perhaps the most appreciated little touch is the guidebook the management has put together for guest use. It points the way to some of the area's natural attractions, including Smelt Sands and Cape Perpetua. A state park trail behind both properties leads over the rockbound coast to a driftwood-laden beach.

The aptly named **SeeVue** (95590 U.S. 101, 541/547-3227, www.seevue.com) has long been a favorite window on the Pacific for stormwatchers and whale-watchers. This 10-room complex thrives today thanks to an eminently affordable combination of comfort and a location just six miles south of Yachats eateries and gallery-hopping and three miles south of Cape Perpetua. Assuming you can pull yourself away from watching the waves, there's also prime beachcombing and wildlife viewing close by. The most exceptional view here is from the Crow's Nest ($50–85), depending on seasonal availability. It sleeps 2–4 and features nautical memorabilia and a set of binoculars. In the same price range for two people, the antiques and housekeeping facilities in Granny's Room is the ultimate in storm-watching coziness. All units here boast Pacific perspectives and thematic decor. There are nonsmoking rooms and some housekeeping units. Friendly, knowledgeable innkeepers here push this place into the upper stratosphere of lodging values anywhere in Oregon. They also accept pets.

Inns

For the ultimate in seclusion, the **Oregon House** (94288 U.S. 101, 541/547-3329, www.oregonhouse.com), eight miles south of Yachats, overlooks the Pacific from a bluff and offers guests a reflective phone-free, TV-less atmosphere. Twelve apartments (housed in five different buildings) with baths and kitchens, some with fireplaces and whirlpool tubs, are perfect for groups. In fact, they specialize in groups but also offer the apartments for individuals. No pets are allowed; quiet children are okay. Stroll the three acres of gardens or head down the private path to the beach.

Another place where rock and tide get top billing is **Ocean Haven** (94770 U.S. 101, 541/547-3583, www.oceanhaven.com, $75–120). Located halfway between Florence and Yachats in a section of coast that one travel writer hyped as the "Amalfi Drive of the Americas," this classic beach house has virtually no motel-type amenities (no TVs or phones in rooms). Pets (which might spook Coast Range wildlife) and smoking are verboten. This is a peaceful nature-lover's retreat with panoramic views, friendly innkeepers, and a well-stocked library. The North View and South View rooms each boast two walls of glass on the ocean, and the beach below has tidal pools to explore. But the Shag's Nest, a cozy cabin with a bedside view of the water and a fireplace, is the ticket for a romantic weekend.

Bed-and-Breakfasts

A few classic bed-and-breakfasts south of Yachats rate a mention for those willing to spend a little more for comfort, location, and privacy. Seven miles south of Yachats, the **Sea Quest Inn** (95354 U.S. 101, 541/547-3782 or 800/341-4878, www.seaq.com, $160 and up) is an antique-filled aerie above the pounding surf. Private entrances and a location adjacent to Ten Mile Creek in this contemporary cedar-and-glass inn make rates well worth it. The newly added "Tis Sweete" is a 1,000-square-foot suite with a king-size canopy bed, a woodburning fireplace, 25-foot-high windows, and a wrap-around deck all located on a private wing for a mere $350 per night (2 people). The host couple's exceptional service and attention to detail make every visitor feel special. From the fine cognac and wines in the evening, the fruit, scones, and popcorn in the commons, to the chocolates and bottled water in your room, the inn is well stocked with quality goodies catering to your whim and pleasure. Breakfasts are delicacy-laden presentations superior to many hotel fine-dining rooms. The wrap-around deck affords superlative views of the beach, and telescopes and binoculars are always on hand for spotting whales and other marine life. Many guests return each year, so be sure to book well in advance. The inn is not appropriate for children under 14 years of age.

In the same area and price range are **Ziggurat** (95330 U.S. 101, 541/547-3925), a four-story glass and wood pyramidlike structure with an abundance of sunlight and comforts

(800-square-foot suites with such extras as a sauna, a baby grand piano, and a wood stove); and the **Kittiwake** (95368 U.S. 101, 541/547-4470), a sprawling, contemporary, beachfront home with spectacular views of the Pacific.

Look for all of these properties six miles south of Yachats at mile marker 171 near Ten Mile Creek. At all of these establishments, you might find such seasonal breakfast fare as local berries and smoked sturgeon. Unlike many of their counterparts elsewhere, most Yachats-area bed-and-breakfasts don't require you to share a bathroom. However, it's also worth noting that the welcome mats are seldom out for children and pets. Rates are around $170 and may require a two-night minimum stay.

Campgrounds
Set along Cape Creek in the Cape Perpetua Scenic Area, the Forest Service's **Cape Perpetua Campground** (reservations 877/444-6777, www.reserveusa.com, open May–Oct., $15) has 38 sites for tents and trailers or motor homes up to 22 feet long. Picnic tables and fire grills are provided. Flush toilets, piped water, and sanitary services are available; reservations are necessary for groups. The Forest Service rangers put on slide-illustrated campfire talks here and at Tillicum Beach during the summer.

Just south, **Neptune State Park** (800/551-6949) has several free beachfront hiker/biker sites.

Four miles farther south you can turn east off U.S. 101 and follow Forest Service Road 56 to get to **Rock Creek Campground** (reservations 877/444-6777, www.reserveusa.com, open May–Oct., $15). The nightly fee gets you a small out-of-the-way campground one-quarter mile from the ocean. Most of the 16 sites are for tents, but a few accommodate small RVs. Fire grills and picnic tables are provided; flush toilets and piped water are available. Several miles farther up Ten Mile Creek is **Ten Mile Creek Campground.** With no reservations and no fee, this small, secluded campground has four sites for tents and small RVs. You'll find fire grills, picnic tables, and primitive sanitary facilities, but no piped water. It's just 15 minutes off the highway, but it feels more remote.

If you're on a budget, try **Lanham Bike Camp,** which involves a hike in from Rock Creek but doesn't charge a fee. There's everything you need to make it through the night at the 10 primitive sites here, but bring your own water. The sites are open all year and don't require reservations.

FOOD
Fine Dining
Right on the main highway is **La Serre** (2nd and Beach, 541/547-3420, closed Tues. and all of Jan., less than $20). A bright skylit restaurant with lots of plants (La Serre means "the greenhouse") creates an appropriate setting for cuisine that eschews deep-fat frying and is heavy on the whole wheat. This may not suggest gourmet continental fare, but somehow La Serre pulls it off. With entrées running the gamut from strawberry-ricotta crêpes to charbroiled steaks, the menu manages to please the Brie-and-chardonnay set as well as their children. Their salmon or crab cakes, oven-roasted marinated free-range chicken, Manhattan clam chowder, bouillabaisse, and clam puffs appetizer will sate anyone who just likes good food. For dessert, try the flourless chocolate cake. On chilly evenings, wash it all down with a coffee nudge. Come back Sunday for a memorable breakfast.

On a bluff overlooking Smelt Sands Beach is the glass-enclosed **Adobe Resort** (1555 U.S. 101, 541/547-3141). Two side-by-side semicircular dining rooms, with windows on the crashing surf, are a great place to start the day for breakfast or end it with a romantic evening repast. Ask about the loft, where elevated coastal views provide photo ops and are the perfect place to nurse a drink (you have to carry your own food up there)—but a Sunday champagne brunch served 9 A.M.–1 P.M. and three meals a day are the real highlights here. For breakfast, start off right with one of several seafood omelets. For lunch, try the grilled Yaquina Bay oysters. For dinner, the Adobe baked crab pot and various kinds of fettuccine are the ticket.

Casual Fare
Right beside the highway, the **Joes' Town Center Café** (U.S. 101 and 4th St., 541/547-4244,

8 A.M.–3 P.M. daily except Wed.) gives the appearance of an old cedar beach house with some modern architectural flourishes. You can sit downstairs near the potbellied stove and bustling counter or upstairs in a windowed loft. On sunny days, kick back on the outside deck. Wherever you plop down, enjoy the full breakfast or lunch, featuring homemade soups and baked goods.

Steak and Seafood
Elaborate picnic eats are available from the **Yachats Crab and Chowder House** "To Go" shop (131 U.S. 101, 541/547-4132, 11 A.M.– 8 P.M. Mon.–Sat.). Pick up fresh half crab and garlic bread, rock cod and halibut fish and chips, as well as assorted breads, meats, and cheeses. Along with clam chowder, the restaurant also makes hearty chowders with Dungeness crab or smoked salmon. And remember, wherever you decide to picnic, chances are the view in the restaurant is at least as good, and there's usually plenty of seating. Known for its chowder, the **Landmark Restaurant** (U.S. 101, 541/547-3215) also has a good selection of fresh fish entrées and some of the most remarkable views on the coast.

Leroy's Blue Whale (541/547-3397) self-described "family restaurants" can be counted on for low prices for American food. Culinary flourishes are limited to a smoked salmon and jack cheese omelet for breakfast and dinner-time seafood specials such as squid rings and prawns sautéed in wine and butter. Leroy's stays open in January, when many of the other eateries in Yachats close early or suspend operation for the month.

The Drift Inn Pub (U.S. 101, 541/457-4477) is carefully restored tavern offering seafood dishes, crunchy salads, fish and chips, and other pub grub in a casual atmosphere.

Market
Make-it-yourselfers will find the right ingredients at **Clark's Market** (U.S. 101). You may also bump into the town mayor and other local VIPs.

Baked Goods
On the Rise Bakery, next door to the chamber of commerce on U.S. 101, offers grainy goodies.

SHOPPING

For such a small burg, Yachats is chockablock with little shops and boutiques. On the north end of Yachats on U.S. 101, **By-The-Sea Books** (887 U.S. 101, 541/547-4455, 10 A.M.–5 P.M., closed Tues.) can edify your curiosity about the area with regional titles or supply the perfect page-turner for that rainy winter day by the woodstove. There are 10,000 used books here and a large collection of new bestsellers. Browsers are encouraged with rocking chairs, coffee, cookies, and a corner dedicated to small children.

Overlooking the bay, just off 2nd Street, **Raindogs** (162 Beach St., 866/RAIN-DOG or 866/724-6364) is run by a friendly couple and has something for just about everybody: jewelry, cookbooks, home accessories, educational toys, pet gear, body and bath supplies, CDs, and more.

Across the highway, **Yachats Mercantile** (130 U.S. 101, 541/547-3060) can fix you up with the beach toys, camping gear, and other odds and ends you forgot to pack for your trip.

INFORMATION AND SERVICES

The **Yachats Area Chamber of Commerce** (241 U.S. 101, P.O. Box 728, Yachats 97498, 541/547-3530 or 800/929-0477, www.yachats.org, 10 A.M.–4 P.M. daily Mar.–Sept., Thurs.–Sun. the rest of the year) has a central location on the highway, next to Clark's Market, and a loquacious staff. Ask them about fishing, rockhounding, birdwatching, and beachcombing in the area.

The **Central Oregon Coast Association** (541/265-2064 or 800/767-2064, www.coastvisitor .com) maintains a useful website with details on Yachats and the rest of coastal Lincoln County.

The bus stop is also in the parking lot of the Clark's Market complex (U.S. 101 and W. 2nd). Here you can catch **Lincoln County Transit** buses (541/265-4900), which run four times a day Monday–Saturday between Yachats and Newport, with a link to Lincoln City.

For your banking and walk-up teller needs, try **National Security Bank Yachats Branch** (348 U.S. 101 N.).

Waldport and Vicinity

Originally a stronghold of the Alsea Indians, Waldport also has had incarnations as a gold rush town, salmon-canning center, and lumber port. This town of about 2,000, whose name means "forest port" in German, is pretty quiet today. The chamber of commerce touts Waldport's livability, suggesting that the town's "relative obscurity" has spared it the fate of more crowded tourist hot-spots. This may also be explained by a nondescript main drag that gives no hint of surrounding beaches and prime fishing and crabbing spots. A recent influx of retirees has spurred new home–building, but this place is still decidedly low-key. For those passing through, Waldport provides a low-cost alternative to the big-name destinations; in Waldport, you won't have to fight for a parking spot or make reservations months in advance.

SIGHTS AND RECREATION

Alsea Bay Bridge Historical Interpretive Center

This small museum-cum-visitors center, operated by the Oregon Parks and Recreation Department and Waldport Chamber of Commerce, stands along the highway on the south side of the river. Exhibits here tell the story of how the sleek 1991 bridge replaced the aging Conde McCullough span across the bay, which has since been demolished. Displays about transportation methods along the central coast since the 1800s, information on the Alsea tribe, and a telescope trained on the seals and waterfowl on the bay are worth a quick stop. In addition, Oregon Parks and Recreation guides lead bridge tours and give clamming and crabbing demonstrations during the summer.

The center (541/563-2002) is open 9 A.M.– 5 P.M. daily in summer, 9 A.M.–4 P.M. Tuesday– Saturday the rest of the year. Admission is free.

Seal Rock State Recreation Site

Four miles north of town, Seal Rock attracts beachcombers and agate-hunters, as well as folks

who come to explore the tidepools and observe the seals on offshore rocks. The park's name derives from a seal-shaped rock in the cluster of interesting formations in the tidewater. The picnic area is set in a shady area behind the sandy beach. During Christmas and spring breaks, the volunteers of Whale Watching Spoken Here are on hand to help visitors spot passing grays 10 A.M.–1 P.M. The park is open for day use only; call 800/551-6949 for information.

Ona Beach State Park

A couple of miles north of Seal Rock, this beguiling park on the west side of the highway includes a forested picnic area with a quarter-mile trail and a footbridge over Beaver Creek leading to a fine stretch of beach. The park is open for day use only; call 800/551-6949 for information.

Drift Creek Wilderness

Seven miles east of Waldport are the nearly 5,800 acres of the Drift Creek Wilderness, which protects the Coast Range's largest remaining stands of old-growth rainforest. Here you can see giant Sitka spruce and western hemlock hundreds of years old, nourished by up to 120 inches of rain per year. These trees are the "climax forest" in the Douglas fir ecosystem. They seldom reach old-growth status because the timber industry tends to replant only fir seedlings after logging operations. There is also perhaps the largest population of spotted owls in the state here, along with bald eagles, Roosevelt elk, and black bear. Drift Creek sustains wild runs of chinook, steelhead, and coho, which come up the Alsea River.

Steep ridges and their drainages, as well as small meadows, make up the topography, which is accessed via a couple of hiking trails. The trailhead closest to Waldport is the **Harris Ranch Trail,** which descends 1,200 feet in two miles to a meadow near Drift Creek. The local access to Harris Ranch and Horse Creek trails leaves ORE 34 at the Alsea River crossing seven miles east of Waldport. Here, pick up Risely Creek Road (Forest Service Road 3446) and FS Road 346. The wilderness is administered by the Siuslaw National Forest–Waldport Ranger Station (541/ 563-3211) which can supply specific directions to the different trailheads into this increasingly rare ecosystem.

Fishing

Waldport's recreational raison d'être is fishing. World-class clamming and Dungeness crabbing in Alsea Bay and the Alsea River's famous salmon, steelhead, and cutthroat trout runs account for a high percentage of visits to the area. Before commercial fishing on the river was shut down in 1957, as much as 137,000 pounds of chinook were netted in a season. The wild fall chinook run remains healthy and starts up in late August. Catch-and-release for sea-run cutthroats starts in mid-August, while steelhead are in the river December–March. Crabbers without boats can take advantage of the Port of Waldport docks.

Gene-O's Guide Service (P.O. Box 43, Waldport 97374, 541/563-3171) calls on four decades of experience to help you reel in salmon and steelhead. Dock of the Bay Marina (1245 NE Mill, 541/563-2003) and Kozy Kove Marina (9646 Alsea Hwy.) rent and sell crabbing and fishing supplies and can guide you to the best spots.

Golf

Crestview Hills Golf Course (1680 Crestline Dr., Waldport, 541/563-3020 or 888/538-4463, open year-round, green fees $14 for 9 holes, $20 for 18 holes) is a public nine-hole course one mile south of Waldport.

ACCOMMODATIONS

"Cottage" is a word often used to describe accommodations between Yachats and Waldport. It may be a duplex or self-contained cabin-type lodging, generally by a beach. The prices gener

> *Waldport's recreational raison d'être is fishing. World-class clamming and Dungeness crabbing in Alsea Bay and the Alsea River's famous salmon, steelhead, and cutthroat trout runs account for a high percentage of visits to the area.*

ally range $70–150 for units with kitchen facilities, fireplaces, and oceanfront locations.

Vacation Rentals

Other lodging options are the rental houses of **Horizon Property** (541/563-5151). Oceanfront digs are available and prices are extremely reasonable. For more information, call the **Central Oregon Coast Association** (800/767-2064).

Motels

The **Terry-a-While Motel** (7160 SW U.S. 101, 541/563-3377, www.terry-a-while.com, $50–110) has well-appointed rooms that range in style (modern to vintage) and size (the newer four-plex is ideal for families).

The beachfront **Edgewater Cottages** (3978 SW U.S. 101, 541/563-2240, www .edgewatercottages.com, $75–85) come complete with view, full kitchen, and a wood-burning fireplace. Ask about the minimum-stay policy before booking. For similarly equipped rooms, try **Cape Cod Cottages** (4150 SW U.S. 101, 541/563-2106, www.dreamwater.com, $69–89).

Hotel

Formerly the Bayshore Inn, the **Evening Star Resort** (902 NW Bayshore Dr., 541/563-7700 or 877/327-6500, www.eveningstarresort.com, $59–150) prides itself on great service. Half of the 84 rooms enjoy sweeping views of the bay, bridge, and town, and all are equipped with either one or two queen-sized beds and the usual amenities. There's also a dining room and cocktail lounge, with occasional entertainment, and a fitness room.

Bed-and-Breakfast

The historic **Cliff House** (1450 Adahi Rd., 541/563-2506, www.cliffhouseoregon.com, $110–225) may appear to be rustic, but its bluff location can't be beat to set a romantic mood. Four rooms, some with whirlpools, are decorated with antiques—even the woodstoves are period. No pets are allowed, and children are best left at home with a family member or the sitter.

Campgrounds

Two excellent campgrounds sit about four miles south of Waldport on U.S. 101 along the beach. **Beachside State Park** (information 541/563-3220 or 800/551-6949, reservations 800/452-5687) is located near one-half mile of beach not far from Alsea Bay and Alsea River. This is a paradise for rock fishers, surfcasters, clammers, and crabbers. For $16–19 per night from mid-April to mid-October, there are 50 tent sites, 32 sites for RVs up to 30 feet long, and some hiker/biker sites. Beachside fills up fast, with such amenities as a laundry room and hot showers, so reserve early for space between Memorial Day and Labor Day.

One-half mile down U.S. 101, the Forest Service has comparable site offerings at **Tillicum Beach** (reservations 877/444-6777, www.reserveusa.com, $15). Set right along the ocean, the campground is open all year but requires reservations. You have the full range of creature comforts here, plus ranger campfire programs in summer. Forest Service roads from Tillicum Beach access Coast Range fishing streams, which are detailed in a Forest Service map. You'll also appreciate the strip of vegetation blocking the cool evening winds that whip up off the ocean here.

If Beachside and Tillicum are filled to overflowing, you might want to set up a base camp in the Coast Range along ORE 34—especially if you have fishing or hiking in the Drift Creek Wilderness in mind. Just go east of Waldport 17 miles on ORE 34 to the Siuslaw National Forest's **Blackberry Campground** (reservations 877/444-6777, www.reserveusa.com, $10). The 33 sites are open year-round for tents and RVs, most of them on the river. A boat ramp, flush toilets, and piped water are on-site. This is a good base for a fishing trip.

FOOD

Forget fine dining in Waldport—this is an eat 'n' run town. Unless you want to drive to the Yachats branch, **Leroy's Blue Whale** (541/563-3445) located right on U.S. 101 is one of few choices.

Standard American

Grand Central Pizza (245 U.S. 101, 541/563-3232) is a favorite with the locals, across the street from the 76 gas station—you can't miss it. *Oregon Coast* magazine voted this the best pie on the coast. In addition to spaghetti dinners, lasagna, and pizza, the homemade garlic rolls, selection of microbrews, fish and chips, and grinder sandwiches are also noteworthy. Best of all, the largest appetites can be sated here for less than $10.

For a hearty breakfast and other meal specials served in a sport-lovers atmosphere, replete with big-screen TV, the **Flounder Inn Tavern** (U.S. 101, 541/563-2266) offers customers lots of pub grub choices, including fish and chips and a popular roasted chicken dinner.

These self-described "family-friendly restaurants" can be counted on for low prices and a varied menu of American food. Vickie's Big Wheel (541/563-3640), at the sound end of the Alsea Bridge, is such a place, with the self-proclaimed "best cheeseburger on the coast." These places stay open in January when many of the other eateries in nearby Yachats close early or suspend operation for the month.

For food served in a bar setting, there's the **Salty Dawg Bar and Grill** (360 E. Port St., 541/563-2555), with traditional American fare and some Mexican specialties. Or, a few miles east of Waldport on Highway 34, go to **Buck's Ranch House** (3349 Alsea Hwy., 541/563-2825) and order up a steak or fried ling cod, or head over to the smoker-friendly bar for a drink.

Upriver Dining

If you're interested in a unique dining experience, follow ORE 34 along the Alsea River for nine miles to a most unlikely site for a good restaurant. Attached to a trailer court and convenience store is the **Kozy Kove Kafe** (9464 ORE 34, Tidewater 97390, 541/528-3251, 9 A.M.–5 P.M. Wed.–Sun.). The dining room and lounge float on a bed of logs by a riverbank and are well placed to observe Australian black swans, elk, salmon jumping in September, and other wildlife. Breakfasts (three-egg omelets with ingredients such as Cajun-smoked salmon and herb cream cheese) are hearty, and lunch and dinner focus on fresh seafood, steak, and prime rib. Clam chowder and strawberry shortcake are recommended accompaniments. Mexican (try the "fajitas with the flame") and Italian entrées add spice to this retreat.

Japanese

Yuzen (U.S. 101, Seal Rock, 541/563-4766, lunch until 2 P.M. and dinner 4–9 P.M. Tues.–Sun.), five miles north of Waldport, is a Japanese restaurant with an oddly Bavarian facade. Well worth a stop, this country-style Japanese food at moderate to expensive prices attracts crowds, so avoid peak dining hours. In addition to sushi and miso soup, lesser-known fare such as fish noodle soup, minced pork or rock shrimp dumplings, and *syo-yaki* (a small, whole broiled fish encrusted in salt) leave room for new discoveries. To enjoy a high-priced gourmet treat at a moderate price here, we recommend sharing an order of *shabu shabu* (paper-thin beef, fresh vegetables, and tofu boiled in a pot and served with three gourmet sauces). With salad and dessert, three people could get away with paying less than $15 apiece.

INFORMATION AND SERVICES

Information

The Walport Chamber of Commerce operates a **visitors center** (P.O. Box 669, Waldport 97394, 541/563-2133, www.pioneer.net/~waldport) in the Alsea Bay Bridge Historical Interpretive Center, just south of the river. The chamber is open 9 A.M.–5 P.M. daily in summer, 9 A.M.–4 P.M. Tuesday–Saturday the rest of the year.

The **Siuslaw National Forest–Waldport Ranger Station** (1094 SW U.S. 101, Waldport 97394, 541/563-3211) can provide information on area camping and hiking, including the trails in the Drift Creek Wilderness.

For banking and walk-up ATM, the Waldport branch of **Bank of Newport** (433 Hwy. 34) can provide these services.

Transportation

ORE 34 runs east from Waldport, following the Alsea River for several miles before veering northeast to Corvallis, about 65 miles away.

Waldport gets bus service from **Greyhound (800/231-2222) and Lincoln County Transit** (541/265-4900). Stops are at the Waldport Ranger Station (1094 U.S. 101) and the Waldport Senior Center (265 Elsie Hwy.). The Lincoln County buses run four times a day Monday–Saturday between Yachats and Newport.

Newport and Vicinity

In January 1852, a storm grounded the schooner *Juliet* near Yaquina (pronounced yah-KWIN-nah) Bay, where her captain and crew were stranded for two months. When they finally made their way inland to the Willamette Valley, they reported on their discovery of an abundance of tiny, sweet-tasting oysters in the bay. Within a decade, commercial oyster farms were established here, and these were the first major impetus to growth and settlement in Newport. The tasty morsels that delighted diners in San Francisco and at New York's Waldorf-Astoria Hotel are almost gone now, but the oyster industry continues in a limited way harvesting introduced species.

The port bustles with the activity of Oregon's largest commercial fishing fleet and second-largest recreational fleet. New factories to process *surimi* (a fish paste popular in Japan) and whiting have provided hundreds of jobs here, and a state-of-the-art aquarium that once housed Keiko the whale (from the movie *Free Willy*) brings in tourist dollars. In this vein, new wildlife observation facilities and improved access to tidepools north of town at Yaquina Head promise to make this park a highlight of the coast. The shops, galleries, and restaurants along Newport's historic Bayfront, together with the Performing Arts Center and quieter charm of Nye Beach, keep up a tourism tradition that goes back to when this town was the "honeymoon capital of Oregon." Today, Newport (pop. 9,960) boasts more oceanfront hotel rooms than any place between San Francisco and Seattle, except perhaps for Lincoln City. This can make for traffic jams on holiday weekends, but it's a small price to pay for proximity to some of the coast's best agate-hunting beaches, cultural programs, and restaurants.

SIGHTS

Oregon State University Hatfield Marine Science Center

Just south of the Yaquina Bay Bridge, head east on the road that parallels the bay to the OSU Hatfield Marine Science Center (Marine Science Dr., Newport 97365, 541/867-0100, http://hmsc.oregonstate.edu). This research and education facility is a low-key but still interesting complement to the very popular Oregon Coast Aquarium, located one-half mile south. At the door to greet you is an octopus in an open tank pointing the way to oceanography exhibits and a hands-on area where you can experience the feel of starfish, anemones, and other sea creatures. The back hallway has educational dioramas, and a theater shows marine-science films throughout the day. If you proceed left from the octopus tank, you'll see tanks with different sea ecosystems. Beyond the walls of the museum, guided field trips are offered (for a fee) to explore estuary, beach, and coastal forest habitats at various times of the year (check with the front desk or the website for details). The bookstore has a good selection of nature-focused books, posters, games, and gifts.

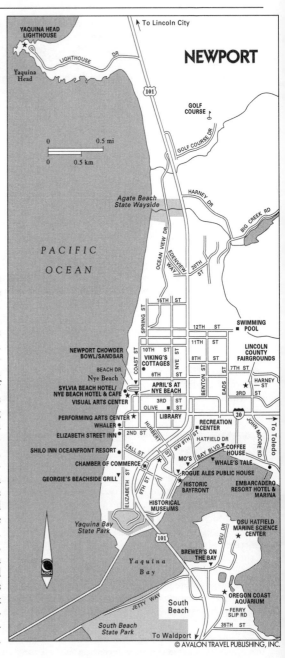

The Marine Science Center is open 10 A.M.–5 P.M. daily in summer and 10 A.M.–4 P.M. Thursday–Monday the rest of the year. During Whale Watch weeks (Christmas break and spring break), the center temporarily returns to its summer hours. Admission is free, but a $3 donation is suggested to support the center and its programs.

The Oregon Coast Aquarium

There are 6,000 miles of water between the Oregon coast and Japan—the largest stretch of open ocean on earth. You can hear *our* side of the story at the Oregon Coast Aquarium (2820 SE Ferry Slip Rd., Newport 97305, 541/867-3474, www.aquarium.org), one of the most popular attractions in the state.

The aquarium initially featured 40,000 square feet of galleries devoted to wetland communities, near-shore and marine ecosystems, and an environmental center. Although it was respected as a top-notch educational facility, it lacked "star power" until the 1996 arrival of Keiko, a 7,720-pound, 32-foot-long orca who starred in *Free Willy*. Understandably, his presence overshadowed four acres of sea lions, sea otters, tidepools, and undersea caves, as well as the largest walk-in seabird aviary in the Americas. Now there is an attraction that might make people forget that the whale-sized attraction moved to Iceland in 1998 for his reentry into the wild.

One of the gems of the aquarium is "Passages of the Deep," a 200-foot-long, acrylic tunnel offering 360-degree underwater views in three diverse habitats, from "Orford Reef" to "Halibut Flats" to "Open Sea," where you're surrounded by free-swimming sharks. The "Jewels of the Sea" exhibit showcases several dozen kinds of jellyfish in an almost psychedelic display.

"At the Jetty" is the aquarium's largest permanent indoor exhibit to date. Visitors look through a window into a 35,000-gallon tank to watch white sturgeon and coho and chinook salmon swimming among large basalt boulders that simulate a coastal jetty, such as these anadromous fish in the wild might pass through on their upriver journey to their spawning grounds.

Of the several hundred species of Pacific Northwest fish, birds, and mammals on display in the rest of the facility, don't miss the sea otters, wolf eel, leopard sharks, lion's mane jellyfish, and the tufted puffins. The younger set will enjoy the sea cave with simulated wave action, which houses a resident octopus.

Indigenous simulated ecosystems help articulate the region's biology. The centerpiece of the Wetland's Gallery, for example, is a cross-section of the salt marsh subject to the periodic ebb and flow of tides. Another ecological niche is illustrated by a 4,730-gallon tank in the Sandy Shores exhibit. Here, you can see smelt, perch, and leopard sharks navigate amid human-made rocks and piers. The Rock Shores Gallery adds another dimension to the experience with an open tidepool that allows visitors to handle starfish, sea anemones, and the like. In the outside aviary and sea mammal pools, latex molds of rocky outcroppings provide perches for birds, otters, and sea lions (some of these animals were rescued from such debacles as the *Exxon Valdez* oil spill).

In addition to leaving here with a heightened understanding of the coast biome, you might also come away with something from the museum shop's first-rate collection of regional books and oceanographic tomes or perhaps some crystals or gemstones. The Mermaid Café is also onsite, emphasizing such Oregon fare as Tillamook dairy products, seasonal fruits, and seafood. Outside in the summer, enjoy barbecued burgers and hot dogs and teriyaki shish kebabs.

The aquarium is open daily year-round (except Christmas Day): 9 A.M.–6 P.M. Memorial Day–Labor Day, 10 A.M.–5 P.M. the rest of the year. Admission is $10.75 adults, $9.50 seniors, $6.50 ages 4–13, free ages four and under. Advance tickets are recommended on weekends, major holidays, and during the summer. To get there from U.S. 101, turn east on OSU Drive or 32nd Street, south of the Yaquina Bay Bridge, and follow Ferry Slip Road to the parking lot.

Oregon Coast History Center

For a glimpse into the rich past of Lincoln County, stop at the Oregon Coast History Center (545 SW 9th St., Newport 97365, 541/265-7509, 10 A.M.–5 P.M. Tues.–Sun. June–Sept., 11 A.M.–4 P.M. Oct.–May, free), which incorporates the Log

© MARK MORRIS

The keeper's cottage at the Yaquina Bay Lighthouse has been restored with 1870s vintage furnishings.

Cabin Museum and the adjacent Queen Anne–style Burrows House, a former boardinghouse built in 1895. It's located one-half block east of the chamber of commerce on U.S. 101. The logging, farming, pioneer life, and maritime exhibits (particularly Newport shipwrecks) are interesting, but the Siletz Indian baskets and other Native American artifacts steal the show.

Here you can learn the heartbreaking story of the hardships—forced displacement, inadequate housing, insufficient food, and poor medical facilities—that plagued the diverse tribes that made up the Confederated Siletz Indian Reservation. These dozen tribes were defeated during the Rogue Indian Wars and other conflicts of the 1850s. In 1856, 2,000 of these coastal natives were marched to a north coast reservation site. At the end of one year their numbers had dwindled to 600.

The Bayfront

Newport's Old Town Bayfront District can be easy to miss if you're not alert. At the north end of the Yaquina Bay Bridge, look for the signs pointing off U.S. 101, which lead you down the hill to

Bay Boulevard, the Bayfront's main drag. Alternately, turn southeast off the highway a few blocks north onto Hurbert Street; this runs into Canyon Way, which ends at Bay. On summer weekends, forget about parking anywhere here unless you arrive early. Spots close by the boulevard can often be found, however, along Canyon Way, the hillside access route to downtown.

Until 1936, ferries shuttled people and vehicles to and from Newport's waterfront. With the completion of the Yaquina Bay Bridge that year, however, traffic bypassed the old town area. Commerce and development moved to the highway corridor, and the Bayfront faded in importance. Within the last couple of decades, the pendulum has swung back, and the Bayfront District is now one of Newport's prime attractions, with some of its best restaurants and watering holes, shopping, and tourist facilities.

One of the first things that will strike you about the Bayfront today is that it's still a working neighborhood, not a sanitized re-creation of a real seaport. Chowderhouses, galleries, and shops stand shoulder to shoulder with fish-pro-

© MARK MORRIS

Conde B. McCullough's elegant 1936 bridge over Yaquina Bay

cessing plants and canneries, and the air is filled with the cries of fishmongers purveying wharfside walkaway cocktails and the harmonious discord of sea lions and harbor seals. On the waterfront, sport anglers step off charter boats with their catches, and you can observe vessels laden with everything from wood products to whale-watchers out in the bay. Unfortunately, the stringent catch limits and cost of equipment make this less of a working port every year. In deference to Oregon commercial anglers and other endangered species, wall murals memorialize fishing boats and whales here on the Bayfront.

Yaquina Bay State Park

In 1871, a lighthouse was built here on a bluff overlooking the mouth of Yaquina Bay, and the lighthouse keeper, his wife, and seven children moved into the two-story wood-frame structure. It soon became apparent, however, that the location was not ideal because the light could not be seen by ships approaching the harbor from the north, and the station was abandoned after just three years, after the light at Yaquina Head was completed. The building was slated for demolition in 1934, when local residents formed

the Lincoln County Historical Society to preserve it. In 1997, the government decided to turn Yaquina Bay's beacon back on.

Today, the handsomely restored structure and surrounding grounds make up Yaquina Bay State Park (541/574-3129 or 800/551-6949), in a beautiful location at the north end of the Yaquina Bay Bridge. It's the oldest building in Newport and the last wooden lighthouse on the Oregon coast. The living quarters, replete with period furnishings, are open daily noon–4 P.M.; admission is free. Be sure to ask the volunteers about the resident ghost here.

From the parking area, you have an excellent photo op of the bay and the bridge. The park is a good place to have a picnic, or you can descend the trails to the beach and dig for razor clams or hunt for agates and petrified wood.

Nye Beach

The 1890s-era tourism boom that came to Newport's Bayfront spilled over into Nye Beach. In 1891, the city built a wooden sidewalk connecting the two neighborhoods, and soon "summer people" were filling the cedar cottages here. In the next century, thanks to an improved

wheelchair-accessible tidepools, Yaquina Head Outstanding Natural Area

river-and-land route from Corvallis, health faddists (who came for hot seawater baths in the sanatorium) and honeymooners soon joined the mix.

Located one mile north from the Bayfront, to the west of U.S. 101 (look for signs on the highway), this one-time favorite retreat for wealthy Portlanders has undergone a revival in recent years. Rough times and rougher weather had reduced luxurious beach houses here to a cluster of weather-beaten shacks until a performing arts center went up two decades ago. On the heels of the development of this first-rate cultural facility, the conversion of a 1910 hotel into a kind of literary hostel (see the listing for Sylvia Beach Hotel in the Accommodations section) has encouraged other restorations and plenty of new construction. Culture vultures, beach lovers, and people-watchers now flock to Nye Beach. Some larger resort and chain hotels have sprung up among the Cape Cod cottages, aging hippies, artists, and friendly fisherfolk, and not everyone is happy about the developments here, as such signs as "The Real Nye Beach—R.I.P." attest. Still, there's plenty of character and charm in this neighborhood, which feels a world

away from the Coast Highway commercial strip just a few blocks to the east.

Yaquina Head Outstanding Natural Area

Five miles north of Newport, rocky Yaquina Head juts out to sea. Tools dating back 5,000 years have been unearthed at Yaquina Head. Many were made from elk and deer antler and bone, as well as stone. Clam and mussel shells from middens in the area evidence a diet rich in shellfish for the area's ancient inhabitants.

Today, much of the headland is encompassed in the Yaquina Head Outstanding Natural Area (P.O. Box 936, Newport 97365, 541/574-3100), managed by the Bureau of Land Management (BLM). Outstanding is the word for this place, and a visitor could easily spend several hours out here exploring all the site has to offer.

At its outer tip stands **Yaquina Head Light-house,** the coast's tallest beacon. In the early 1870s, materials intended for construction of a lighthouse several miles north at Otter Crest were mistakenly delivered here. The 93-foot tower began operation in 1873 and replaced the poorly located lighthouse south of here at the mouth of Newport's harbor. Walk up the 114 cast-iron steps for a spectacular panorama of the headland and surrounding coast. The lighthouse is open daily, weather permitting.

Below, an observation deck provides views of seals, sea lions, gray whales, and seabirds. Of the half-dozen varieties of pelagic birds that cluster on Colony Rock—a large monolith in the shallows 200 yards offshore—the tufted puffin is the most colorful. It's sometimes called a sea parrot because of its large yellow-orange bill. Puffins arrive here in April and are most visible early in the day on the rock's grassy patches. The most ubiquitous species here are common murres, guillemots, and cormorants. The murre's white breasts and bellies contrast with their darker bills and elongated backs. The guillemots resemble pigeons, but with white wing patches and bright red webbed feet. The cormorants look like prehistoric pelicans.

East of the lighthouse, the large Interpretive Center (541/574-3116, open 10 A.M.–5 P.M. daily in summer, until 4 P.M. the rest of the year) features exhibits on local ecosystems, Indian culture, and historical artifacts such as a 19th-century lighthouse keeper's journal. Other highlights include a life-size replica of the Fresnel lens that shines from the top of the nearby lighthouse, a sea cave simulation with a life-size mural of a California gray whale (accompanied by an exhibit detailing its migratory pattern), as well as statues of birds and harbor seals, and information on tidepool inhabitants.

Close by, wheelchair-friendly paths give access to tidepools, augmented by the hand of man, in an abandoned basalt quarry on the south side of the headland. Enjoy sea stars, purple urchins, anemones, and hermit crabs at low tide.

The fee to enter Yaquina Head is $5 per car, which is valid for three days. The Pacific Coast Passport is also valid here.

Beaches

North of town, **Agate Beach** is a broad swath of coastline famed for its agate-hunting opportunities (see the sidebar "Agate-Hunting") and its views of nearby Yaquina Head. In ad-

---

AGATE-HUNTING

Hunting for agate after winter storms is a passion at several Oregon beaches, particularly around Newport. Before the Ice Age, metals, oxides, and silicates were fused together to create this type of quartz. Red, amber, blue, and other tones sometimes form stripes or spots in the translucent rocks. One of the best places to find these treasures is on the beach north of Hotel Newport, appropriately called Agate Beach. Nearby Moolack Beach and the beach at Seal Rock, north of Waldport, as well as area estuaries and streambeds, are more spots worth a look October–May. Procure the free pamphlet *Agates: Their Formation and How to Hunt for Them* from the Greater Newport Chamber of Commerce before setting out.

---

dition to the semiprecious stones, the contemplative appeals of Agate Beach inspired no less a figure than Ernest Bloch, the noted Swiss composer who lived here from 1940 until his death in 1959. Famed violinist Yehudi Menuhin spoke of Bloch and the locale thusly: "Agate Beach is a wild forlorn stretch of coastline looking down upon waves coming in all the way from Asia to break on the shore, a place which suited the grandeur and intensity of Bloch's character." Each summer, the Ernest Bloch Music Festival pays tribute to the spirit and music of this man.

Moolack Beach, two miles north of Yaquina Head, is a favorite with kite flyers and agate hunters. Another 1.5 miles north, at **Beverly Beach,** 20-million-year-old fossils have been found in the sandstone cliffs above the shore. Beverly Beach also attracts waders, unique for Oregon's chilly waters. Offshore sandbars temper the waves and the weather, so it's not as rough or as cold as many coastal locales. This long stretch of sand (panoramic photos are best taken from Yaquina Head Lighthouse looking north) is rated among America's 50 best beaches in a list that considers scenic and recreational appeals.

The beach at **Yaquina Bay State Park,** accessible via a trail from the bluff-top parking area, is a popular spot for clam-digging and agate-hunting.

Two miles south of the Yaquina Bay Bridge, **South Beach State Park** draws beachcombers, anglers, and picnickers to its miles of broad, sandy beach. The large campground here is the closest available to Newport.

Toledo

Aficionados of antiquities can head east of Newport six miles up the Yaquina River on Highway 20 to Toledo, where "junque" shops abound. This small town's fortunes have risen and fallen with the timber cut. At one time, the world's largest spruce mill was here, but in the era of big timber's swan song, dealers of collectibles have sprouted up to take advantage of coast-bound traffic from the Willamette Valley. Most of the antique shops are located on Main Street. Recently, timber has enjoyed a resurgence here, with the mill getting old-growth logs submerged in Yaquina Bay during World War II.

RECREATION

Fishing

Newport is one of the top spots on the coast for charter fishing, and opportunities are plentiful here at the home port of Oregon's second-largest recreational fleet. Bottom fishing (year-round), tuna fishing (Aug.–Oct.), crabbing (year-round), and salmon and halibut fishing (seasonal) are all possible. Typical rates here are $55 for a half day of bottom fishing, $100 for a full day; $100 for an eight-hour salmon outing; $175 for 12 hours of tuna fishing; $150 for a 12-hour halibut charter.

In addition to a full menu of fishing excursions, most Newport operators also offer whale-watching charters. These include **Newport Marina Store and Charters** (2212 OSU Dr., South Beach, 541/867-4470 or 877/867-4470, www.newportmarinacharters.com), which offers a combination crabbing and fishing trip, $65 for six hours; **Newport Tradewinds** (653 SW Bay Blvd., 541/265-2101 or 800/676-7819, www.newporttradewinds.com); and **Sea Gull Charters, Inc.** (343 SW Bay Blvd., 541/265-7441 or 800/865-7441, www.seagullcharters.com).

For those who prefer to take matters into their own hands, the clamming and Dungeness crabbing are superlative in Yaquina Bay. If you haven't done this before, local tackle shops, such as the Newport Marina Store in South Beach, will rent crab pots or rings and offer instruction. The best time to dig clams is at an extremely low tide. At that time, look for clammers grabbing up cockles in the shallows of the bay. Tide tables are available from the chamber of commerce and many local businesses.

Whale-Watching

In addition to the fishing charter companies, which all offer whale-watching tours, the best company on the coast in terms of having state-of-the-art equipment and natural-history interpretation is **Marine Discovery Tours** (345 SW Bay Blvd., 800/903-BOAT or 800/903-2628, www.marinediscovery.com, two-hour SeaLife tour $25 adults, $20 ages 13–16, $14 ages 4–12). Whale-watching, seal- and bird-watching, an oyster bed tour, estuary and ocean exploration, and a harbor tour, narrated by naturalist guides, exemplify their offerings. Their 65-foot *Discovery* features videocameras that magnify the fascinating interplay between smaller life forms, but the real attractions can be appreciated by the naked eye. Landlubbers will especially relish the full crab pots pulled up from the deep and the resident pod of whales often visible north of Yaquina Bay off Yaquina Head.

During the prime whale-watching weeks of late December and late March, volunteers from Whale Watching Spoken Here staff the **Don A. Davis City Kiosk** in Nye Beach to answer questions and help you spot whales.

Golf

The public course closest to Newport is nine-hole **Agate Beach Golf Course** (4100 North Coast Hwy., 541/265-7331, open year-round, green fees $14 for 9 holes, $28 for 18 holes), just north of town. The views of Yaquina Head alone are worth a visit.

Bike Rental

In Nye Beach, **The Bike Shop** (223 NW Nye St., 541/265-2481) has a good selection for rent.

Other Recreation

Newport Parks and Recreation Department operates the **Municipal Swimming Pool** (1212 NE Fogarty, 541/265-7770), which opens in June. Public **tennis courts** are located one block north of the pool. The **Newport Recreation Center** (225 SE Avery St., 541/265-7783) offers a variety of organized and drop-in activities, including basketball, volleyball, soccer, tennis, and roller skating.

ENTERTAINMENT

Overlooking the sea in Nye Beach, the **Newport Performing Arts Center** (777 W. Olive, 541/265-2787, www.coastarts.org/pac), the coast's largest performance venue, hosts local and national entertainment in the 400-seat Alice Silverman Theatre and the smaller Studio Theatre. At the same address is the **Oregon Coast Council for the Arts,** (541/265-9231 or 888/701-7123, www.coastarts.org), which puts out a free monthly newsletter and has ticket information on the PAC venues. It also has updates on the **Newport Visual Arts Center** (777 NW Beach Dr., 541/265-6540), located right above the beach two blocks north at the Nye Beach turnaround. The two floors and two galleries here offer art-education programs and exhibition space for paintings, sculpture, and other works, often with a maritime theme. Runyan Gallery is open 11 A.M.–6 P.M. Tuesday–Sunday. Upstairs Gallery is open noon–4 P.M. Tuesday–Saturday. Admission is free.

In addition to its impressive schedule of music, dance, drama, and other arts, the Performing Arts Center screens a series of imported and art films—the ones you probably won't find at Newport's multiplex: **Newport Cinema** (5836 N. Coast Hwy., 541/265-2111).

In the Bayfront District, Mariner Square (250 SW Bay Blvd., 541/265-2206) is a complex of three attractions that mostly appeal to kids: **Ripley's Believe It or Not!, The Waxworks,** and **The Undersea Gardens.** Admission per attraction is $6.95 adults, $3.95 children; discounts are offered to hardy souls who want to take in all three.

EVENTS

The biggest bash here (and one of the largest events of its kind in the country) is late February's **Newport Seafood and Wine Festival** (541/265-8801 or 800/262-7844, $6–9, ages 21 and over only), which features dozens of food booths and scores of Oregon wineries serving up these palate pleasers, along with music and crafts, at the South Beach Marina (across Yaquina Bay from the Bayfront). A huge tent joins the exhibition hall, wherein festivalgoers wash down delights from the deep with Oregon vintages.

The second event of note is **Loyalty Days and Sea Fair** (541/265-8801 or 800/262-7844) in early May, focusing on sailboat races, a chicken feed, and a parade. What began during the Depression as the Crab Festival, intended to stimulate the market for Dungeness crab, was recast during the depths of the Red Scare of the 1950s as a public expression of patriotism. These days, that aspect still undergirds the events, as evidenced by visiting naval vessels, but it's really just a big community party stretching over four days, with carnival rides, boat tours, yacht races, bed races, a car show, a parade, and the coronation of the Crab Queen. An admission fee is charged.

Each summer, the lectures, recitals, and concerts of the **Ernest Bloch Music Festival** (information 541/765-3142, tickets 541/265-2787, www.coastarts.org/pac) are eagerly anticipated by classical music lovers. Usually, it takes place from the end of June through mid-July, at the Newport Performing Arts Center (777 W. Olive St.), with related performances at other locales along the central coast. Along with Bloch's compositions, works by Schubert, Ravel, Saint-Saëns, and other icons of classical music are performed by top musicians in this acoustically superior hall. This event and Lincoln City's Cascade Head Chamber Music Festival are considered the coast's preeminent classical music offerings. Ticket prices range from free to $25.

The **Fourth of July fireworks** display, shot off from the South Beach Marina, is a crowd-pleasing spectacle. Vantage points include Yaquina Bay State Park, the bridge, and the beach. July is also the month for the **Lincoln County Fair and Rodeo** (541/265-6237), held over four days on the third weekend of the month, at the Lincoln County Fairgrounds, on the east side of town one block north of Highway 20.

"Suds & Surf" is the theme at the annual mid-October **Newport Microbrew Festival** (541/265-8801 or 800/262-7844, $6, ages 21 and over only), held at the Rogue Ales Brewery (2320 OSU Dr., Newport, 541/867-3660), at South Beach Marina, just south of the bridge. This event, Oregon's second-largest microbrew festival, brings together 30 of the Northwest's finest craft breweries, complemented by musical entertainment and a variety of food and arts-and-crafts booths. The festival also features commercial and home-brew competitions.

ACCOMMODATIONS

Motels

Viking's Cottages (729 NW Coast St., 541/265-2477 or 800/480-2477, www.vikingsoregoncoast .com, $70–200) has Cape Cod–style cabins with kitchens, recommended for those who want to experience 1920s Nye Beach houses with modern conveniences and kitchens. Most have no phones, however, and only showers. The decks and stairs to the beach are what they're more about anyway. Most cost less than $100 per night, and the large ones cost $200 and sleep 6–8 people.

Built in the 1940s and recently refurbished, the **Agate Beach Motel** (175 NW Gilbert Way, 541/265-8746 or 800/755-5674, www .agatebeachmotel.com, $85–145) has 10 simple but charming beachfront units overlooking Agate Beach, each with a private bedroom, kitchen, living room, and sundeck. Drop-ins are welcome, but reservations are recommended.

Hostel

The **Brown Squirrel Hostel** (44 SW Brook St., 541/265-3729, $15–20) charges a minimal fee for a room with shared bath and bunk beds (bring your sleeping bag). It's one block from the beach.

Hotels

The Nye Beach community is the place to go for a taste of tradition and salt air. Close by are excellent restaurants, the Performing Arts Center, and, of course, the beach.

The **Sylvia Beach Hotel** (267 NW Cliff St., 541/265-5428, rooms $83–173, dorm bed $25) combines the camaraderie of a hostel with the intimate charm of a bed-and-breakfast. Built in the era when the Corvallis–Yaquina Bay train and seven-seater Studebaker touring cars from Portland ferried the summer folks to Nye Beach, this hostelry was considered the height of luxury. Known as the Cliff House and later on as the Gilmore Hotel, even a "Honeymoon Capital of Oregon" sobriquet could not forestall its eventually being overshadowed by newer, more elaborate resorts.

Its rebirth as the Sylvia Beach Hotel was expedited by a National Historic Landmark designation and a literary theme that has attracted an enthusiastic following. The 20 guest rooms have been named after different authors and furnished with decor evocative of each respective literary legacy. The Edgar Allen Poe Room, for instance, has a pendulum guillotine blade, stuffed ravens, and who knows what else, given Poe's recurring theme of cementing family relations. The Hemingway Room features mounted hunting trophies. The Tennessee Williams Room sets the stage with a ceiling fan, a glass menagerie, and mosquito netting, while the Agatha Christie Room drops such clues as shoes underneath the curtains and capsules marked "Poison" in the medicine cabinet.

The Sylvia Beach would be just another cute idea were it not for an imaginative innkeeper who even facilitates guest interactions. This often comes to pass over the tasty dinners in the hotel's Tables of Content restaurant (see the Food section). Hot spiced wine is served, along with a great view of Yaquina Head Lighthouse, in the library at 10 P.M., which often leads to conversations far into the night.

Most of the rooms ("bestsellers") run $118, with several oceanfront suites ("classics") featuring a fireplace and deck going for $173. Novels go for $83. Particularly recommended is the Mark Twain Suite, featuring an outside patio

Sylvia Beach Hotel in Newport Beach's hip Nye Beach district

facing south. This exposure acts as a buffer to the north winds of summer. All of these rates include a full breakfast and reflect double occupancy. Single patrons pay $10 less. At breakfast, you have a choice of entrées and share a table with eight other guests, so misanthropes beware! The fact that no smoking, pets, or radios are allowed on the premises should also be mentioned. Small children are discouraged. And if you're looking for a budget room, Sylvia Beach features dormitory bunk beds for $25 per night. Even if you don't stay here, you're invited to come by for a look at unoccupied rooms whose doors are always left open for this purpose.

To get there, turn off U.S. 101 on NW 3rd and follow it down to the beach, where NW 3rd and Cliff streets meet. Then look for a large four-story dark green vintage wooden structure with a red roof on a bluff above the surf.

Two doors down, another retreat from the ordinary is **The Nye Beach Hotel & Café** (219 NW Cliff St., 541/265-3334, $65 and up). Eighteen rooms feature all the modern amenities (ex-

cept phones), fireplaces, and willow loveseats on oceanview balconies; then add whimsical decor evocative of the era when Newport was Oregon's self-proclaimed Honeymoon Capital. The small bistro-café, a bright, airy restaurant serving creative, multiethnic small plates, is the perfect Valentine's Day getaway. It also has a sunset-friendly outside deck.

Surprisingly, some of the least expensive view rooms in town are available at the **Shilo Inn Oceanfront Resort** (536 SW Elizabeth St., 541/265-7701 or 800/222-2244, $95–165). This chain inn offers 149 standard-equipped rooms, as well as two on-site restaurants and two indoor pools, and it's kid- and pet-friendly.

Just down the street is the **Elizabeth Street Inn** (232 SW Elizabeth St., 541/265-9400 or 877/265-9400, www.elizabethstreetinn.com, $99–199) on a bluff overlooking the ocean. All of the rooms in this newer property face the ocean and have private balconies. They come fully equipped with all the modern conveniences. Guests also get a complimentary continental

CENTRAL COAST

breakfast and have use of the indoor pool, spa, and fitness room.

For comfort, you can't beat **The Whaler** (155 SW Elizabeth St., 541/265-9261 or 800/433-9444, www.whalernewport.com, $109 and up). With 73 rooms—each with a view and some with fireplaces, wet bars, and private balconies—guests are treated to fresh-popped popcorn, pool facilities, and continental breakfast.

The ever-popular **Embarcadero Resort Hotel & Marina** (1000 SE Bay Blvd., 541/265-8521 or 800/547-4779, www.embarcadero-resort.com, $80 and up), overlooking Yaquina Bay, has an assortment of suites and townhouses with full kitchens and fireplaces. Off-water studios start at $80, and rates go up from there.

The **Best Western Agate Beach Inn** (3019 N. Coast Hwy., 541/265-9411 or 800/547-3310, www.newportbestwestern.com, up to $119 in summer) is yet another oceanfront hotel, but with a fine view overlooking Yaquina Head Lighthouse. Replete with a grill and sports bar, this inn features guest rooms with all of the imaginable amenities, including a data port.

Bed-and-Breakfast

You may not find any riverboat gamblers aboard the **Newport Belle Bed & Breakfast** (H Dock, Newport Marina, 541/867-6290 or 800/348-1922, www.newportbelle.com, $100–145), a recently constructed sternwheel riverboat designed as a floating inn, but this 97-foot-long B&B evokes the ambiance of the sternwheeler heyday. Choose from five generous staterooms, each with its own personality and private bath. Three of the rooms have queen-size beds, one room has a king, and the family room has a full and a twin bed. Most have fabulous vistas of the bustling marina and bridge area. In the evening, guests either retire to their staterooms, enjoy the open afterdeck, or socialize in the main salon, where they are also treated to a gourmet breakfast every morning. No pets, children, or smoking are allowed. Soft-soled shoes required.

Campgrounds

The campgrounds at South Beach State Park and Beverly Beach State Park could well be the most popular places to stay of their kind on the Oregon coast. Their proximity to Newport, the absence of other camping in the area, and the special features of each explain their appeal.

Beverly Beach (information 541/265-9278 or 800/452-5687, reservations 800/452-5687, open year-round) has 152 tent sites, 127 RV spaces (both $17–21), and some yurts set seven miles north of Newport on the east side of the highway in a mossy glade. Across the road is a tunnel leading to a beach. **Devil's Punchbowl** and **Otter Crest** are one and two miles up the highway, respectively. All of the amenities are provided in the fees.

South Beach State Park (information 541/867-4715 or 800/551-6949, reservations 800/452-5687, open mid-Apr.–mid-Oct., $17–21, hiker/biker spaces $5) is just south of the Yaquina Bay Bridge, occupying a long beach with opportunities for fishing, agate hunting, windsurfing (for experts), horseback riding, and hiking. It has the full range of creature comforts, including laundry.

FOOD

Markets

This is a town for serious eaters—folks who know good food and don't mind paying a tad more for it. It's also the kind of place where there are wharfside vendors, as well as fast-food joints and a 24-hour **Safeway** (220 U.S. 101, 541/265-2930) or **Fred Meyer** (150 NE 20th St., 541/265-4581) to do it on the cheap. The **Oceana Natural Foods Co-op** (152 SE 2nd St., 541/265-8285) is a place to stock up on bulk and organic foods if you're planning a picnic. There are also sandwiches, soups, salads, juices, and so on served on-site here. Because you'll probably be spending most of your time at either Nye Beach or the Bayfront, eateries in those neighborhoods highlight this section.

About seven miles east of the Bayfront, the **Oregon Oyster Farms** (6878 Yaquina Bay Rd., Newport, 541/265-5078, 9 A.M.–5 P.M. daily) is the only remaining commercial outlet of Yaquina Bay oysters. Visitors are welcome to observe the farming and processing of these succulent shellfish. Try oysters on the half-shell, or sample the smoked oysters on a stick. To get there, follow Bay Boulevard east from the Bayfront.

June–October, you can pick up the freshest garden produce the area has to offer, plus baked goods, honey, and other delectables, at the Lincoln County Small Farmers' Association's **Saturday Farmers Market,** held in the parking area of the Newport Armory (41 SW U.S. 101, 541/574-4040), on the east side of the highway just behind City Hall. It kicks off at 9 A.M.

Seafood

The Newport Bayfront is where Mohava Niemi first opened the original **Mo's** (622 SW Bay Blvd., 541/265-2979, www.moschowder.com) several decades ago. When word got out about the good food and low prices, Mo's small homey place soon had more business than it could handle. In response to the overflow, **Mo's Annex** (541/265-7512) was created across the street. While both establishments feature such favorites as oyster stew and peanut butter cream pie, the Annex bay window has the best view.

Another solid choice for those who crave fresh seafood is the **Whale's Tale** (452 SW Bay Blvd., 541/265-8660, open daily). **Newport Chowder Bowl** (728 NW Beach Dr., 541/265-7477, $5–18) is perfect after a long beach walk. A first-rate salad bar, garlic bread, and award-winning chowder make an excellent lunch. Next door, the **Sandbar** (722 NW Beach Dr., 541/265-6032) is a casual family restaurant with dining on two ocean-view levels. Prime rib is served nightly, along with burgers, steaks, live crab, and other seafood dishes.

April's at Nye Beach (749 NW 3rd St., 541/265-6855, dinner only Wed.–Sun., $12–25) is a small, stylish café with big Mediterranean flavors close to the Sylvia Beach Hotel. Fish soup and portabello mushrooms in cheese-laden cannelloni are standouts in a creative menu. Housemade bruschetta and steamed Manila clams are excellent appetizers. For dessert have an eclair dipped in chocolate ganache and topped with slivered almonds. Affordable wines by the glass (around $5) add to one of Newport's best dining experiences.

Georgie's Beachside Grill (744 SW Elizabeth St., 541/265-9800, $20 and under) in Nye Beach's Hallmark Inn has the best ocean view in town, as well as good food. The salmon hash and smoked seafood pasta are highlights. The restaurant also features Cajun/creole (try the catfish or shrimp creole) and Jamaican seafood specials for dinner.

Northwest

Canyon Way Bookstore and Restaurant (1216 SW Canyon Way, 541/265-8319, dinner $20) has been a mainstay of Newport's culinary and cultural scenes for several decades. A combination restaurant, art gallery, clothing boutique, and 20,000-title bookstore, it has something for everybody here. Instead of going the haute cuisine route, the budget-conscious might prefer to feast on homemade quiche and croissants from the carryout shop after browsing the wide-ranging selection of travel titles in the front-room bookstore. These can be savored with a cup of espresso. In addition to the bakery selections in the carryout shop, there is other low-priced luncheon fare. In the evening, early dinners almost halve the later menu prices for the same order. Menu highlights include prawns Provençale, Yaquina Bay oysters, crab cakes, and a good Oregon-centered wine list. You'll also appreciate little extras such as an outdoor patio dining and works by local artists adorning Canyon Way's walls.

You don't have to be a guest to have a meal at the **Tables of Content,** the excellent restaurant at the Sylvia Beach Hotel (267 NW Cliff St.). There's a nice view of the breakers, good company, and it's a good dollar value for creatively prepared Northwest cuisine. Each night, there are several entrée selections with an appetizer, salad, bread, beverages (alcohol extra), and dessert for less than $20, prix fixe. Diners share tables and are encouraged to break the ice with a game called Two Truths and a Lie, in which they regale each other with several stories, the object being to distinguish which one is true. Reservations are mandatory.

Standard American

Rogue Ales Public House (748 SW Bay Blvd., 541/265-3188) is across the Bay in Old Town, serving seafood salads, shrimp melt sandwiches, pizza, fish and chips, and seasonal fish dishes. The menu tops out with cioppino. In addition to washing down all of the above with renowned Rogue ales, there's Keiko Draft root beer, a creamy concoction laced with honey and vanilla.

Farther east down Bay Boulevard is a wonderful morning haunt, **The Coffee House** (156 SW Bay Blvd., 541/265-6263, open daily for breakfast and lunch). Gourmet pastry and such creative brunch fare as a wild mushroom omelet, crab cakes Florentine, various crêpes, and oysters lightly breaded with Japanese panko bread crumbs are complemented by the best espresso drinks in Newport. The homey confines of this place are a nice escape from the tourist trappings nearby. In fair weather, the outside deck is a relaxing spot for soaking in some rays while you gaze out on the harbor.

Champagne Sunday brunch overlooking the bay at the **Embarcadero** (1000 SE Bay Blvd., 541/265-8521) lets you fill up on all the breakfast entrées, fresh seafood, and bubbly you can handle. Count on this place for good service and the freshest fish available. Weekdays, seafood omelets and frittatas are noteworthy on the breakfast menu. Lunch also features a nice selection of salads, sandwiches, and entrées made with the anglers' fresh catch in roughly the same price range. Otherwise, burgers, sandwiches, and fish and chips typify the offerings for lunch. At night, fresh seafood entrées dominate the menu. Reservations are recommended for Sunday brunch 10 A.M.–2 P.M. and later for dinner.

Lighthouse Deli, (640 U.S. 101, South Beach, 541/867-6800) has fish and chips in a batter that's light enough to not obscure the flavor of fresh salmon, halibut, cod, and so on. If you're looking for a family stop after the Aquarium (just south of the Aquarium turnoff), this is it.

Enjoy excellent pizza, seafood, pasta, and other pub grub at **Brewer's on the Bay** (2320 OSU Dr., 541/867-3660, open until 5 P.M.), at the Rogue Ales Brewery. Visit the brewery itself, the most decorated microbrewery in the state, for daily tours and tastings.

Southern Pacific railroad brochure of Yaquina Bay, 1903

COURTESY OF SALEM (OREGON) PUBLIC LIBRARY HISTORIC PHOTOGRAPH COLLECTIONS

INFORMATION AND SERVICES

Information

The **Greater Newport Chamber of Commerce** (555 SW U.S. 101, Newport 97365, 541/265-8801 or 800/541/262-7844, www.newportchamber .org) has lots of literature and helpful staff. The office is open 8:30 A.M.–5 P.M. Monday–Friday, 10 A.M.–4 P.M. weekends, June–September.

The **Central Oregon Coast Association** (541/265-2064 or 800/767-2064, www.coastvisitor .com) maintains a useful website with details on Newport and the rest of Lincoln County. The City of Newport operates another informative website, **Get to Know Newport,** at www .discovernewport.com.

A National Public Radio station, **KLCO,** a local translator station for Eugene's KLCC, is heard on your dial at 90.5 FM.

Services

Given the size of this city, there's more likelihood of needing to call the **police** (541/265-5352) than in many other coastal locales. Other useful numbers include **Pacific Communities Hospital** (930 SW Abbey, 541/265-2244) and the **Lincoln County Ambulance** (541/265-3175). The Coast Guard **marine conditions** line is 541/265-5511.

Eileen's Coin Laundry (1078 N. Coast Hwy., 541/265-5474) is open 6 A.M.–11 P.M. daily. The **Newport Public Library** (35 NW Nye St., 541/265-2153) is open 10 A.M.–9 P.M. Monday–Thursday, 10 A.M.–6 P.M. Friday–Saturday, and 1–4 P.M. Sunday. The **post office** (310 SW 2nd St., Newport 97365, 541/265-5542), is one block west of the highway. For ATM services, head to **Bank of America**'s walk-up teller on 10 S. Coast Highway at Olive.

Internet Access

For quick and easy access to the Web, try **Ore-gonfast.net** (428 SW U.S. 101, 541/574-1642), with its high-speed connection for $6 per hour.

Transportation

Greyhound (956 W. 10th St., 541/265-2253) handles long-distance service along U.S. 101. **Valley Retriever** (541/265-2253) buses connect Newport with Corvallis Monday–Saturday. On weekdays, **Lincoln County Transit** (541/265-4900, www.co.lincoln.or.us/transit/) runs buses four times daily, north to Lincoln City and south to Yachats, with numerous stops en route through Newport. A brochure with schedules and fare info is available in commercial establishments all over town.

The **Newport Municipal Airport** (135 SE 84th St., South Beach, 800/424-3655) has sightseeing and charter flights available.

Newport's car rental agency of choice is **Enterprise Rent a Car** (27 S. Coast U.S. 101, 541/574-1999).

Depoe Bay and Vicinity

In *Blue Highways,* William Least Heat-Moon characterized Depoe Bay thusly: "Depoe Bay used to be a picturesque fishing village; now it was just picturesque. The fish houses, but for one seasonal company, were gone, the fleet gone, and in their stead had come sport-fishing boats and souvenir ashtray and T-shirt shops."

To be fair, tourists have always come here since the establishment of the town. In fact, for all intents and purposes, the town didn't really exist until the completion of the Roosevelt Highway (U.S. 101) in 1927, which opened the area to car travelers. Before that time, the area had been mainly occupied by a few members of the Siletz Reservation. One of the group worked at the U.S. Army depot and called himself Charlie Depot. The town was named after him, eventually taking on the current spelling.

Depoe Bay is in the heart of the so-called Twenty Miracle Miles, describing the attractive stretch of rockbound coast from south of Depoe Bay north up to the broad beaches of Lincoln City. Regardless of what you think of the short commercial strip along the highway here, the scenic appeal of Depoe's location is impossible to ignore. The rocky outer bay, flanked by headlands to the north and south, is pierced by a narrow channel through the basalt cliffs leading to the inner harbor. This six-acre pond is notable as the world's smallest natural navigable harbor. It's home to an active sport-fishing fleet, as well as a concentration of whale-watching charters that has earned Depoe Bay its sobriquet as Oregon's Whale-Watching Capital.

SIGHTS
The Bayfront and Harbor

Depoe Bay is situated along a truly beautiful coastline that cannot be fully appreciated from the highway. A quarter-mile seawall and promenade invite a stroll. For a panorama of the harbor, continue along the sidewalks across the gracefully arching concrete bridge, designed by Conde McCullough and built in 1927. Other nice perspectives are offered from residential streets west of U.S. 101; try Ellingson Street, south of the bridge, and Sunset Street at the north end of the bay. Perhaps the most all-encompassing overlook is offered by the glass-enclosed rooftop lookout (open to the public) on top of the **Oregon Coast Aquarium Store,** located right at the harbor entrance. Two "spouting horns," natural blowholes in the rocks north of the harbor entrance, can send plumes of spray 60 feet into the air when the tide and waves are right.

East of the bridge is Depoe Bay's claim to international fame, the world's smallest navigable natural harbor. This distinction is announced by a sign citing its recognition by the *Guinness Book of World Records*. This boat basin is also exceptional because it's a harbor within a harbor. This topography is the result of wave action cutting into the basalt over eons until a 50-foot passageway leading to a six-acre inland lagoon was created. In addition to whale-watching, folks congregate on the bridge between the ocean and the harbor to watch boats maneuver into the enclosure. Depoe Bay's Harbor was scenic enough to be selected as the sight from which Jack Nicholson commandeered a yacht for his mental patient crew in the movie version of *One Flew Over the Cuckoo's Nest*.

Boiler Bay State Scenic Viewpoint

One-half mile north of town is Boiler Bay, so named because of the boiler left from the 1910 wreck of the *J. Marhoffer*. The ship caught fire three miles offshore and drifted into the bay. The remains of the boiler are visible at low tide. This rock-rimmed bay is a favorite spot for rock fishing, birding, and whale-watching. A trail leads down to some excellent tidepools.

Whale Cove

One-half mile south of Depoe Bay, a picturesque bay has been scooped out of the sandstone bluffs. The tranquility of the calendar-photo-come-to-life here is deceptive. There's considerable evidence to suggest that this tiny embayment—and not California's Marin County—was the site of Francis Drake's 1579 landing (see the sidebar "Drake's Lost Harbor?"), but the jury is still out. During Prohibition, bootleggers used the protected cove as a clandestine port. In the 1980s, a court decision allowing property owners to restrict access to Whale Cove set a precedent undermining public ownership of other Oregon beaches. (More recently, however, this trend was counteracted by another high court decision that prevented a Cannon Beach innkeeper from building on a public beach.)

Rocky Creek State Scenic Viewpoint overlooks Whale Cove. There are picnic tables, and it's a good spot for whale-watching, but there's no access down to the beach.

Otter Crest Loop

The rocky bluffs of this coastal stretch take on an even more dramatic aspect as you leave the highway at the Otter Crest Loop, a winding three-mile section of the old Coast Highway, two miles south of Depoe Bay.

From atop **Cape Foulweather,** the visibility can extend 40 miles on a clear day. The view south to Yaquina Head and its lighthouse is a photographer's fantasy of headlands, coves, and offshore monoliths. Bronze plaques in the parking lot tell of Captain Cook naming the 500-foot-high headland during a bout with storm-tossed seas on March 7, 1778. Comic relief from the coast's parade of historical plaques comes with another tablet bearing the inscription, "On this site in 1897, nothing happened."

The Lookout gift shop on the north side of the promontory is a good place to buy Japanese fishing floats for a few bucks. The million-dollar view from inside the shop is easily one of the most spectacular windows on the ocean to be found anywhere.

Another mile south, in the hamlet of Otter Rock, you'll find another of the Oregon coast's several diabolically named natural features, the **Devil's Punchbowl.** The urnlike sandstone formation, filled with swirling water,

DRAKE'S LOST HARBOR?

In 1996, the media exploded with stories raising the possibility that the tiny hamlet of Whale Cove, two miles south of Depoe Bay, could supplant Plymouth Rock as the birthplace of a nation. Rotting timbers from what is theorized to have been a stockade built by Sir Francis Drake in 1579 were unearthed in an area where stories have long circulated that the English privateer made landfall.

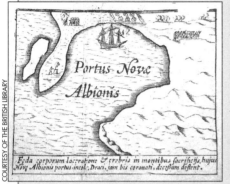

COURTESY OF THE BRITISH LIBRARY

E da corporum laceratione & crebris in montibus sacrificiis, hujus Novæ Albionis portus incol:, Draci, jam bis coronati, decessum deflent.

This 1589 map of Portus Novae Albionis (Drake's harbor) by Jodocus Hondius is the spitting image of Whale Cove.

Over the years, these notions have been fueled by several tantalizing pieces of evidence: an unsigned ship log from Drake's voyage in a museum in England that identified 44 degrees north latitude—the same as Whale Cove—as a landing site; an English shilling dating from 1560 found on the central Oregon coast in 1982; a photo from the 1930s showing a local resident with a distinctly English sword he unearthed; and a ship's cutlass found in Newport in the early 19th century bearing the markings of a 16th-century English arsenal. Moreover, excavations of a nearby Indian village thought to have been buried in the year 1600 turned up brass items, blades, and Venetian beads.

Sailing *Golden Hynde*, the only one of his five-ship fleet to survive the stormy straits around Cape Horn, Drake harassed Spanish settlements throughout Latin America and plundered Spanish ships wherever he met them. Sailing west from Mexico on its return to England via the Cape of Good Hope, the treasure-laden *Golden Hynde* was beset by storms, and Drake had to retreat to land to make repairs. Conventional history has held that he made landfall around San Francisco, most likely on the Marin County coast.

Ward, however, believes that Drake continued his voyage farther north and sailed into the Strait of Juan de Fuca, thinking he had found the fabled Northwest Passage. Turning around before he realized his mistake, Drake then headed south down the Washington and Oregon coasts, where he found a sandy cove in which to drop anchor and make repairs before the long journey home.

On Drake's return to England after four years at sea, news of his exploits were suppressed. Queen Elizabeth confiscated the logs and charts, and it would be 10 years before an official account of the voyage would be published. Then, Drake's New Albion was described as being around 38 degrees north latitude (in northern California), in an attempt, Ward believes, to fool the Spanish into thinking the Northwest Passage was much farther south.

After Elizabeth's death in 1603, however, new charts began to appear that placed the landing site much farther north, and early 17th-century charts show a small, shallow bay labeled "Novus Albionis" (New Albion), which is an uncannily accurate depiction of Whale Cove.

Since the initial blizzard of publicity, there has been no final word from the archaeologists and historians involved in corroborating these claims. Because most history books have placed New Albion, Drake's fabled lost settlement, near San Francisco, researchers will not be too quick to claim otherwise without definitive research.

© MARK MORRIS

view from Cape Foulweather

has been sculpted by centuries of waves flooding into what had been a cave until its roof collapsed. The inexorable process continues today, thanks to the ebb and flow of the Pacific through two openings in the wall of the cauldron. A state park viewpoint gives you a ringside seat on this frothy confrontation between rock and tide. When the water recedes, you can see purple sea urchins and starfish in the tidepools of the **Marine Gardens** 100 feet to the north.

To the south of the Punchbowl vantage point are picnic tables and a wooden walkway down to the beach. Close by, in the Otter Rock **Mo's** restaurant, a seat occupied by "The Boss" himself, Bruce Springsteen, on June 11, 1987, is enshrined. Also in Otter Rock, the **Flying Dutchman Winery** (541/765-2553, 11 A.M.–6 P.M. daily) makes limited batches of handcrafted wines and offers tastings and tours.

Back on U.S. 101, a mile's drive south brings you to Beverly Beach State Park.

ACCOMMODATIONS

Lodgings in popular Depoe Bay require advance reservations on most weekends and holidays. In a part of the coast that is dense with lodging, we see a need to list only those that spectacularly highlight the major reasons to come here.

Hotels

The Surfrider Resort (3115 NW U.S. 101, 764-2311 or 800/662-2378, www.surfriderresort .com, $69–139) is a few miles north of town on picturesque Fogarty Creek's rockbound coast. Although it's been around for a while and is not too elaborate, its setting and other appeals mandate a mention: oceanfront suites/rooms with decks (lower in off-season), some with whirlpool tubs, kitchens, and fireplaces. A good restaurant, an indoor pool, hot tub, and midweek specials (two nights with breakfast, $159) also are noteworthy. Locals say the steaks in the restaurant are the best on the coast, and the view from the dining room is special.

The Inn at Arch Rock (70 NW Sunset St., 800/767-1835, www.innatarchrock.com, rooms $69–269, condos $199) comprises a cluster of white clapboard buildings that overlooks the bay from its clifftop perch at the north end of town. Lodging options include thirteen oceanfront rooms and three two-bedroom condo units next door that sleep six guests.

Located about three miles south of Depoe Bay, at one of the most scenic spots on the spectacular Otter Crest Loop (or anywhere on the central coast, for that matter), is the **Inn at Otter Crest** (301 Otter Crest Loop, Otter Rock, 541/765-2111 or 800/452-2101, www .innatottercrest.com, $100–139), a condo resort perched close to the edge of the sandstone bluffs at the ocean's edge. There is a two-night minimum on holidays and weekends. The Flying Dutchman dining room (see the Food section) faces 500-foot Cape Foulweather to the north and is a wonderful place to watch the sunset or scan the sea for whales.

Formerly Gracie's Landing, now **Gracie's Sea Hag Inn** (235 SE Bay View Ave., 541/765-2322 or 800/228-0448, www.gracieslanding.com, $89–135), this small inn overlooks the harbor—affording views of sea otters, ducks, and geese while the whale-watching and fishing boats come and go. All rooms have a harbor view and include a hot breakfast. The inn is also dog-friendly.

Bed-and-Breakfast

The Channel House (35 Ellingson St., 541/765-2140 or 800/447-2140, www.channelhouse.com, $90–260) is our choice for a central coast contemplative retreat or a honeymoon getaway. With three rooms and nine spacious suites boasting expansive, dramatic views of the ocean, private decks with outdoor whirlpool tubs (in most rooms), fireplaces, plush robes, and other amenities, the stage is set for a seaside vigil or romance. This bluff-top B&B (there isn't a beach below, just miles of ocean and surrounding cliffs) may not look prepossessing from the outside, but inside the place is all windows and angles. Imagine *Architectural Digest* with a nautical theme. Named for the 50-foot channel into the harbor north of the inn, this is the best place in the country to commune with whales, passing boats, winter storms, and the setting sun. The fact that some of the suites can accommodate four people lays out the welcome mat for families (but no pets or young children) or friends and couples traveling together. A continental breakfast with tasty baked goods in an oceanside dining area is included in the rates. To fully appreciate this gem of a lodging before you book, consult its photo-filled website.

FOOD

Seafood

Head to the locally popular **Gracie's Sea Hag Restaurant** (58 U.S. 101, 541/765-2734, $11–25). Their seafood hors d'oeuvres (fried whitefish, scallops, oysters, smoked tuna, and boiled baby shrimp) give ample testimony to their claim that it's "seafood so fresh the ocean hasn't missed it yet." Another popular dish is salmon stuffed with crab and shrimp, baked in wine and herb butter. A lavish salad bar, a Friday night all-you-can-eat seafood buffet, and a recipe for clam chowder fêted by the *New York Times* has also generated good word of mouth.

Tidal Raves (279 NW U.S. 101, 541/765-2995, lunch $5–10, dinner $10–18) boasts the best views in town and a casual ambience. Tidal Raves is open for lunch and dinner with tasty food at moderate prices. In addition to fresh fish and other seafood dishes such as Thai prawns and oyster spinach bisque, the restaurant's pasta specialties are uniformly excellent. The Pasta Rave features crab, shrimp, ling cod, snapper, and more on a bed of linguine with pesto. The Dungeness crab casserole is also noteworthy. For dessert don't miss warm chocolate chunk cookie with Tillamook Vanilla Bean ice cream.

Casual Fare

The **Spouting Horn** (541/765-2261), overlooking the harbor, serves breakfast, lunch, and dinner 11:30 A.M.–9 P.M. Monday, 8 A.M.–9 P.M. Wednesday–Sunday. Try the amazing deep-dish blackberry pie.

The **Nautical Nook** (22 Bay St., 541/765-8999, 6:30 A.M.–9 P.M. daily), located next door to Tradewinds fishing charters, is a full-service restaurant specializing in humongous burgers, seafood, pasta, and pizza. They have an espresso bar and a beer and wine list, and this hometown haunt also delivers meals from Otter Rock to Salishan. Note that opening hours may vary in relation to fishing season.

The **Flying Dutchman** (301 Otter Crest Loop, Otter Rock, 541/765-2111), in South Depoe at the Inn at Otter Crest (see Accommodations section), faces 500-foot-high Cape Foulweather to the north. Classical cuisine is served here at dinnertime, and more reasonably priced sandwiches and salads (less then $10) can be enjoyed at lunch. Breakfast is also served from 8 A.M., but the real highlight is the evening repast. Dinnertime favorites include the blackened prime rib and seafood fettuccine. The restaurant's bluffside aerie makes a great place to watch the sunset or look for whales.

RECREATION

With open ocean minutes from port here, catching a salmon or seeing a whale is possible as soon as you leave the harbor. Most charter operators here offer both fishing and whale-watching excursions. Bottom-fishing trips average $55 for a five-hour run, salmon fishing about $100 for a seven- or eight-hour day, and whale-watching excursions run about $15–25 per person per hour.

Some well-established companies here include **Dockside Charters** (541/765-2545 or 800/733-8915, www.docksidedepoebay.com), which offers one-hour trips aboard their 50-foot excursion boat for $15 per adult and on 25-foot rigid-hull inflatables for $25 per adult. **Tradewinds Charters** (541/765-2345 or 800/445-8730, www.tradewindscharters.com) offers one- and two-hour trips December–Feburary and March–May. Rates run $15–45 for adults on their fleet of 30- to 52-foot boats and an 18-foot Zodiac. A 12-hour tuna charter costs $160. **Zodiac Adventures** (800/571-6463, www.zodiacadventures.com) runs whale-watching tours only on a 24-foot Zodiac for $25 per person per hour.

EVENTS

The **Depoe Bay Classic Wooden Boat Show, Crab Feed, and Ducky Derby** is held the last weekend in April. Several dozen wooden craft, both restored and newly constructed vessels, ranging from kayaks to skiffs and dinghies to larger fishing boats, are displayed in the harbor and the adjacent City Park. Rowing races, boat-building workshops, crab races, and other activities are scheduled. At the big Crab Feed (10 A.M.–5 P.M. Sat. and Sun., $14 full dinner), see some 1,500 pounds of crab, plus side dishes, devoured at the Community Hall. The Ducky Derby is a raffle in which you purchase "tickets" in the form of rubber duckies, which race down the harbor's feeder stream vying for prizes. Surprisingly, this event is the only such boat show we know of on the coast, which seems a great shame, given the role that boats and ships have played in the history of the Oregon coast. For more information, contact the chamber of commerce.

The **Fleet of Flowers** happens each Memorial Day in the harbor to honor those lost at sea and in military service. More than 20,000 people come to witness a blanket of blossoms cast upon the waters.

The **Depoe Bay Salmon Bake** (10 A.M.–5 P.M. on the third Sat. of Sept., adults $13–14, kids $7–8) is held at Depoe Bay City Park, flanking the rear of the boat basin. Some 3,000 pounds of fresh ocean fish are caught and cooked Indian-style—on alder stakes over an open fire—and served with all the trimmings. The feast is savored to the accompaniment of live entertainment. It always seems to rain on the day of this event, but that's life on the Oregon coast.

INFORMATION AND SERVICES

On the east side of the highway, opposite the seawall, the **Depoe Bay Chamber of Commerce** (70 NE U.S. 101, Depoe Bay 97341, 541/765-2889 or 877/485-8348, www.depoebaychamber.org, 11 A.M.–3 P.M. weekdays, 9 A.M.–4 P.M. weekends) offers some printed matter about the town, as well as the central coast in general.

The *Depoe Bay Beacon*, a tabloid published twice a month and sold locally for two bits, offers interesting insight into local goings-on. The police report will have you shaking your head in wonder.

The Coast Guard **marine weather service** (541/765-2122) can be contacted around the clock.

Transportation

Three northbound and southbound **Greyhound** buses (800/231-2222) hit Depoe Bay each day. The southbound stops at the Fire Hall on U.S. 101 at the north end of town, whereas northbound coaches stop at Whistlestop Market (U.S. 101 and Schoolhouse Rd.) and Liberty Market (466 NE U.S. 101). On weekdays, **Lincoln County Transit** (541/265-4900, www.co.lincoln.or.us/transit/) runs buses four times daily, north to Lincoln City and south to Yachats.

Lincoln City and Vicinity

Back in 1964, five burgs that straddled seven miles of beachfront between Siletz Bay and the Salmon River came together and incorporated as Lincoln City. In commemoration, a 14-foot bronze statue of Abraham Lincoln was donated to the city by an Illinois sculptress. *The Lank Lawyer Reading in His Saddle While His Horse Grazes* originally occupied a city park; Governor Mark Hatfield and actor Raymond Massey, who had portrayed Honest Abe in a 1940 film, came for the dedication. Today, the statue stands in a non-descript lot at NE 22nd and Quay Avenue. Look for the sign on U.S. 101 near the Dairy Queen pointing the way.

In the following decades, what were discrete towns have grown and melded into an uninterrupted conurbation with a population of about 6,800 (which can balloon to 30,000 on a busy weekend). While the resulting sprawl and "zoned commercial" signs can be maddening at times, the most visited town on the coast must be doing something right. Perhaps it's the proximity to Portland and Salem, or the area's *two* Indian-run casinos. Perhaps it's the broad, long (over seven miles), and sandy beach, or the superlative wildlife viewing around Siletz Bay. Or maybe it's the attraction of Devil's Lake State Park, a gem without equal among coastal freshwater playgrounds. Add prime kite-flying, some of the better restaurants on the coast, and bibliophile and antique haunts, and it's clear that there's more to the area than the pull of saltwater taffy and outlet malls.

SIGHTS AND RECREATION

The Beach

Lincoln City boasts seven uninterrupted miles of sandy beach, but you have to go looking for most of it. From Siletz Bay north to Road's End State Recreation Area, there are more than a dozen access points. You can head west from U.S. 101 on just about any side street to get there. High coastal bluffs lining the north-central portion of town, though, may mean a climb

down (and back up) long flights of stairs cut into the cliff. For something approaching solitude on a crowded day, follow Logan Road west from the highway near the north end of town to **Road's End State Recreation Area;** tidepools and a secluded cove add to the allure. This stretch is popular with windsurfers.

Tidepool explorers should also check out the rock formations at SW 11th Street (Canyon Drive Park), NW 15th Street, and SW 32nd.

The **D River Wayside,** a small park on the beach in more or less the middle of town, is a state park property where you can watch what locals claim is the "world's shortest river" empty into the ocean. Flowing just 120 feet from its source, Devil's Lake, to its mouth at the Pacific, it's short, all right, and despite its unspectacular appearance, was a cause célèbre when the *Guinness Book of World Records* withdrew the D's claim to fame in favor of a Montana waterway, the Roe. Local schoolkids rallied to the D's defense with an amended measurement, but the Roe, at a mere 53 feet long, carries the imprimatur from *Guinness* as the most diminutive stream. As another bit of geographic trivia, this is an unexpectedly hotly contested category, with partisans pushing their contenders in Texas, Arizona, and New Zealand. In addition to seeing D River flow from "D" Lake into "D" ocean, you can fly a kite on the beach here. It's one of the easier beach-access points, between stretches of high, motel-topped bluffs, so it can get a little crowded.

Another convenient beach-access point is off SW 51st Street at the south end of town, just before **Siletz Bay.** A large parking area here in what's known as the Taft District stands beside the driftwood-strewn shore of the bay, where you can often see a group of harbor seals chasing their dinner or coming in for a closer look at you. It's a short walk to the ocean.

Time was when it was common for storms and currents to wash up that ultimate beach-comber's prize—**glass fishing floats**—on the Oregon coast. Used by Japanese anglers to buoy their nets, the blue or green glass spheres, ranging

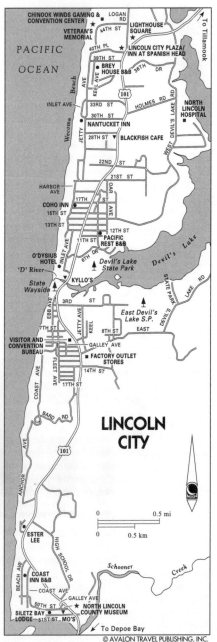

from as small as two inches up to two feet in diameter, have been mostly replaced by plastic or foam floats and are now a rare find. Since 1999, however, Lincoln City has improved the beachcomber's odds by distributing more than 2,000 glass floats along its beaches, between October and Memorial Day. Handcrafted by Northwest glass artists, each of the colorful floats is signed and numbered and placed by volunteers on the beaches above the high-tide line. If you find one, you can call or stop in at the visitors center for a certificate and information about the artist who created it.

Devil's Lake

Devil's Lake, just east of town, is the recreation center of Lincoln City. In addition to windsurfing and hydroplaning, eight species of fish can be caught here, including catfish, yellow perch, crappie, largemouth bass, and trout. Chinese grass carps were introduced to the lake to help control the rampant aquatic weeds. There's also good bird-watching on and around this shallow, 678-acre lake, which attracts flocks of migratory geese, ducks, and other waterfowl. Species to look for include canvasbacks, Canada geese, widgeons, gadwalls, grebes, and mallards. Bald eagles and ospreys also nest in the trees bordering the lake.

The lake takes its name from a local Indian legend. The story tells that when Siletz warriors paddled a canoe across the lake one moonlit night, a tentacled beast erupted from the still water and pulled the men under. It's said that boaters today who cross the moon's reflection in the middle of the lake tempt the same fate, but so far the lake's devil has remained silent for years.

Of the five access points, East Devil's Lake Road off U.S. 101 northeast of town offers a scenic route around the lake's east side before rejoining U.S. 101 near the day-use portion of the state park at the south end of the lake. To reach the camping area of **Devil's Lake State Recreation Area,** take NE 6th Drive east from U.S. 101, about one-quarter mile north of the D River. The day-use area has a boat ramp, and there's a moorage dock across the lake adjacent to the campground.

KESEY'S LEGACY

Two miles south of Lincoln City, you'll come to the turnoff for ORE 229 along the Siletz River. If you drive down the north side of the river about 1.25 miles, on the opposite shore you'll note a Victorian-ish house that's built to last. It was constructed for the movie version of Ken Kesey's *Sometimes a Great Notion*. The 1971 film, a so-so adaptation of a memorable novel, starred Paul Newman, Lee Remick, Henry Fonda, and Michael Sarrazin. The plot concerns the never-say-die spirit of an anti-union timber baron, his not-always-supportive family, and life in the mythical Coast Range logging community of Wakonda. A huge porch once fronted the riverbank, heavily reinforced against the elements. It was taken down in the decade after the movie was made, but it lives on in the pages of the book. Much of the movie was shot in this area, with café scenes taking place at Mo's on Newport's bayfront. Other scenes were shot near Florence.

tells the story of this area through exhibits of old-time logging machinery, homesteading tools, fishing, military life, and Indian history. Check out the early fashion mannequins and a World War II mine that was washed ashore.

Golf and Tennis

At the north end of town is 18-hole **Lakeside Golf Club** (3245 NE 50th St., 541/994-8442, green fees $18 for nine holes, $30 for a full day).

Serious devotees can head seven miles south to **Westin Salishan Golf Links** (U.S. 101, Gleneden Beach 97388, 541/764-3632 or 800/890-8037, green fees $75–95 May–Oct. and $55 the rest of the year, cart rental $20) to play the award-winning 18-hole course set in the foothills of the Coast Range and bordered by Siletz Bay and the sea. Keep in mind that this is a Scottish links course, where the roughs are really rough.

Tennis players can enjoy the public outdoor courts at NW 28th. These are about half the price of the Salishan (541/764-3633), which averages about $15 per person for a 75-minute set.

Mountain bikes, canoes, and paddleboats can be rented at the **Blue Heron Landing** (4006 W. Devil's Lake Rd., Lincoln City 97367, 541/994-4708).

Chinook Winds Casino

One of the biggest draws in town is the Chinook Winds (1777 NW 44th St., Lincoln City 97367, 541/996-5825 or 888/244-6665, www.chinookwindscasino.com), operated by the Confederated Tribes of Siletz Indians, near the north end of town. In addition to daily 24-hour slots, blackjack, poker, keno, bingo, craps, and roulette, the casino has two on-site restaurants and a busy schedule of big-name (or formerly big-name) entertainment. Recent shows, for example, have included the Beach Boys, George Carlin, and Don McLean.

North Lincoln County Historical Museum

This modest museum (4907 SW U.S. 101, 541/996-6614, noon–4 P.M. Tues.–Sat., free)

ACCOMMODATIONS

Of the cheek-by-jowl selection of lodgings in Lincoln City, we're partial to the hotels at the south end of town and near Siletz Bay. Although the views are not always expansive, the beachfront isn't as crowded here as it is from the D River north, and you're far from casino traffic. If you want something closer to the gaming tables, there are more than 1,000 other rooms in this town.

Motels

The Ester Lee (3803 SW U.S. 101, 541/996-3606 or 888/996-3606, www.esterlee.com, $46–151) is a decades-old family motel complex along with some cottages on a bluff above miles of beachfront. All rooms have ocean views and fireplaces, and some have kitchens and whirlpool tubs. Pets are allowed. It's nothing fancy, but good value for the money. Rates depend on the season and day of the week.

Another pet-friendly place, the **Coho Inn** (1635 NW Harbor, 541/994-3684 or 800/848-7006, www.thecohoinn.com, studios $60–136, family suites $84–167) has 50 oceanfront units with fireplaces, kitchens, and continental breakfast. Pets are allowed for an extra fee.

Lodge

When asked to choose *the* place to stay on the Oregon coast, most Oregonians would recommend the **Salishan Lodge** (7760 N. U.S. 101, Gleneden Beach, 541/764-2371 or 888/SALISHAN, www.salishanlodge.com, $215–365 in summer, $119–295 the rest of the year). Named for a widespread native dialect in the Oregon Territory, this former Westin resort is one of a dozen properties in the nation that consistently receives a four-star and a five-diamond rating. Almost every year, *Condé Nast Traveler* magazine rates Salishan as one of the top resorts in the country.

Strictly speaking, the resort is more of a Coast Range mountain lodge than a beach resort. Although distant Siletz Bay views might edify those in search of the postcard stereotype of Oregon's upper left edge, most folks quickly learn to appreciate the peace of the forest and golf course here. This paradigm shift is facilitated by art and landscape architecture that convey the vision of John Gray, who built Salishan and such other Northwest properties as Skamania and Sunriver from native materials with respect for the surrounding environment. After making a fortune from the chainsaw business, Gray decided to leave more of a legacy than just stumps.

Even if you don't stay here, the grounds and facilities are worth a look. The art gallery is free and features some of the best Oregon artists (also check out master wood carver Leroy Setziol's bas-relief panels in the dining room). The forested trails behind the golf course (rated among the top 75 in the United States) showcase the rainforested foothills of the Coast Range and the waterfowl near Siletz Bay. Across the street, the Salishan Marketplace features first-rate galleries and a good bookstore, Allegory Books.

The Salishan still fetches top-drawer prices and attracts well-heeled nature lovers, corporate expense-account clientele, folks enjoying a special occasion, and serious golfers. You'll also find everyday folks and seminar attendees on winter weekend specials at half the summertime rates. Ask about multiday packages for big savings on your room rate.

Although the resort does not have ocean frontage or rooms appreciably larger or more ornate than those at many other upscale digs, the occupancy rate is high year-round. With advance notice, you can even bring your dog. From cedarshake, self-contained units in the upper level of the complex to the smaller luxury motel rooms overlooking the golf course, you'll find nicely appointed interiors in earthy colors.

In addition to the recreational and aesthetic appeals of the resort, the **Dining Room** is also responsible for Salishan's lofty reputation. Consistently touted as one of the top three restaurants in the state, it has become famous for its creative interpretations of seasonal Northwest delicacies and its 12,000-bottle wine cellar (famous for the world's largest collection of Oregon pinot noir). The latter is open for tours, as are the grounds, whose plant life is described by pamphlets available at the front desk. Fliers on area nature trails, art, and other topics are also available.

Hotels

For a small luxury hotel, where golf is not the focus, **The O'dysius Hotel** (120 NW Inlet Court, 541/994-4121 or 800/869-8069, www.odysius.com, $149–311) offers 30 oceanview units furnished with period antiques. Guests meet in the lobby every afternoon to sample Oregon wine. The hotel accepts pets, provides concierge and massage service, and offers continental breakfast. Handicapped-accessible facilities are available.

If you've been fantasizing about rolling out of bed, slipping on your robe—coffee in hand—and walking out onto a semi-private stretch of beach, then the **Inn at Spanish Head** (4009 SW U.S. 101, 541/996-2161 or 800/452-8127, www.spanishhead.com, $84 and up, discounts for longer stays) may be your best bet. Oregon's only resort hotel situated right on the beach, the inn takes its place—large and looming—against the backdrop of rugged cliffs. Whether in a suite, studio, or bedroom unit, every room has an ocean view. On-site amenities include **Fathoms,** the 10th-floor restaurant/bar serving up Northwest favorites, and a fireplace lounge, meeting rooms, a heated outdoor pool, saunas, a spa, and an exercise room.

With five newer units, **The Nantucket Inn** (3135 NW Inlet Ave., 541/996-9300, www .thenantucketinn.com, $99–139 off-season) provides guests with oceanfront accommodations just steps from the beach; some rooms come equipped with kitchens, whirlpool tubs, and fireplaces. A continental breakfast is served.

The **Siletz Bay Lodge** (1012 SW 51st St., 541/996-6111 or 888/430-2100, www .siletzbaylodge.com, $79–155 in summer), on the north end of Siletz Bay on a driftwood-strewn beach, is a family-friendly and wheelchair-accessible (with elevators) lodging in a location that's ideal for bird-watching and viewing seals. About half of the standard rooms have balconies, with delightful views of the bay and the sun going down over Salishan Spit. Spa rooms and suites are also available if you happen to be in town for a romantic getaway. Such in-room amenities as microwaves, refrigerators, and coffeemakers are offered, and a continental breakfast (7–10 A.M.) is included in the rates. There is three-night minimum stay during holidays.

Bed-and-Breakfasts

Lincoln City has its share of B&Bs from which to choose. Close to the beach, **Brey House B&B** (3725 NW Keel Ave., 541/994-7123, www.breyhouse.com, $85–165) is one of the oldest B&Bs on the Oregon coast. Shirley Brey has owned the three-story Cape Cod–style home, built in 1940, for 16 years. Be sure to sample their excellent breakfast, which is served in a light-filled room overlooking the ocean. True to its motto, this place is "just across from the ocean," with four bedrooms (all with private baths and entrances). Not appropriate for children.

The light and bright **Coast Inn B&B** (4507 SW Coast Ave., 888/994-7932 or 541/994-7932, www.oregoncoastinn.com, $95–125) offers non-smoking guest rooms and a hot breakfast in a sprawling Craftsman-style home located in his-

toric Taft Heights, south of Spanish Head. Siletz Bay is a short walk, as is public beach access. Entirely remodeled in 2001, this home features comfortable new furnishings and homey decor. **Pacific Rest B&B** (1611 NE 11th St., 541/994-2337, $100–175) is a newer home with large suites, located on a hillside just above Highway 101. If you have younger children and want the B&B experience, this is your best bet because owners Ray and Judy Waetjen welcome the young'uns.

The **Salmonberry B&B** (61008 North Cascades Hwy., Marblemount, 360/873-4016, $150–175) has three guest accommodations and is located in a coastal woodland, just a short walk from the southern edges of Siletz Bay. Each individually decorated room has a queen-sized bed, down comforter, sitting area, private bath, TV, and VCR. Room rates include breakfast, complimentary evening wine and cheese, and unlimited use of all guest spa facilities, including a heated indoor swimming pool, sauna, and whirlpool bath.

To rent vacation homes throughout Lincoln County, contact **Lincoln City Visitor and Convention Bureau,** 800/452-2151. Or, try **Pacific Retreats** (3126-A NE U.S. 101, 800/473-4833, www.pacificretreats.com), which features a selection of vacation home rentals.

Campgrounds

Several wilderness retreats are worth noting in the Lincoln City area. One remote escape is at **Van Duzer Wayside,** about 12 miles east of town on ORE 18, which offers a dozen primitive (and free) hiker/biker sites in a beautiful forest near the Salmon River.

More free rustic sites can be found about eight miles north of town and just south of Neskowin. To get there, just look for the Scenic Drive sign east of U.S. 101 and follow County Road 12 for four miles. From there, travel about 100 yards west on Forest Service Road 12131 and you'll see the campground set along **Neskowin Creek.** To find out about the trails in the surrounding rainforest, contact the Siuslaw National Forest in Hebo (541/392-3161). The campground is open mid-April to mid-October—bring your own water or water-purification kit. The nearby scenic drive continues up into an area of huge trees captioned by Forest Service placards explaining the ecology.

More elaborate camping is available at **Devil's Lake State Park** (1452 NE 6th St., Lincoln City 97367, information 541/994-2002, reservations 800/452-5687, mid-Apr.–late Oct.), with 68 tent sites and 32 RV sites with full hookups serviced with all the amenities, including showers, a café, and a laundry room. The fee is $17–21 per night, $29 for yurts, $4 for hiker/biker spaces. This campground is just off U.S. 101 at the northeast end of town, between the ocean and the 678-acre Devil's Lake.

Devil's Lake RV Park (4041 NE West Devil's Lake Rd., 541/994-3400), near Lakeside Golf, has 80 paved sites with full hookups for $17–21; no tent camping is allowed.

FOOD

Lincoln City offers surprisingly many cost-effective and palate-pleasing dining options. Some of the best are located near the north end of town. South of the D River (city center), there's a cluster of pricier gourmet eateries that merit special consideration.

Steak and Seafood

Despite a coastal gourmet restaurant row between Depoe Bay and Lincoln City where dinner tabs are comparable to Portland's upscale restaurants, affordable yet tasty options do exist here, as exemplified by the **Kernville Steak and Seafood House** (186 Siletz Hwy., Kernville, 541/994-6200). Besides decent food at a good value, this place looks out onto the river and surrounding hills through huge picture windows. Blue heron and deer are frequent dinner companions, but the real attractions are the half-dozen nightly seafood specials (all moderate price range), which often showcase fresh-caught shellfish and premium aged beef. Finding this dinner house is tricky because of its inconspicuous facade on the south side of the river. Head one mile south of Lincoln City, on the Siletz Highway just east of Highway 101.

If this coastal restaurant row tour is eating a hole in your wallet, there's always tried-and-true **Mo's** (860 SW 51st St., 541/996-2535). As usual, count on good clam chowder and full fish dinners, as well as superlative views of the water. Or try **Figaro's Pizza** (4095 NW Logan Rd., 541/994-4443) for family dining options such as pizza, lasagna, and salad. Open for lunch and dinner, with reasonable prices.

The best smoked fish in these parts can be had at **Barnacle Bill's Seafood Store** (2174 U.S. 101, 541/994-3022). The smoked sturgeon here is half the price it is on the East Coast, and although it's not thin-sliced New York deli style, it has a more delicate flavor. Look for a little storefront on the east side of the highway in the middle of town.

If restaurants south of town tend toward expensive, and budget palaces are everywhere up north, it follows that somewhere in the middle of Lincoln City, you'll find moderately priced alternatives. **Kyllo's** (1110 NW 1st Ct., 541/994-3179) specializes in broiled, sautéed, and baked seafood, plus excellent homemade desserts. The former can be washed down by Oregon microbrews and wines. Seafood dinners are in the $20–30 range, and lunch is often about half that. Locals say they've had good luck with the specials, which are new and different every night. The restaurant is visible from U.S 101 as you drive by the D River Wayside. With views of the water on all sides, this restaurant is a good place to linger. Avoid peak dining hours, because no reservations are taken.

The reasonable prices at Salishan Lodge's (see Accommodations section) **Cedar Tree** restaurant are a welcome surprise. This casual restaurant might be less elaborate and half the price of Salishan's five-star Dining Room, but its Northwest cuisine comes from the same kitchen. Complete breakfasts won't lighten the wallet too much. For a few pennies more, the hot smoked chinook salmon hash is a highlight. Affordable lunchtime specialties include oyster stew and a Reuben sandwich. For dinner, splurge on the potlatch salmon or an Angus New York strip steak. With a window on Siletz Bay, you don't even have to dress up or make reservations. The Cedar Tree has also reintroduced Salishan's popular Friday seafood buffets in summer.

Fine Dining

At the adjoining Salishan **Dining Room,** special emphasis is placed on seasonal seafood, game, and other regional delicacies. Dinner here can be quite pricey, but the elegance of the setting, expansive wine list, and creative dishes have long made this a coastal dining destination.

One-half mile south of Salishan (five miles equidistant from Depoe Bay and Lincoln City) are two other Gleneden Beach eateries with considerable appeal. The **Side Door Café** (6675 Gleneden Beach Loop, 541/764-3825) combines a gourmet restaurant with a musical venue. The airy yet cozy-feeling dining room features a menu where rock spring rolls, bouillabaise, and parmesan-encrusted halibut exemplify the menu offerings. The adjoining state-of-the-art Eden Hall theater might feature a Northwest artist with a national reputation, such as jazz singer Nancy King or Portland-based Delta blues artist Kelly Joe Phelps.

The **Bay House** (5911 SW U.S. 101, 541/996-3222, www.bayhouserestaurant.com) is a place food critics describe as "intimate" and "elegant." You might also add "expensive." The menu changes seasonally and is posted on their website. Local gourmets will tell you, however, that the Dungeness crab with artichoke hearts and spinach and the rack of lamb are well worth the price. Oenophiles will want to look at the wine list singled out in *The Wine Spectator.* The tab at the Bay House is definitely worth it, especially if you're fortunate to be dining in view of the sunset over Siletz Bay.

Casual Fare

Café Roma Bookstore and Coffeehouse (1437 NW U.S. 101, 541/994-6616) brings an air of refinement to Lincoln City. Fresh home-baked pastries and desserts, fresh-roasted gourmet coffees and espresso drinks, as well as a collection of interesting books, make this a wonderful retreat on a cold and drizzly day.

The **Blackfish Café** (2733 NW U.S. 101, 541/996-1007) also has managed to be included

in the short list of prime coastal dining destinations. The reason is chef Rob Pounding, whose use of local produce and fresh products enabled Salishan to scale culinary heights in the previous decade. This orientation is repeated in this beach bistro with a menu that might feature Willamette Valley pork in huckleberry compote and troll-caught chinook salmon with Oregon blue cheese mashed potatoes. In addition to the emphasis on fresh, homegrown, and creative, there is no shortage of humbler fare such as the self-proclaimed "best" clam chowder on the coast and halibut fish and chips.

Food to the North

The **Lighthouse Brew Pub** (4157 U.S. 101 N., 541/994-7238) is a welcome rehash of the McMenamin formula so successful in the Willamette Valley. Just look for a lighthouse replica in a parking lot on the northwest side of 101 across from McDonald's. Pizza bread, burgers, sandwiches, and chili can be washed down by McMenamin's own ales or some other quality brew, as well as hard cider and wine. Live music at night is an added plus.

Dory Cove Restaurant (5819 Logan Rd., 541/994-5180, noon–8 P.M.) near Road's End State Park has prices that are a little higher than Mo's, but the range of broiled seafood entrées (halibut fish and chips recommended), chowder, and salmonburger/oysterburger/cheeseburger fantasies make this place an overwhelming favorite with locals.

If you're en route to the wine country or the Willamette Valley or just want a respite from resort traffic, a place that appeals to everybody is the **Otis Café** (1259 Salmon River Hwy., 541/994-9560) at the Otis Junction on ORE 18 two miles east of U.S. 101. Here, innovative variations on American road food have been warmly embraced by everyone from local loggers to yuppies (and *New York Times* food critics) stopping off on the drive between Portland and the coast. In September, salmon-fishing devotees can be seen lining up here at 6:30 A.M. Breakfast in this unpretentious café, five miles northeast of Lincoln City, is such an institution that long waits on the porch are the rule on weekend mornings. The reasons why include the thick-crusted molasses bread that comes with many orders, buttermilk waffles, and their legendary hash browns under melted Rogue Valley white cheddar. A half portion for one dollar less is the equivalent of all-you-can-eat fare, so walk the beach at Neskowin before tackling the unabridged version. Large portions, low prices, and a culinary touch that turns pork chops and rhubarb pie into epicurean delights are in full evidence at lunch and dinner.

Two Indian gaming casinos are located within 25 miles of one another and offer dining alternatives to the coast-bound traveler. Both **Chinook Winds** (1777 NW 44th St., Lincoln City, 888/CHINOOK or 888/244-6665, 541/966-5825), and **Spirit Mountain** (800/760-7977), about 25 miles east of Lincoln City on ORE 22 in Grande Ronde, have many dining options. Each offers generous full buffets for breakfast, lunch, and dinner, and both have fine-dining, full-service restaurants offering moderate to expensive prices. Both casinos have nightly buffets in the $15 range. Chinook Winds also offers a Friday night seafood buffet and a Sunday champagne brunch. Chinook Winds' ocean views are also worth noting. Both casinos have outlets for 24-hour dining.

ENTERTAINMENT AND EVENTS

Crabs and Chowder

A novel way to shake off the winter doldrums of mid-January is at the **Crustacean Classics** ($5 per person, $10 family of four), a three-day weekend event combining a chowder cook-off, wine tasting, and live crab races. A kids' food-sculpting competition, beverage-serving contest, live music, and crab luncheon add to the fun. Held in the Factory Stores at Lincoln City (1500 SE East Devil's Lake Rd., 541/996-5000).

Kite Festivals

Lincoln City calls itself the kite capital of the world, pointing to its position midway between the pole and the equator, which gives the area predictable wind patterns. The town holds not one but two kite fiestas at the D River Wayside each year. The spring Kite Festival takes place

the first weekend in May; the fall festival is held the third weekend in September. The event is famous for giant spin socks, some as long as 150 feet. Call 541/994-3070 or 800/452-2151 (in Oregon) for more information.

Cascade Head Chamber Music Festival

The **Cascade Head Chamber Music Festival** (P.O. Box 605, Lincoln City 97367, 541/994-5333 or 877/994-5333, www.cascadeheadmusic.org) is another Oregon kulturfest that brings together world-class artists in an informal setting. Events are hosted at St. Peter the Fisherman Lutheran Church (1226 SW 13th St., 541/994-2007), under the direction of Sergiu Luca, a famed violinist who draws on decades of international experience and the friendship of virtuosi who fly in from all corners of the globe to make music on the Oregon coast. Old-world artists such as Beethoven and Brahms, as well as contemporary composers, are featured in a series of June concerts (usually two per week over a several-week period). To order tickets, contact the festival ticket office (541/994-5333), or get them at the gallery in Salishan or the Lincoln City Visitor and Convention Bureau. Tickets run around $15 and may not always be available at the door.

Sandcastle-Building Contest

Lincoln City's version of this popular coastal event happens off SW 51st, in the historic Taft District alongside Siletz Bay. Scheduled for the first Saturday in August. Call 541/996-3800 for complete details.

Eden Hall and Side Door Café

Housed within the renovated Gleneden Brick and Tile Factory, five miles south of Lincoln City in Gleneden Beach, Eden Hall and the Side Door Café (6645 Gleneden Beach Loop Rd., 541/764-3826 for performance info, 541/764-3825 for restaurant, www.edenhall.com) stages live theater and hosts an impressively eclectic roster of regional and touring musicians. This spacious, airy warehouse has an excellent sound system and is a wonderful place to take in a concert, with an emphasis on jazz, folk, and blues. For details on the adjacent Side Door Café, see the Food section.

Theater and Movies

Lincoln City's homegrown theater company, **Theatre West** (3536 SE U.S. 101, Lincoln City, 541/994-5663, www.theatrewest.com), produces a half-dozen entertainments each year, with an emphasis on comedies, plus musicals and drama.

Catch first-run flicks at the **Bijou Theatre** (1624 NE U.S. 101, 541/994-8255), an old-time movie house dating back to the 1930s, making it a rare old survivor around here. The six-screen **Regal Cinemas** (3755 SE High School Dr., 541/994-7649), just east of U.S. 101 in the south end of town, is its modern competitor.

SHOPPING

A couple of miles south of town, **Alder House III** is a glass-blowing operation and gallery open to the public. The variety of shapes and colors produced are fascinating aspects of this ancient craft that the artisans here will explain to you. Alder House is open mid-March through November, daily 10 A.M.–5 P.M. Their high-quality creations are on sale at bargain prices. The road to this establishment is indicated by signs on U.S. 101 three miles south of Lincoln City, three-quarters mile east on Immonen Road.

With some 65 shops, the **Factory Stores at Lincoln City** (1500 SE East Devil's Lake Rd., 541/996-5000), near the south end of town, is the largest outlet mall on the Oregon coast and has become something of a regional destination. Shops here include the ones you'd expect—London Fog, Samsonite, Eddie Bauer, etc.—plus some regional treats such as the tasting room/espresso shop at **Chateau Benoit** (541/996-3981), where you can sample Oregon wines, and **Pendleton Woolen Mills** (541/994-2496).

Catch the Wind (266 SE U.S. 101, 541/994-9500) has a shop here, as well as in Newport and Florence, selling kites, windsocks, and all the materials you need to create your own colorful flying contraption. This one is conveniently close to the D River Wayside, site of Lincoln City's twice-annual kite festivals.

INFORMATION AND SERVICES

A little south of the D River, the helpful **Lincoln City Visitor and Convention Bureau** (801 SW U.S. 101, 541/994-8378 or 800/452-2151) is open 9 A.M.–5 P.M. Monday–Saturday, 10 A.M.–4 P.M. Sunday. **Driftwood Public Library** (541/996-2277) is in the same municipal complex.

The **Central Oregon Coast Association** (541/265-2064 or 800/767-2064, www.coastvisitor.com) maintains a useful website with details on Lincoln City and the rest of coastal Lincoln County.

The **Traveler's Convenience Center** (660 SE U.S. 101), one mile south of the D River, has a coin laundry. The **post office** (541/994-2128) is two blocks east of U.S. 101 on East Devil's Lake Road.

The local walk-up teller is housed in the **Bank of America** building (1931 NW U.S. 101); there's another at the Factory Stores location.

Internet Access

For those who can't resist the urge to surf (the Internet, that is) the **B&B Package Express** (960 SE U.S. 101, 541/994-7272, closed Sunday) is not technically a cyber café, but it is a place to get online. They also have fax, copying, shipping (UPS, FedEx, Airborne), and a notary public. Rates are $6 per hour, with a $3 minimum.

Also in town, the **Cyber Garden and Tea House** (1826 NE U.S. 101, 541/994-3067, open daily) hosts five workstations with DSL connections along with numerous connections for personal laptops. A comfy place, with stuffed chairs and serving coffee, tea, and pastries, they offer a few other electronic services as well, such as printing, copying, faxing, and scanning. The hourly rate runs $9 or $5 per half-hour.

Transportation

Lincoln City–bound travelers from Portland (via 99W) and Salem (via ORE 22) pass through the scenic wine and orchard country to connect with ORE 18. This is one of the most dangerous roads to drive in the state, so extra care is called for on this two-laner.

About 25 miles east of Lincoln City is the state's number-one visitor attraction, **Spirit Mountain Casino** (P.O. Box 39, Grand Ronde 97347, 800/760-7977, http://spiritmountain.com), operated by the Confederated Tribes of Grand Ronde. In 2002, the casino drew 3.3 million people. Games of chance include daily 24-hour slots, craps, blackjack, poker, keno, and bingo.

Another dozen miles farther west, you pass through the **Van Duzer Forest Wayside,** a prime spot on the Salmon River for a picnic. Two miles before U.S. 101 is the hamlet of **Otis,** best known to travelers for appealing comfort food at the Otis Café.

Greyhound (800/231-2222) and **Lincoln County Transit** (541/265-4900, www.co.lincoln.or.us/transit/) buses stop in town. The latter line goes as far south as Yachats; they offer weekday service only and are closed on major holidays.

Peak traffic times in Lincoln City can result in 25,000 cars per day crawling through town. As an alternative to rush hour on U.S. 101, you could try detouring on NE West Devil's Lake Road or NE East Devil's Lake Road, which bypass the worst congestion.

For car rentals, contact **Robben Rent a Car** (3244 NE U.S. 101). For a list of car rental agencies on the coast and elsewhere in Oregon, check www.american-car.net/car-rental/OR.

North Coast

The north coast, from Lincoln City to the Columbia River, is little more than an hour's drive from Salem and Portland, so the region draws the greatest numbers of visitors. Still, apart from the weekend crush at Lincoln City, Cannon Beach, and Seaside, there's more than enough elbow room for everyone along this enchanting and varied coast.

Just north of Lincoln City, Cascade Head beckons hikers to explore its rare prairie headlands ecosystem. It's just inside Tillamook County, an area that's home to more cows than people and is synonymous with delicious dairy products—cheese and ice cream in particular. The Coast Highway wends inland through its lush pastureland between Neskowin and the town of Tillam-

ook. It's a pleasant enough stretch, but the Three Capes Scenic Loop, a 35-mile scenic coastal detour, is a more attractive alternative for both motorists and cyclists. At Pacific City, at the southern end of the Three Capes Loop, commercial anglers launch their dories right off the sandy beach and through the surf in the lee of Cape Kiwanda and mammoth Haystack Rock—a sight not seen anywhere else on the West Coast. The spectacular views and bird-watching from Lookout and Meares, the other two eponymous capes of the scenic loop, round out the attraction of this beautiful drive.

In Tillamook, it's no surprise that the town's biggest visitor attraction is cheese-related. More than a million people a year come to the Tillamook

Columbia River, seen from Coxcomb Hill in Astoria

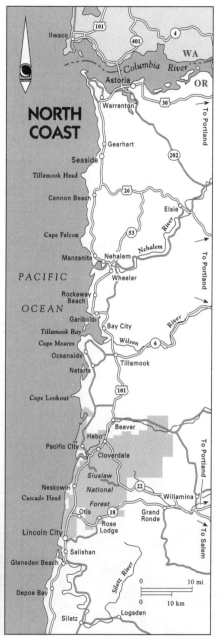

NORTH COAST

© AVALON TRAVEL PUBLISHING, INC.

Cheese Factory to tour the cheese-making operations and sample the excellent results. The Tillamook Air Museum is another popular diversion, housing an outstanding collection of vintage and modern aircraft in gargantuan Hangar B, the largest wooden structure in the world. Tillamook Bay, fed by five rivers, yields great harvests of oysters and crab, while the active Garibaldi charter fleet targets salmon in the bay and in the offshore waters.

Not far north, the Nehalem Bay area attracts more anglers, crabbers, and kayakers, as well as discriminating diners who come from far and wide to enjoy some surprisingly sophisticated cuisine. Close by, Oswald West State Park is a gem protecting old-growth forest and handsome little pocket beaches, as well as, some believe, a Spanish pirate treasure buried on Neahkahnie Mountain.

Cannon Beach and Seaside are two extremely popular resort towns that are polar opposites of one another. Cannon Beach, an understated enclave of tastefully weathered cedar-shingled architecture, is chockablock with art galleries, boutiques, and upscale lodgings and restaurants. Seaside is Oregon's quintessential family-friendly beach resort, with a long boardwalk, candy and gift shops, and noisy game arcades.

At the coast's far northwestern tip, where the mighty Columbia River meets the Pacific, visitors to Fort Stevens State Park can inspect the skeleton of a century-old shipwreck, as well as a military fort active from the Civil War to World War II. Fort Clatsop National Memorial includes a re-creation of the Corps of Discovery's winter 1805–1806 quarters—a must-stop for Lewis and Clark buffs and a focal point of bicentennial activities.

A few miles away, the former shipping and canning center of Astoria is rediscovering its own potential, with a lively arts scene, adventurous cuisine, and brightly painted Victorian homes hosting overnighters for bed and breakfast. Its long-idled waterfront is growing busy again with tourist attractions—most notably the wonderful Maritime Museum, one of the best in the west.

Neskowin and Cascade Head

NESKOWIN

The tiny vacation village of Neskowin (rhymes with "let's go in") has a quiet appeal based on a beautiful beach and two golf courses in the shadow of 1,500-foot-high Cascade Head. It's the polar opposite of busy Lincoln City, 15 miles south. There's not much to do here but relax on the uncrowded beach and enjoy the views of Cascade Head and the dark beauty of **Proposal Rock,** a stony, forested hillock that stands right at the edge of the surf, with Neskowin Creek curving around it. The feature was named by Neskowin's first postmistress, whose daughter received a marriage proposal nearby.

Golf

Neskowin boasts twice as many golf courses as restaurants, which is to say, two. **Hawk Creek Golf Course** (48480 U.S. 101 S., 503/392-4120, $12 for nine holes) is a hilly, nine-hole course on the east side of the highway. West of the highway, **Neskowin Beach Golf Course** (48405 Hawk St., 503/392-3377, green fees $12.50) has streams and water hazards adding a challenge to most of the nine holes.

Accommodations

From the outside, **The Chelan** (48750 Breakers Blvd., 503/392-3270, $110–125) resembles a lovingly landscaped Mediterranean villa perched on a dune above the Pacific. The nine two-bedroom condo units are well worth the price, with fireplaces, kitchens, and views. **Proposal Rock Inn** (U.S. 101 S., Neskowin 97149, 503/392-3115, rooms $44–89, suites $89–135) backs up on Hawk Creek and commands a fine view of the beach and the eponymous rock. Two-room oceanview suites with a full kitchen fetch higher prices than the standard rooms.

Free, rustic **campsites** can be found about eight miles north of town and just south of Neskowin. To get there, just look for the Scenic Drive sign east of U.S. 101 and follow County Road 12 for four miles. From there, travel about 100 yards west on Forest Service Road 12131, and you'll see the campground set along Neskowin Creek. To find out about the trails in the surrounding rainforest, call or write the Siuslaw National Forest (Hebo, OR 97121, 541/392-3161). The campground is open mid-April to mid-October—bring your own water or water-purification kit. The nearby scenic drive continues up into an area of huge trees captioned by Forest Service placards explaining the ecology.

Food

The **Neskowin Marketplace** is a grocery-deli-general store right off the highway. Neskowin's only restaurant, fortunately, serves great food at moderate prices. The **Hawk Creek Cafe** (503/392-3838, 8 A.M.–9 P.M. daily) has a friendly atmosphere and an inviting deck perched right over the creek. Count on filling omelets for breakfast; sandwiches, burgers, and wood-fired pizza for lunch; and grilled fish and steaks for dinner.

CASCADE HEAD
Cascade Head Scenic Research Area

About 10 miles north of Lincoln City, the 11,890-acre Cascade Head Experimental Forest was set aside in 1934 for scientific study of typical coastal Sitka spruce and western hemlock forests found along the Oregon coast. In 1974, Congress established the 9,670-acre Cascade Head Scenic Research Area, which includes the western half of the forest, several prairie headlands, and the Salmon River estuary. In 1980, the entire area was designated a Biosphere Reserve as part of the United Nations Biosphere Reserve system.

The headlands, reaching as high as 1,800 feet, are unusual for their extensive prairies still dominated by native grasses: red fescue, wild rye, and Pacific reedgrass. The Nechesney Indians, who inhabited the area as long as 12,000 years ago, purposely burned forest tracts around Cascade Head to provide browse for deer and to

![Cascade Head photograph](© MARK MORRIS)

Cascade Head and the Salmon River estuary, north of Lincoln City

reduce the possibility of larger, uncontrollable blazes. These human-made alterations are complemented by the inherent dryness of south-facing slopes that receive increased exposure to sun. In contrast to these grasslands, the northern part of the headland is the domain of giant spruces and firs because it catches the brunt of the heavy rainfalls and lingering fogs. Endemic wildflowers include coastal paintbrush, goldenrod, streambank lupine, rare hairy checkermallow, and blue violet, a plant critical to the survival of the Oregon silverspot butterfly, a threatened species found in only six locations. Deer, elk, coyote, snowshoe hare, and the Pacific giant salamander find refuge here, while bald eagles, great horned owls, and peregrine falcons may be seen hunting above the grassy slopes. Today, in addition to its biological importance, the area is a mecca for some 6,000 hikers annually and for anglers who target the salmon and steelhead runs on the Salmon River.

On the north side of the Salmon River, turn west from U.S. 101 onto **Three Rocks Road** for a scenic driving detour on the south side of Cascade Head. The paved road curves about 2.5 miles above the wetlands and widening channel of the Salmon River estuary, passes Savage Road, and ends at a parking area and boat launch at Knight County Park. From the park, the road turns to gravel and narrows (not suitable for RVs or trailers) and continues about another one-half mile to its end, at a spectacular overlook across the estuary.

Cascade Head also offers some rewardingly scenic hikes, with rainforest pathways and wildflower meadows giving way to dramatic ocean views. The **Cascade Head Trail** runs six miles roughly parallel to the highway, with a south trailhead near the intersection of Three Rocks Road and U.S. 101 and a north trailhead at Falls Creek, on U.S. 101 about one mile south of Neskowin. It passes through old-growth forest and offers coastal views near its north end.

A short but brisk hike to the top of the headland on a **Nature Conservancy trail** begins near Knight County Park. Leave your car at the park and walk about one-half mile up Savage Road to the trailhead. It's 1.7 miles one way, with a 1,100-foot elevation gain. No dogs or bicycles are allowed on the trail.

About three miles north of Three Rocks Road, gravel Cascade Head Road (Forest Service Rd. 1861) leads four miles west of U.S. 101 to the **Hart's Cove trailhead.** The first part of the trail runs through arching red alder treetops and 250-year-old Sitka spruces with five-foot diameters. The understory of mosses and ferns is nourished by 100-inch rainfalls. Next, the trail emerges into open grasslands. The hilly, five-mile round-trip hike finally leads to an oceanfront meadow overlooking Hart's Cove, where the barking of sea lions might greet you. This trail can have plenty of mud, so boots are recommended as you tromp through the rainforest. Note that the trail is closed Janurary 15–July 15.

Sitka Center for Art and Ecology

The region in the shadow of Cascade Head can be explored in even greater depth thanks to the Sitka Center for Art and Ecology (P.O. Box 65, Otis 97368, 541/994-5485, www.sitkacenter .org), located off Savage Road on the south side of the headland. Classes are offered June–August in art and nature as an expression of the strong relationship between the two. Experts in everything from local plant communities to Siletz Indian baskets conduct outdoor workshops on the grounds of Cascade Head Ranch. Classes can last from a couple of days to a week, and fees vary as well.

Three Capes Scenic Loop

The Three Capes Scenic Loop, a 35-mile byway off U.S. 101 between Pacific City and Tillamook, is considered by many to be the preeminent scenic area on the north coast of Oregon. While the beauty of Cape Kiwanda, Cape Lookout, and Cape Meares certainly justifies leaving the main highway, it would be an overstatement to portray this drive as a thrill-a-minute detour on the order of the south coast's Boardman Park or the central coast's Otter Crest Loop. Instead of fronting the ocean, the road connecting the capes winds mostly through dairy country, small beach towns, and second-growth forest.

What's special about this scenic loop are the three capes themselves, and unless you get out of the car and walk on the trails, you'll miss the aesthetic appeals and the distinctiveness of each headland's ecosystem. The wave-battered bluffs of Cape Kiwanda, the precipitous overlooks along the Cape Lookout Highway, and the curious Octopus Tree at Cape Meares are the perfect antidotes to the inland towns along U.S. 101. Most of the lodging and dining options in the Three Capes area are clustered in Pacific City and at the other end in Netarts and Oceanside. In between, it's mostly sand dunes, isolated beaches, rainforest, and pasture.

CAPE KIWANDA

North of Neskowin, U.S. 101 passes through pastoral landscapes befitting Tillamook County's nickname, "the Land of Cheese, Trees, and Ocean Breeze." If you've tasted Tillamook ice cream or award-winning cheddar cheese, chances are the mere sight of the cows grazing on the lush grasses here will have you thinking about your next meal. The trees and ocean breeze components begin to take form on the Three Capes Scenic Loop turnoff (Brooten Road) about eight miles north of Neskowin. The route leads a couple of miles along Nestucca Bay and the Nestucca River, one of the best salmon and steelhead streams in the state. Strong runs of spring and fall chinook on the Nestucca and the Little Nestucca rivers can yield lunkers above 50 pounds.

As you approach the shore in Pacific City, the sight of **Haystack Rock** will immediately grab your attention. At 327 feet, this sea stack is nearly 100 feet taller than the like-named rock in Cannon Beach. Standing a mile offshore, this monolith has a brooding, enigmatic quality that constantly draws the eye to it. Look closely, and you'll understand why some folks called it Teacup Rock.

The tawny sandstone escarpment of Cape Kiwanda juts one-half mile out to sea and frames the north end of the beach. In storm-tossed waters, this cape is the undisputed king of rock-and-roll if you go by coffee-table books and calendar photos. While other sandstone promontories on the north coast have been ground into sandy beaches by the pounding surf, it's been theorized that Kiwanda has endured thanks to the buffer of Haystack Rock. In any case, hang-gliding aficionados are glad the cape is here. They scale its shoulders and set themselves aloft off the north face to glide above the beach and dunes.

PACIFIC CITY

This small town of about 1,000 at the base of Cape Kiwanda attracts growing numbers of vacationers and retirees but remains true to its 19th-century origins as a working fishing village. In addition to the knockout seascapes and recreation, if you come here at the right times you may be treated to a unique spectacle—the launch or return of the **dory fleet.** It's a tradition dating back to the 1920s, when gillnetting was banned on the Nestucca River to protect the dwindling salmon runs. To retain their livelihood, commercial anglers began to haul flat-bottomed, double-ended dories down to the beach on horse-drawn wagons, then rowed out through the surf to fish. These days, trucks and trailers get the boats to and from the beach, and outboard motors have replaced oar power, enabling the dories to get 50 miles out to sea from Pacific City. If you come here around 6 A.M., you can watch them taking off. The fleet's late-afternoon return attracts a crowd that comes to see the dory operators skidding their crafts as far as possible up the beach to the waiting boat trailers. Other people meet the dories to buy salmon and tuna direct.

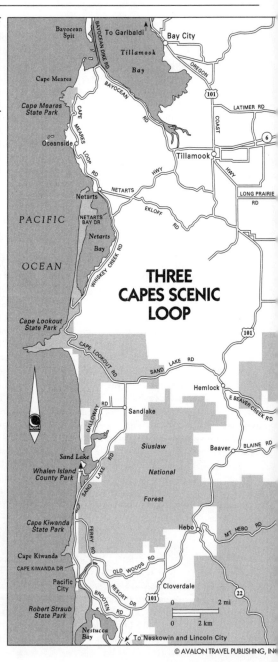

THREE CAPES SCENIC LOOP

In late July, the **Dory Festival** celebrates the area's fleet. The three-day fête includes craft and food booths, a pancake breakfast, a fishing derby, and other activities. Visitors also have the opportunity to ride out through the surf in a dory, for about $10 per person. For more information, call the chamber of commerce (503/965-6161). If you want to join the anglers at other times of year, contact the **Haystack Fishing Club** (888/965-7555), across from the beach near the Inn at Cape Kiwanda, where you can book with Joe Hay, the only licensed dory outfitter in the world. Troll for salmon or ling cod, whale-watch, or just enjoy the ride.

In addition, the Pacific City area is besieged by surfers, who enjoy some of the longest waves on the Oregon coast. **Robert Straub State Park,** just south of town, offers access to Nestucca Bay and to the dunes and a long, uninterrupted stretch of beach.

Accommodations

The nicest motel on the Three Capes route is **The Inn at Cape Kiwanda** (33105 Cape Kiwanda Dr., Pacific City, 503/965-6366 and 888/965-7001, www.innatcapekiwanda.com, $159–299 in summer, $109–219 Nov. 1–Apr. 30). All rooms face a beautiful beach and Cape Kiwanda's giant sand dune. If it's too rainy to go outside, fireplaces and spacious, well-appointed rooms make for great storm-watching. Inquire about special packages that offer discounts on rooms, as well as meals at the Pelican Pub across the road. Rooms with whirlpool tubs are available here, and pets are permitted in some rooms.

Five blocks from the beach, the **Inn at Pacific City** (35215 Brooten Rd., Pacific City, 503/965-6366 or 888/722-2489, $78–85 May–Oct., half price the rest of the year) is a low-slung, shingle-clad compound. Across the street, at the **Pacific City Inn** (35280 Brooten Rd., 503/965-6464 or 866/567-3466), rooms fetch $79–95 in summer ($49–65 off-season), with two-room suites for $119–139 in summer. Both of these motels allow pets for an additional $9 nightly.

Food

Our advice is to fill up your tummy in Pacific City before heading north on the sparsely populated Capes Loop. While a few outlets of undistinguished diner food might keep you alive until Oceanside—the other outpost of civilization on the north end of the Loop—the Capes' midsection is more a feast for the eyes.

Mexican and Seafood: Los Caporales (35025 Brooten Rd., Pacific City, 503/965-6999, open from 11 A.M. Wed.–Sun.) serves up bountiful plates of Mexican food and seafood—so generous that the combination plates ($7–10) could feed several people. The restaurant's name refers to foremen at a cattle ranch, perhaps explaining portions fit for wrangler-sized appetites.

If hanging plants, a piano, and Nestucca River frontage don't make you feel at home, the apple pie and other wholesome fare at the **Riverhouse** (34450 Brooten Rd., Pacific City, 503/965-6722) probably will. In addition to comfort food at lunch, dinner is a fine-dining experience where you don't have to get dressed up. The burgers and open-face sandwich combinations are priced on the high side ($9–13) but are the perfect pick-me-ups after a morning of fishing or beachcombing along the Nestucca River estuary. Dinners (most around $20) focus on fish and shellfish, with a couple of beef choices. Steamer clams simmered in vermouth make a hearty starter. Or try a salad with their sweet blue cheese dressing, which has enough of a following throughout western Oregon that it's sold in regional supermarkets. Weekends feature the eclectic offerings of live musicians on Saturday night and a wonderful Sunday brunch. Come early, because seating is limited in this 11-table restaurant.

Casual Fare: Close by, at the **Grateful Bread Bakery** (34085 Brooten Rd., Pacific City, 503/965-7337, 8 A.M.–8:30 P.M. Thurs.–Mon.), the challah, carrot cake, marionberry strudel, and other homemade baked goods deserve special mention. This is a good place to fill a thermos with the bakery's excellent coffee and grab a baguette for a picnic atop one of the capes. The full breakfast menu offers a range of tasty omelets, served with oven-roasted spuds at great

© MARK MORRIS

prices. The Salmon Scramble is another winner. Lunch here might include thin-crust New York–style pizza paying homage to the owners' East Coast roots, Tillamook cheese chowder, or dill shrimp salad sandwich. You can do breakfast or lunch well here for little more than $7. Dinners feature dory-caught cod prepared breaded and grilled or blackened, as well as salmon, chicken, and steak.

A popular and well-known Pacific City hangout is the **Pelican Pub and Brewery** (33180 Cape Kiwanda Dr., Pacific City, 503/965-7007, www.pelicanbrewery.com). Set in a most enviable spot right on the beach opposite Cape Kiwanda and Haystack Rock, this brewpub has the best coastal view of any brewpub in Oregon, with an eclectic, mouthwatering menu to match. Halibut fish and chips, gourmet pizzas, steamed clams, barbecue pork ribs, and hazelnut-crusted salmon are some of the standouts. The pub's brews, including Tsunami Stout, Doryman's Dark Ale, India Pelican Ale, and MacPelican's Scottish Style Ale, have garnered stacks of awards. Watching the sun set behind Haystack Rock, while supping on a pint of Doryman's and a bowl of chowder (another award-winner), is a recipe for pure contentment.

CAPE LOOKOUT

Sand Lake

The scenic route continues north from Pacific City on Cape Drive about six miles to the hamlet of Sand Lake. Extensive sand dunes surrounding the Sand Lake estuary here suddenly transition to the rainforest slopes on top of nearby Cape Lookout. The dunes and beach attract squadrons of dune buggy enthusiasts. Camping is available year-round at **Sand Beach Campground** (Galloway Rd., 877/444-6777), which has basic sites for tenters and RVs. This dramatic area is popular with hikers, too. **Into The Sunset** (503/965-6326) organizes personalized guided horseback excursions; the "full moon ride" is highly recommended.

Cape Lookout Hikes

A couple miles farther north, look for the large parking area for the 2.5-mile trail to the tip of Cape Lookout. An orientation map at the trailhead details the trail options. Two trails go down to the water's edge, while the trailhead at the northwest corner of the parking lot leads out to land's end. The 2.5-mile-long, one-mile-wide cape juts out from the coast, so hikers feel as if they're on the prow of a giant ship suspended 500 feet above the ocean on all sides. Here, more than anywhere else on the Oregon coast, you get the sense of being on the edge of the continent. Giant spruce, western red cedars, and hemlocks surround the gently hilly trail to the tip of the cape. In March, Cape Lookout is a popular vantage point for whale-watching. June through August, a bevy of wildflowers and birds further enhance the rolling terrain en route to the tip of this headland, and in late summer red huckleberries line the path.

Halfway to the overlook, there are views north to Cape Meares over the Netarts sandspit. Even if you settle for a mere 15-minute stroll down the trail, you can look southward beyond Haystack Rock to Cascade Head. Right about where the trees open up, look for a bronze plaque commemorating the crash of a World War II plane (with nearly a dozen casualties) embedded into the rock wall bordering the right-hand (north) side of the trail at eye level. If you're unable to take this hike, there are two unmarked turnouts along the highway between the sand dunes and Cape Lookout parking lot that let you survey the terrain south to Cape Kiwanda.

Cape Lookout State Park

On the north side of the cape is the campground and beach extension of expansive Cape Lookout State Park (13000 Whiskey Creek Rd. W., Tillamook 97141, 503/842-4981 information, 800/452-5687 reservations), which also encompasses the entire cape and the five-mile-long Netarts Spit within its boundaries. The park has 176 tent sites ($16) and 38 full-hookup sites ($20), as well as 10 yurts ($27), three cabins (with bathrooms, kitchen, TV/VCR, $65), and a hiker/biker camp ($4); discounts apply October–April. Amenities include showers, flush toilets, laundry, and evening programs. Reservations and deposit are required at this popular campground. Eight miles of hiking trails include a trail beginning at the registration booth leading to a ridge above the ocean. Another trail heads north through a variety of estuarine habitats along the sandspit separating Netarts Bay from the Pacific. The former is a popular site for agate hunters, clammers, and crabbers. There is also a $3 day-use fee, covered by the Coast Passport.

CAPE MEARES

North from Cape Lookout State Park, the trees along the Three Capes route open at a couple of turnouts, offering beguiling views to the north of the seven-mile-long Netarts Spit, Netarts Bay, and Three Arch Rocks just offshore. The road quickly drops down and skirts the shallow bay, which drains and fills with the tides. Netarts Bay and its mudflats are popular with clamdiggers and with anglers and crabbers, who can launch boats from Netarts Landing at the northeast corner of the bay. **Netarts Bay RV Park and Marina** (2260 Bilyeu, Netarts, 503/842-7774) and **Big Spruce RV Park** (4850 Netarts Hwy. W., 503/842-7443) rent motorboats and crabbing supplies.

NETARTS

Tiny Netarts (pop. approx. 200) has an enviable location overlooking the bay and the Pacific beyond. Along with nearby Oceanside, it's the closest coastal settlement from Tillamook and makes for a fine, quiet getaway.

Accommodations and Food

The **Terimore** (5105 Crab Ave., Netarts 97143, 503/842-4623 or 800/635-1821, $45–100) is situated a short walk from the water at the north end of Netarts Bay. Other than some units with fireplaces and kitchens, there are few frills here, but for fair rates you'll find yourself close to the water and within easy driving distance of Cape Lookout trails and a beach walk away from Roseanna's, the Capes Loop's best restaurant. A pets-allowed policy (in some rooms) and a coin laundry are two other appreciated practicalities. Wood-paneled kitchen units with bay and ocean views run $80–100 ($60–80 in winter), while no-view kitchen cottages run $45–75 ($35–60 in winter). Ask about special offers in the off-season, November–April.

Happy Camp (P.O. Box 52, 845 Happy Camp Rd., Netarts 97143, 503/842-4012, open year-round, $16) has 30 tent sites and 38 RV sites. All the amenities are available, and reservations are accepted.

You'll find several lunch and dinner spots to choose from. The view of Cape Lookout is tops at **The Schooner** (2065 Netarts Bay Rd., 503/842-4988, open daily), which serves breakfast (starting at 8 A.M.), lunch, and dinner (seafood and steak).

OCEANSIDE

The road between Netarts and Cape Meares heads into the pricey beach-house community of Oceanside (pop. approx. 250). Many of the homes are built into the cliff overlooking the ocean, Sausalito-style. This motif reaches its apex atop Maxwell Point. You can peer several hundred feet down at **Three Arch Rocks Wildlife Refuge,** part-time home to one of the continent's largest and most varied collections of shorebirds. A herd

© MARK MORRIS

Netarts Bay, with Three Arch Rocks in the distance

of sea lions also populates this trio of sea stacks from time to time.

Accommodations

While low prices and a window on the water can be found at **Ocean Front Cabins** (1610 Pacific Ave., Oceanside, 503/842-6081 or 888/845-8470, $50–75), the older, smallish rooms here might at first give some travelers pause. Nonetheless, for as little as $50 (with a kitchenette, $60; two-bedded rooms with full kitchens, $75), you'll find yourself literally within a stone's throw of Oceanside's beachcombing and dining highlights.

The aptly named **House on the Hill** (P.O. Box 187, Oceanside 97134, 503/842-6030, standard units $95–185, $120–225 kitchen units), also called the Clifftop Inn, is perched on a bluff at Maxwell Point, where you get the seclusion and cliffside ocean grandeur of this headland. Discounts off-season knock about 25 percent off the rates. Most of the 16 units here are not especially elaborate, but the sweeping view is easily worth whatever you pay for the room. The office maintains a little museum with sea specimens and newspaper articles about the area, as well as

a telescope focused on the offshore Three Arch Rocks bird refuge several hundred feet below.

Another good lodging option is **Bender Vacation Rental Properties** (503/233-4363, $70–175, two-night minimum), boasting six units with cliffside ocean views, large private decks, and full kitchens (except for one unit). Other amenities include fireplaces, TVs, VCRs, and microwaves. Pets are welcome at most locations.

Food

Roseanna's Oceanside Café (1490 Pacific Ave. NW, Oceanside, 503/842-7351) is a popular draw for Three Capes travelers and garners high marks from just about everyone. At first, the weather-beaten cedar-shake exterior might lead you to expect an old general store, as indeed it was decades ago. Once you're inside, however, the ornate decor leaves little doubt that this place takes its new identity seriously. From an elevated perch above the breakers, you'll be treated to expertly prepared steak and seafood followed by sumptuous desserts. Dishes centered on local oysters and fresh salmon are the specialties frequently touted by the staff. The menu is surprisingly extensive, as is the wine list, but be forewarned—the bills can be high at Roseanna's (around $30 per person for dinner) and the service leisurely, so you might just want to enjoy lunchtime gourmet sandwiches. Better yet, come for the blackberry cobbler dessert; order it warm, so the Tillamook Vanilla Bean ice cream on top melts down the sides, and watch the waves over a long cup of coffee.

The **Anchor Tavern** (1495 Pacific Ave., Oceanside, 503/842-2041) is a nearby alternative for food by the beach. Along with microbrews, specialties are smoked meats, barbecue ribs, clam chowder, pizza, and burgers. A light meal with a microbrew won't set you back more than $10. Hanging above the bar is a wide-angle photo of Hartford, Connecticut. The four-foot-long picture depicts the kind of urban sprawl that will make you glad you're here.

Oceanside Espresso (1610 Pacific Ave., Oceanside, 503/842-1919) is at the north end of the main drag on a bluff above the beach. While finding gourmet coffee drinks in this part of the coast can sometimes seem like searching for the Holy Grail, this place has something else going for it—windows overlooking the surf in front of Three Arch Rocks. Light breakfast with fresh-baked pastries, lunchtime homemade soup and sandwiches, and the works of local artists adorning the walls all make a stop worthwhile.

CAPE MEARES SCENIC VIEWPOINT

With stunning views, picnic tables, a newly restored lighthouse, and a uniquely contorted tree a short walk from the parking lot, Cape Meares Scenic Viewpoint is the user-friendliest site on the Three Capes Loop. The park was named for English navigator John Meares, who

mapped many points along this coast in a 1788 voyage. The famed **Octopus Tree** is less than one-quarter mile up a forested hill. The tentacle-like extensions of this Sitka spruce have also been compared to the arms of a candelabra. Another writer likened this tree to a gargantuan spider in a near-fetal position. The 10-foot diameter of its base supports five-foot-thick trunks, each of which is large enough to be a single tree. Scientists have propounded several theories for the cause of its unusual shape, including everything from wind and weather to insects damaging the spruce when it was young. An Indian legend about the spruce contends that it was shaped this way so that the branches could hold the canoes of a chief's dead family. Supposedly, the bodies were buried near the tree. This was a traditional practice among the tribes of the area, who referred to species formed thusly as "council trees."

Beyond the tree you can look back at Oceanside and Three Arch Rocks Refuge. The sweep of Pacific shore and offshore monoliths makes a fitting finale to your sojourn along the Three Capes Loop, but be sure to also stroll the short paved trail down to the lighthouse, which begins at the parking lot and provides dramatic views of an offshore wildlife refuge, Cape Meares Rocks. Bring binoculars to see tufted puffins, pelagic cormorants, seals, and sea lions. The landward portion of the refuge protects rare old-growth evergreens.

The restored interior of **Cape Meares Lighthouse,** built in 1890, is open 11 A.M.–4 P.M. daily May–September. This beacon was replaced as a functioning light in 1963 by the automated facility located behind it, and it now houses a gift shop. A free tour is occasionally staffed by volunteers, who might tell you about how the lighthouse was built here by mistake and offer a peek into the prismatic Fresnel lenses.

Tillamook and the Tillamook Bay Area

Without much sun or surf, what could possibly draw enough visitors to the town of Tillamook (pop. 4,270) to make it one of Oregon's top three tourism attractions? Superficially speaking, tours of a cheese factory and a World War II blimp hangar, in a town flanked by mudflats and rain-soaked dairy country, shouldn't pull in more than a million tourists a year—but they do. As anyone who has driven to Tillamook via the scenic Three Capes Loop or past Neahkahnie Mountain on U.S. 101 can attest, those tasty morsels of jack and cheddar provide the perfect complement to the surrounding region's scenic beauty.

Tillamook County is home to more than 26,000 cows, which easily outnumber the county's human population. They're the foundation of the Tillamook County Creamery Association's famous cheddar cheese and other dairy products, which generate about $85 million in annual sales. Other important contributors to the local economy are fishing and oyster farming.

Aesthetic and gastronomic appeals notwithstanding, Capt. Robert Gray was merely looking for safe harbor when he pulled into the area of present-day Garibaldi, on the north side of Tillamook Bay, in 1788. He originally mistook the bay for the mouth of the Columbia, the "great river of the northwest" he was seeking. After some exploration of the area, he realized his mistake, and after a skirmish with Indians in which a member of his crew was killed, Gray departed. Some historians cite this as the first American landing on Oregon soil.

In any case, the region—whose name in Indian parlance means "Land of Many Waters"—has been written up in several other footnotes of history. In the early 1900s, Tillamook Bay's sandspit became the site of a popular resort known as Bay Ocean. This complex was once envisioned as the Atlantic City of the Pacific coast. Over the years, however, changes in ocean currents resulting from construction of a new jetty caused the sandspit to wash away, and by 1932 few traces remained of the three-story hotel, natatorium, cabins, scores of private homes, and the world's largest heated indoor swimming pool. As any old-timer on the coast will tell you, "Woe betide those who build their castles on the sand."

In 1933, a wildfire devastated forests in the Coast Range east of town in what was the worst disaster in the state's history. The Tillamook Burn raged for four weeks, reducing massive acreage of old growth to rows of charred stumps. The fire pushed a cloud of ash 40,000 feet into the air. Ashfall was recorded 500 miles out to sea and as far east as Yellowstone National Park in Wyoming, while Oregon's upper left edge lived in semidarkness for weeks. Fires in 1939 and 1945 further ravaged the area, leaving a total of 355,000 acres destroyed by the three blazes. More than 72 million seedlings planted by a community reforestation effort in the years that followed have produced an impressive stand of trees in these forests today.

In 1940–1942, partially in response to a Japanese submarine firing on Fort Stevens in Astoria, the U.S. Navy built two blimp hangars south of town, the two largest wooden structures ever built, according to the *Guinness Book of World Records*. Of the five naval air stations on the Pacific coast, the Tillamook blimp guard patrolled the waters from northern California to the San Juan Islands and escorted ships into Puget Sound. All kinds of blimp stories abound in Tillamook bars, but only one wartime encounter has been documented. Recently declassified records confirm that blimps were involved in the sinking of what was believed to be two Japanese submarines off Cape Meares. In late May 1943, two of the high-flying craft, assisted by U.S. Navy subchasers and destroyers, dropped several depth charges on the submarines, which are still lying on the ocean floor.

Until 1946, when the station was decommissioned, naval presence here created a boomtown. Bars and businesses flourished, and civilian jobs were easy to come by. After the war years, Tillamook County returned to the economic trinity of "cheese, trees, and ocean breeze" that has sustained the region to the present day.

© MARK MORRIS

These gals and more than 26,000 of their pals outnumber Tillamook County's human residents and enable an $85-million-a-year dairy industry.

SIGHTS

Tillamook Cheese Factory

With more than a million visitors a year, the Tillamook Cheese Factory (4175 U.S. 101 N., Tillamook 97141, 503/842-4481, 8 A.M.–8 P.M. daily in summer, 8 A.M.–6 P.M. Labor Day–mid-June) is far and away the county's biggest drawing card. The plant welcomes visitors with a reproduction of the *Morningstar,* the schooner that transported locally made butter and cheese in the late 1800s and now adorns the label of every Tillamook product. The quaint vessel symbolizing Tillamook cheesemaking's humble beginnings stands in stark contrast to the technology and sophistication that go into making this world-famous gourmet product today.

Inside the plant, a self-guided tour follows the movement of curds and whey to the "cheddaring table." Whey is drained from the curds, which are then cut and folded. These processes are coordinated by white-uniformed workers in a stadium-sized factory. As you look down on the antiseptic scene from the glassed-in observation area, it's

hard to imagine this as the birthplace of many a pizza and grilled-cheese sandwich. A taste of a few samples, however, proves it's true. Tillamook ice cream has been touted by the *New York Times* as superior to Häagen-Dazs, and their extra-premium aged sharp white cheddar was rated by the National Milk Producers in 1997 as the country's best cheese.

User-friendly informational placards and historical displays recount Tillamook Valley's dairy history from 1851, when settlers began importing cows. The problem then was how to ship the milk to San Francisco and Portland. Even though salting butter to preserve it allowed exportation, ships still faced the difficulty of negotiating the treacherous Tillamook bar. In 1894, Peter McIntosh introduced techniques here to make cheddar cheese, whose long shelf life enabled it to be transported overland.

In the early 1900s, the Tillamook County Creamery Association absorbed smaller operations and opened the modern plant in 1949. Today, Tillamook produces tens of millions of pounds of cheese annually, including Monterey jack, Swiss, and multiple variations of their

NORTH COAST FONDUE

Here's a tasty way to enjoy the famous cheese, trees, and ocean breeze of Oregon's north coast: When visiting the Tillamook Cheese Factory, purchase a 10-ounce bar of Tillamook extra sharp cheddar. They are often on special for just a couple of bucks. These so-called seconds may look funky, but their cosmetic blemishes are actually an indication of additional aging that enrich the flavor, and they can be easily trimmed. You might consider getting an extra bar or two to keep in your cooler to take home with you. You'll also need a bottle of beer. Every beer imparts its own distinctive finish. The Oregon ales in particular work best for this recipe (some of our favorites are Newport Pale Ale, Bridgeport Blue Heron, or Bridgeport Coho). Finally, you'll need a good loaf of bread, preferably sourdough or a crusty baguette.

Rest assured that a fancy fondue pot with a denatured alcohol burner is not required to produce and enjoy this venerable dish. It can just as easily be prepared on a campfire in a well-blackened Boy Scout pot. A camp stove also works quite well if you don't have access to a kitchen.

Begin by slicing the French bread into pieces about an inch square, so that each piece has some crust to hold it together. Then cut up the entire cheese bar into small cubes and toss them into a saucepan. Add about a half cup of beer to start. You can add more later, depending on how thick or thin you like your fondue. Melt the cheese on low temperature, stirring to obtain a creamy texture. Season to taste with pepper. Grab a fork, stab a piece of bread, dip it in, and feast.

"American Milk Producer's Best Cheese in America" award-winning white cheddar. Pepperoni, butter, cheese soup, milk, and other products are also available. There's a gift shop (more Holstein-themed tchochkes than you've probably dreamed of) and a full-service restaurant here, but the big attraction is the ice cream counter. Have a double-scoop chocolate peanut butter cone—worth every penny.

Blue Heron French Cheese Company

A quarter-million people a year visit Tillamook County's *second* most popular attraction, the Blue Heron French Cheese Company (2001 Blue Heron Dr., 503/842-8282, 8 A.M.–8 P.M. daily in summer, shorter hours the rest of the year), located one mile south of the Tillamook Cheese Factory. Housed in a large white barn, Blue Heron is famous for its Brie, although the cheese is no longer produced on-site. In addition to cheeses and other gourmet foods, the shop sells gift baskets, and more than 90 varieties of Oregon wines are available in their wine-tasting room. A deli serves lunches of homemade soups and salads. For kids, there's a petting farm with the usual barnyard suspects.

Tillamook Air Museum

South of town off U.S. 101, you can't possibly miss the enormous Quonset hut–like building east of the highway. The world-class aircraft collection of the Tillamook Air Museum (6030 Hangar Rd., 503/842-1130, 10 A.M.–5 P.M. daily, $9.50 adults, $8.50 seniors, $5.50 ages 13–17, $2 ages 7–12) is housed in and around Hangar B of the decommissioned Tillamook Naval Air Station. At 1,072 feet long, 206 feet wide, and 192 feet high, it's the largest wooden structure in the world. During World War II, this and another gargantuan hangar on the site (which burned down in 1992) sheltered eight K-class blimps, each 242 feet long.

Inside the seven-acre structure, you can learn about the role the big blimps played during wartime, as well as how they are used today. In addition, there's a large collection of World War II fighter planes (many one-of-a-kind models), as well as photos and artifacts from the naval air station days. Be sure to check out the cyclo-crane, a combination blimp/plane/helicopter. This was devised in the 1980s to aid in remote logging operations; it ended up being an $8 million bust.

If possible, bring binoculars here to see the interesting latticework of rafters and Navy-uniformed mannequins on the catwalks 20 stories up. To get there from downtown, take U.S. 101 South two miles, make a left at the flashing yellow light, and follow the signs.

Tillamook County Pioneer Museum

East of the highway in the heart of downtown, Tillamook County Pioneer Museum (2106 2nd St., 503/842-4553, 8 A.M.–5 P.M. Mon.–Sat., noon–5 P.M. Sun., Apr.–Sept., $3 adults, $7 families, $2 seniors, $.50 ages 12–17) is famous for its taxidermic exhibits and memorabilia from pioneer households. Particularly intriguing are hunks of ancient beeswax with odd inscriptions recovered from near Neahkahnie Mountain. Old photos are also worth the admission price. The old courtroom on the second floor has one of the best displays of natural history in the state. There are many beautiful dioramas, plus shells, insects, nest eggs, and taxidermy. The Beals Memorial Room houses a famous rock and mineral collection along with fossils. The main floor and the basement highlight human history with antique kitchen tools, old-time logging equipment, Indian artifacts and basketry, historic modes of conveyance (from stagecoaches to cars), and simulated pioneer households. In short, this is probably Oregon's best pioneer history museum.

Oregon Coast Explorer Train

A delightful way to see Tillamook Bay, the beach, Nehalem Bay, and the Nehalem River Valley is on board this excursion train, pulled by a gleaming, restored 1910 engine by Heisler Locomotive Works. The train (503/842-8206, www.potb.org/oregoncoastexplorer.htm, $12) makes weekend runs between Tillamook and Mohler (home of the Nehalem Bay Winery), via Bay City, Garibaldi, Rockaway, and Wheeler. In addition, the train offers coast supper runs, picnic runs inland from Garibaldi to the Salmonberry Canyon Wilderness, Fall Foliage excursions, and special "Santa" trips in December. The main season kicks off in late May and lasts through September, but the Explorer operates a reduced schedule at other times of the year.

Munson Creek Falls

Seven miles south of Tillamook, a 1.5-mile access road turns east from U.S. 101, leading to the highest waterfall in the Oregon Coast Range. Munson Creek Falls drops 266 feet over mossy cliffs surrounded by an old-growth forest. A very narrow, bumpy dirt road then takes you to the parking lot. A quarter-mile trail leads to the base of the falls, while another, slightly longer trail leads to a higher viewpoint; wooden walkways clinging to the cliff lead to a small viewing platform. This is a spectacle in all seasons, but come in winter when the falls pour down with greater fury. Note that motor homes and trailers cannot get into the park because the lot is too small.

RECREATION
Fishing

Among Oregon anglers, Tillamook County is known for its steelhead and salmon. Motorists along U.S. 101 know that the fall chinook run has arrived when fishing boats cluster outside the Tillamook Bay entrance near Garibaldi. As the season wears on, the fish—affectionately called "hogs" because they sometimes weigh in at more than 50 pounds—make their way inland up the five coastal rivers—the Trask, Wilson, Tillamook, Kilchis, and Miami—that flow into Tillamook Bay. At their peak, the runs create such competition for favorite holes that the process of sparring for them is jocularly referred to as combat fishing, as fishing boats anchor up gunwale to gunwale to form a fish-stopping palisade called a "hogline." Smokehouses and gas stations dot the outer reaches of the bay to cater to this fall influx.

The Guide Shop Inc. (12140 Wilson River Hwy., 503/842-3474) can arrange for a full day of fishing for chinook and silver salmon, steelhead, sturgeon, or trout; rates are about $150 per person for 1–4 anglers.

Golf

Golfers choose between two public courses in Tillamook. About two miles north of Tillamook, east of U.S. 101, is the **Bay Breeze Golf Course** (2325 Latimer Rd., 503/842-1166, green

M

NORTH COAST

fees $10 for nine holes on weekends). Another two miles north is the **Alderbrook Golf Course** (7300 Alderbrook Rd., 503/842-6413, green fees $24 for 18 holes on weekends).

More Outdoor Recreation

Besides fishing, the Tillamook State Forest holds plenty of other recreational opportunities. From a distance, the forest seems like a tree plantation, but hidden waterfalls, old railroad trestles from the days of logging trains, and moss-covered oaks in the Salmonberry River Canyon will convince you otherwise. Bird-watchers and mushroom pickers can easily penetrate this thicket thanks to 1,000 miles of maintained roads and old railroad grades. Two challenging trails off ORE 6, **King Mountain,** 25 miles east of Tillamook, and **Elk Mountain,** 28 miles east of Tillamook, climb through lands affected by the Tillamook Burn, but with scenic views throughout. Thanks to salvage logging in the wake of the disaster and subsequent replanting, myriad trails crisscross forests of Douglas and noble fir, hemlock, and red alder. A pamphlet entitled *Tillamook Forest Trails* is put out by the Oregon Department of Forestry, Tillamook District (4907 E. 3rd St., Tillamook 97141, 503/842-2543).

Bird-watchers flock to Tillamook Bay June–November to sight pelicans, sandpipers, tufted puffins, blue herons, and a variety of shorebirds. Prime time is before high tide, but step lively because this waterway was originally called "quicksand bay."

EVENTS

The **Tillamook County Fair** (503/398-5119) takes place the second week of August and represents more than 75 years of tradition. The **Dairy Festival** (for information: Tillamook Chamber of Commerce, 503/842-7525) takes place throughout June with rodeos, parades, and evocations of the Swiss-German roots of the region's settlers. Lederhosen, polka bands, sausages, and thousands of cheese-crazed tourists make this a lively celebration of the end of a long rainy season.

ACCOMMODATIONS

Hotels

Most travelers seem to pass through Tillamook on their way to someplace else, but there are a few lodging choices. **Best Western Inn & Suites** (1722 N. Makinster Rd., Tillamook 97141, 503/842-7599 or 800/299-4817, $94–150) is close to everything. Rooms have data ports, refrigerators, microwaves, irons and ironing boards, coffeemakers, plus cable TV. Amenities include an indoor pool, sauna, and hot tub, plus complimentary continental breakfast. **Shilo Inn** (2515 N. Main Ave., Tillamook 97141, 503/842-7971 or 800/222-2244, $75–129) has an indoor pool, spa, sauna, steam room, fitness center, restaurant, and lounge on-site. Ask about special discounts.

Campgrounds

Kilchis County Park (503/842-8662, closed Sept.–May, $10) has primitive riverside sites near good steelhead and salmon fishing on the Kilchis River. To get there, go up Kilchis River Road about 10 miles northeast of Tillamook. East of Tillamook, campers will find a half-dozen **state forestry park** campgrounds (503/842-2545) strung along Highway 6 on the Wilson River or its feeder streams, ranging from primitive to basic. Overnight costs range from free to $10.

FOOD

Tillamook restaurant fare draws on the local bounty from the sea and surrounding farm country. Dungeness crab, bay shrimp, clams, and oysters are indigenous to the area, and a burgeoning number of wine and gourmet outlets throughout Tillamook County can make for a surprisingly interesting taste tour. But the best food is found out in the county's smaller towns, in Oceanside, Manzanita, Nehalem, and Pacific City.

Local Delicacies

Eleven miles south of Tillamook on U.S. 101, near Beaver Road in Hebo, **Bear Creek Artichokes** (503/398-5411) is a large roadside fruit stand purveying the locally grown artichokes, as well as an astounding variety of herbs, perennials, and fruit. The cherries, marionberries, blackberries, and plums are recommended, as are the homemade fruit jams, apple dumplings, and scones. Although artichokes are a crop not usually seen outside of California, they thrive here. California artichokes traditionally come into Oregon markets from March–June, whereas the 'chokes grown around Tillamook ripen August–October. The Oregon variety is meatier and slightly sweeter. You can buy them here in season or look for them at farmers markets, Safeway, and Cub Foods.

Another source for the county's freshest produce is the **Tillamook Farmers Market** in downtown Tillamook. It runs every Saturday, late June through early October, on Laurel Avenue.

The **Farmhouse Café** at the Tillamook Cheese Factory serves breakfast and lunch from 8 A.M. daily. The deli at the **Blue Heron French Cheese Company** fixes sandwiches, soups, and salads daily. On the west side of U.S. 101, between the two cheese meccas, lunchtime do-it-yourselfers might check the locally raised and cured meat and smoked salmon at **Debbie D's Sausage Factory** (503/842-2622).

INFORMATION AND SERVICES

The **Tillamook Chamber of Commerce** (3705 U.S. 101 N., Tillamook 97191, 503/842-7525, www.tillamookchamber.org) is located across the parking lot from the cheese factory. Open 9 A.M.–5 P.M. Monday–Friday, 10 A.M.–3 P.M. Saturday, 10 A.M.–2 P.M. Sunday, mid-June– September.

Other useful numbers include the **Tillamook Crisis and Resource Center** (503/842-9486), **Tillamook Ambulance** (503/842-4444), and the **county sheriff** (503/842-2561).

BAY CITY

Casual passersby wouldn't figure tiny Bay City, five miles north of Tillamook, as a key stop on a Tillamook County gourmet tour, but those in the know hit the brakes here for excellent seafood, especially oysters. Motoring through

Bay City, you'll notice piles of oyster shells on the roadside, destined to be ground up into chicken feed. Predictably, local menu entrées with grilled Tillamook Bay oysters are a good bet.

Food

Pacific Oyster (5150 Oyster Bay Dr., 503/377-2323) lends credence to this assertion with grilled oysters, or enjoy them smoked, cocktail style, or on the half-shell. Crab cakes, halibut burgers, and clam chowder are also highlights in an extensive menu of fresh seafood. Takeout lunches are in the $6.50–8 range and can be enjoyed outside on the jetty close to interpretive placards that explain this environment.

Downie's Café (9320 5th St., 503/377-2220) is a greasy-spoon favorite among anglers. Whether it's homemade buttermilk pancakes for breakfast or the famous oyster burger ($6.50) for lunch, you'll leave full and satisfied. Finish off with a slice of homemade pie, especially pumpkin with Tillamook ice cream. To get to Downie's, look for the mural facade of Artspace Café on the east side of U.S. 101 opposite Tillamook Bay. Turn at Artspace onto 5th Street and drive two blocks to its intersection with C Street.

Artspace Café and Gallery (U.S. 101 at 5th, 503/377-2782, 4–9 P.M. Fri., 11 A.M.–8 P.M. Sat., 11 A.M.–3 P.M. Sun.) is another great place for oysters (try the oyster burgers and oysters Italia). There are also fresh fish, pasta dishes, chicken, and vegetarian offerings ($6.25–16.75). Occasional live music, a nice selection of beer, wine, and coffee drinks, paintings by Northwest artists on the walls, and the chance to create your own masterpiece courtesy of tableside crayons and paper make for a cultural interlude. While you're there, get caught up on Tillamook Bay politics with a copy of the free tabloid *Bay City Slug,* a pugnacious monthly that proudly proclaims itself "The Paper That Hates Progress."

GARIBALDI

Tillamook Bay's commercial fishing fleet is concentrated in this little port town (pop. 970) near the north end of the bay. Garibaldi, named in

© MARK MORRIS

crab traps, Garibaldi

1879 by the local postmaster for the Italian patriot, is a fish-processing center: Crabs, shrimp, fresh salmon, lingcod, and bottom fish (halibut, cabezon, rockfish, and sea perch) are the specialties here. At the marina, **Bayocean Seafood** (608 Commercial Dr., 503/322-3316) gets it right off the boats, so the selection is both low-priced and fresh. Likewise the crab, fish, and other seafood available next door at **Oregon Gourmet** (606 Commercial Dr., 503/322-2544). If you want it fresher, you'll have to catch it yourself.

And the town's fishing and crabbing piers *do* attract hordes who want to catch their own. Rent crab traps, kayaks, and other gear at the **Garibaldi Marina** (302 Mooring Basin Rd., 503/322-3312). In addition to dock fishing, guide and charter services offer salmon and halibut fishing, bird-watching, and whale-watching excursions. North of Garibaldi on U.S. 101, the bay entrance is a good place to see brown pelicans, harlequin ducks, oyster-catchers, and guillemots. The Miami River marsh, south of town, is a bird-watching paradise at low tide, when ducks and shorebirds hunt for food.

Fishing

The **Miami River** and **Kilchis River,** which empty into Tillamook Bay south of Garibaldi, get the state's only two significant runs of chum salmon, a species that is much more common from Washington northward. There's a catch-and-release season for them mid-September to mid-November. Both rivers also get runs of spring chinook and are open for steelhead most of the year.

Several charter companies have offices at the marina. **Troller Charters** (304 Mooring Basin, 503/322-3666) offers fishing excursions (a full day of salmon or halibut fishing for $70) and wildlife-viewing or whale-watching trips ($20 per person). Other outfits include **Garibaldi Charters** (607 Garibaldi Ave., 503/322-0007), and **Siggi G. Ocean Charters** (611 S. Commercial, 503/322-3285).

ROCKAWAY BEACH

This town of 1,200 was established as a summer resort in the 1920s by Portlanders who wanted a coastal getaway. And so it remains today—a quiet spot without much going on besides walks on the seven miles of sandy beach, a **Kite Festival** in mid-May, and an **Arts and Crafts Fair** in mid-August. Shallow **Lake Lytle,** on the east side of the highway, offers spring and early summer fishing for trout, bass, and crappie. The **Visitor Information Center** (503/355-8108), lodged in a bright red caboose in the center of town, can fill you in on other goings-on.

Accommodations

The Inn on Manhattan Beach (105 NW 23rd Ave., Rockaway Beach 97136, 503/355-2301 or 800/368-6499, $79–149 in summer, $49–99 off-season) is a small, comfortable, beachside motel toward the north end of town, run by the same folks at the Nehalem River Inn. Studios and one- or two-bedroom suites feature jetted spas and plush beds, with French doors opening onto private decks. Some units have kitchenettes.

The Inn at Rockaway Beach (104 U.S. 101 S., 503/355-2400 or 800/265-4291, rooms $59–89 in summer, $45–65 off-season) is a motel in a structure that dates back to 1912, when it was built to house railroad workers. Five one-room units and four two-bedroom suites are available; suites, with sitting rooms and kitchenettes, sleep up to seven.

The **Tradewinds Motel** (523 N. Pacific, Rockaway, 503/355-2112 or 800/824-0938, $47–95) is a family-friendly place on the beach, with a small picnic area and children's playground. All rooms are equipped with refrigerators, coffeemakers, and cable TV, while the oceanfront rooms also have fireplaces, full kitchens, and private balconies.

Food

Look to Rockaway's **Beach Pancake and Dinner House** (202 U.S. 101 N., 503/355-2411, open daily at 7 A.M.) for big portions at moderate prices. Locals tout the chicken and dumplings ($7.50). Other features include Mexican dishes, fresh oysters, and breakfast all day ($4.50–13). Photos and paintings by local artists cover the walls at **R and R Espresso & Café** (120 U.S. 101 N., 503/355-3315), which opens daily at 6 A.M. for coffee and baked goods; lunch includes salads and panini.

Internet Access

In Rockaway Beach, the **Online Resource Center** (480 U.S. 101 S., 503/355-3832) is open daily and provides full Internet access for $7 per hour, as well as laptop connections, coffees, snacks, soft drinks, and copying services.

Nehalem Bay Area

WHEELER

Wheeler (pop. 350) is a little town astride the Nehalem River where most accommodations are low-cost efficiencies for visiting fisherfolk, but the 10 rooms of the **Wheeler on the Bay Lodge and Marina** (580 Marine Dr., 503/368-5858 or 800/469-3204, $75–135), on U.S. 101 on the shore of Nehalem Bay, has other appeals. Seven rooms have bay views, five have spas, and all have different decor. There's also a video store, kayak rentals, dock tie-ups ($6 per night), and on-site massages, and they can help arrange fishing charters. Across the street, you can rent sea kayaks, recreational kayaks, surfboards, and other gear from **Nehalem Bay Kayak Co.** (503/368-

6055). They also organize guided paddle tours of the bay on Saturdays and Tuesdays.

Accommodations and Food

The Old Wheeler Hotel Bed & Breakfast (495 U.S. 101, Wheeler 97147, 503/368-6000 or 877/653-4683, $75–220 May–Sept.), a 1920s landmark across the road from the bay, has discounts available on weekdays and during the off-season. On weekends, a Swedish massage in the hotel's new massage room starts at $25 for a half-hour—just the thing after a long day of kayaking or fishing.

In a tiny cottage with seven tables (and bayview outdoor seating on the deck when possible) off the main drag, the **Treasure Café**

(92 Rorvik St., 503/368-7740, open for breakfast Thurs.–Sun., $5–9; dinner 6–9 P.M. on summer weekends only, $14–17), just off U.S. 101, offers hearty dishes that'll prepare you for whatever you've got planned for the day. How do scrambled eggs served with pan-fried locally farmed oysters, prawns benedict, hazelnut waffles, and buttermilk biscuits with homemade sausage gravy sound on a brisk, foggy morning? Try to get there before it opens at 9 A.M. on Thursday and Friday (8 A.M. Sat.–Sun.) to avoid the breakfast crush. Dinner entrées include tiger prawns in a variety of preparations, cioppino, grilled fish, pasta, pork tenderloin, and barbecue babyback ribs. Cash and checks only are accepted.

NEHALEM

Tiny Nehalem (pop. 230), occupying just a few blocks along U.S. 101 on the north bank of the Nehalem River, has developed several gift and antique shops and restaurants and a few surprise attractions in keeping with its new identity as a tourist town. Sizable runs of spring and fall chinook salmon and winter steelhead make this a popular destination for anglers. In August, locals claim you could just about cross the river stepping from boat to boat when the fish are in. Just southwest of town, the county maintains a boat-launch facility and dock, providing access to the river and to the bay downstream. The bay and slow-moving river also invite exploration by kayak and canoe; bring your own, or rent them in Nehalem. The sternwheeler *Nehalem Belle* (35995 U.S. 101 N., 503/368-7047) offers short cruises down the river into Nehalem Bay and back, serving picnic lunches and family-style buffet suppers while the skipper narrates local and natural history. Call for departure times and prices.

Accommodations

Nehalem offers a couple of interesting lodging choices. If you'd like to overnight close to the river—*on* the river—try the **Nehalem Bay Floating Motel** (503/368-7047). Choose among one-of-a-kind lodgings, including a 35-foot barge (sleeps 4–6 and has a separate bedroom, $135

nightly), a 47-foot converted tug (sleeps three, $135 per night), and a classic 41-foot Chris-Craft yacht, all moored on the river just off the highway in Nehalem. All units include linens, towels, kitchenettes with dishes, gas barbecues, cable TV, and videos, plus free use of kayaks, golf clubs, and boat moorage at their docks. Reservations are recommended.

An easily overlooked hideaway a short drive off U.S. 101 southeast of Nehalem is **The Nehalem River Inn Lodge** (34910 ORE 53, 503/355-2301 or 800/368-6499, www.river-inn.com, $99–149). Perched right on the South Fork of the Nehalem, this one-time roadhouse dating back to the 1930s has been converted into a four-unit riverside retreat with a surprise trump card—an outstanding restaurant (see the Food section) serving gourmet Northwest cuisine made from local ingredients. Each of the sunny, comfortable units has a private bath, cable TV, and a deck affording views of the river, the surrounding pasturelands, and mountains. The romantic white Riverside Cottage is a two-room suite with a kitchenette, fireplace, and a two-person spa. Eagle's Aerie also comprises two rooms, with a queen-size bed and twin hide-a-bed, plus kitchenette. The spacious Cormorant's Watch features a fireplace, king-size bed, jetted tub, and sweeping views from large picture windows, while the smaller Heron's Lookout sleeps one to two in its queen-sized bed. The inn also rents kayaks, which you can launch from the private dock to paddle up and down the river on a wildlife safari; you may spot otters, elk, bald eagles, and even seals that venture upriver from the bay. The inn is open year-round, while the dining room is open spring to fall.

Food

The **Nehalem River Inn's Restaurant and Wine Cellar** (34910 ORE 53, 503/355-2301 or 800/368-6499, www.river-inn.com) is one of the best places on the coast to experience fresh and inventive Northwest cuisine. After plying his craft on cruise ships and at top hotels, chef Stephen Tinkham returned to his native Tillamook County to establish the Inn in 1995. Taking full advantage of the regional ingredients available to him, Tinkham has created one of

THE WRECK OF THE GLENESSLIN

The sea was calm and the winds mild along the north Oregon coast on the afternoon of October 1, 1913, when locals observed a square-rigged ship sailing perilously close to the Nehalem shore. The Liverpool-built three-master *Glenesslin,* bound for Portland, was one of a dying breed of large sailing ships on the high seas, which were quickly being replaced by steam-powered vessels. Built in 1885, she was a fine ship and fast: Her 74-day passage from Portland, Oregon, to Port Elizabeth, South Africa, was never surpassed by another square-rigger. But on this day, in the twilight of sail, seasoned and reliable crews were scarce—the *Glenesslin*'s first and second officers were but 22 years old—and inexperience led to disaster.

the *Glenesslin,* still under full sail, on the rocks below Neahkahnie Mountain

According to maritime author James A. Gibbs, in his fascinating *Shipwrecks of the Pacific Coast,* the *Glenesslin,* under full sail, suddenly turned east toward the base of Neahkahnie Mountain. Losing the wind under the lee of Cape Falcon, Gibbs theorizes, the ship lost headway and the crew were unable to bring her about. As she neared the shore, an underwater reef ripped open her bottom plates. The crew shot a line to shore, and with the help of local rescuers, all 21 hands made it safely to land—many of them, it was said, under the influence of strong drink. As breakers pounded her stern, grinding her against the rocks, the ship soon began to break up. A Nehalem man bought the dying vessel for $100, but there was little hope of salvaging much.

In the lengthy official inquiry that followed, the captain and second mate were judged negligent in their duty, and the first mate reprimanded. The ship's underwriter initially balked at covering the loss, claiming that the ship had been intentionally wrecked in a scheme to collect the insurance, but they eventually paid up. It was a heartbreaking end for a beautiful and storied ship.

---

the coast's largest and most sophisticated menus, blending Northwest seafood, game, locally grown organic produce, wild mushrooms, and other ingredients to create dishes that will turn the heads of even the most discriminating diners. The other wonderful news about the Nehalem River Inn Restaurant is that prices are refreshingly reasonable: main courses range $12.50–26.50, with a wide choice of appetizers, soups, and salads $3–11.50. Although seafood takes center stage here, non–fish eaters will also find tempting choices. Entrées offered on a typical evening might include shrimp-stuffed halibut paupiettes with hazelnut pesto and wild fiddleheads, cognac-flamed venison tenderloin on juniper rusks with chanterelle mushrooms duxelles, Grand Marnier–flamed roast confit of duckling with Oregon gooseberry citronette and fresh lavender, and butternut squash agnolotti with pine nuts, sun-dried tomatoes, Parmesan, and tarragon. Start off with an appetizer such as spiced petite river crayfish with cayenne chipotle aioli, a specialty salad such as wild sorrel and organic greens with huckleberry vinaigrette, or a soup such as oyster stew with white mire poix or alder-smoked salmon chowder. Complement your meal with a bottle from a well-selected wine list favoring Oregon

NORTH COAST

wineries, including its own private-label wines. The dreamy desserts also highlight what's fresh and regional, including wild coast huckleberry cheesecake and Oregon marionberry peach melba. You could drive many a mile to sit down to a more flavorful and satisfying meal. Loyal customers make the journey from up and down the coast from asfar as Lincoln City and Astoria, and even from Portland, a two-hour drive away. The restaurant serves dinner only and opens for weekends in April, then operates nightly from Memorial Day to mid-September. Reservations are recommended.

On the riverside in Nehalem, the **Nehalem Dock Restaurant** (35815 U.S. 101 N., 503/368-5557, 11:30 A.M.–8 P.M. Sun.–Thurs., until 9 P.M. Fri. and Sat.) is an enjoyable spot for a casual lunch or dinner, with pastoral views from the dining room and adjoining deck. Burgers, fish and chips, crab cakes, and salmon, halibut, and prawn dishes are served with some creative twists. Owner-chef Tom Inouye, a world-class skateboarder, displays an impressive collection of skateboards and surfboards, which cover most of the walls and ceilings. If you come by boat, you can tie up at the public dock next door.

Winery

One-quarter mile back toward U.S. 101, the **Nehalem Bay Winery** (34965 ORE 53, 503/368-9463, www.nehalembaywinery.com) offers tastings and sales of its varietals, as well as fruit and berry wines (pinot noir, gewurztraminer, and blackberry). You can tour the grounds here and picnic 10 A.M.–6 P.M. daily or enjoy the tasting room's welcoming milieu. Saturdays and Sundays May–October, you can board the *Oregon Coast Explorer,* a vintage excursion train that runs between Tillamook and the winery. To get to the winery, look for the ORE 53 sign on U.S. 101 and head east 1.5 miles.

MANZANITA AND VICINITY

Huddled along an expansive curve of beach at the foot of Neahkahnie Mountain, quiet Manzanita (pop. 785) makes a pleasant stop for lunch or for the weekend. As one of the few

towns along the north Oregon coast that's not located directly on U.S. 101, Manzanita seems to feel more peaceful and secluded than most others. When adjacent coastal areas are fogbound, the seven-mile-long Manzanita Beach usually enjoys sunshine because of the shelter of Neahkahnie Mountain. It also has good surfing and windsurfing.

Nehalem Bay State Park

Just south of Manzanita, and occupying the entire sandy appendage of Nehalem Spit, is scenic, sprawling **Nehalem Bay Campground** (503/368-5943 information, 800/452-5687 reservations, open year-round), a favorite with beginning windsurfers, bikers, beachcombers, and anglers. To get there, turn south at Bayshore Junction just before U.S. 101 heads east into the town of Nehalem. Sandwiched between the bay and a four-mile beach stretching from Manzanita to the mouth of the Nehalem River are six full-hookup sites, 270 electrical with water sites, going for $16–20, plus some bargain hiker/biker sites ($4) and hot showers. There are 18 yurts for $27, a horse camp (17 sites with corrals, $12), and even a fly-in camp (six primitive sites) adjacent to the airstrip. A $3 daily day-use fee applies to noncampers. Park amenities include evening programs, flush toilets, and piped water. As big as this park is, it does fill up in summer, so reservations are recommended (particularly during July and August). Campers here often head over to the **Bunkhouse** (36315 U.S. 101, 503/368-6183) for ample and tasty breakfasts.

Oswald West State Park

Just north of Manzanita, **Neahkahnie Mountain** towers nearly 1,700 feet up from the edge of the sea. U.S. 101 climbs up and over its shoulders, to an elevation of 700 feet, and the vistas from a half-dozen pullouts (highest along the Oregon coast) are spectacular—but do try to keep your eyes on the snaking road until you've parked your car. This stretch of the highway, built by the Works Progress Administration (WPA) in the 1930s, was constructed by blasting a roadbed from the rock face and buttressing it

THE LOST TREASURE
OF NEAHKAHNIE MOUNTAIN

Local legends tell of Spanish pirates burying a treasure at Neahkahnie Mountain. One story relates that the crew of a shipwrecked Manila galleon salvaged its cargo of gold and beeswax (a valuable commodity in trade with Asia) by burying it in the side of the mountain. To deter Indians from the site, the pirates killed a black man and buried him on top of the cargo. While this account taken from native histories has never been substantiated, a piece of crudely inscribed beeswax retrieved from the Neahkahnie region carbon-dated 1500–1700 A.D. (on display at Tillamook's Pioneer Museum) keeps speculation alive. Further intrigue was added by the 1993 discovery of

© MARK MORRIS

the view from Neahkahnie Mountain: historic rockwork and Manzanita Beach

an ancient wooden rigging block. Found in the mud at the mouth of the Nehalem River, it was determined by a Spanish maritime expert to have been from a Manila galleon during that same time period. Lewis and Clark's 1805 reports of a Chinook Indian with red hair, and similar accounts from the Vancouver Expedition's 1792 encounter with a redheaded native who claimed his late father had been a shipwrecked Spanish sailor, would tend to corroborate the likelihood of this shipwreck and treasure stories passed down in native oral histories.

with stonework walls on the precarious cliffs. Soaring a thousand feet above, on the east side of the highway, is the peak named for the Tillamook tribe's fire spirit, Neah-Kah-Nie. The faint-hearted or acrophobic certainly couldn't have lasted long on this job. The handiwork of these roadbuilders and masons can be admired at several pullouts, along with the breath-taking vista of Manzanita Beach, Nehalem Spit, and some 17 miles south to Cape Meares.

Most of the mountain, and the prominent headlands of Cape Falcon, are encompassed within the 2,500-acre gem of Oswald West State Park. Several hiking trails weave through the park, including the 13 miles of the Oregon Coast Trail linking Arch Cape to the north with Manzanita. From the main parking lot on the east side of U.S. 101, a half-mile trail follows Short Sand Creek to **Short Sand Beach.** From Short Sand Beach, you can pick up the three-mile, old-growth-lined Cape Falcon Trail to the highway, or

you might want to just linger at Smuggler's Cove, which is a popular spot for surfers year-round. Rainforests of hemlock, cedar, and gigantic Sitka spruce crowd the secluded, boulder-strewn shoreline. At daybreak or dusk, keep an eye out for Roosevelt elk.

One mile south of the main parking lot is the access road to the **Neahkahnie Mountain Summit Trail** on the east side of the highway. It's not well marked; look for a subdivision on the golf course to the west. Drive the gravel road up one-quarter mile to the trailhead parking lot and begin a moderately difficult 1.5-mile ascent. Allow about 45 minutes to get to the top. The summit view south to Cape Meares and east to the Nehalem Valley ranks as one of the finest on the coast.

Whether you believe in the stories of lost pirate wealth buried somewhere on Neahkahnie Mountain (see the sidebar "The Lost Treasure of Neahkahnie Mountain"), there is real treasure

NORTH COAST

today for all who venture here, in the intangible currency of extraordinary natural beauty. The state park bears the name of Governor Oswald West, whose far-sighted 1913 beach bill was instrumental in protecting Oregon's virgin shoreline. That same year, Neahkahnie Mountain was the site of another shipwreck, in somewhat mysterious circumstances. (See the sidebar "The Wreck of the Glenesslin.")

To camp at Oswald West State Park (800/551-6949), you walk 0.3 mile from the campers' parking lot to 30 primitive campsites in a grove of old-growth conifers backdropped by high cliffs. You can use the wheelbarrows at the parking lot and campground to cart your gear back and forth. Camping is allowed March–October and costs $10–14 per night. There are flush toilets, but this campground is the only state park without electrical hookups.

Accommodations

Overnighters can choose from a variety of tasteful vacation cottages, B&Bs, and other lodgings in Manzanita. Advance reservations at most are a must, especially in summer, and many require two- to three-night stays during the high season and on some holidays. A good alternative to motels for families here are the rentals available from the several property management agencies in town. Among these is **Ribbon Investment Firm** (430 Laneda Ave., Manzanita 97130, 888/503-6009, www .ribboninvestmentfirm.com), with more than 40 fully furnished homes to let, running $75–195 per night. **OceanEdge Specialty Rentals** (P.O. Box 116, Manzanita 97130, 503/368-3343) offers about a dozen Manzanita properties, all on the beach or with ocean views, $160–260 per night in summer.

If you're looking for an upscale-but-worth-it retreat, the cedar-clad **Inn at Manzanita** (67 Laneda Ave., Manzanita 97130, 503/368-6754, $120–160 d summer, weekends, and holidays, lower rates Sun.–Thurs. off-season), set in a Japanese-accented garden just a short walk from the beach, promises guests (no children) the three Rs: recreation, relaxation, romance. Each of its 13 wood-paneled rooms features a gas fire-

place and two-person spa; most rooms have a balcony, offering glimpses through the evergreens of the nearby beach. Fresh flowers daily, robes, and other amenities help you feel pampered. Despite being in the middle of town near restaurants and the beach, a feeling of luxurious seclusion prevails. A two-night minimum stay is required on weekends and July 1–Labor Day, and discounts are available.

Six blocks from the beach, the five spacious and airy cabins of **Coast Cabins** (635 Laneda Ave., 503/368-7113, $125–225 in summer, about 20 percent lower off-season) comfortably sleep one to two (two-story Cabin 5 is designed for up to four persons) and offer kitchenettes or full kitchens, satellite TV, and goose-down pillows and comforters. Two-night minimum for advance reservations in summer and weekends all year. Pets are allowed in some cabins for a $20 nightly fee.

The Arbors Bed-and-Breakfast (78 Idaho Ave., 503/368-7566 or 888/664-9587, $105–115), one block from the beach, offers two cozy rooms with private bath in a handsome, Craftsman-style cottage built in the early 1920s.

Food

Among the numerous eateries strung along Manzanita's main street, Laneda Avenue, gourmets flock from far and wide to the **Blue Sky Café** (154 Laneda Ave., 503/368-5712). Casual in atmosphere but serious about good food, Blue Sky's seasonally rotating menu uses organic vegetables, wild mushrooms, and fresh seafood to create elegant multiethnic dishes. A skylit, art-filled interior and attentive service complement Blue Sky's culinary cutting edge. Expect to pay around $12–25 for main courses. No credit cards are accepted. Summer hours are 5:30–9:30 P.M. Monday–Saturday, 9 A.M.–2 p.m. and 5:30–9:30 P.M. Sunday, closed Monday and Tuesday off-season.

Across the street, **Gale's** (165 Laneda Ave., 503/368-4253) is a reliable place for a fresh seafood dinner just based on their preparation of Oregon's tricky razor clams ($16.95 with dinner accompaniments). Whether it's a salmon fillet dinner or a Dungeness crab dinner salad (each

$16.95), the menu's other denizens of the deep appear to have come out of the sea that very day. There's also steak and chicken in the same price range and a full bar. There's usually live music, often blues bands from Portland, here on weekends.

Left Coast Siesta (288 Laneda Ave., 503/368-7997, closed Mon.–Tues.) specializes in design-your-own-burritos, the perfect takeout for a filling lunch or dinner. Options include spicy beef, spicy chicken, tequila-lime chicken, or black beans to put into a selection of flavored tortillas. They also have tacos and enchiladas. Budget diners can eat well here for less than $6. And even though they advertise "fast, healthy, and fresh," Left Coast doesn't sacrifice flavor. And if you like it *caliente,* this is the place for you: Left Coast Siesta stocks a hot sauce bar with 200-plus different types of the hot stuff.

Even closer to the water, **Marzano's** (60 Laneda Ave., 503/368-5593) serves the coast's best slices of gourmet pizza, with prices to match—$15–24 for large-size whole pies. The roasted vegetable pizza is recommended, and the smoked prosciutto with aged Montegrappa cheese is another winner. The understated decor here is dominated by reproductions of French advertising posters. Between Marzano's near-beachfront location and the half-mile of Laneda to U.S. 101, there seem to be more places serving espresso drinks per capita here than in any other town on the entire coast. Best of the lot is **Manzanita News and Espresso** (500 Laneda Ave.), whose quiches, sandwiches, muffins, and remarkable selection of magazines and newspapers are also appreciated. This is our recommendation for the place to start your day.

House renters, budget diners, and picnickers can take advantage of the excellent produce and impressive (for a coastal market) grocery section at **Manzanita Grocery & Deli** (2nd and Laneda, open until 8 P.M.). One block away, **Mother Nature's Natural Foods Store** (10 A.M.–7 P.M. Mon.–Sat.) stocks natural groceries, coffees and teas, bulk foods, wine, and beer.

Cannon Beach and Vicinity

In 1846, the USS *Shark* met its end on the Columbia River Bar. The ship broke apart, and a section of deck bearing a small cannon and an iron capstan drifted south, finally washing ashore south of the current city limits at Arch Cape. And so this town got its name, which it adopted in 1922. Replicas of the hardware now stand near that spot, while the originals are preserved at the Cannon Beach Historical Society Museum.

In 1873, stagecoach and railroad tycoon Ben Holladay helped create Oregon's first coastal tourist mecca, Seaside, while ignoring its attractive neighbor in the shadow of Haystack Rock. In the 20th century, Cannon Beach evolved into a bohemian alternative to the hustle and bustle of the family-oriented resort scene to the north. Before the recent era of development, this place was a quaint backwater attracting laid-back artists, summer-home residents, and the overflow from pricier digs in Seaside. Today, the low-key charm and atmosphere conducive to artistic expression are threatened by a massive visitor influx and price increases. While such vital signs as a first-rate theater, a good bookstore, cheek-by-jowl art galleries, and fine restaurants are still in ample evidence in Cannon Beach, your view of them from the other side of the street might be blocked by a convoy of Winnebagos.

In *Travels With Charlie,* John Steinbeck bemoaned how present-day Carmel, California, would be eschewed by the very people who gave the town the appealing sobriquet of "artist colony." This same thing could well happen to the Carmel of the Oregon coast, Cannon Beach, unless the growth that began in 1980 is slowed. Within a decade, the number of motel rooms here has doubled, as has the number of visitors on a busy weekend (now averaging 10,000–12,000).

Nonetheless, the broad, three-mile stretch of beach dominated by the impressive monolith of Haystack Rock still provides a contemplative experience—although you might have to walk a

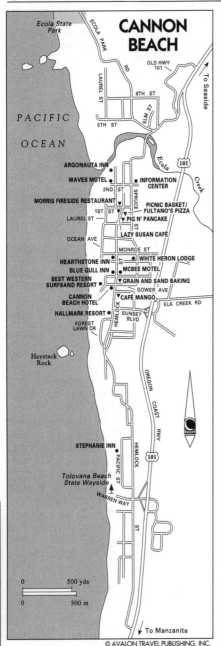

CANNON BEACH

Ecola State Park

ECOLA PARK RD

OLD HWY 101

To Seaside

LAUREL ST

6TH ST

ELM ST

PACIFIC

5TH ST

OCEAN

Ecola Creek

101

ARGONAUTA INN

WAVES MOTEL
2ND ST

INFORMATION CENTER

MORRIS FIRESIDE RESTAURANT

SPRUCE ST

1ST ST

PICNIC BASKET/ FULTANO'S PIZZA

LAUREL ST

PIG N' PANCAKE

OCEAN AVE

LAZY SUSAN CAFÉ

MONROE ST

HEARTHSTONE INN

WHITE HERON LODGE

BLUE GULL INN

MCBEE MOTEL

BEST WESTERN SURFSAND RESORT

GRAIN AND SAND BAKING

GOWER AVE

CANNON BEACH HOTEL

CAFÉ MANGO

ELK CREEK RD

HALLMARK RESORT

SUNSET BLVD

HEMLOCK

FOREST LAWN DR

Haystack Rock

OREGON COAST HWY

Moon

STEPHANIE INN

HEMLOCK

PACIFIC ST

101

Tolovana Beach State Wayside

WARREN WAY

ST

0   500 yds
0   500 m

To Manzanita

© AVALON TRAVEL PUBLISHING, INC.

NORTH COAST

half mile from your parking place to get to it. And if you're patient and resourceful enough to find a space for your wheels, the finest gallery-hopping, crafts, and shopping on the coast await. The town is small enough for strolling, only 1.3 miles long, and its location removed from U.S. 101 spares it the kind of blight seen on the main drags of other coastal tourist towns.

Wood shingles and understated earth tones dominate the architecture of tastefully rendered galleries, bookstores, and bistros. Throngs of walkers along Hemlock Street, the main drag, also distinguish this burg from the typical coastal strip town whose heart and soul have been pierced by U.S. 101. You have to go clear to the north end of Cannon Beach to find a gas station, and even then you're liable to bypass its stone-cottage facade.

SIGHTS
South of Cannon Beach

A few miles north of Oswald West State Park's main parking lot is the Arch Cape Tunnel, cut right through the mountain. This marks the end of the state park but not the beauty. As you head north, views of **Hug Point State Park** and pristine beaches will have you ready to pull over. In summer, this can be a good escape from the crowds at Cannon Beach. Time your visit to coincide with low tide, when all manner of marine life in tidepools will be exposed. Also at low tide, you may see remains of an 800-foot-long, Model T–sized road blasted into the base of Hug Point, an early precursor to U.S. 101. The cliffs are gouged with caves and crevasses that also invite exploring, but be mindful of the tides so you don't find yourself stranded. Hug Point got its name in the days when stagecoaches used the beach as a highway; they had to dash between the waves, hugging the jutting headland to get around.

Another three miles north is **Tolovana Beach Wayside.** Picnic facilities and the view of Haystack Rock aren't the only reasons to come here. This is an excellent base from which to walk south down to Hug Point or north one mile into Cannon Beach.

SALEM (OREGON) PUBLIC LIBRARY HISTORIC PHOTOGRAPH COLLECTIONS

Tillamook Rock Light

The historic Tillamook Rock Lighthouse, a mile out to sea from Tillamook Head, was a crucial guide to mariners for 76 years. Today, it's a privately owned columbarium (repository for cremated human remains).

Haystack Rock

As you get closer to town, Haystack Rock looms larger. This is the third-highest seastack in the world, measuring 235 feet high. As part of the Oregon Islands National Wildlife Refuge, it has wilderness status and is off-limits to climbing. Puffins and other seabirds nest on its steep faces, and intertidal organisms thrive in the tidepools around the base. The surrounding tidepools, within a radius of 300 yards from the base of the monolith, are designated a "marine garden"; it's open to exploration, but with strict no-collecting (of anything) and no-harassment (of any living organisms) protections in effect. Flanking the mountain are two rock formations known as the Needles. These spires had two other counterparts at the turn of the 20th century that have gradually been leveled by weathering and erosion. Old-timers will tell you that a trail to the top of Haystack was dynamited by the government in 1968 to keep people off this bird rookery. It also reduced the number of intrepid hikers trapped on the rock at high tide.

The **Haystack Rock Awareness Program** (503/436-1581, www.haystackrock.org) spon- sors free interpretive programs here June–August; call or check their website for the schedule and details. Although these talks are interesting and informative, the beach also speaks to you with its own distinctive voices. You can't miss the cacophony of seabirds at sunset and, if you listen closely, the winter phenomenon of "singing sands" created by wind blowing over the beach.

Klootchy Creek

From the north end of town, it's not far to the junction of U.S. 101 and U.S. 26. The latter goes 80 miles east to Portland, but many coastal travelers just travel two miles on U.S. 26 to visit Klootchy Creek Park. In an old-growth spruce and fir forest you'll find the **world's tallest Sitka spruce.** Standing 216 feet high and 52 feet in circumference, it's believed to be more than seven centuries old. To find the tree, look for signs on the north side of the highway shortly after leaving Cannon Beach. A wooden boardwalk protects the tree's root system and lets you approach the tree while sparing you the muddy terrain.

NORTH COAST

Haysbuck Rock, Cannon Beach

Ecola State Park

Ecola State Park is just north of the Cannon Beach townsite. Thick conifer forests line the access road to Ecola Point. This forested cliff has many trails leading down to the water. The view south takes in Haystack Rock and the overlapping peaks of the Coast Range extending to Neahkahnie Mountain. This is one of the most photographed views on the coast. Out to sea, the sight of sea lions basking on surf-drenched rocks (mid-Apr.–July) or migrating gray whales (December and March) and orcas (May) are seasonal highlights. From Ecola Point, trails lead north to horseshoe-shaped **Indian Beach,** a favorite with surfers. Some prefer to drive there as a prelude to hiking up Tillamook Head, considered by Lewis and Clark to be the region's most beautiful viewpoint.

The name Ecola means "whale" in Chinook jargon and was first used as a place name by William Clark, referring to a creek in the area. Lewis and Clark's journals note a 105-foot beached whale found somewhere within present-day Ecola Park's southern border, Crescent Beach. This area represents the southern-

most extent of Lewis and Clark's coastal Oregon travels.

There is a $3 day-use fee at the park. The Oregon Coast Annual Passport and Oregon Coast 5-Day Passport are also honored.

Cannon Beach History Center

Permanent exhibits at the small Cannon Beach History Center (corner of Spruce and Sunset, 503/436-9301, 1–5 P.M. Wed.–Sat., $1–2) chronicles the town's timeline, from prehistory to the modern expansion of tourism and recreation. The original, eponymous cannon from the ill-fated *Shark* is also on display here.

Les Shirley Park

In addition to being the probable location of the whale carcass observed by Lewis and Clark, city-owned Les Shirley Park has interpretive signs to explain the interaction of ocean and fresh water that occurs in Ecola Creek estuary. To reach the park after leaving town on the beach loop to U.S. 101, turn left on 5th Street at the foot of the hill. Pass the sign for Ecola State Park; Les Shirley Park is a few more blocks ahead.

NORTH COAST

RECREATION
Riding
Sea Ranch Stables (415 Old U.S. 101, 503/436-2815, 9 A.M.–5 P.M.), at the north entrance to Cannon Beach off U.S. 101, rents horses for beach rides mid-May to Labor Day. Horses are allowed on the beach anywhere along the coast using public access points. Sea Ranch offers several one- to two-hour guided rides, including night rides on the beach.

Saddle Mountain Hiking
Another reason to head east from Cannon Beach is the hike up 3,283-foot Saddle Mountain. To get to the trailhead, take U.S. 26 from its junction with U.S. 101 for 10 miles and turn left on the prominently indicated Saddle Mountain Road. Although it's paved, this road is not suitable for RVs or wide-bodied vehicles. After seven twisting miles, you'll come to the trailhead of the highest peak in this part of the Coast Range. The trail is steep and gains more than 1,600 feet in 2.5 miles. Wet conditions can make the going difficult (allow four hours round-trip), and the scenery en route is not always exceptional, but the view from the top is worth it.

On a clear day, hikers can see some 50 miles of the Oregon and Washington coastlines, including the Columbia River. Also possible are spectacular views of Mt. Rainier, Mt. St. Helens, Mt. Hood, and, unfortunately, miles of clearcuts. If you go between May and August you'll be treated to a wildflower display that'll surprise you. On the upper part of the trail, plant species that pushed south from Alaska and Canada during the last Ice Age thrive. The cool, moist climate here keeps them from dying out as they did at lower elevations. Some early blooms include pink coast fawn lily, monkey flower, wild rose, wood violet, bleeding heart, oxalis, Indian paintbrush, and trillium. Cable handrails provide safety on the narrow final quarter-mile trail to the summit.

Bike Rental
Mike's Bike Shop (248 N. Spruce St., 503/436-1266) has rentals for $3–6 per hour. Mike's specializes in mountain bikes, which can also be returned at a Warrenton outlet. You'll also find three-wheel beach-cycles for rent at the north end of town. These are fun for zipping up and down the hard-packed sand when the tide is down.

EVENTS AND ENTERTAINMENT
Events
The **Puffin Kite Festival,** one of several kite events held on the coast, takes advantage of late April's blustery winds. Individuals and teams demonstrate flying techniques and compete for prizes; and for kids, there's a treasure hunt, sandcastle building, and face painting. The festival is held just north of Haystack Rock, in front of the Surfsand Resort, which sponsors the event.

The half-dozen or so other sand-sculpting contests that take place on the Oregon coast pale in comparison to Cannon Beach's annual **Sandcastle Day.** In 1964, a tsunami washed out a bridge, and the isolated residents of Cannon Beach organized the first contest as a way to amuse their children. Now in its fifth decade, this is the state's oldest and most prestigious competition of its kind. Tens of thousands of spectators show up to watch 1,000-plus competitors fashion their sculptures with the aid of buckets, shovels, squirt guns, and any natural material found on the beach. The resulting sculptures are often amazingly complex and inventive. This event is free to spectators, but entrants pay a fee. Recent winners included Egyptian pyramids and a gigantic sea turtle. The event usually coincides with the lowest-tide Saturday in June. Call 503/436-2623 to find out the exact date of this collapsible art show, which takes place north of Haystack Rock. Building begins in the early morning; winners are announced at noon. The American Legion serves a big breakfast buffet at 1216 S. Hemlock St., open to all.

The **Artist and Lecture Series** features notable regional writers, poets, artists, and others reading from their works or speaking on their craft in spring and fall. Dates and locations are posted around town, or contact the Cannon Beach Arts Association (1064 S. Hemlock St., Cannon Beach 97110, 503/436-0744) for a schedule.

In July and August, the well-regarded **Haystack Summer Program in the Arts** (503/464-4812, www.haystack.pdx.edu) offers classes and workshops in painting, music, gardening, and writing, including the annual Pacific Northwest Children's Book Conference. In addition, evening readings, art exhibits, and lectures are open to the public.

For a weekend in early November, writers, singers, composers, painters, and sculptors take over the town for the **Stormy Weather Arts Festival** (503/436-2623). Events include music on the streets, plays, a Saturday afternoon Art Walk, and the Quick Draw in which artists have one hour to paint, complete, and frame a piece while the audience watches. The art is then sold by auction.

Music and Theater

Going strong for more than 30 years, the **Coaster Theatre Playhouse** (108 N. Hemlock St., Cannon Beach 97110, 503/436-1242, http://coastertheatre.com) stages a varied bill of musicals, dramas, mysteries, comedies, concerts, and other entertainments. It's open year-round, in a building that started in the 1920s as a skating rink cum silent-movie house. Tickets run $14–16.

Beginning in July, the city park, at Spruce and 2nd streets, hosts **Concerts in the Park,** a series of jazz, rhythm and blues, and popular music, on Sunday afternoons at the bandstand 2–4 P.M. Well-chosen jazz and folk acts frequently grace the **Bald Eagle Coffee House** (1287 S. Hemlock St., 503/436-0522) on weekends.

ACCOMMODATIONS

If you're not willing to make storm-watching an acquired taste, do not reserve Cannon Beach lodgings from mid-January through early March. During this time much of the annual rainfall total of 80 inches is recorded. Should high room rates or crowds on weekends other times of the year be a deterrent, remember that Cannon Beach is only 1.5 hours from Portland, perfect for a day trip.

Vacation Rentals

Several local property management companies offer a large selection of furnished rental homes—ranging from grand oceanfront homes to quaint, secluded cottages. **Cannon Beach Property Management** (3188 S. Hemlock St., 877/386-3402 or 503/436-2021, www.cbpm.com) allows visitors to tour its list of homes via the web, as does **Cannon Beach Vacation Rentals** (P.O. Box 723, 866/436-0940, www.visitcb.com). Rates for both range $65–400.

Motels

About a one-minute walk to the beach, with friendly management and a great vibe, the **Blue Gull Inn** (632 S. Hemlock St., 503/436-2714 or 800/507-2714, $79–170) offers a choice between a beach house or less expensive motel units. These come with housekeeping facilities. The modern cottages have in-room whirlpool tubs, fireplaces, and full kitchens. A sauna and laundry room are on the grounds. Cottages for larger groups are also available. The **McBee Motel** (888 S. Hemlock St., 503/436-0247, $39–130) is less elaborate and less expensive, but close enough to town and far enough from traffic to be worth considering. McBee accepts pets in its homey cottages. For somewhat more money than you'd pay at these places, you can get the intimacy and flavor of a bed-and-breakfast.

For a homey atmosphere, try the **Argonauta Inn** or **The Waves Motel** (both located at 188 W. 2nd St., 503/436-2205 or 800/822-2468, www.thewavesmotel.com, $79–359). The Argonauta is made up of four houses in the middle of downtown and has five furnished units just 150 feet from the beach. A cluster of six buildings makes up The Waves, with units to fit the needs of families, couples, or larger groups.

Built in the 1920s, the nine-gabled **Wave Crest Motel** (4008 S. Hemlock St., 503/436-2842, $40–75) is a pet- and smoke-free European-style hotel that caters to adults who have no interest in cable TV but share a penchant for sing-alongs around the piano, a good book, witty conversation, and old-fashioned card games. Coffee, tea, and pastries are served in the morning. Some rooms have private bathrooms; others share.

Hotels

For a family-oriented oceanfront lodge, try **Sea Sprite Guest Lodgings** (P.O. Box 933, Cannon Beach 97110, 503/436-2266 or 866/828-1050, www.seasprite.com, $73–300). With a beachfront location just south of Haystack Rock, plus kitchens, TVs, and spectacular views, it's not surprising that this place commands high rates during the regular season. What *is* surprising is the off-season discount of up to 40 percent off these rates, Sunday–Thursday, November–April. These family-style beach cabins are a throwback to the Oregon coast of an earlier era. Inside you'll find such homey touches as fireplaces, games, books, periodicals, and rockers. Outside you have flowers, picnic tables, and the best of Cannon Beach shopping and beachcombing in close proximity. Choose from one of six oceanfront cabins, which hold up to two, six, or eight—depending on your choice. The Hemlock House can also be rented—up and down, or just the upper portion. Upstairs sleeps eight, while the newly remodeled daylight lower level will sleep an additional four people. To get there, take the Beach Loop (Hemlock St.) south of town and turn west at Nebesna Street.

If the Sea Sprite is full, the same management will steer you to the **Hearthstone Inn** (107 E. Jackson St., 503/536-1392, $75–85), which also features off-season specials. While this romantic, rustic lodging doesn't have the Haystack Rock views of the Sea Sprite, it's closer to downtown shopping.

The **Cannon Beach Hotel** (1116 Hemlock St., 503/436-1392, $50–190) is a converted 1910 loggers' boardinghouse with 30 rooms and a small café and restaurant on the premises. Continental breakfasts are included in the rates, and lunch and dinner can be enjoyed here apart from the lodging package. The most expensive rooms have fireplaces, whirlpools, and partial ocean views. Meals are available in the restaurant adjacent to the lobby. As with all Cannon Beach accommodations, be sure to reserve well in advance.

The **Best Western Surfsand Resort** (Oceanfront and Gower Streets, 503/436-2274 or 800/547-6100, $160 and up) offers a great combination of location and amenities in Cannon Beach. You can park your car upon arrival and walk to downtown galleries or enjoy Haystack Rock just outside your door. Other neighbors include the Wayfarer Restaurant (award-winning clam chowder and seafood), as well as Hane Grain and Sand Bakery (a combination art gallery and first-rate bakery). The Surfsand's array of lodging options run the gamut from spacious oceanfront rooms, many with such features as kitchens, fireplaces, and spas (in addition to use of the Cannon Beach Athletic Club and an indoor pool and spa) to houses in the Coast Range. Such comforts and conveniences come with a price, but Cannon Beach is one town whose many charms rate a deluxe treatment like this one.

Just a few minutes' walk from downtown, **Ecola Creek Lodge** (208 E. 5th St., 503/436-2776 or 800/873-2749, www.cannonbeachlodge.com, $80–199) is a Cape Cod–style inn set of 22 unique units, within four buildings with stained glass, lawns, fountains, flower gardens, and a lily pond. Major renovation of the property was completed in January 2000. Les Shirley Park and Ecola Creek separate the lodge from the beach.

The oceanfront **Hallmark Resort** (1400 S. Hemlock St., 888/448-4449 or 503/436-1566, www.hallmarkinns.com, $59–349) boasts romantic views of Haystock Rock. With convention and meeting facilities, a pool, and on-site massages available, this is a service-oriented resort geared to accommodate large groups, families, and couples. In-room fireplaces add a romantic touch.

For a more private experience and just steps from the ocean, **The White Heron Lodge** (356 N. Spruce St., 503/436-2205 or 800/822-2468, $169–199) comprises two fully furnished oceanfront Victorian-style homes, both of which sleep up to four. Each of the suites looks directly out to the Pacific. Wide sandy beaches and large grass front yards make it a great location for families, especially those with small children. Located on a residential dead-end street, the lodge is only one block from the action.

Bed-and-Breakfast

In Cannon Beach, the two-bedroom B&B called the **Tern Inn** (3663 S. Hemlock St., 503/436-528, $125–175) is close enough to the beach for good views. Rooms have private baths, private entrances, and a full breakfast with home-baked goodies. Reserve at least one month in advance.

Campgrounds

For easier access to Cannon Beach's natural wonders, camping offers nature at a bargain price. Although camping is not permitted on the beach or in Cannon Beach city parks, there are plenty of options for RV, tent, and outdoors enthusiasts. The **Sea Ranch RV Park** (415 Old U.S. 101, 503/436-2815, www.cannon-beach.net/searanch) has grassy sites nestled among the trees, also home to horses, ducks, rabbits, and raccoons. Open year-round with both full and partial hookups for RVs, campsites include a picnic table and fire ring (firewood sold on the premises), access to restrooms with hot showers—all just three blocks from the beach and downtown. Sites run $20–30, depending on the number of people. Cabins are also available for $65. Pets are welcome, but they must be on a leash. Reservations are recommended.

For a more pampered experience, check out the **RV Resort at Cannon Beach** (345 Elk Creek Rd., 503/436-2231 or 800/847-2231, www.cbrvresort.com). Open year-round, with 100 full hookups, an indoor pool and spa, free cable TV, on-site convenience store, launderette, restroom, and meeting room, this resort features a Saturday Night Weenie Roast during the summer. Call for rates.

The family-run **Wright's for Camping** (334 Reservoir Rd., 503/436-2347, www.wrightsforcamping.com, $18 and up) has quite a history. In the 1930s, the Wrights would come from Portland to camp in this area. Then in 1946, Pop Wright bought 10 acres in Cannon Beach from a friend. After running a successful construction company in town, Wright and his wife turned their 10-acre site into a campground. Choose from 19 sites, with picnic tables, restrooms, laundry room, fire rings, and handicapped-accessible facilities. Leashed pets are okay.

FOOD

As you might expect, eating out can get expensive here. However, there are some ways to beat the costs, and, there are a few justifiable splurges.

Local Delicacies

The **Mariner Market** (139 N. Hemlock St., 503/436-2442, 9 A.M.–9 P.M.) is an antique-filled grocery that's fully stocked with fresh meat, fruit, and vegetables. They carry organic produce and natural food products, as well as a deli with fast-food takeout items. The Mariner's prices beat the tab at several other markets in town.

In the fishing business for more than 25 years, **Ecola Seafoods** (208 N. Spruce St., 503/436-9130) features fresh-catch Dungeness crab and bay shrimp cocktails. Or sample their smoked salmon and fish and chips, as well as a decent clam chowder. You'll find it across from the public parking lots and restrooms.

Casual Fare

Bill's Tavern (188 N. Hemlock St., 503/436-2202), once a legendary watering hole, is now a more traditional remodeled brewhouse. Although some people pine for the original establishment's homier decor, they come for the best in-house brews in town. Sweet, thick onion rings, greasy but good fries, one-third-pound burgers, sautéed prawns, and grilled oysters are the bill of fare.

Try the wood-paneled, skylit **Lazy Susan Café** (126 N. Hemlock St., 503/436-2816) for any-time breakfast (eggs with a side of bread pudding), lunch (sandwiches and salads), and light dinner (hot seafood salad). There's also the fresh fish catch of the day and pizza. Head over to the **Lazy Susan Grill & Scoop** (156 N. Hemlock St.) for lunch or to wash it all down with espresso or a soda fountain concoction at this spacious family-friendly establishment. Open until 5 P.M. (8 P.M. on weekends).

Café Mango (1235 S. Hemlock St., 503/436-2393, 7:30 A.M.–2:30 P.M. daily) is another breakfast/lunch mainstay, locally famous for such dishes as Amish oatcake waffles, blueberry cornmeal pancakes, frittatas, bagels and lox, and creative omelets. Such Mexican dishes as pozole soup, chilaquiles, and a breakfast burrito stuffed with homemade refried beans and eggs are also winners in this homey restaurant. Fresh fruit smoothies, homemade ketchup and jam, as well as extensive vegetarian options with organic ingredients also explain Midtown's cult status.

Morris' Fireside Restaurant (207 N. Hemlock St., 503/436-2917, 8 A.M.–3 P.M. daily) is an attractive log building where pot roasts, steak, and seafood are featured along with "logger" breakfasts. Portions are large, and prices are moderate.

The local **Pig 'N Pancake** (223 S. Hemlock St., 503/436-2851, open for breakfast and lunch daily) has large picture windows overlooking a leafy ravine, and offers 35 varieties of breakfast (including homemade pancakes), served anytime. For lunch, try the soups, chowder, or halibut fish and chips.

Several afterthoughts deserving of serious consideration are the ice cream and soda bar at **Picnic Basket** (183 N. Hemlock St., 503/436-1470); compare your favorite ice cream flavor at **Osburn's Ice Creamery** (240 N. Hemlock St., 503/436-2578). The latter is adjacent to **Osburn's Grocery and Deli** (503/436-2234), which makes sandwiches that can easily satisfy two. Summertime specials on local produce and people-watching from old classroom chairs on Osburn's porch are Cannon Beach traditions.

Fultano's Pizza (200 N. Hemlock St., 503/436-9717) sits unobtrusively off to the right near the corner of 2nd and Hemlock on your way to the beach. If you're hungry, aromas of fresh cheese, garlic, and free-baked dough will draw you inside this brick enclave. Pizza by the slice with an array of toppings, hefty salads, an all-you-can-eat salad bar, pasta dishes, and oven-baked subs all hold their own with most establishments of this ilk in Oregon.

Finally, there are several good bakeries in town, but **Grain and Sand Baking** (1064 Hemlock St., 503/436-0120) rates the nod if you're looking for a lunch with cosmopolitan flair. With first-rate coffee and fresh juices to wash down muffins, scones, and inexpensively priced light meals (black bean empanadas, homemade lasagna, portabello mushroom quiche, and home-made soups typify the offerings) and an adjoining gallery devoted to local artists, this is a special spot. Best of all, you're close enough to Haystack Rock for a picnic.

Northwest and Seafood

Hankering for some authentic West Coast chowder? Head to **Dooger's Seafood and Grill** (1371 S. Hemlock St., 503/436-2225, www.cannonbeach.net/doogers, open for breakfast, lunch, and dinner, $11–16) for award-winning seafood, or purchase one of their famous "Chowder Kits." For $12 plus shipping, the kit includes a 51-ounce can of clams, five ounces of potatoes, and all the spices. All you need to do is add water and cream. You can even order it online at their website.

Whether or not you're staying at **The Stephanie Inn** (2740 S. Pacific St., 503/436-2221 or 800/633-3466), you are welcome to join guests in the dining room for an expensive four-course prix-fixe dinner featuring innovative Northwest cuisine. The atmosphere boasts mountain views, open wood beams, a river-rock fireplace, and cozy seating. Because of limited seating, reserve well ahead of time.

Mo's at Tolovana (195 Warren Way, 503/436-1111) sits next to Tolovana Park and boasts a restaurant site once selected by *Pacific Northwest* magazine as having "the most romantic view on the Oregon coast." Add this to Mo's reliable formula of fresh fish and rich clam chowder at very reasonable prices in a family-friendly atmosphere, and you can't miss.

GALLERIES AND SHOPS
Art

Cannon Beach has long attracted artists and artisans, and here art lovers and purchasers will find nearly two dozen outlets for their work. Most of the many Cannon Beach galleries and boutiques are concentrated along Hemlock Street, where you can hardly swing a Winsor & Newton No. 12 hogbristle brush without hitting one. Not surprisingly, the seashore is the subject and inspiration of many works you'll see here, with Haystack Rock frequently depicted in various media. Cannon Beach Information Center has a guide to all the galleries in town, or you can just stroll and discover them for yourself. A few favorites are:

The **Cannon Beach Gallery** (1064 S. Hemlock St., 503/436-0744) features the works of local and Northwest artists in changing monthly exhibits. **DragonFire Interactive Studio & Gallery** (123 S. Hemlock St., 503/436-1533) is a teaching studio, offering classes on weekends in various media. Throughout the summer, everyone is invited to come and express his or her creativity, tipple some wine, and listen to live music at the Saturday-night "Paint Party," hosted by local artists 6–10 P.M.

At the north end of town, **White Bird Gallery** (251 N. Hemlock St., 503/436-2681) is one of Cannon Beach's oldest, in operation since 1971, and casts a wide net with paintings, sculpture, prints, photography, glass, ceramics, and jewelry. Next door in Heather's Court, the **Artists Gallerie** (271 N. Hemlock St., #3, 503/436-0336) is a working studio showing the works of four painters whose styles range from realist to pure abstraction. Also at Heather's Court, the **Uffelman Gallery** (503/436-2404) showcases the strikingly modern still lifes of Jeff Uffelman, which transform such mundane ingredients as a handful of peapods or peeled cucumbers into mesmerizing images. **Valley Bronze** (186 N. Hemlock St., 503/436-2118) shows sculptures cast at the world-famous foundry in Joseph, Oregon, as well as paintings and diverse works from other prominent artists.

Specialty Shops

Much of the attraction in Cannon Beach is window shopping up and down Hemlock Street, which, in addition to galleries, is lined with clothing stores, gift shops, and other boutiques. Cannon Beach supports two fine kite stores one block apart, where you can gear up for the big Puffin Kite Festival: **Once Upon a Breeze** (240 N. Spruce St., 503/436-1112) and **Wind Dancer** (210 N. Hemlock St., 503/436-8612). The **Cannon Beach Book Company** (130 N. Hemlock St., 503/436-1301) is one of the better bookstores on the coast. This is the place to pick up regional titles or a good novel (lots of mysteries) for that rainy weekend.

In the **Cannon Beach Mall**, two shops specialize in European imports: **A Stór** (175 E. 2nd St., 503/436-0664) carries handcrafted items from Ireland, including hand-knit sweaters, pottery, and jewelry; **Aagesen's Imports** (183 N. Hemlock St., 503/436-1737) focuses on Scandinavian imports. **Ecola Square** (123 S. Hemlock St.) has a clutch of boutiques focused on nature and the outdoors: The **Wild Bird Shop** (bird feeders, birdhouses, etc.), **Shorelines, NW** (shells), and **Nature Arts & Sounds** (fountains and supplies).

INFORMATION AND SERVICES

The chamber of commerce operates the **Cannon Beach Information Center** (201 E. 2nd, Cannon Beach 97110, 503/436-2623, www.cannonbeach.org, 11 A.M.–5 P.M. Mon.–Sat., 10 A.M.–4 P.M. Sun.). This facility is close to the public restrooms (2nd and Spruce) and basketball and tennis courts. The **post office** (155 N. Hemlock St., 503/436-2822) is open 9 A.M.–5 P.M. Monday–Friday.

Sandpiper Medical Walk-in Clinic (171 N. Larch St., 503/436-1142) offers medical care for the whole family and minor emergency services. It's located in Sandpiper Square behind the stores on the main drag.

Getting There and Around

From U.S. 101, there's a choice of four entrances to the beach loop (also known as U.S. 101 Alternate, a section of the old Oregon Coast Highway) to take you into town. As you wade into the town's shops, galleries, and restaurants, the beach loop becomes Hemlock Street, the main drag of Cannon Beach. Sunset Empire Transportation District operates **TheBus** (503/861-7433), which serves Cannon Beach, Seaside, Astoria-Warrenton, and points in between. **Parking** can be hard to come by, especially on weekends, but you'll find public lots south of town at Tolovana Park and in town at Hemlock at 1st Street and on 2nd Street.

The free **Cannon Beach Shuttle** runs every half-hour on a 6.5-mile loop, from Les Shirley Park on the north end of town to Tolovana Park, and operates 10 A.M.–6 P.M. daily, with extended summer hours.

Seaside and Gearhart

Seaside is Oregon's quintessential, and oldest, family beach resort. The beach is long and flat, sheltered by a scenic headland, with lifeguards on duty during summer, beachside playground equipment, and the West Coast's only boardwalk north of Santa Cruz, California. Ice cream parlors, game arcades, eateries, and gift shops crowd shoulder to shoulder along the main drag, Broadway; the aroma of cotton candy and French fries lend a heady incense to the salt air, and the clatter of bumper cars and other entertainments can induce sensory overload. Atlantic City it's not—thank goodness—but on a crowded summer day the resort evokes the feeling of a carnival midway by the sea. During spring break, when Northwest high school and college students arrive, the population of 6,200 can quadruple almost overnight.

South of town, the presence of clammers and waders in the shallows and surfers negotiating the swells also recalls the liveliness of a southern California or Atlantic shorefront instead of the remote peacefulness of many Oregon beaches. East Coast visitors often liken Cannon Beach to Provincetown, and Seaside to Coney Island—before their declines as destination resorts. Neighboring Gearhart, a mainly residential community (pop. 995) just to the north, has a few lodgings away from the bustle of Seaside, as well as a venerable 18-hole golf course.

Located along the Necanicum River, in the shadow of majestic Tillamook Head, Seaside has attracted tourists since the early 1870s, when transportation magnate Ben Holladay sensed the potential of a resort hotel near the water. But better transportation was needed to get customers to the place. At that time, the way to get to Seaside was first by boat from Portland down the Columbia River to Skipanon (now Warrenton), and from there by carriage south to Seaside. To speed the connection, Holladay constructed a railroad line from Skipanon to Seaside. To escape Portland's summer heat, families would make the boat and railroad journey to spend their summer in Seaside. Most men would go back to Portland to work during

Seaside beach scene, circa 1940

COURTESY OF THE OREGON STATE ARCHIVES

NORTH COAST

the week, returning to the coast on Friday to visit the family. Every weekend the families would gather at the railroad station to greet him, then see him off again for his trip back to Portland. It wasn't long before the train became known as the "Daddy Train." As roads between Portland and the coast were constructed, the car took over, and the railroad carried its last dad in 1939.

Before becoming the state's first coastal resort, Seaside's fame as the end of the Lewis and Clark Trail made it a national landmark. In recent years, the town has become more than just a retreat for Portland families. Oregon's apostle of haute cuisine, the late James Beard, used to hold a celebrated cooking class here each summer. This opened the door for writers' retreats, art classes, and business conventions. If these occasions or a family outing should bring you to Seaside, you'll enjoy the spirit of fun if you don't mind plenty of company on summer weekends.

SIGHTS
The Prom and Broadway

Sightseeing in Seaside means bustling up and down Broadway and strolling leisurely along the Prom. This two-mile boardwalk, extending from Avenue U north to 12th Avenue, was constructed in 1921 to replace the rotten planks from a wooden walkway built in 1908 and to protect ocean properties from the waves. It makes for a pleasant walk alongside the beach and offers good vantages from which to contemplate the sand, surf, and massive contours of 1,200-foot-high Tillamook Head to the south. Midway along the Prom is the **Turnaround,** a concrete and brick traffic circle that is the west end of

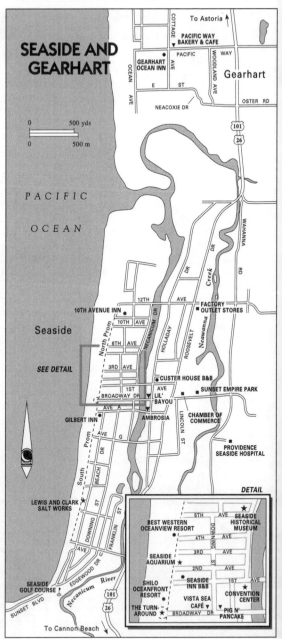

THE GREAT NORTHWEST SHOE SWAP

Designer kites, Japanese glass fishing floats, berry jams, myrtlewood bowls, and objets d'art culled from galleries are among the gift-shopping treasures typically found on the Oregon coast. But in 1991, a unique event added a new wrinkle to the scene. It all started when a cargo of Nike athletic shoes washed up on north coast beaches, the result of the wreck of an Asian ship. The Japanese current swept the shoes down from the North Pacific to be deposited on Clatsop County beaches. Before long, beachcombers here were forming "shoe swap" clubs to match up sizes and styles in pairs. With extensive washing, these shoes were almost good as new, or at least good enough to sell for less than the $50–120 asking price at conventional outlets. From Cannon Beach north, the flotsam footwear was adver-tised on launderette bulletin boards, in community newspapers, and by hawkers on the street. Nike, Beaverton's multibillion-dollar shoemaker, did nothing to spoil this party, reveling instead in the publicity generated by the incident.

In March 1996, another beachcomber's bonanza hit the Oregon coast. This time, it was both athletic shoes and toys from a ship that burned in Asian waters 15 months before. These encounters with flotsam footwear have provided oceanographers with important data on ocean currents. Such incidents have also heartened proponents of "transoceanic diffusion," the theory that contends that aeons-old Asian boat migrations supplemented Eastern Hemisphere visitors crossing a land-ice bridge in the area of the present-day Bering Strait.

Broadway. A bronze statue of Lewis and Clark gazing ever seaward proclaims this point the end of the trail for their expedition, although in fact they explored a bit farther south, beyond Tillamook Head. Eight blocks south of the Turnaround, between Beach Drive and the Prom is a replica of the Lewis and Clark salt cairn (see Lewis and Clark Salt Works, below).

Running east from the Turnaround, Broadway—Seaside's central traffic artery—runs one-half mile to Roosevelt Avenue (U.S. 101) through a dizzy gamut of tourist attractions. Along Broadway, in a four-block area running west of U.S. 101 and bordered by the Necanicum River and 1st Avenue, and Avenue A, you'll find some fancy Victorian frame houses, some of the few old buildings that survived the 1912 fire that destroyed much of the town.

Seaside Historical Museum

If you tire of having a good time on Broadway and the beach, make your way to the Seaside Historical Museum (570 Necanicum Dr., 503/738-7065, 10 A.M.–4 P.M. Mon.–Sat. late Mar.–Oct. and noon–3 P.M. the rest of the year, noon–3 P.M. Sun. year-round, $2 adults, $1 kids), six blocks north of Broadway, where the Clatsop Indian artifacts and exhibits on early tourism

in Seaside will impart more of a sense of history than anything else in town.

Seaside Aquarium

Right on the Prom north of the Turnaround is the Seaside Aquarium (200 N. Prom, 503/738-6211, 9 A.M.–5 P.M. daily Mar.–Oct., 9 A.M.–5 P.M. Wed.–Sun. in winter, $3 ages 6–13, $6 ages 14 and up). It's not quite the Oregon Coast Aquarium in Newport, but if you're not going to make it that far south, it's an okay introduction to sea life for young children. Back in the era of the Daddy Train, this place served as a natatorium but was converted to its current use in 1937. Today the pool is filled with the raucously barking results of one of the best captive-breeding programs for seals in the world. In addition, one hundred species of marine life include 20-ray sea stars, crabs, ferocious-looking wolf eels and moray eels, and octopus.

Lewis and Clark Salt Works

Near the south end of the Prom are the reconstructed salt works of Lewis and Clark. While camped at Fort Clatsop during the winter of 1805–1806, the captains sent a detachment south to find a suitable place for rendering salt from seawater. Their supply was nearly exhausted, and

Lewis and Clark statue at Seaside's Turnaround

RECREATION

Following Lewis and Clark

From the south end of Seaside, you can walk in the footsteps of Lewis and Clark on an exhilarating hike over **Tillamook Head.** In January 1806, neighboring Indians told of a beached whale lying several miles south of their encampment. William Clark and a few companions, including Sacagawea, set off in an attempt to find it and trade for blubber and whale oil, which fueled the expedition's lanterns. Climbing Tillamook Head from the north, the party crested the promontory. Clark was moved enough by the view to later write about it in his journal:

I beheld the grandest and most pleasing prospect which my eyes ever surveyed. Immediately in front of us is the ocean breaking in fury. To this boisterous scene the Columbia with its tributaries and studded on both sides with the Chinook and Clatsop villages forms a charming contrast, while beneath our feet are stretched the rich prairies.

the precious commodity was a necessity for preserving and seasoning their food on the expedition's return journey. At the south end of present-day Seaside, five men built a cairnlike stone oven near a settlement of Clatsop and Killamox Indians, and set about boiling seawater nonstop for seven weeks to produce 3.5 bushels (about 112 quarts) of salt for the trip back east. Truth be told, the stone oven isn't much to look at, but for Lewis and Clark buffs, this is an important site.

As a point of vexillological trivia, the salt works and Fort Clatsop are the only places besides Baltimore's Fort William McHenry to fly the flag that was the United States' banner 1795–1818. The 15 stars and 15 stripes represent the original 13 states, plus Vermont and Kentucky. It soon became clear that a stripe for every state would be unworkable, and in 1818, Congress redesigned the national banner with 13 stripes for the original colonies and one star for each state.

They eventually found the whale, south of Tillamook Head. Ecola Point and State Park here are named for it, after the Chinook word for "whale," *ecola* or *ekkoli.* By the time Clark arrived, however, the whale had been reduced to little more than a skeleton by the industrious Tillamook Indians, who used every part of the beast they could harvest. Clark measured the leviathan at 105 feet, which, if accurate, could only mean it was a blue whale, the largest animal on earth and an extraordinary windfall for the Indians. He found the Tillamooks busily engaged in boiling the blubber in a large wooden trough by means of hot stones. The oil, when extracted, was stored in bladders. He had to bargain hard for a share, and wrote this of the negotiations:

The Tillamooks, although they possessed large quantities of this blubber and oil, were so penurious that they disposed of it with great reluctance, and in small quantities only; insomuch that my utmost exertions, aided by the party, with the small

NORTH COAST

stock of merchandise I had taken with me, were not able to procure more blubber than about 300 pounds and a few gallons of oil. Small as this stock is, I prize it highly; and thank Providence for directing the whale to us; and think Him much more kind to us than He was to Jonah having sent this monster to be swallowed by us, instead of swallowing of us, as Jonah's did.

Today, you can experience the view that so impressed Clark on the **Tillamook Head National Recreation Trail,** which runs seven miles through Ecola State Park. Before setting out, you could arrange to have a friend drive down to **Indian Beach** to pick you up at the end of this three- to five-hour trek. Or you can be picked up another mile south at the Ecola Point parking lot. To get to the trailhead, drive to the south end of Seaside to Avenue U past the golf course to Edgewood Street and turn left, then continue until you reach the parking lot at the end of the road. Nearby is an area known as **the Cove,** frequented by surfers (prevailing winds favor winter surfing rather than summer) and anglers. As you head up the forested trail on the north side of Tillamook Head, you can look back over the Seaside townsite. In about 20 minutes, you'll be gazing down at the ocean from cliffs 1,000 feet above. A few hours later, you'll hike down onto Indian Beach, arriving near the restrooms.

Fish and Wildlife

Just because you're smack-dab in the middle of a family resort town doesn't mean you can't enjoy some of nature's bounty—anglers can reel in trout, salmon, and steelhead from the Necanicum River right in the center of downtown. The **12th Avenue Bridge** is a popular spot for fishing and crabbing. **Cullaby Lake,** on the east side of U.S. 101 about four miles north of Gearhart, offers fishing for crappies, bluegills, perch, catfish, and largemouth bass. At 88 acres, Cullaby is the largest of the many lakes on the Clatsop Plains. Two parks on the lake, **Carnahan Park** and **Cullaby Lake County Park,** have boat ramps, picnic areas, and other facilities. Cullaby is the only practical place to

water-ski in the area. One-half mile west of the highway, **Sunset Beach Park** on Neacoxie Lake (also known as Sunset Lake) has a boat ramp, picnic tables, and a playground. Anglers come for warm-water fish species, plus rainbow trout stocked in the spring.

Bird-watchers revel in **Necanicum Estuary Park,** at the 1900 block of N. Holladay Drive, across the street from Seaside High School. Local students have built a viewing platform, stairs to the beach, a boardwalk, and interpretive signs. Great blue and green herons and numerous migratory bird species flock to the grassy marshes and slow tidal waters near the mouth of the Necanicum River. Occasionally, Roosevelt elk, black-tailed deer, river otters, beavers, minks, and muskrats can also be sighted.

Water Sports

Despite the lifeguard on duty in summer, swimming at Seaside's beach isn't the most comfortable unless you're used to the North Sea. Warm-blooded swimmers can head to the pool and spa at **Sunset Empire Park** (1140 E. Broadway St., 503/738-3311, open daily). Gearhart boasts a quieter beach than Seaside. At Quatat Park, you can rent **kayaks, canoes, and pedal boats** for exploring the Necanicum River.

The surfing venues north of Tillamook Head, Indian Basin, near Short Sands Beach in Oswald West State Park, and in Manzanita can be enjoyed with surfboard and equipment rentals from **Cleanline Surf Shop** (719 1st Ave., 503/738-7888), which also rents Boogieboards, as well as wetsuits, boots, and flippers.

Bike Rentals

Seaside has a bumper crop of places that rent bicycles, all for similar rates. The **Prom Bike Shop** (622 12th Ave., 503/738-8251) charges $3–6 per hour. Others are **Wheel Fun Rentals Spoke I** (21 N. Columbia St., 503/717-4337), **Wheel Fun Rentals Spoke 2** (151 Ave. A, 503/738-7212), **Iron Coach Bike Rentals** (220 S. Columbia St., 503/738-9458), and **Distinctive Outdoor Fun For All** (407 S. Holladay Dr., 503/738-8447).

Golf

Golfers can escape to public courses south of Seaside and north in the small town of Gearhart. At **Seaside Golf Course** (451 Ave. U, 503/738-5261, green fees $9–10 for nine holes). The British links–style course at **Gearhart Golf Links** (Marion St., 503/738-3538) was established in 1882, making it one of the oldest on the West Coast. Green fees are $35 for the 18-hole course. The **Highlands at Gearhart** (1 Highland Rd., 503/738-5248, green fees $18 for 18 holes) is another public nine-hole course, with ocean views from most holes.

Other Recreation

In Seaside, the high school (1901 N. Holladay Dr.) and Broadway School (1120 Broadway St.) have free **tennis courts** with lights. There are also free public courts in Gearhart. Gearhart also has a **bowling alley,** Recreation Lanes, on the west side of U.S. 101 just north of the road to downtown, which reportedly serves the best hamburgers, halibut fish and chips, and homemade pie around.

EVENTS AND ENTERTAINMENT

Seaside predates any other town on the Oregon coast as a place built with good times in mind. A zoo and racetrack were among Seaside's first structures. Today, the town hosts the annual **Oregon Dixieland Jubilee** (800/394-3303, www.jazzseaside.com) at the end of February. This event has been gaining momentum for more than 20 years and appeals to fans of Dixieland and traditional jazz. The town celebrates the **Fourth of July** with a parade, picnic, and social at the Seaside Museum and a big fireworks show on the beach. In early September, the **Hot Rod Happenin'** (503/717-1914) and **Roadster Show** (800/394-3303) bring classic cars from all over to downtown and the Civic and Convention Center (1st Ave. at Necanicum). The third week in September, the **Seaside Sand Sculpture and Beach Festival** is good fun.

Saturday afternoons, there are **free concerts** downtown at Quatat Park. **Cannes Cinema**

(U.S. 101 at 12th Ave.) is a five-screen multiplex showing the usual.

ACCOMMODATIONS

Whatever your price range, you'll have to reserve ahead for a room in Seaside during the summer, weekends, and holidays (especially spring break). If you do, chances are you'll be able to find the specs you're looking for, given the area's array of lodgings—more than three dozen motels, a few B&Bs, and many vacation rentals. If you don't, come prepared to camp. The Seaside Visitors Bureau has a helpful website (www.seasideor.com) with comprehensive listings.

Vacation Rentals

A good option for families and groups might be one of the several dozen vacation rentals. Check with the Seaside Visitors Bureau, or contact one of the rental agencies: **Oceanside Vacation Rental** (503/738-7767 or 800/840-7764), **D. B. Rentals** (503/717-9516 or 800/203-1681), **Northwind Property Management** (503/738-5532 or 800/488-3301).

Motels

Motel 6 (2369 S. Roosevelt, 503/738-6269, $59 d) is on U.S. 101 about one-half mile south of Broadway. The **Comfort Inn** (545 Broadway Ave., Seaside, 503/738-3011, $75–140) is right on the Necanicum River. Rooms feature fireplaces, spa baths, microwaves, fridges, and balconies overlooking the river.

Gearhart offers a respite from the bustle of Seaside. The **Gearhart Ocean Inn** (67 N. Cottage St., 503/738-7373, $49–109) offers off-season specials October–April for your choice of 11 New England–style wooden cottages with comforters, wicker chairs, throw rugs, and a location close to the beach. The two-story deluxe units have kitchens and hardwood floors. Pets are allowed in some units. This spruced-up old motor court is one of the best values on the North Coast.

Hostel

The cheapest place in town is the **Seaside International Hostel** (930 N. Holladay Dr.,

503/738-7911 or 800/909-4776, $16–59). Unlike the other hostels, it doesn't close down during the day, there's an espresso bar, and the Necanicum River runs through the backyard. Close by is the Necanicum Estuary Park described later in this chapter. There are shared rooms with 4–6 bunks and private rooms. To get there from U.S. 101, make a left at the city center sign, turn on Holladay, and continue north. When you get to 9th Avenue, look for the hostel on the left. There's no curfew here.

Hotels

The **Shilo Oceanfront Resort** (30 N. Prom, 503/738-9571 or 800/222-2244, $100 and up) is right by the Prom turnaround and is a justifiable splurge for the oceanfront rooms that have balconies, fireplaces, and kitchenettes. A restaurant with windows on the water (good Sunday brunch) and an oceanview spa/pool/health club make it worth the price. The lounge features DJ music.

Best Western Oceanview Resort (414 N. Prom, Seaside, 503/738-3264 or 800/234-8439, $71–205) is another large hotel/motel right on the beach. Amenities include an on-site restaurant and lounge, heated pool, and spa; most rooms face the ocean.

Bed-and-Breakfasts

Although motels dominate the lodging scene in Seaside, a few B&Bs offer an alternative. Our top award for creativity goes to the **Seaside Inn B&B** (581 S. Prom, 503/319-3300 or 800/772-7766, $115–295). This four-story, shingle-sided structure stands right on the beach, with its north gable skewered by a clock tower. Each of the 15 guest rooms is decorated in a unique theme: The queen-sized bed in the '50s and '60s Rock & Roll room, for example, is incorporated into the tail end of a '59 Oldsmobile ($115–189). Other themes include the Bubble Room ($120–199), Sports Corner ($110–185), and the Clock Tower Suite ($160–295). Most have a spectacular ocean view.

The Gilbert Inn (341 Beach Dr., 503/738-9770 or 800/410-9770, $105–125 May–Sept., 15–20 percent less off-season) is a well-preserved 1892 Queen Anne, located just one block south of Broadway and one block from the beach. Period furnishings adorn the 10 guest rooms, which all have private bath, down comforters, and other nice touches; the third-floor "Garret" sleeps up to four in a queen and two twin beds, with ocean views from the dormer window. Rates include a full breakfast.

North of Broadway, the **10th Avenue Inn** (125 10th Ave., 503/738-0643 or 800/745-2378, $89–129) is a comfortable 1908 home built just a few steps from the beach. In the parlor, a baby grand piano, guitar, and other instruments are available for musically inclined guests. The three guest rooms have king-sized beds, attached baths, TVs, and small refrigerators. Next door is the **Doll House,** a sweet two-bedroom cottage (ideal for four adults plus two or three children) with a full kitchen and a deck with barbecue grill, which is operated by the same folks. It goes for $800 per week in summer (minimum week's rental), $150 per night off-season (two-night minimum).

The **Custer House Bed & Breakfast** (811 1st Ave., 503/738-7825 or 800/467-0201, $80–85) is another Victorian, one block east of the Necanicum River. The three guest rooms all have a private bath, and rates include a full breakfast.

FOOD

While a stroll down Broadway might have you thinking that cotton candy, corn dogs, and saltwater taffy are the staples of Seaside cuisine, several eateries here can satisfy taste and nutrition, as well as the broad-based clientele of this beach town.

Casual Fare

For breakfast, the Swedish pancakes and crab-and-cheese omelets at **Pig 'N Pancake** (323 Broadway St., 503/738-7243) are tops. If you're seriously hungry, try the Frisbee-sized cinnamon rolls. At last count, you could choose from 33 different breakfast variations at this place. Although you might think it's just another franchise on the main drag, you can count on this local chain (with outlets in Astoria and Cannon Beach) for three solid meals every day of the week. Locals rave about **Corpeny's Coffee House and Bakery** (2281 Beach Dr., 503/738-7353), where creative omelets can be had all day, in addition to salads, baked goods, and coffee drinks.

The Stand (109 N. Holladay Dr., 503/738-6592) features the satisfying and inexpensive Mexican fare that you'd find on the streetcart *loncherias* of Guadalajara. The carnitas taco is a mouthful of seasoned pork only exceeded perhaps by its beefy counterpart, the carne asada taco. The chili verde burrito, as well as enchiladas, tamales, and other specialties, can be enjoyed in the tiled confines of the restaurant.

Steak and Seafood

The **Vista Sea Café** (150 Broadway St., 503/738-8108) is known for pizza with ingredients such as artichokes, feta, chorizo, and pesto, plus topnotch clam chowder with homemade beer bread. Its location one block from the Turnaround makes it especially convenient.

Dooger's (505 Broadway St., 503/738-3773), which also has an outlet in Cannon Beach, has won acclaim for its clam chowder. Local clams and oysters, fresh Dungeness crab legs, sautéed shrimp, and marionberry cobbler are also the basis of Dooger's do-good reputation. The **Bell Buoy of Seaside** (1800 Holladay Dr., 503/738-6354) is a seafood market that makes an excellent razor clam chowder. Much of their seafood is brought in by their own fleet, and they'll pack for overnight shipping.

A rarity in these parts, **Lil' Bayou** (20 N. Holladay Dr., 503/717-0624) dishes up authentic muffalettas, jambalaya, blackened catfish, gumbo, and a host of other Cajun and creole standards, right down to side dishes of collard greens, at reasonable prices. Lunch entrées run $5–8, while most dinners are $12–15, topping out at $19.95 for an 18-ounce New York strip steak with Jack Daniel's sauce. Finish off with a slice of sweet potato pecan pie or Aunt B's cheesecake. Ooooh-weeee.

Seaside's toniest dinner house is probably **Ambrosia** (210 S. Holladay Dr., 503/738-7199). A good way to kick off your meal is with a selection from their martini menu, which offers a dozen variations on the standard. The N'Awlins, made with pepper vodka and jalapeño-stuffed olives, is an eye-opener. Entrées include fish, chicken, pork, and duck dishes, and pastas incorporating crab, shrimp, and clams; prices range $13–22, although the beef choices are stiffly priced at $25–27.

Dining in Gearhart

If the ambience of Seaside on a holiday weekend palls, try the **Pacific Way Bakery and Café** (601 Pacific Way, Gearhart, 503/738-0245). Gearhart is an appealing out-of-the-way place just north of Seaside, one-half mile west of U.S. 101. This is the area where famed food writer James Beard was raised. Beard would probably give Pacific Way's croissants five stars, so flaky and buttery are these breakfast-time mainstays. They take center stage again at lunch, providing the foundations for delectable sandwich fillings. Particularly recommended are the smoked salmon and cream cheese with thin-sliced red onion on croissant, the cioppino, and Caesar salad. Pasta, crusty pizzas, and seafood dishes (including thick seafood stew), as well as crêpes, also pop up at lunch and dinnertime. Ribeye steak and local razor clams are other frequent dinnertime highlights in this surprisingly urbane little café hidden behind a rustic old storefront. For bakery takeout fare, the baguettes and apple turnovers are tops.

INFORMATION AND SERVICES

The **Seaside Chamber of Commerce and Visitors Bureau** (7 N. Roosevelt St., Seaside 97138, 503/738-6391 or 800/444-6740, www .seasidechamber.com) is open 8 A.M.–5 P.M. daily. The **post office** is at 300 Avenue A, Seaside 97138.

The **police** (1090 S. Roosevelt Dr., 503/738-6311) make their presence known by handing out bagels and chatting with young people during spring break.

Providence Seaside Hospital (725 S. Wahanna Rd., 503/717-7000) has 24-hour service and an emergency room.

Public restrooms are located at the Turnaround and one block from the Prom at the intersection of 12th Avenue and Necanicum Drive.

Seaside is very walkable, but for $2, you can ride around town on the brightly painted **Seaside Street Car,** which runs hourly. Sunset Empire Transportation District also operates **TheBus** (503/861-7433), which serves Cannon Beach, Seaside, Astoria-Warrenton, and points in between.

Seaside's **Digital Design** (111 Broadway St., Ste. 3, 503/717-8350, open daily), located on the Seaside strip, is a cyber café featuring coffee or espresso along with Internet connections (at $5 per hour) and digital printing.

Find an **ATM** at Bank of America (300 S. Holladay Rd.).

Astoria and Vicinity

With its river and ocean access and abundance of natural resources, Astoria was long a traditional meeting place for the Native American tribes of this region. These features continue to lure travelers seeking prime recreational opportunities to this historic seaport town. Many visitors are aware of Astoria's legacy as the oldest permanent U.S. settlement west of the Rockies; its glory days are preserved by museums, historical exhibits, and pastel-colored Victorian homes weathered by the sea air. Hollywood has chosen Astoria's picturesque neighborhoods to simulate an idealized all-American city on close to a dozen occasions. This often creates the expectation of a Williamsburg of the West, where the portrayal of history and heritage is a focal point of the local identity. The reality of modern-day Astoria, however, is more accurately captured in a locally popular bumper sticker that defiantly proclaims, "We Ain't Quaint!"

The preserved pioneer past and attractive Victorian homes may soften the rough edges of a once-bustling port that has seen better days, but not enough to let anyone mistake blue-collar Astoria for an ersatz tourist town. The decommissioning of the U.S. Naval station after World War II, the decline in the logging and fishing industries, and the closure of several dozen canneries on the waterfront have had lasting effects on this town of 10,000 people. Empty storefronts here tell the story of a resource-based economy bruised by progress, but there's plenty of pluck left in this old dowager, and her best years may be yet to come. Astoria hath many charms: Historic buildings downtown are undergoing restoration, cruise ships are calling, fine restaurants are multiplying, a lively music and arts scene is thriving, and there's new life along the waterfront, anchored by the excellent Columbia River Maritime Museum.

The waters surrounding Astoria define the town as much as the steep hills it's built on. Along its northern side, the mighty Columbia, four miles wide, is a mega-highway carrying a steady flow of traffic, from small pleasure boats to massive cargo ships one-quarter mile long. Soaring high over the river is an engineering marvel that's impossible to miss from most locations in town. At just over four miles long, the Astoria-Megler Bridge, completed in 1966, is the longest bridge in Oregon and the longest bridge of its type (cantilever through truss) in the world. On Astoria's south side, the Young's River, flowing down from the Coast Range, broadens into Young's Bay, separating Astoria from its neighbor Warrenton (pop. 4,040) to the west.

A few miles to the northwest, the Columbia River finally meets the Pacific, 1,243 miles from its headwaters in British Columbia. Where the tremendous outflow (average 118 million gallons per minute) of the River of the West encounters the ocean tides, conditions can be treacherous, and the sometimes monstrous waves around the bar have claimed more than 2,000 vessels over the years. This rivermouth could well be the biggest widow-maker on the high seas, earning it the title Graveyard of the Pacific. Lewis and Clark referred to it as "that seven-shouldered horror" in a journal entry from the winter of 1805–1806.

HISTORY

The Clatsop Indians, a Chinook-speaking tribe, lived in this area for thousands of years before Astoria's written history began. When Lewis and Clark arrived in 1805, the Clatsops numbered about 400 people, living in three villages on the south side of the Columbia River, but began a steady decline soon after contact with whites.

The region was first chronicled by Don Bruno de Heceta, a Spanish explorer who sailed near the Columbia's mouth in August 1775. He named it the Bay of the Assumption of Our Lady, but the strong current prevented his ship from entering. American presence on the Columbia began with Captain Robert Gray's discovery of the river in May 1792, which he christened after his fur-trading ship, *Columbia Rediviva*.

Thereafter, Lewis and Clark's famous expedition of 1803–1806, with its winter encampment at Fort Clatsop, south of present-day Astoria, helped incorporate the Pacific Northwest as part of a new nation. In 1811, John Jacob Astor's agents built Fort Astoria on a hillside in what would eventually grow into Astoria—the first American settlement west of the Rockies. Despite temporary occupation by the British between 1813 and 1818, the fort and a shaky American presence were able to hold on until settlers came to farm the region during the Oregon Trail era of the 1840s. During the Civil War, Fort Stevens was built to guard against a Confederate naval incursion.

From that time until the 1900s, immigrants of Scandinavian descent predominated. Commerce grew with the export of lumber and foodstuffs to gold rush–era San Francisco and the Far East. Salmon canneries became the mainstay of Astoria's economy during the 1870s, helping it grow into Oregon's second-largest city—and a notorious shanghaiing port. Over the ensuing decades, logging, fishing, and shipbuilding coaxed the population up to 20,000 by World War II.

Some believe that the port city might have grown to rival San Francisco or Seattle had it not been for the setback of a devastating fire in

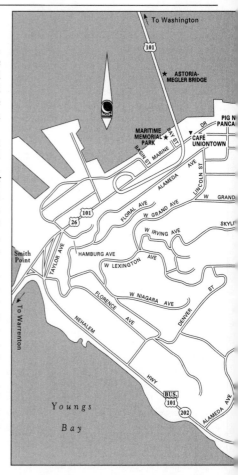

1922. In the early morning hours of December 8, a pool hall on Commercial Street caught fire, and the flames spread rapidly among the wooden buildings, many supported on wooden pilings, of Astoria's business district. By daybreak, more than 200 businesses in a 32-block area had been reduced to smoldering heaps. The downtown was rebuilt in the ensuing years, largely in brick and stone, but the devastation changed the fate of Astoria.

Near the end of World War II, a Japanese submarine's shelling of Fort Stevens made it the only fortification on American soil to have sus-

Columbia   River

ASTORIA

8TH STREET
VIEWING TOWER

CHAMBER OF
COMMERCE   MARINE   DR   WET DOG
                                        CAFÉ   14TH
                                                    STREET
                                                    PIER   COLUMBIA RIVER
                                                                MARITIME MUSEUM   UPPERTOWN FIREFIGHTERS
                                                                                       MUSEUM/ASTORIA CHILDREN'S
                                                                                       MUSEUM
BOND   ST   T. PAUL'S   AMTRAK
                                        URBAN CAFÉ   SILVER SALMON GRILLE   MARINE   DR   DEPOT
COMMERCIAL   ST   DUANE   HERITAGE
                                        HOTEL ELLIOTT   LIBERTY   MUSEUM   ASTORIA
        FLAVEL HOUSE ★   ● CLEMENTINE'S B&B   THEATER   AQUATIC
                                                            EXCHANGE   ST   CENTER
        FRANKLIN AVE   FRANKLIN   ●
                                        STREET B&B   ROSE RIVER
        GRAND   AVE   INN B&B
                                        ROSEBRIAR   CATHEDRAL
        HARRISON   AVE   HOTEL   IRVING   AVE   TREE

        JEROME   AVE
KENSINGTON   AVE   CLATSOP
                                                        LEXINGTON   AVE   COMMUNITY
                                                                                   COLLEGE
LEXINGTON   AVE
                                                    COXCOMB   Coxcomb
        NIAGARA   AVE   DR   ASTORIA   Hill
                                                                    COLUMN ▲
                                                    JAMES   ST
KLASKANINE   AVE
                                            WILLIAMSPORT   RD   PIPELINE   RD
MCCLURE   AVE

                    0   0.25 mi

                    0   0.25 km

                    202

↓ To County Fairgrounds

© AVALON TRAVEL PUBLISHING, INC.

tained an attack in a world war. After the war, the region's fortunes ebbed and flowed with its resource-based economy. In an attempt to supplement that economy with tourism, the State Highway Division began constructing the Astoria-Megler Bridge in 1962 to connect Oregon and Washington. When it opened in 1966, the bridge provided the final link in 1,625-mile-long U.S. 101.

Unfortunately, preserving Astoria's glory days could not make up for the closing of the canneries and the decline of logging and fishing, although in recent years the long-dormant sardine fishery has resumed, helping to revive the fish-packing industry. The modern era has been characterized by a steady cultivation of tourism dollars, resulting in the thoughtful development of the waterfront, including the two-mile River Walk and plans for a conference center at the port. Astoria is becoming an increasingly popular port-of-call for cruise ships, with more than a dozen visiting in 2003. Whether or not Astoria's ship ever comes in, let's hope the unpretentious charm of this hillside city-by-the-sea will not be lost in the process.

ASTORIA-WARRENTON AND VICINITY

Clatsop Spit

WA
OR

Columbia River

Pt. Adams

WRECK OF ★
PETER IREDALE

Hammond

Fort Stevens
State Park

101

FORT STEVENS HWY

COLUMBIA RIVER HWY

30

RIDGE RD

Smith
Point

Astoria

0 ——— 1 mi

0 ——— 1 km

202

NEHALEM

Warrenton

101

BUS.
101

Youngs Bay

PACIFIC OCEAN

OREGON COAST HWY

HWY

WARRENTON-

ASTORIA

HWY

Young's River

FORT CLATSOP
NATIONAL MEMORIAL

★

Lewis and Clark River

LEWIS AND CLARK RD

YOUNGS RIVER

YOUNGS RIVER LOOP RD

202

101
26

FORT CLATSOP RD

↙ To Seaside

© AVALON TRAVEL PUBLISHING, INC.

SIGHTS

Astoria Column

The best introduction to Astoria and environs is undoubtedly the 360-degree panorama from atop the 125-foot-tall Astoria Column (503/325-2963, open dawn–dusk daily) on Coxcomb Hill, the highest point in town. Patterned after the Trajan Column in Rome, the reinforced-concrete tower was built in 1926 as a joint project of the Great Northern Railroad and the descendants of John Jacob Astor to commemorate the westward sweep of discovery and migration. The sgraffito frieze spiraling up the exterior illustrates Robert Gray's 1792 discovery of the Columbia River, the establishment of American claims to the Northwest Territory, the arrival of the Great Northern Railway, and other scenes of Northwest history. The vista from the surrounding hill-top park is impressive enough, but for the ultimate experience, the climb up 164 steps to the tower's top is worth the effort.

Before ascending, get oriented with the annotated bronze relief map in front of the column, which notes the distances and directions to landmarks near and far. From this vantage point, you can see across the rooftops of the town, the Astoria Bridge, giant freighters gliding up and down the Columbia, and a long sweep of the Washington shore. To the northwest are the Columbia Bar and Cape Disappointment. On clear days, look northeast to Mt. St. Helens and to Mt. Hood on the far eastern horizon. Looking over Young's Bay south and west of Astoria, the Clatsop Plains extend to Tillamook Head and Saddleback Mountain.

Get to the Astoria Column from downtown by following 16th Street south (uphill) to Jerome

NORTH COAST

This 1886 woodcut, looking toward the northeast, shows Astoria as a growing seaport.

COURTESY OF GODFATHER'S BOOKS

Avenue. Turn west (right) one block and continue up 15th Street to the park entrance on Coxcomb Drive. A $1 parking fee is requested at the visitors center.

Walking Tour

After getting a bird's-eye view from Coxcomb Hill, you might want to take a closer look at Astoria on foot. The town is home to dozens of beautifully restored 19th-century and early-20th-century houses. A walking tour of many of them is laid out in a guidebook written by a local historian and available for $3 at the Heritage Museum (1618 Exchange St.). You can book a guided tour through **Historical Tours of Astoria** (612 Florence Ave., 503/325-3005).

If you want to forgo the purchase and let the architectural scenery do the talking, here's a suggested route: From the Flavel House Museum, at 8th Street and Duane, start walking south on 8th Street and turn left on Franklin Avenue. Continue east to 11th Street, then detour south one block on 11th Street to Grand Avenue, east on Grand, north on 12th Street, and back to Franklin, continuing your eastward trek. Walk to 17th Street, then south again to Grand, double back on Grand two blocks to 15th Street, then

walk north on 15th to Exchange Street and east on Exchange to 17th, where you'll be just two blocks from the Columbia River Maritime Museum. The route takes you past 74 historical buildings and sites.

On the Waterfront

Although most of Astoria's waterfront is lined with warehouses, industry, and docks, the **6th Street Riverpark** and River Walk will get you front-row views of the river. The park is a local favorite from which to watch ships from the sheltered observation platform and to fish for Columbia River salmon. The Lewis and Clark Bicentennial headquarters is here; placards around the park display information about the Lewis and Clark Expedition and the area's Chinook natives. Walk east from Pier 6, past the fish-packing plants, for an interesting—if malodorous and noisy (thanks to the sea lions)—perspective on what is still a working commercial fishing port. The 11th Street Pier has been developed with a restaurant and shops, and the 14th Street Pier and 17th Street Dock are two other convenient access points for watching cargo ships, sea lions, and fishing boats.

The **River Walk** provides riverside passage for pedestrians and cyclists along a three-mile stretch

ASTORIA GOES TO THE MOVIES

In recent decades, the Victorian homes and ocean view in Astoria's hillside neighborhoods and the surrounding maritime settings have provided the backdrop for such fanciful modern sagas as *Free Willy I* and *II, Kindergarten Cop, Teenage Mutant Ninja Turtles III, Short Circuit, Come See the Paradise,* and *The Goonies.* The latter, a cult favorite of sorts shot in 1985, concerns a gang of local kids hunting for pirate's treasure, and happy memories of the movie continue to attract a steady stream of visitors looking for the locations used in the film. A guide to movie locations is available at the Oregon Welcome Center in Astoria, the Heritage Museum, Flavel House Museum, and the Warrenton Visitors Center.

between the Port of Astoria and the community of Alderbrook. Eventually, the path will extend another two miles eastward to Tongue Point and west past the Port of Astoria to Smith Point.

An excellent way to cover some of the same ground, accompanied by color commentary on sights and local history, is by taking a 40-minute ride on Old Number 300, the **Astoria Riverfront Trolley** (503/325-6311, 3 P.M.–9 P.M. Mon.–Thurs., noon–9 P.M. Fri.–Sun.), which runs on Astoria's original train tracks alongside the River Walk as far east as the East Mooring Basin. The lovingly restored 1913 trolley originally served San Antonio and later ran between Portland and Lake Oswego in the 1980s. Off-season, it operates weekends only until dark. During heavy rains, the antique trolley may stay put in its newly constructed barn. It costs $1 to ride the trolley as long as you stay on board; the $2 All-Day Fare lets you get on and off as often as you like.

Columbia River Maritime Museum

On the waterfront. a few blocks east of downtown Astoria, the Columbia River Maritime Museum (1792 Marine Dr., 503/325-2323, www.crmm.org, 9:30 A.M.–5 P.M. daily except

Thanksgiving and Christmas Day, $8 adults, $7 seniors, $4 ages 6–17, free ages six and under) is hard to miss. The roof of the 44,000-square-foot museum simulates the curvature of cresting waves, and the gigantic 25,000-pound anchor out front is also hard to ignore. This eye-catching facade is more than matched by what's inside. The museum's recent $5 million expansion features an award-winning film that introduces visitors to the region's maritime history and includes displays on the Coast Guard, salmon fishing, tugboats, and canneries of Astoria. Floor-to-ceiling windows in the Great Hall allow visitors to watch the river traffic in comfort.

The eras when Indian canoes plied the Columbia, Lewis and Clark camped on its shores, and dramatic shipwrecks occurred on its bar are recounted with scale models, exquisitely detailed miniatures of ships, paintings, and artifacts. The most dramatic exhibit is of a 44-foot U.S. Coast Guard motor lifeboat, poised precariously on a wave in a life-size re-creation of a rescue on the Columbia River Bar. The chance to walk the bridge of a World War II destroyer, steer a tugboat, or tie a cleat hitch and other useful knots imparts a hands-on aspect to the experience. Local lighthouses, the evolution of boat design, and harpoons are the focus of other exhibits here. There are also some artifacts from the *Peter Iredale* and other ships that have met their ends on the Oregon coast. Scrimshaw, fishing and cannery memorabilia, a small watercolor of the harbor by a crewmember on Robert Gray's 1792 voyage of discovery, and sea charts dating as far back as 1587 also highlight your visit.

Your ticket also gains you admission aboard the 128-foot Lightship *Columbia,* now permanently berthed alongside the museum building. This vessel served as a floating lighthouse, marking the entrance to the mouth of the river and helping many ships navigate the dangerous waters. After almost three decades of service, it was replaced in 1979 by an unstaffed 42-foot-high navigational buoy. The gift shop has a great collection of books on Astoria's history, as well as other maritime topics.

The 25,000-pound anchor from a U.S. Navy battleship outside the Columbia River Maritime Museum dwarfs a young visitor.

Uppertown Firefighters Museum and Astoria Children's Museum

Sharing space in a historic redbrick building (formerly the North Pacific Brewery, built in 1896) at 30th and Marine Drive are two museums that will especially appeal to kids. Admission of $3 adults or $2 seniors and AAA members gets you into both. The museums are usually open 11 A.M.–2 P.M. Wednesday–Saturday, but hours can vary.

The Uppertown Firefighters Museum (503/325-2203) displays an extensive collection of firefighting equipment from 1873 to 1963. Featured are hand-pulled, horse-drawn, and motorized fire engines, including a 1912 American LaFrance fire truck, a Stutz fire engine, and a 1946 Mack fire truck. The photos and information about the devastating fires of 1893 and 1922 are fascinating.

The Astoria Children's Museum (503/325-8669), provides hands-on activities and other fun and educational programs for kids. Permanent exhibits include a child-sized grocery store and an active toddler area. Additional special activities are scheduled during school breaks and summer vacation.

The Heritage Museum and Research Library

The Clatsop County Historical Society operates the Heritage Museum (1618 Exchange St., Astoria 97103, 503/325-2203, 10 A.M.–5 P.M. daily May–Sept., $4 adults, $2.50 seniors, $2 ages 6–12). Housed in the handsome neo-classical building that was originally Astoria's city hall, it has several galleries filled with antiquities, tools, vintage photographs, and archives chronicling various aspects of life in Clatsop County. The museum's new centerpiece exhibit concentrates on the culture of the local Clatsop and Chinook tribes, from before European contact to the present day. Other exhibits highlight the natural history, geology, early immigrants and settlers in the region, and the development of commerce in such enterprises as fishing, fish packing, logging, and lumber. The research library has recently expanded and is open to the public.

Fort Astoria

In a tiny park at the corner of 15th and Exchange streets, a reproduction of a rough-hewn log blockhouse and mural commemorate the spot where Astoria began, when John J. Astor's fur traders originally constructed a small fort in 1811. It's worth a quick stop for buffs of early Northwest history.

Flavel House Museum

Captain George Flavel, Astoria's first millionaire, amassed a fortune in the mid-19th century through his Columbia Bar piloting monopoly, and later expanded his empire through shipping, banking, and real estate. Between 1884 and 1886, he had a home built in the center of Astoria, overlooking the Columbia River, where he retired with his wife and two daughters. From its fourth-story cupola, Flavel could watch the comings and goings of his sailing fleet. Although the captain died in 1893, members of the family

the George Flavel House, a masterpiece of
Queen Anne architecture

lived in the house until 1933. The amazing story
of the Flavel family was depicted in colorful detail by Calvin Trillin in a February 1993 issue
of *The New Yorker*.

When the Clatsop County Historical Society
assumed stewardship in 1951, the mansion was
slated for demolition, to be paved over as a parking lot for the adjacent courthouse. Fortunately,
thanks to the efforts of the historical society and
many volunteers, the house still stands today, at
the corner of 8th Street and Duane, a splendidly
extravagant Queen Anne mansion that reflects
the rich style and elegance of the late Victorian era
and the lives of Astoria's most prominent family.
Known locally as "the house with the red roof," it
has withstood more than a century of storms off
the Columbia River estuary. This landmark for
incoming ships is now the foremost monument
to Astoria's golden age as the leading port in the
Northwest.

The property encompasses a full city block
and includes a rehabilitated carriage house and
surrounding gardens. With its intricate woodwork inside and out, period furnishings, and art,
along with its extravagantly rendered gables, cornices, and porches, the Flavel House ranks with
the Carson Mansion in Eureka, California, as a
Victorian showplace. The 14-foot ceilings, Persian
rugs, and an array of imported tiles are upstaged
only by the fireplaces framed in exotic hardwoods in every room. The recently restored Carriage House is now an orientation center for
visitors, with exhibits, an interpretive video, and
museum store.

Visitors to The Flavel House Museum (441
8th St., 503/325-2203, open 10 A.M.–5 P.M. daily
May–Sept., 11 A.M.–4 P.M. Oct.–Apr.) should
stop first at the Carriage House to purchase tickets: $5 adults, $4 seniors and students, $2 ages
6–17, free ages five and younger.

Twilight Creek Eagle Sanctuary/ Lewis and Clark National Wildlife Refuge

Six miles east of Astoria in the Burnside area is the
Twilight Creek Eagle Sanctuary. To get there,
drive east on U.S. 30 and turn left at Burnside.
Another left one-half mile later takes you to the
viewing platform, which overlooks the 35,000
acres of mudflats, tidal marshes, and islands
(which Lewis and Clark called "Seal Islands") of
the Lewis and Clark National Wildlife Refuge.
Bald eagles live here year-round, with 30–35 active nest sites. The area provides wintering and
resting habitat for waterfowl (including an estimated 1,000 tundra swans in winter), shorebirds, and songbirds. Beavers, raccoons, weasels,
mink, muskrats, and river otters live on the islands; harbor seals and California sea lions feed in
the rich estuary waters and use the sandbars and
mudflats as haul-out sites at low tides.

Fort Clatsop National Memorial

On November 7, 1805, after a journey of nearly
19 months and 4,000 miles, the Lewis and Clark
Expedition thought they had at last reached their
destination, the Pacific Ocean. "Ocian in View!
O! the joy," wrote William Clark in his journal.
Alas, they were close, but from the Washington
side of the Columbia River they had mistaken its
broad mouth for the sea itself. Hindered by waves
and foul weather, it would take nearly another

Fort Clatsop interior

week before they actually beheld the Pacific. They explored farther west, to Cape Disappointment, and spent 10 uncomfortable days exposed to the elements on the north shore of the Columbia, then decided to move south for a more suitable location to pass the coming winter.

They chose a thickly forested rise alongside the Netul River (now the Lewis and Clark River), a few miles south of present-day Astoria, for their campsite. There the Corps of Discovery quickly set about felling trees and building two parallel rows of cabins, joined by a gated palisade. The finished compound measured about 50 feet square. The party of 33 people, including one African American, a Native American woman, and her baby, moved into the seven small rooms on Christmas Eve and named their stockade Fort Clatsop for the nearby tribe.

The winter of 1805–1806 was one of the worst on record—cold, wet, rainy, and generally miserable. Of the 106 days the group spent at the site, it rained on all but 12. The January 18, 1806, journal entry of expedition member Private Joseph Whitehouse was typical of the comments recorded during the stay: "It rained hard all last night, & still continued the same this morning. It continued Raining during the whole of this day."

While at Fort Clatsop, the men stored meat and other supplies, sewed moccasins and new garments, and traded with the local Indians, all the while coping with the constant damp, illness and injuries, and merciless plagues of fleas. As soon as the weather permitted, on March 23, 1806, they finally departed on their homeward journey to St. Louis.

Within a few years, the elements had erased all traces of Fort Clatsop, and its exact location was lost. In 1955, local history buffs took their best guess and built a replica of the fort, based on the notes and sketches of Captain Clark. In 1999, an anthropologist discovered a 148-year-old map identifying the location of Lewis and Clark's winter encampment, and as it turns out the modern reproduction is sited very close to the original.

Today, in addition to the log replica of the fort, a well-equipped visitors center, museum, and other attractions make Fort Clatsop National Memorial (92343 Fort Clatsop Rd., Astoria 97103, 503/861-2471, www.nps.gov/focl, 8 A.M.–6 P.M. daily in summer, 8 A.M.–5 P.M. the rest of the year, closed Christmas) a must-see for anyone interested in this pivotal chapter of American history. The expedition's story is nicely narrated here with displays, artifacts, slides, and films, but the summertime living-history reenactments are the main reason to come. Paths lead through the grove of old-growth Sitka spruce, with interpretive placards identifying native plants. A short walk from the fort leads to the riverside, where dugout canoes are modeled on those used by the corps while in this area.

The winter of 1805–1806 put a premium on wilderness survival skills, some of which are exhibited here by rangers in costume, 9 A.M.–5:30 P.M. daily from Memorial Day to Labor Day. You can see them tanning hides, making buckskin clothing and moccasins, and molding tallow candles and lead bullets. In addition, visitors may occasionally participate in constructing a dugout canoe or try their luck at starting a fire by striking flint on steel. For a taste of what Lewis and Clark and their party experienced here, a visit on a cold, wet, wintry day, when every branch and leaf is dripping with rain, is an opportunity to better appreciate their fortitude.

This 125-acre park sits six miles southwest of Astoria and three miles east of U.S. 101 on the Lewis and Clark River. To get there from Astoria, take Marine Drive and head west across Young's Bay to Warrenton. On the other side of the bay, look for signs for the Fort Clatsop turnoff. Then turn left off the Coast Highway and follow the direction markers.

Admission at press time is $3 per person or $5 per carload, good for seven days' admission, but entrance fees will probably rise during the 2004–2006 bicentennial observations. The Oregon Coast Annual Passport and Oregon Coast 5-Day Passport are honored here. Park officials expect that the annual quarter-million visitors will increase by up to 70 percent during the bicentennial, and a new, larger parking lot is being built three-quarters mile from the visitors center; trails and shuttles will connect the two, and plans are also in the works to add a kayak and canoe landing at the lot. Once that lot fills, visitors will have to board special shuttle buses in Astoria, Warrenton, Fort Stevens, Seaside, and Cannon

Beach. For details, contact the park or the Sunset Empire Transportation District, locally known as TheBus (503/861-RIDE or 800/776-6406, www.ridethebus.org). Park entrance will include the cost of the ride.

Fort Stevens State Park

Ten miles west of Astoria, at the far northwest corner of the state, this Civil War–era outpost was one of three military installations (the others were Forts Canby and Columbia in Washington) built to safeguard the mouth of the Columbia River. Established shortly before the Confederates surrendered on April 9, 1865, Fort Stevens served for 84 years, until just after the end of World War II. Today, the remaining fortifications and other buildings are preserved along with 3,700 acres of woodland, lakes, wetlands, miles of sand beaches, and three miles of Columbia River frontage.

The fort's creation was not the only outgrowth of the Civil War on the West Coast. The year before, Lincoln had founded the city of Port Angeles, Washington, for "lighthouse purposes."

Battery Russell, at Fort Stevens State Park

Given the subsequent creation of Fort Stevens shortly thereafter, it's a logical assumption that lighthouse purposes also meant watching out for Confederate ships and the British, whom the Union feared would ally with the South. The remote northwest Oregon coast may seem a world away from the bloody battles of the Civil War, until you consider that the last shots of the conflict were fired even farther away, in the Bering Strait: On June 5, 1865, the *Shenandoah* attacked a fleet of Yankee whalers because the Confederate skipper was unaware of the Appomattox treaty, which had ended the war two months before.

Although Fort Stevens did not see action in the Civil War, it sustained an attack in a later conflict. On June 21, 1942, a Japanese submarine fired 17 shells on the gun emplacements at Battery Russell, making it the only U.S. fortification in the 48 states to be bombed by a foreign power since the

War of 1812. No damage was incurred, and the Army didn't return fire. Shortly after World War II, the fort was deactivated and the armaments were removed.

Today, the site features a memorial rose garden, the Fort Stevens Military Museum (Hammond 97121, 503/861-1671 or 800/551-6949, 10 A.M.–6 P.M. daily Memorial Day–Labor Day, 10 A.M.–4 P.M. Wed.–Sun. the rest of the year, free) with old photos, weapons exhibits, and maps, as well as seven different batteries (fortifications) and other structures left over from almost a century of service. Climbing to the commander's station for a scenic view of the Columbia River and South Jetty are popular visitor activities. The massive gun batteries, built of weathered gray concrete and rusting iron, eerily silent amid the thick woodlands, also invite exploration; small children should be closely supervised because there are steep stairways, high ledges, and other hazards.

THE PETER IREDALE

One of the best known of the hundreds of ships wrecked on the Oregon coast over the centuries is that of the British schooner *Peter Iredale*. This 278-foot four-master, fashioned of steel plates on an iron frame, was built in Liverpool in 1890 and came to her untimely end on the beach south of Clatsop Spit on October 25, 1906. En route from Mexico to pick up a load of wheat on the Columbia River, the vessel ran aground during high seas and a northwesterly squall. All hands

were rescued and, with little damage to the hull, hopes initially ran high that the ship could be towed back to sea and salvaged. That effort proved fruitless, and eventually the ship was written off as a total loss. Today, nearly a century later, the remains of her rusting skeleton protruding from the sands of Fort Stevens State Park are a familiar sight to most who have traveled the north coast. Signs within Fort Stevens State Park lead the way to the parking area close to the wreck.

the *Peter Iredale* on November 13, 1906, three weeks after the wreck . . .

. . . and in 2003

During summer, guided tours of the underground Battery Mishler ($2) and a narrated tour of the fort's 37 acres on a two-ton U.S. Army truck ($2.50) are also available. The summer programs include Civil War reenactments and archaeological digs; consult the visitors center for schedules.

Nine miles of bike trails and six miles of hiking trails link the historic area to the rest of the park and provide access to Battery Russell and the 1906 wreck of the British schooner *Peter Iredale* (see special topic). You can also bike to the campground one mile south of the Military Museum.

Parking is available at four lots about a mile apart from one another at the foot of the dunes. The beach runs north to the Columbia River, where excellent surf fishing, bird-watching, and a view of the mouth of the river await. South of the campground (east of the *Peter Iredale*) there's a self-guided nature trail around part of the two-mile shoreline of **Coffenbury Lake.** The lake also has two swimming beaches with bathhouses and fishing for trout and perch.

To get there from U.S. 101, drive west on Harbor Street through Warrenton on Route 104 (Ft. Stevens Highway) to the suburb of Hammond, and follow the signs to the park. There is a $3 parking day-use fee, which is covered by the Oregon Coast Annual Passport and Oregon Coast 5-Day Passport.

RECREATION
Fishing Charters
More than any other industry, commercial fishing has dominated Astoria throughout its history. Salmon canneries lined the waterfront at the turn of the 20th century. Albacore and longline shark fishing put dinner on the table in the 1930s and 1940s. In the modern era, commercial fishing has turned to sole, rockfish, flounder, and less-well-known bottom fish. If it's not enough to watch these commercial operations from the dock, try joining a charter. **Tiki Charters** (503/325-7818, www.tikicharters.com) will take you out to drop your line for salmon and sturgeon. Trips depart from the West Mooring Basin in Astoria. River tours are also available.

Given the retail price of fresh salmon, you could theoretically pay for a charter trip by landing a single fish. **Gale Force Guides** (Warrenton, 503/861-1494) takes sport anglers fishing for salmon in either salt or fresh water, depending on the season. On your own, go after trout, bass, catfish, steelhead, and sturgeon in freshwater lakes, streams, and rivers. Ling cod, rockfish, surfperch, or other bottom fish can be pursued at sea, off jetties, or along ocean beaches.

Hiking
An in-town hike that's not too strenuous begins at 28th Street and Irving, and meanders up the hill to the Astoria Column. If you drive to the trailhead, park along 28th. It's about a one-mile walk to the top. En route is the **Cathedral Tree,** an old-growth fir with a sort of Gothic arch formed at its roots.

The **Oregon Coast Trail** starts (or ends) at Clatsop Spit, at the north end of Fort Stevens State Park. The most northerly stretch extends south along the beach for 14 miles to Gearhart. It's a flat, easy walk, and your journey could well be highlighted by a sighting of the endangered silver-spot butterfly. It now frequents just six sites, including four in Oregon, with Clatsop County being one of them. The endangered status of this species protects it under law and has stopped developers from building resorts on coastal meadows and dunes north of Gearhart. Look for a small orange butterfly with silvery spots on the undersides of its wings. You also might encounter cars on the beach. This section of shoreline is, inexplicably, the longest stretch of coastline open to motor vehicles in Oregon. Call the State Parks and Recreation Department (800/551-6949) for an up-to-date report on trail conditions before starting out.

Fort Stevens State Park has six miles of hiking trails, through woods, wetlands, and dunes. One popular hike here is the two-mile loop around **Coffenbury Lake.**

The Astoria Aquatic Center
The Astoria Aquatic Center (20th and Marine Dr., 503/325-7027, 5:30 A.M.–8 P.M. Mon.–Thurs., 5:30 A.M.–7 P.M. Fri., noon–7 P.M. Sat.,

noon–4 P.M. Sun.) houses four pools, including a 100-foot water slide with a 20-foot drop and lazy river current; a six-lane, 25-yard lap pool; adult hydro spa pool; kiddies' wading pool; locker rooms; and a variety of fitness equipment. Pool hours are subject to change and may be extended during summer months.

EVENTS AND ENTERTAINMENT

For the lowdown on all the happenings in and around Astoria, get your hands on a copy of *Hipfish*, Astoria's spirited monthly tabloid that's distributed free all over town.

Fisher Poets Gathering

Modeled after Elko, Nevada's popular Cowboy Poets Gathering, the Fisher Poets Gathering (Clatsop Community College, www.clatsopcollege.com/fisherpoets) provides a forum in which men and women involved in the fishing and other maritime industries share their poems, stories, songs, and artwork in a convivial seaport setting. Inaugurated in 1998, the annual February event draws writers and artists from up and down the Pacific coast and farther afield for readings, art shows, concerts, book signings, workshops, films, silent auction, and other activities at pubs, galleries, theaters, and other venues around town. Participation isn't limited to fisherfolk, but extends to anyone with a connection to maritime activity, and themes range from the rigors (and humor) of life on the water to environmental issues. Admission is by donation ($5) at the ticket booth of the Columbian Theater (11th and Marine Dr.).

Astoria-Warrenton Crab and Seafood Festival

The Crab and Seafood Festival (information 503/325-6311 or 800/875-6807, 4–9 P.M. Fri., 10 A.M.–8 P.M. Sat., 11 A.M.–4 P.M. Sun., $5–7 adults, $3 ages 62 and up, $1 kids 12 and under), held the last weekend in April at the Clatsop County Fairgrounds, is a hugely popular event that brings in crowds from miles around. Scores of booths feature a cornucopia of seafood and other cuisine, regional beers and Oregon wines,

and arts and crafts. Activities include continuous entertainment, crab races, a petting zoo, and kids' activities. A traditional crab dinner caps off the evening.

To get to the fairgrounds from Astoria, take U.S. 202 and drive 4.5 miles to Walluski Loop Road and watch for signs. Parking is limited at the fairgrounds. Frequent shuttle service takes folks between the fairgrounds, Park & Ride lots, the Port of Astoria, and local hotels and campgrounds.

Scandinavian Midsummer Festival

The legacy of the thousands of Scandinavians who arrived to work in the mills and canneries of Astoria in the late 19th and early 20th centuries is still strong in Astoria, with public steam baths, *lutefisk, smorrebrod* platters, and church services in Finnish. Today, the biggest event in town is the Scandinavian Midsummer Festival (P.O. Box 7, Astoria 97103, 503/325-6311, $6 adults, $2 children ages 6 and up), which usually takes place the third weekend of June, Friday–Sunday. Local Danes, Finns, Icelanders, Norwegians, and Swedes come together to celebrate their heritage. Costumed participants dance around a flowered midsummer pole (a fertility rite), burn a bonfire to destroy evil spirits, and have tugs-of-war pitting Scandinavian nationalities against each other. Food, dancing, crafts, and a parade bring the whole town out to the Clatsop County Fairgrounds on Walluski Loop Road just off ORE 202.

Silver Salmon Celebration

If you miss the spring Crab Festival, get a second shot in mid-October at the Silver Salmon Celebration (Astoria-Warrenton Area Chamber of Commerce, 503/325-6311), held at the foot of Basin Street, near Astoria's West End Mooring Basin. Get fresh salmon right off the boat, and enjoy seafood delicacies, beer and wine tasting, arts and crafts, live music, and lots of activities for little ones.

Astoria Regatta Week

An Astoria tradition since 1894, Regatta Week is considered the Pacific Northwest's longest-running festival. Held on the waterfront in early August, the five-day Regatta (Astoria Regatta Association, P.O. Box 24, Astoria 97103, www.astoriaregatta.org) kicks off with the regatta queen's coronation and reception. Attractions include live entertainment, a grand land parade, historic home tours, ship tours and boat rides, sailboat and dragon boat races, a classic car show, a salmon barbecue, arts and crafts, food booths, a beer garden, and a twilight boat parade.

Astor Street Opry Company

Astoria's long-running *Shanghaied in Astoria,* which is based on the town's dubious distinction as a notorious shanghai port during the late 1800s, is a good old-fashioned melodrama. Chase scenes, bar fights, and a liberal sprinkling of Scandinavian jokes will have you laughing, in between applauding the hero and booing the villain. Performed with gusto by the Astor Street Opry Company (279 W. Marine Dr., Astoria, 503/325-6104), the show has been going on for two decades. Shows are performed Thursday–Saturday evenings, mid-July to mid-September, in the converted Old Finnish Meat Market building. Tickets are $8–16, available at the door.

Liberty Theater

The handsome Liberty Theater (www.libertytheater.org), whose colonnaded facades along Commercial and 12th streets converge at the corner box office, is a vibrant symbol of Astoria's ongoing rejuvenation. The ornate Mediterranean-style building in the heart of downtown began its life in 1925 as a venue for silent films, vaudeville acts, and lectures. The theater continued as a first-run movie house, but after decades of neglect, this grande dame was showing her age badly, and it looked as though the Liberty would eventually meet the sad fate of so many fine old movie palaces. Happily, though, a nonprofit organization began efforts in the 1990s to restore the theater to its original elegance and equipping it to be a state-of-the-art performing arts center. Work is ongoing, but already the Liberty hosts concerts, recitals, theater, and other events.

River Theater

A local cultural treasure, located underneath the Astoria Bridge, the nonprofit River Theater (230 W. Marine Dr., 503/325-7487, www.rivertheater.com) has staged a new edition of its original "Simple Salmon" sketch comedy series every April since 1998. Part writing competition, part theatrical production, the cast acts out sketches submitted by the public and the audience votes for their favorites. Open-mike readings, dinner theater, live community-radio (KMUN) broadcasts, and plays from Shakespeare to Ionesco fill out the changing bill of fare. In addition, the River Theater hosts an impressively eclectic lineup of local and touring musicians, covering most of the bases with Celtic, bluegrass, folk, blues, and jazz, with pop, punk, rock, and gospel tossed in for good measure. Check their website or *Hipfish* for scheduled events.

Other Venues

The **VooDoo Room** (corner of 11th and Marine Dr., 503/325-2233, open from 5 P.M. daily), adjacent to the Columbian Café and Theater, presents local and visiting bands (rock, alt-country, blues) and serves cocktails with pizza and other light fare. **Clatsop Community College** (1653 Jerome Ave., Astoria 97103, 503/338-2473, www.clatsopcollege.com/arts&ideas) sponsors an eclectic program of music, film, dance, theater, and art offerings in its Arts and Ideas series. Most performances occur at the Astoria Performing Arts Center (16th and Franklin).

Movies

Adjacent to the Columbian Café, the **Columbian Theatre** (corner of 11th and Marine Dr., 503/325-3516) screens the big movies you may have missed a month before in their first run. Dine on beer, wine, pizza, and other munchies while you watch. Shows are nightly at 7 P.M.; $3 general admission, $2 seniors and kids.

Astoria Gateway Cinema (1875 Marine Dr., 503/338-6575) is a modern movie multiplex, showing the usual stuff, where you can pass an afternoon trying to forget the interminable winter rains.

Bookstores

Several bookstores in town invite serious browsing, buying, and intellectual stimulation. **Kneedeep in Books** (1052 Commercial St., 503/325-9722) specializes in used books and remainders, as well as new books. On the next block, **Godfather's Books and Espresso** (1108 Commercial, 503/325-8143) sells a mix of new and used books and has a case full of excellent antique maps and prints depicting the Columbia River and north coast. The espresso bar is a good place to dry out on a rainy afternoon and catch up on local gossip. **Lucy's Books** (348 12th St., 503/325-4210) is a small but big-hearted locally owned bookshop with an emphasis on Northwest regional subjects. Owner Laura Snyder hosts readings by local and visiting writers and publishes an entertaining quarterly newsletter and book reviews.

ACCOMMODATIONS

With its wealth of large, elegant houses in its Victorian neighborhoods, it's not surprising that Astoria has more B&Bs than any other town on the Oregon coast. The historic former homes of merchants, politicians, sea captains, and salmon canners number among Astoria's bed-and-breakfast offerings. In addition, you'll find a pair of fine old renovated hotels, a wide selection of motels, and camping options not far from town.

Motels

You'll find about a dozen motels to choose from in and around Astoria, most of them located along U.S. 30, otherwise known as Marine Drive, in the northwest section of town. Most are fairly similar and don't have the charm that the town's B&Bs offer, but they're generally a bit less expensive and are reasonably close to downtown.

The **Crest Motel** (5366 Leif Erickson Dr./U.S. 30, 503/325-3141 or 800/421-3141, standard rooms $62–84, view rooms $81–115) offers cliffside river views, a coin-operated laundry, and a whirlpool set in a gazebo overlooking the river. View rooms are worth the extra money. Lower rates apply in off-season, and discounts are available for AAA members and seniors. About one-half mile closer to town, **Comfort Suites** (3420 Leif Erickson Dr./U.S. 30, 503/325-2000, $69–139), has river-view rooms with microwaves, fridges, and free HBO; continental breakfast is served 6–10 A.M. Facilities include a heated pool, spa, sauna, exercise room, and laundry.

Two blocks from the West Mooring Basin and its charter docks, the **Astoria Dunes Motel** (288 W. Marine Drive, 503/325-7111 or 800/441-3319, $48 in summer, $75 the rest of the year) has 58 rooms, an indoor heated pool and whirlpool tub, and king and queen-sized beds.

About one-half mile east of the Astoria-Megler Bridge, the **Rivershore Motel** (59 W. Marine Dr., 503/325-2921, $58–88) has 43 rooms with coffeemakers, microwaves, refrigerators, and Internet access. Some rooms include kitchens. July through early September, rooms with one to two queen-sized beds run $58–78; kitchen units are $68–88. Rates drop about 25 percent the rest of the year.

The sprawling **Red Lion** (400 Industry St., 503/325-7373 or 800/RED-LION, $59–99) is located right at the Mooring Basin Marina, just off Marina Drive. These motel units seem a bit worse for wear, but you can't get any closer to the river, and view rooms have a front-row seat on the passing ship traffic. The Romantic Getaway to Astoria package includes a view room, champagne, and dinner for two in the on-site **Seafare Restaurant,** all for $109–119.

At the west end of town, the **Best Western Astoria Inn** (555 Hamburg St., 503/325-2205 or 800/621-0641, $63–169) has 73 rooms in a five-story structure overlooking Young's Bay. Facilities include an indoor pool, sauna, hot tubs, and laundry room.

Across the bay in Warrenton, the **Shilo Inn Astoria/Warrenton** (1609 E. Harbor Dr., Warrenton, 503/861-2181, $72–175) is a convenient base for exploring Fort Clatsop and Fort Stevens. The 63 mini-suites include a microwave, refrigerator, and satellite TV with premium channels. A heated indoor pool, spa, sauna, steam room, fitness center, restaurant, and lounge are available on-site.

Hotels

Built as a private Georgian-style residence in 1902, then converted into a convent in the 1950s, the elegant **Rosebriar Hotel** (636 14th St., 503/325-7427 or 800/482-0224, www.rosebriar.net, $59–169 d) was renovated into a small, comfortable hotel in the early '90s. Set on a quiet neighborhood street a few blocks uphill from the Maritime Museum, the large bowfront windows of the parlor/lobby and many of the upstairs rooms command a sweeping view of the town and river below. Original woodwork, tastefully understated decor and furnishings, and cordial service make a stay here quite pleasant.

You have a choice of three rooms with baths or seven without (facilities down the hall). Discounts are offered for three-night stays; call or check the website for packages and other specials. A full breakfast is also included, served in the spacious dining room. The recently opened Captain's Suite includes a kitchenette, large master bath, soaking tub overlooking the Columbia, and a sitting room with fireplace ($249). The 1885 carriage house cottage adjacent to the main hotel is self-contained with its own kitchen, plus fireplace, whirlpool tub, and private patio. The Rosebriar is one of Astoria's most popular lodgings, so it's a good idea to reserve at least 10 days in advance during summer.

After a $4.3 million, two-year renovation, the **Hotel Elliott** (357 12th St., 877/378-1924, www.hotelelliott.com, $105–275) reinvented itself in 2003 as a tony boutique hotel in the heart of downtown Astoria. The Elliott first opened in 1924, and its current incarnation preserved much of the original charm of its Craftsman-era details, including the mahogany-clad lobby, handcrafted cabinetry, wood and marble fireplaces and stone floors in all bathrooms, plus such 21st-century modern conveniences as high-speed Internet access and big-screen TVs. The hotel has 21 standard rooms, six standard suites, and five premium suites, including the five-room Presidential Suite ($650) with access to a rooftop garden. An original banner painted across the hotel's north side proudly proclaims: Hotel Elliott— Wonderful Beds. The new Elliott has made a point of living up to this claim, with goose-down pillows, luxurious 440-count Egyptian-cotton sheets, featherbeds, and top-of-the-line mattresses to ensure a memorable slumber.

Bed-and-Breakfasts

One block east of the Rosebriar, the **Rose River Inn B&B** (1510 Franklin Ave., 503/325-7175, rooms $85–110, suites $120–130) offers two river-view suites and two guest rooms in a large, cheerfully painted Victorian, decorated with European antiques and art and surrounded by a neatly tended garden. Each room includes a clawfoot tub, and the River Suite also has a Finnish sauna. Road-weary travelers should consider a massage from innkeeper Kati, a licensed massage therapist from Helsinki.

Franklin Street Bed-and-Breakfast (1140 Franklin St., 503/325-4314, www.franklin-st-station-bb.com, $80–135 d) is a grand, four-story Victorian built in 1900. Six rooms and suites, five with private bath, accommodate up to 14 guests. The view from the fourth-floor Starlight Suite is unmatched, and there's even a telescope for up-close ship spotting. The Hide-Away Suite includes its own complete kitchen, dining area, living room, and private entry. Rich woodwork and local art are appreciated extras. It's within easy walking distance of downtown, and breakfast is included in the rates. A minimum two-night stay is required on weekends, and 10-day advance reservations have become necessary because of the popularity of this place.

The Astoria Inn (3391 Irving Ave., 503/325-8153 or 800/718-8153, www.astoriainnbb.com, $70–$85) is a rambling 1890s National Historic Landmark perched on a hilltop with views of incoming and outgoing ships. An interior decor evocative of the 19th century and a second-floor library with comfy wing chairs also make this place recommended. Each of the four rooms has a queen-sized bed with private bath. Good breakfasts such as sourdough French toast soaked in Grand Marnier are included in the rate.

Clementine's Bed-and-Breakfast (847 Exchange St., 800/521-6801, www.clementines-bb.com, rooms $85–150, suites $150–155), a handsome two-story home built in the Italianate style in 1888, stands in good company across the street from the Flavel House and is on Astoria's Historic Homes Walking Tour. From the gardens around the house come the fresh flowers that accent the guest rooms and common areas, as do the herbs that spice the delicious gourmet breakfasts that are a special highlight of a stay here. There are five rooms in the main house, all with feather beds and private bath; upper-story rooms have private balconies with river views.

In addition, two spacious, sunny suites are available in the Moose Temple Lodge, adjacent to the main house. Built in 1850, this is the oldest extant building in Astoria; it was the Moose Temple from 1900 to 1940 and later served as a Mormon church. Renovated with skylights, wood floors, and fireplaces, small kitchens, and several beds, these are ideal for families or other groups. Pets are welcome. September–May, Clementine's offers packages combining cooking classes with one- or two-night stays. Courses include bread- and pastry-making and theme classes such as "A Weekend in Provence." Clementine's requires a two-night minimum stay on weekends mid-May to mid-October and on holiday weekends. Single-night stays are fine the rest of the year, and discounts are available off-season.

A 10-minute drive west of Astoria, adjacent to the Fort Stevens Historic Area in quiet Hammond, the **Officer's Inn Bed-and-Breakfast** (540 Russell Pl., Hammond, 503/861-2524 or 800/377-2524, www.officersinn.net, $79–99) was built in 1905 and formerly housed Army officers and their families before the fort was decommissioned. A broad porch running the full length of the building overlooks the fort's original parade grounds. The 8,000-square-foot inn offers eight guest units, all with private baths and king- or queen-sized beds; two-bedroom family suites each have a queen-sized bed and two double beds.

Campgrounds

Families flock to **Fort Stevens State Park** (800/452-5687 for reservations, open year-round). With 253 tent sites, 343 RV sites, and a special area for walk-in campers and bicyclists, the campground is the largest in the state park sys-

tem. With the park's amenities and other attractions, this is the perfect base camp from which to take advantage of the region. Just be sure to avoid spring break (around March 23–29) if you wish to be spared the rites of spring enacted here by Oregon teenagers. Reservations are accepted here, and a $17–22 fee is charged. Yurts can be had for $29, hiker-biker sites for $4.

Across the road from the state park, **Astoria Warrenton Seaside KOA** (1100 NW Ridge Rd., Hammond 97121, 503/861-2606 or 800/562-8506) has 310 sites, with 54 cabins. Summer rates (Apr.–Sept.) are $25.95–33.95 for basic tent sites, $39.95–49.95 for deluxe RV sites with all the hookups; one-room cabins (sleep five) run $45.95–55.95, two-room cabins (sleep six) run $55.95–65.95. Prices drop about 10 percent the rest of the year. Amenities include an indoor pool and hot tub, game room, mini-golf, and bike rentals.

FOOD

Over the past several years, Astoria has begun to develop a reputation for excellent dining at fair prices, with several restaurants standing out for their creative and consistently delicious fare. Espresso fans will also be pleased to know that there are no fewer than 20 outlets for the stuff in town, with hole-in-the-wall cafés seemingly down every side street. Part of the fun is finding them.

From Mother's Day to early October, follow local tradition and stroll leisurely up and down 12th Street, between Marine Drive and Duane Street, where vendors offer farm-fresh produce, crafts, and specialty foods. **Astoria's Sunday Market** is held 10 A.M.–3 P.M. each Sunday. Local musicians perform everything from bluegrass to Bach at the international food court in the Wells Fargo parking lot at 12th and Marine Drive.

Markets

For do-it-yourselfers, Oregon's number-one retail chain, **Fred Meyer** (1451 U.S. 101, Warrenton, 503/861-3003), has a deli that stocks salads, meats, cheeses, French bread, and other takeout items. This store is also known for good deals on clothes, camping equipment, and hardware. Across the bay in Astoria is a **Safeway** (1153 Duane St., 503/325-4662).

Two blocks west is Astoria's healthy headquarters, the **Astoria Community Store** (1389 Duane St., 503/325-0027, 9 A.M.–6 P.M. Mon.–Sat., 9 A.M.–3 P.M. Sun.). This is the place to stock up on organic produce, naturopathic products, and all manner of good-for-you goodies.

In a falsefront clapboard building near the waterfront is one of Oregon's most esteemed purveyors of gourmet smoked fish, established in 1920. **Josephson's Smokehouse** (106 Marine Dr., 503/325-2190, www.josephsons.com) produces Scandinavian cold-smoked salmon without dyes or preservatives, so it is seldom sold through retail outlets. Instead, Josephson's caters to mail-order clientele and fine restaurants that serve the product upon arrival. You can buy direct here at a cheaper (but not cheap) price than the mail-order rates. Pickled salmon, salmon jerky, sturgeon caviar, crab, oysters, and a variety of alder-smoked and canned fish are also sold here. On typically foggy days in midwinter, there's nothing finer than a cup of very thick Josephson's clam chowder.

Casual Fare

As widely appreciated as it is small, the **Columbian Café** (1114 Marine Dr., 503/325-2233, 8 A.M.–2 P.M. Mon.–Fri., 9 A.M. to 2 P.M. weekends, dinner 5 P.M. until they're done Wed.–Sat.) is where the meatless 1960s meet cutting-edge Northwest cuisine. The good selection of pasta entrées, crêpes, and fresh catch of the day are all expertly prepared and moderately priced. The chef here is also famous for Uriah's St. Diablo jelly, which comes in garlic, jalapeño, and red-pepper flavors. These jellies are available here and sold throughout the state. You may also enjoy the free-flowing political repartee with the staff and regulars in this cramped (several booths and a lunch counter) but friendly and popular place. Breakfast is a highlight here. Dinners run $10–20, with most lunches and breakfasts $4–8.

Adjacent are the Columbian Theatre, which shows second-run flicks that you can enjoy with beer, wine, and pizza, and the VooDoo Room, one of Astoria's most active live music clubs. See the Events and Entertainment section for more info.

A state travel magazine has named the **Ship Inn** (One 2nd St., 503/325-0033) as the best pub in Oregon, and another regional publication gave it a thumbs-up for its seafood and business lunches ($6–14). Despite its unprepossessing exterior, the Ship is popular with locals and visitors who appreciate good fish and chips, cheese plates, Cornish pasties, and other English specialties such as steak-and-kidney pie and bangers and mash, and imported brews. A welcoming fire, great waterfront views, and live music, including jazz and bluegrass, also provide conviviality here.

In a beautifully restored 1892 Victorian on the hillside above town, the **Home Spirit Bakery** (1585 Exchange St., 503/325-6846, 9 A.M.–3:30 P.M. Tues.–Sat., 5:30–8 P.M. Thurs.–Sat.) is a special find that's quickly become a local favorite. The bakery and café sells highly esteemed sourdough loaves and flaky pastries, and lunches focused on quiche (asparagus is yummy, $4.95), salads, and sandwiches made with their own croissants ($5.50). Dinner is a prix-fixe affair ($21): Salads and starters might include roasted peppers, fiddleheads, capers, and olives on garden lettuces with potato and leek tart; entrée choices could be farro risotto with roasted asparagus and spring vegetables, blackwattle fish pie, raspberry chicken, or pork loin stuffed with feta cheese and winter greens; finish up by selecting a dessert such as homemade sorbet, key lime pie, or tiramisu. Reservations are recommended.

Housed in a former warehouse, one of the few downtown buildings to survive the 1922 fire, **Pier 11 Feed Store Restaurant** (77 11th Ave., 503/325-0729, 11 A.M.–9 P.M. Mon.–Sat., 9 A.M.–9 P.M. Sun., until 10 P.M. nightly in summer) has a great view of the Columbia through its huge picture windows and a wood-framed interior that conjures a shrine to the ancient mariner (look for the wooden sea serpent near the bar). Entrées ($12–22) lean toward the school of breaded and fried, but steamed clams, baked halibut, and clam chowder are among the alternatives. You can also get good prime rib and steak and dine affordably at lunch ($4.50–12).

"Eat well, laugh often, and love much" is the motto that neatly sums up the vibe at the easygoing **T. Paul's Urban Café** (1119 Commercial St., 503/338-5133, 9 A.M.–9 P.M. Mon.–Thurs., 9 A.M.–11 P.M. Fri.–Sat.). The menu of hip diner food with fresh Northwest twists includes towering turkey sandwiches, bay shrimp ceviche, Caribbean jerk quesadilla, prawn pasta, and clam chowder. Coffee drinks, beer, and wine are available.

Astoria's only brewpub, the **Wet Dog Café** (144 11th St., 503/325-6975, 11 A.M.–11 P.M. Mon.–Thurs. and Sun., 11 A.M.–2 A.M. Fri.–Sat., kitchen closes at 9 P.M.), is home to the Pacific Rim Brewery, maker of eight hand-crafted microbrews, ranging from the golden Pacific Pale ale to the full-bodied Sow Your Wild Oatmeal Stout. There's also a full bar. Housed in a cavernous remodeled former waterfront warehouse, with good views out the big windows. Food is basic pub grub: fish and chips, burgers, pizzas, sandwiches, and salads, with all-you-can-eat ribs featured on Fridays. Happy hour specials and children's menu are available. The Dog is quiet at weekday lunchtimes, but Thursday to Saturday nights get rowdier, when there's live music.

A good choice for families with kids, the Astoria outlet of **Pig 'N Pancake** (146 W. Bond St., 503/325-3144, 6 A.M.–10 P.M. daily), a small chain (others are in Seaside and Cannon Beach), excels at big, filling breakfasts at reasonable prices ($3.95–9.95). Their specialties are homemade pancakes and waffles, available in a dozen varieties, including potato, Swedish (thin, crispy pancakes with lingonberries), and pecan-filled; and, of course, pigs in a blanket. Lunch relies mainly on sandwiches (with some seafood twists such as Dungeness crab on an English muffin, topped with melted cheese), chowder, and salads, while dinners branch out with pasta, stir-fry, prime rib, and halibut and salmon served grilled, broiled, or steamed.

Fine Dining

In the days when transportation here was mostly by water, Astoria's neighborhoods developed unique personalities. One of these was Uniontown, located west of the present downtown, where Scandinavian anglers and longshoremen hung out near the fish-processing plants. Underneath the Astoria Bridge in this waterfront district, **Café Uniontown** (218 W. Marine Dr., 503/323-8708, Tues.–Fri. for lunch, Tues.–Sun. for dinner) boasts an upscale menu with such seasonal offerings as raspberry hazelnut chicken breast; oven-roasted lobster tail; portabella, ricotta, and garlic ravioli; and bacon-wrapped filet mignon. Special requests can be accommodated. Wednesday is Rib Night, when $14.95 buys all you can eat. Live music on weekends could be bluegrass or jazz piano. Check out the 1907 vintage bar in the restaurant's lounge, where weekend songfests can end your evening on a high note.

For a bit of a splurge, local seafood aficionados recommend the **Silver Salmon Grille** (1185 Commercial St., 503/338-6640, open daily at 11 A.M.) for fine dining in an atmosphere that's somewhat formal but not starchy. Attractive murals of the eponymous fish adorn the walls inside and out, and salmon takes the pride of place on the dinner menu as well, in a variety of preparations that are fresh and cooked to a T. The Silver Salmon Supreme, for example, is a fillet filled with Dungeness crab, bay shrimp, and smoked Gouda, oven-poached in white wine and lemon for $21.95. Additional seafood items such as butter-grilled razor clams ($18.95), several beef choices such as London broil ($16.95), pork and chicken, and pasta dishes fill out the extensive menu. A selection of Northwest microbrews and a wine list favoring Oregon and French vintages nicely complements the entrées. The lunch menu reprises many of the dinner selections for $8.95–13.95, along with filling sandwiches and burgers ($5.95–9.95).

In a century-old converted cannery building on Pier 6, **Gunderson's Cannery Café** (One 6th St., 503/325-8642, lunch $5–12, dinner $9.50–25) seats you as close to the waterfront as you can get without a boat. This 13-table mauve and pink restaurant serves an innovative bill of fare that's popular with locals and knowledgeable out-of-towners. Whether you have crab cakes in red pepper pesto or pecan-crusted halibut, leave room for the desserts you'll pass in the display case at the entrance. The lunch menu features a Halibut Burger, generous Caesar salads, pizzas on homemade focaccia crust, and what many consider to be Astoria's best clam chowder. Winter hours are 11 A.M.–8 P.M. Tuesday–Saturday, 9 A.M.–6 P.M. Sunday. Summer hours are 11 A.M.–8:30 P.M. Monday–Saturday, 9 A.M. Sunday for breakfast and brunch. Outdoor seating usually starts in March.

Winery

Close to the Flavel House, the **Shallon Tasting Room** (1598 Duane St., 503/325-5978, noon–6 P.M. daily) invites you to sample this vineyard's specialty fruit wines. Try the chocolate-orange wine, as well as other unique wines produced from whey. The winemaker is effusive and knowledgeable and will show you around while you sip.

INFORMATION AND SERVICES

Visitor Information

The **Astoria Chamber of Commerce** (P.O. Box 176, 111 W. Marine Dr., Astoria 97103, 503/325-6311 or 800/875-6807, www.oldoregon.com, 8 A.M.–6 P.M. daily in summer, 9 A.M.–5 P.M. Mon.–Fri. Oct.–Apr.) operates the Oregon Welcome Center at its offices, providing a plethora of brochures and maps for visitors to Astoria and other destinations on the north Oregon coast and southwest Washington. They will send you a free guidebook with plenty of handy information.

Car Rentals

Astoria has the greatest number of car rental agencies on the coast—two. Try **Hertz** (1492 Duane St., 503/325-7700) or **Enterprise Rent A Car** (644 W. Marine Dr., 503/325-6500).

Newspapers and Radio

With 10,000 people, Astoria is the largest city and the media hub of the north coast. The local newspaper, the *Daily Astorian,* is sold around town and is worth a look if only to get the editorial slant of Steve Forrester. This former Washington correspondent's witty commentary on local, regional, and national events pulls no punches. The

North Coast Times Eagle is a political activist monthly that holds forth on coastal issues. It's sold around town and in Powell's Bookstore in Portland. The free monthly *Hipfish* is a publication in the great tradition of the alternative press of the sixties. Whether you agree with their take on regional politics or not, the thoughtful, lively articles and complete entertainment listings will enhance your visit to the North Coast.

Throughout the north coast, **KMUN** (91.9 FM Astoria and Seaside, 89.5 in Cannon Beach) is a public radio station with community-based programming that is especially diverse. Folk, classical, jazz, and rock music, public affairs, radio drama, literature readings, children's bedtime stories, and National Public Radio news will make you want to keep your dial glued to this frequency.

Other Services

The **Astoria Post Office** is located in the Federal Building at 8th and Commercial. The **library** (458 10th Ave., 503/325-7323) is open Tuesday–Sunday.

Clean Services Coin Laundry (823 W. Marine Ave., 503/325-2027) will help you deal with any leftover mud you might have accumulated on your clothes from walking around Fort Clatsop trails after a rainstorm.

Other useful numbers include the **county sheriff** (503/225-2061), the **Coast Guard** (2285 Airport Rd., Warrenton, 503/861-6220), and **Columbia Memorial Hospital** (2111 Exchange St., Astoria, 503/325-4321).

The local **Bank of America** (977 Commercial St.) in Astoria houses an ATM. In Warrenton, head to **Costco** (180 SE Neptune Ave.) for access to an ATM.

TRANSPORTATION

Getting There

Driving directions might help those looking for an efficient way to get to Astoria from Portland. Take I-5 north to exit 36 to Longview. This puts you onto Tennant Boulevard for two miles. Go left at Oregon Way for one mile. Cross the bridge over the Columbia to Rainier, Oregon, and turn

© MARK MORRIS

The 4.1-mile Astoria-Megler Bridge links Oregon and Washington.

right (west) on U.S. 30. From there, it's one hour to Astoria along the soggy bottomlands on the west side of the river. Approaching Astoria on northbound U.S. 101, remember that the highway between Astoria and Seaside is a two-laner much of the way and can make for slow going, especially on weekends.

Amtrak Thruway Motorcoach Service (800/USA-RAIL, www.amtrak.com) runs daily between the north coast and Portland Union Station. Board the coach in Astoria at the Mini-Mart (95 W. Marine Drive). Departure from Astoria is at 8 A.M.; arrival in Portland at 10:15 A.M. Departure from Portland is at 6 P.M.; arrival in Astoria at 8:15 P.M. The bus stops upon request at Seaside, Warrenton, and Gearhart.

In 2003, Amtrak initiated train service between Portland and Astoria for the first time in living memory, with the **Lewis & Clark Explorer.** From late May to early September, the excursion train departs Linnton Station in Northwest Portland (get there by bus from downtown's Union Station at 7:30) Friday–Monday at 7:50 A.M., follows the scenic route along the Columbia on the water-level Burlington Northern tracks, and arrives at Astoria's old train depot on 20th Street off Marine Drive at 11:50 A.M. The train departs Astoria at 4:50 P.M., arriving in

Portland at 8:50 P.M. One-way tickets are $24 general, $20 seniors. Contact Amtrak for reservations and more details. As part of the Lewis and Clark Bicentennial, this special train is slated to run summers through 2005, although Oregon's budget woes could derail those plans.

Getting Around

Getting around Astoria can have its pitfalls for the unsuspecting. Potentially troublesome for visitors are the steep hills and the city's layout of seemingly random one-way streets. Holidays and summer weekends bring heavy traffic along U.S. 30, a.k.a. Leif Erickson Drive (east end of town) and Marine Drive (center and west), Astoria's major traffic artery. In light of the foregoing, you might consider the following alternatives.

For visitors willing to let go of their cars for a while, the Sunset Empire Transportation District, better known as **TheBus** (call 503/861-RIDE or 800/776-6406, www.ridethebus.org) provides reasonably frequent transportation around Astoria and along the coast from Warrenton (including Fort Stevens State Park and Fort Clatsop) to Cannon Beach. Most routes are served every 40–60 minutes, Monday–Saturday. Adult fare is $.75; students, children, and seniors $.50. For routes and schedules, call or check the website.

Resources

Suggested Reading

Natural History

Alt, David, and Donald W. Hyndman. *Roadside Geology of Oregon.* Missoula, MT: Mountain Press Publishing Company, 2003. Part of the fine Roadside Geology Series, the coast chapters describe, in layman's language, the geologic forces that shaped the region.

Evanich, Joseph E., Jr. *Birder's Guide to Oregon.* Portland, OR: Audubon Society of Portland, 2003. A good all-around guide to the state's birdlife, with a useful breakdown of specific coastal locations and details on what species to watch for and when.

Paulson, Dennis. *Shorebirds of the Pacific Northwest.* Seattle, WA: University of Washington Press, 2003. For the specialist rather than the generalist, there is no better book than this richly detailed guide for distinguishing an avocet from a stilt, a plover from a curlew, and identifying any of the dozens of other species found near the water's edge.

Pojar, Jim, and Andy MacKinnon (eds.). *Plants of the Pacific Northwest Coast: Washington, Oregon, British Columbia, and Alaska.* Edmonton, Alberta: Lone Pine Publishing, 2003. A highly regarded guide, illustrated with excellent photos, to the flora of the entire Northwest region.

Sept, J. Duane. *The Beachcomber's Guide to Seashore Life in the Pacific Northwest.* Vancouver, British Columbia: Harbour Publishing Company Limited, 2003. This ideal guide for the casual and curious observer aids in understanding the intertidal zone and in identifying more than 270 species encountered there, including crabs, clams and other mollusks, seaweeds, sea stars, sea anemones, and more.

Yuskavitch, James A. *Oregon Wildlife Viewing Guide.* Helena, MT: Falcon Publishing Company, 1994. Not limited to the coast, this highly regarded resource covers 87 wildlife-viewing areas statewide, with detailed regional maps and tips on successful wildlife watching.

History

Beckham, Steven Dow, and Robert M. Reynolds (photographer). *Lewis & Clark from the Rockies to the Pacific.* Portland, OR: Graphic Arts Center Publishing Co., 2002. Focusing on the second half of the expedition's outward-bound journey, this gorgeously illustrated and insightful book covers Lewis and Clark's trying months spent camped in the rainy woodlands of the north Oregon coast.

Friedman, Ralph. *In Search of Western Oregon.* Caldwell, ID: Caxton Press, 1991. A fascinating read, packed with anecdotes, folklore, historical details, and more, all told in Friedman's engaging style.

Gibbs, James A. *Shipwrecks of the Pacific Coast* Portland, OR: Binford and Mort, 1989. Endlessly fascinating and frequently heartbreaking reading from a master of Northwest maritime lore. Covers all known shipwrecks off the coasts of Oregon, Washington, and California.

Hadlow, Robert W. *Elegant Arches, Soaring Spans: C.B. McCullough Oregon's Master Bridge Builder.* Corvallis, OR: Oregon State University Press, 2003. Driving U.S. 101 along the Oregon coast wouldn't be the same without the dozen beautiful bridges designed by McCullough between the two world wars, and which he called "jeweled clasps in a wonderful string of pearls."

O'Donnell, Terence. *Cannon Beach: A Place by the Sea.* Portland, OR: Oregon Historical Society, 1996. A highly personal historical evocation of life in Cannon Beach and environs.

Recreation

Henderson, Bonnie. *Exploring the Wild Oregon Coast.* Seattle, WA: Mountaineers Books, 1994. Primarily a hiking guide, covering several lesser-known but rewarding hikes, and enriched with an abundance of information on flora and fauna.

Ostertag, Rhonda, and George Ostertag. *75 Hikes in the Oregon's Coast Range and Siskiyous* Seattle, WA: Mountaineers Books, 2003. A well-chosen selection of hikes along the length of the coastal ranges covers a broad variety of terrain and difficulty levels. Detailed trail descriptions and maps make this guide particularly useful.

Stienstra, Tom. *Foghorn Outdoors Oregon Camping.* Emeryville, CA: Avalon Travel Publishing, 2002. Details more than 700 campgrounds across the state, with an excellent selection on the coast. Rich with tips on gear, safety, and other topics.

Description and Travel

Irving, Stephanie (ed.). *Best Places Destinations: Oregon Coast.* Seattle, WA: Sasquatch Books, 2003. Highly selective but reliable recommendations on where to stay, eat, and what to see and do.

Nelson, Sharlene, and Ted Nelson (contributor). *Umbrella Guide to Oregon Lighthouses.* Kenmore, WA: Epicenter Press, 2003. Tells the stories of 11 Oregon coast lighthouses, as well as beacons on the Columbia and Willamette rivers. A good reference for anyone curious about these romantic aids to navigation.

Oberrecht, Kenn. *Driving the Pacific Coast Oregon and Washington: Scenic Driving Tours along Coastal Highways.* Guilford, CT: Globe Pequot Press, 2000. Compact and practical guide covers recreation, shopping, camping, dining, and lodging—with an emphasis on budget options—along U.S. 101, with interesting bits of history thrown into the mix.

Oberrecht, Kenn. *Oregon Coastal Access Guide: A Mile-By-Mile Guide to Scenic and Recreational Attractions.* Corvallis, OR: Oregon State University Press, 2003. Meticulously researched and informative guide to major sights, natural features, and recreational opportunities. Contains no restaurant or lodging info, but is an eminently useful resource for travelers nonetheless.

Internet Resources

Parks and Public Lands

Oregon State Parks
www.oregonstateparks.org
Descriptions, maps, contact information, and more details on all Oregon state parks.

ReserveAmerica
www.reserveamerica.com
The central site for reserving campgrounds in the national forests and Oregon Dunes National Recreation Area.

Siskiyou National Forest
www.fs.fed.us/r6/siskiyou
Details on recreation, camping, and resources in the national forest.

Siuslaw National Forest
www.fs.fed.us/r6/siuslaw
Details on recreation, camping, and resources in the national forest and the Oregon Dunes National Recreation Area.

U.S. Bureau of Land Management
www.or.blm.gov
The BLM manages numerous recreational sites along the coast and the coastal mountains, including the Dean Creek Elk Viewing Area, Yaquina Head Outstanding Natural Area, and Cape Blanco Lighthouse.

Recreation

Oregon Department of Fish and Wildlife
www.dfw.state.or.us
Complete details on fishing and hunting seasons, licenses, regulations, and more. Includes useful species-identification charts.

Oregon State Marine Board
www.boatoregon.com
Extensive information on boating safety, ramps and other facilities, bar conditions, etc.

Tide Predictions
www.saltwatertides.com
Current and future tide-prediction charts for three dozen coastal Oregon locations.

Whale Watching Spoken Here
http://whalespoken.org
Volunteer organization assists visitors with spotting whales at 29 sites from southern Washington to northern California.

Information and Travel Services

AAA Oregon/Idaho
www.aaaoregon.com
For members only, provides travel planning and booking services, plus detailed maps of each coastal county. Their "Oregon Coast Tour Map" is particularly good.

Oregon Coast Visitors Association
www.visittheoregoncoast.com
A good clearinghouse of information for the entire coast, including events listings, weather, and links to all coastal chambers of commerce.

Oregon Tourism Commission
www.traveloregon.com
A good statewide resource for useful free maps and pamphlets and extensive listings of lodgings and activities.

U.S. Coast Guard
www.piersystem.com/external/index.cfm?cid=21
Public information site of the 13th District, serving the Oregon and Washington coasts. Has useful information on boating and water safety.

Transportation

Amtrak
www.amtrak.com
> Operates train service between Portland and Astoria, as well as bus service between Portland and other north coast towns.

Greyhound
www.greyhound.com
> Operates a coast route twice daily between Portland and Brookings.

Oregon Department of Transportation Road Conditions
www.tripcheck.com
> Displays current conditions and advisories.

Chambers of Commerce and Visitors Centers

Astoria-Warrenton Area Chamber
www.oldoregon.com

Bandon Chamber of Commerce
www.bandon.com

Bay Area Chamber of Commerce
www.oregonsbayareachamber.com

Brookings/Harbor Chamber of Commerce
www.brookingsor.com

Cannon Beach Chamber of Commerce
www.cannonbeach.org

Depoe Bay Chamber of Commerce
www.depoebaychamber.org

Florence Area Chamber of Commerce
www.florencechamber.com

Garibaldi Chamber of Commerce
www.garibaldioregon.com

Gold Beach Promotion Committee
www.goldbeach.org

Greater Newport Chamber of Commerce
www.newportchamber.org

Lincoln City Chamber of Commerce
www.oregoncoast.org

Nehalem Bay Area Chamber of Commerce
www.nehalembaychamber.com

Port Orford Chamber of Commerce
www.portorfordoregon.com

Reedsport/Winchester Bay Chamber of Commerce
www.reedsportcc.org

Rockaway Beach Chamber of Commerce
www.rockawaybeach.net

Seaside Oregon Visitor Bureau
www.seasidechamber.com

Tillamook Chamber of Commerce
www.tillamookchamber.org

Waldport Chamber of Commerce
www.pioneer.net/~waldport

Yachats Area Chamber of Commerce
www.yachats.org

Index

Index

A

accommodations: 34–37; *see also specific place*
Agate Beach: 129
agate-hunting: general discussion 129; Paradise Point Beach 73; Whiskey Run Beach 89–90
air travel: 45
alcohol: 39
Alfred A. Loeb State Park: 56
Alsea Bay Bridge: 120
animal rehabilitation: 77
animals: 9–15
aquariums: Oregon Coast Aquarium 97; Seaside Aquarium 189
Arch Rocks: 56
art galleries: Cannon Beach 185–186
artist communities: 177
Astoria: 195–215; accommodations 209–211; as cinematic backdrop 200; climate 4; events 207–208; food 211–214; history 196–197; maps 196–197, 198; services 214; sights 198–206; transportation 214–215
Astoria Aquatic Center: 206
Astoria Children's Museum: 201
Astoria Column: 198–199
Astoria-Megler Bridge: 195
Astoria Regatta Week: 207–208
Astoria Riverfront Trolley: 200
Astoria-Warrenton Crab and Seafood Festival: 207
Astor Street Opry Company: 208
ATV dune rides: 107
auto travel: 47–49

B

bald eagle sanctuaries: 202
banana slugs: 13
Bandon: 75–83; accommodations 80–82; food 82–83; map 76; Old Town 75–76; recreation 78–80
Bandon Dunes Golf Resort: 79
Bandon Marsh National Wildlife Refuge: 78
Battle Rock Park: 71
Bay Area: 84–95; accommodations 92–93; festivals 91–92; food 94–95; history 84; map 85; recreation 90–91; services 95; sights 86–90
Bay City: 169
Bayfront District (Newport): 126–127

Bay Ocean: 164
Beach Bills (1967 and 1972): 3
beachcombing: 21–22, 189
beachgrass, European: 8
beach plants: 8
bears: 12
beavers: 12
bed-and-breakfasts: 35
bicycling: general discussion 23; Bullards Beach

Beaches

general discussion: 3
Agate Beach: 129
Bailey Beach: 63
Beverly Beach: 129
Buena Vista State Park: 63
Bullards Beach State Park: 77–78
Cape Arago State Park: 89
Fort Stevens State Park: 206
Harris Beach State Park: 54–55
Hug Point State Park: 178
Indian Beach: 180
Lincoln City: 143–144
Mill Beach: 55
Moolack Beach: 129
Myers Creek Beach: 63
Neptune State Park: 115
Nesika Beach: 63–64
Nye Beach: 127–128
Ona Beach State Park: 120
Pistol River State Park: 63
public rights: 3
Robert Straub State Park: 159
safety: 42
Sand Beach Campground: 160
Shore Acres State Park: 87–88
Short Sand Beach: 175
South Beach (Gold Beach): 63
South Beach (Newport): 130
Sunset Bay State Park: 87
Whiskey Run Beach: 89–90
Yachats: 114–115
Yaquina Bay State Park: 129

State Park 73–74; Cannon Beach 181; Nehalem Bay State Park 174; rentals 130; Seaside
191; Zuzu's Pedals 115; *see also specific place*
Biosphere Reserve (Cascade Head): 155
Bird Island: 55
birds: 10–11, 77
bird-watching: Bandon Marsh National Wildlife
    Refuge 78; Fort Stevens State Park 206;
    Haystack Rock 10, 179; Necanicum Estuary
    Park 191; Oregon Shorebird Festival 91; sea-
    sons 10; Tillamook Bay 168
Biscuit Fire: 56
black bears: 12
black-tailed deer: 12
blimp hangar: 164, 166
Bloch, Ernest: 129
blowholes: 114–115, 138
Blue Heron French Cheese Company: 166
boating: 43–44
bogs: 8
Boiler Bay State Scenic Viewpoint: 138
Bostonian: 97
Brookings-Harbor: 51–61; accommodations
    58–60; climate 4; food 60–61; Harris Beach
    State Park 54–55; history 51–52; Kalmiopsis
    Wilderness 56–57; map 53; recreation 57–58;
    Samuel H. Boardman State Scenic Corridor
    54–55; services 61; sights 52–57
Bullards Beach State Park: 77–78
bus travel: 45

C
canneries, fish: 18–19, 62, 196
Cannon Beach: 177–186; general discussion
    154; accommodations 182–184; art galleries
    185–186; climate 4; food 184–185; map 178;
    recreation 181; sights 178–180
canoeing: *see* kayaking
Cape Arago State Park: 89
Cape Blanco State Park: 72
Cape Foulweather: 138
Cape Kiwanda: 157–158
Cape Lookout State Park: 160–161
Cape Meares: 161
Cape Meares Scenic Viewpoint: 163
Cape Perpetua: 96, 113–114
Cape Sebastian: 55, 62–63
carnivorous plants: 105
Carpenterville Road: 54
car rentals: 49

Camping

general discussion: 35–37
Astoria: 211
Boice Cope County Park: 73
Bullards Beach State Park: 77
Cannon Beach: 184
Coos Bay: 93
Florence: 109–110
gear: 65
Lincoln City: 147–148
Nehalem Bay State Park: 174
Newport: 134
Oswald West State Park: 176
Port Orford: 73–74
Sand Beach Campground: 160
Waldport: 122
Winchester Bay: 102
Yachats: 118

car travel: 47–49
Cascade Head Scenic Research Area: 155–157
casinos: Chinook Winds Casino 145; Mill
    Casino 91
Cathedral Tree: 206
cedar, Port Orford: 51
Central Coast: 96–152; general discussion
    96–97; Florence 103–112; Lincoln City
    143–152; map 98; Newport 123–137;
    Reedsport/Winchester Bay 97–103; Waldport
    120–123; Yachats 113–119
Chambers of Commerce: 40–41
Charleston: 84
cheese: Blue Heron French Cheese Company
    166; Tillamook Cheese Factory 165
Chetco Valley: 57
Chetco Valley Historical Society Museum: 54
children's activities: Astoria Children's Museum
    201; food sculpting 150; Oregon Coast
    Aquarium 125; Prehistoric Gardens 71–72;
    Sandcastle Day 181; Seaside Aquarium 189;
    West Coast Game Park 78
chinook salmon: 14
Chinook Winds Casino: 145
chun salmon: 14
Civil War forts: 204–205
clamming: general discussion 29; Seaside 187;
    Yaquina Bay State Park 129
classic car festivals: 192

Index

Clatsop Indians: 196
climate: 4–6
Coast Range: 2
Coffenbury Lake: 206
coho salmon: 14
Colony Rock: 129
columbarium, Tillamook Rock Lighthouse: 179
Columbia: 200
Columbia River: general discussion 195; gorge formation 3; mouth 195
Columbia River Maritime Museum: 200
Coos Art Museum: 86–87
Coos Bay: climate 4; flora 7; shipwrecks 86; *see also* Bay Area
Corps of Discovery: *see* Lewis and Clark expedition
crabbing: 29
cranberries: 81
cruises: *Nehalem Belle* 172; Siuslaw River 107
cuisine, coastal: 38

Cullaby Lake: 191
Cummin's Creek Wilderness: 115

D
dangers, coastal: 42–45
Darlingtonia Wayside: 105
Dean Creek Elk Viewing Area: 98
Depoe Bay: 137–142; accommodations 140–141; food 141; sights 137–140; Whale Cove 138, 139
Deuel, Dan: 77
Devil's Elbow: 106
Devil's Lake: 143, 144
Devil's Punchbowl: 138
disabilities, travelers with: 39
diving: 87
Doerner fir: 8
dogsledding: 91, 108
Douglas fir: nation's largest 8; replanting 7

Events and Festivals

general discussion: 32–33
Astoria Regatta Week: 207–208
Astoria-Warrenton Crab and Seafood Festival: 207
Azalea Festival: 58
Beachcomber's Festival: 58
Blackberry Arts Festival: 92
Cascade Head Chamber Music Festival: 150
Chainsaw Sculpture Championships: 101
Chowder, Brews, and Blues: 108
classic car: 192
Crafts on the Coast: 115
Cranberry Festival: 80
Crustacean Classics: 150
Curry County Fair and Rodeo: 66
Dairy Festival: 168
Depoe Bay Ducky Derby: 142
Depoe Bay Salmon Bake: 142
Dory Festival: 159
Dune Mushers Mail Run: 91, 108
Ernest Bloch Music Festival: 131
Festival of Lights: 80
Fleet of Flowers: 142
kite: 150, 171, 181
Loyalty Days and Sea Fair: 131
Nature's Coastal Holiday Light Show: 58

Newport Microbrew Festival: 132
Newport Seafood and Wine Festival: 131
Oregon Coast Music Festival: 92
Oregon Dixieland Jubilee: 192
Oregon Shorebird Festival: 91
Pistol River Wave Basin National Windsurfing Competition: 66
Prefontaine Memorial Run: 92
Rhododendron Festival: 108
sandcastle-building (Lincoln City): 150
Sandcastle Contest (Bandon): 80
Sandcastle Day (Cannon Beach): 181
Scandinavian Midsummer Festival: 207
Seaside Sand Sculpture Festival: 192
Silver Salmon Celebration: 207
Smelt Fry: 115
Southern Oregon Kite Festival: 58
Stormy Weather Arts Festival: 182
Tillamook County Fair: 168
Tsalila: 100
Wild Rivers Festival: 66
Wine and Seafood Festival: 80
Yachats: 115–116
Yachats Village Mushroom Fest: 116
see also specific place

Drake, Sir Francis: 139
Drift Creek Wilderness: 120–121
driving distances: 46
Dune Country: 96, 100–101
dunes: general discussion 3; ATV rides 107; Dune Country 100–101; Jessie M. Honeyman Memorial State Park 104–105; Robert Straub State Park 159; Sand Beach Campground 160; Umpqua Dunes 99
Dungeness crab: 38

E
earthquakes: 44
Ecola State Park: 180
economy: 17
ecosystems: general discussion 7–9; estuaries 89; sand dunes 101; simulated 125; tidepools 9–10
elk: 98
emergency services: 42
endangered animals: salmon 15, 25; sea otters 11; steelhead trout 15; western snowy plover 11
environmental issues: Beach Cleanup 3; beach-grass removal 8; salmon habitat degradation 25
estuaries: Coquille River 78; Necanicum Estuary Park 191; Rogue 62; South Slough Estuarine Research Reserve 89
explorers, European: 16–17

F
Face Rock: 77
farms, cranberry: 81
fauna: 9–15
fir: 7
fire, Astoria: 196
First Peoples: see Native Americans
Fisher Poets Gathering: 207
fishing floats, Japanese: 21, 143–144
fish-processing: 170
Flavel, Captain George: 201–202
Flavel House Museum: 201–202
flora: 7–9
Floras Lake: 73
Florence: 103–112; accommodations 108–110; climate 4; food 110–112; recreation 106–108; sights 104–106
fondue: 166
food: 37–39, see also specific place
forest fires: 56
Fort Astoria: 201
Fort Clatsop National Memorial: 196, 202–204

Fishing

general discussion: 24–29
Bay Area: 90–91
Buffington Memorial City Park: 73
Bullards Beach State Park: 73–74
Cape Arago State Park: 89
Central Coast: 96
charters: 130, 170, 206
Chetco River: 57
Coffenbury Lake: 206
Columbia River: 199
commercial: 123, 153, 206
Coos Bay: 90
Coquille River: 79
Cullaby Lake: 191
Depoe Bay: 142
Dory Festival: 159
dory fleet: 158
Elk River: 73
Fisher Poets Gathering: 207
Fort Stevens State Park: 206

Garrison Lake: 73
Gold Beach area: 65
guided trips: 65, 73
industry: 18–19
Kilchis River: 170
Lake Lytle: 171
Miami River: 170
Newport: 130
Rogue River: 62
runs: 26–28
Seaside: 191
Siltcoos Lake: 107
Sixes River: 73
Tenmile Lake: 99
Tillamook: 167
Tillamook Bay: 169–170
Waldport: 118, 121
Wheeler: 171
Winchester Bay: 99

Fort Stevens: 196–197
Fort Stevens State Park: 154, 204–206
Free Willy: 125
fuel: 49

G
gardens: marine 179; Shore Acres State Park 87, 88
Gardiner: 97
Garibaldi: 169–170
Garrison Lake: 73
Gearhart: 187–195
geography: 2–3
glaciation: 2–3
glass fishing floats: 21
Glenesslin wreck: 173
Gold Beach: 62–70; accommodations 66–68; Cape Sebastian 62–63; climate 5; food 68–69; museums 62; recreation 64–66
Golden and Silver Falls State Park: 90
gold mining: black sand 62; Whiskey Run Beach 89
golf: Bandon Dunes Golf Resort 79; Sandpines Golf Course 107; Seaside 192; Westin Salishan Golf Links 145; *see also specific place*
Grassy Knob Wilderness: 72–73
gratuities: 38
"Graveyard of the Pacific": 195
Gray, Capt. Robert: 164
gray whales: 11–12
Great Northwest Shoe Swap, the: 189

H
Haceta Head Lighthouse: 96, 106
hangar, blimp: 164
hang gliding: 158
Harris Beach State Park: 54–55
Haystack Rock (Cannon Beach): 177, 179
Haystack Rock (Cape Kiwanda): 157
Haystack Rock Awareness Program: 179
hazards: 42
healthcare: 42
hemlock: 7, 155
Heritage Museum (Astoria): 201
high intertidal zone: 9
Highway 101 (U.S. 101): 48–49
historical walking tour, Astoria: 199
history: 16–19
horseback riding: Bandon Beach riding stables 77; Florence 107; Gold Beach 65; Sand Beach Campground 160; Sea Ranch Stables 181

Hiking

general discussion: 24
Astoria: 206
Cape Lookout: 160–161
Cape Perpetua: 113–114
Cascade Head Scenic Research Area: 156–157
Drift Creek Wilderness: 120
Dune Country: 101
Elk Mountain: 168
Fort Stevens State Park: 206
Gold Beach: 65
Indian Sands Trail: 55
Kalmiopsis Wilderness: 56–57
King Mountain: 168
Neahkahnie Mountain: 174–176
Oregon Coast Trail: 206
Redwood Nature Trail: 56
Saddle Mountain: 181
Sand Beach Campground: 160
South Slough Estuarine Research Reserve: 89
Tillamook Head National Recreation Trail: 191
Umpqua Dunes: 99
see also Parks and Wildlife Refuges

House Rock: 55
huckleberry picking: 108
Hughes House: 72
Hug Point State Park: 178
Humbug Mountain: 71
Hume, Robert: 62
hypothermia: 42–43

I
Indian Beach: 180
Indian culture: *see* Native Americans
Indian Sands: 16
industry: fishing 18–19, 62; logging 19; modernizing 197; nineteenth-century 17; oyster 123
information, visitor: 39
Internet access: 42
intertidal zones: 9

JK
J. Marhoffer: 138
Jessie M. Honeyman Memorial State Park: 104–105

jetboats: 64, 66
Kalmiopsis Wilderness: 51, 56–57
kayaking: guided trips 58; Necanicum River 191; Siltcoos River 107; Sunset Bay State Park 87
Keiko: 97, 125
Kesey, Ken: 145
king salmon: 14
kite festivals: 150, 171
Klamath Mountains: 2
Klootchy Creek: 179

L
Lake Marie: 98
Lakeside: 99
language: 16
Les Shirley Park: 180
Lewis and Clark expedition: general discussion 17; bicentennial events 30–31; bicentennial headquarters 199; description of Columbia River mouth 195; encounter a beached whale 190–191; following footsteps of 190–191; at Fort Clatsop 196, 202–203; Lewis and Clark Explorer Train 31; portraits 17; re-created quarters 154; salt works 189–190; southernmost extent of travels 180
Lewis and Clark National Wildlife Refuge: 202
Lewis and Clark Salt Works: 189–190
Liberty Theater: 208
life vests/jackets: 43
lighthouses: Bullards Beach State Park 77; Cape Blanco 72; Cape Meares 163; Coquille River 78; Haceta Head Lighthouse 96, 106; Tillamook Rock Lighthouse 179; Umpqua Lighthouse State Park 98; Yaquina Bay State Park 127; Yaquina Head 129
Lincoln City: 143–152; accommodations 145–148; beach 143–144; climate 5; events 150–151; food 148–150; map 144; services 151–152
litter collection: 3
logging: 19
low intertidal zone: 9

M
mail: 41–42
mammals, land: 12–13
Manzanita: 174–177
"marine gardens": 140, 179
Marine Science Center: 124–125
marshes, coastal salt: 8–9

Museums

Astoria Children's Museum: 201
Chetco Valley Historical Society Museum: 54
Columbia River Maritime Museum: 200
Coos Art Museum: 86–87
Coos County Historical Museum: 87
Coquille River Museum: 76
Curry County Historical Museum: 62
Flavel House Museum: 201–202
Fort Stevens Military Museum: 205
Heritage Museum: 199, 201
Marshfield Sun Printing Museum: 87
North Lincoln County Historical Museum: 145
Oregon Coast History Center: 125–126
Rogue River Museum: 62
Seaside Historical Museum: 189
Siuslaw Pioneer Museum: 104
Tillamook Air Museum: 166
Tillamook County Pioneer Museum: 167
Uppertown Firefighters Museum: 201

matsutake mushrooms: 9
Maybeck, Bernard: 51
microbreweries: 132
mid-intertidal zone: 9
migration, annual whale: 12
Mill Beach: 55
Mill Casino: 84, 91
mineral deposits: 3
mining, potential offshore: 3
Missoula Flood: 3
Mo's Fish Shanty: 37
money: 40–41
Monterey cypress: 54
mountain beavers: 12
Munson Creek Falls: 167
mushrooms: general discussion 9; festivals 116; picking 168
myrtles, Oregon: 7–8
Myrtlewood: 90

N
Native Americans: crafts 157; culture 16; fight with white settlers 18; history 16; Rogue Indian wars 70; Tsalila 100; vision quests 71
Natural Bridges Cove: 55–56
Neahkahnie Mountain: 174–176

Necanicum River: 187
Nehalem: 172–174
Nehalem Bay: 171–177; general discussion 154; accommodations 176; food 176–177; Manzanita 174–177; Nehalem 172–174; Wheeler 171–172
Nehalem Bay State Park: 174
Nehalem Belle: 172
Neskowin: 155
Netarts: 161
Newport: 123–137; accommodations 132–134; Bayfront District 126–127; climate 5; events 131–132; food 134–136; map 124; Oregon Coast Aquarium 125; recreation 130–131; services 137; sights 124–130
North Coast: 153–215; general discussion 153–154; Astoria 195–215; Cannon Beach 177–186; Cascade Head Scenic Research Area 155–157; map 154; Nehalem Bay 171–177; Seaside and Gearhart 187–195; Three Capes Scenic Loop 157–163; Tillamook 164–169
Northwest Forest Pass: 31–32
Northwest Passage, quest for the: 17
nutria: 12
Nye Beach: 127–128

O
Oceanside: 161–163
Octopus Tree: 163
Ona Beach State Park: 120
Oregon Coast Aquarium: 97, 125
Oregon Coast Explorer Train: 167
Oregon Coast Highway: 48–49
Oregon Coast History Center: 125–126
Oregon Coast Trail: 24
Oregon Connection: 90
Oregon Donation Land Act: 70
Oregon Islands National Wildlife Refuge: general discussion 10; Bandon area sea stacks 77; Bird Island 55; Haystack Rock 179
Oregon Pacific Coast Passport: 30
Oregon State University Hatfield Marine Science Center: 124–125
Oswald West State Park: 174–176
Otter Crest Loop: 138–140
otters: 11
oyster industry: 123

P
Pacific City: 158–160
Pacific giant salamander: 13

Parks and Wildlife Refuges

Alfred A. Loeb State Park: 56
Bandon Marsh National Wildlife Refuge: 78
Buena Vista State Park: 63
Bullards Beach State Park: 77–78
Cape Arago State Park: 89
Cape Blanco State Park: 72
Cape Lookout State Park: 161
Cascade Head Scenic Research Area: 155–157
Cummin's Creek Wilderness: 115
Dean Creek Elk Viewing Area: 98
Devil's Elbow: 106
Drift Creek Wilderness: 120, 120–121
Ecola State Park: 180
fees and passes: 29–32
Fort Stevens State Park: 204–206
Grassy Knob Wilderness: 72–73
Harris Beach State Park: 54–55
Hug Point State Park: 178
Jessie M. Honeyman Memorial State Park: 104–105
Kalmiopsis Wilderness: 51, 56–57

Lewis and Clark National Wildlife Refuge: 189–190
Nehalem Bay State Park: 174
Neptune State Park: 115
Oregon Islands National Wildlife Refuge: 10
Oswald West State Park: 174–176
Pistol River State Park: 63
Port Orford Heads State Park: 71
Robert Straub State Park: 159
Samuel Boardman State Park: 51
Shore Acres State Park: 87–88
Siskiyou National Forest: 51
Smelt Sands State Recreation Site: 114
Sunset Bay State Park: 87
Three Arch Rocks Wildlife Refuge: 161–162
Twilight Creek Eagle Sanctuary: 202
Yachats State Recreation Area: 114–115
Yaquina Bay State Park: 127
Yaquina Head Outstanding Natural Area: 128–129

Pacific harbor seals: 11
Peoples, First: *see* Native Americans
Peter Iredale: 205
petting park, animal: 78
phone services: 42
pine needles, identifying: 7
plane travel: 45
plants: 7–9, 105
Port Orford: 70–74; accommodations 73–74; climate 5; food 74; recreation 73; sights 70–73
Port Orford cedar: 51
Port Orford Heads State Park: 71
postal service: 41–42
prairie headlands, Cascade Head: 155–156
prawns: 38
Prefontaine, Steve: 92
Prehistoric Gardens: 71–72
Proposal Rock: 155
public transportation: 45

QR

Quail Prairie Lookout: 57
rafting: Rogue River 62; Siltcoos Lake 107
recreation: 21–34
Redwood Nature Trail: 56
redwoods: 51, 120
Reedsport: 97–103; accommodations 100–102; food 103; recreation 99; sights 97–98
rental cars: 49
resort community, Seaside: 187
River Theater: 208
road conditions: 48–49
Robert Straub State Park: 159
Rockaway Beach: 170–171
Rogue Indian wars: 18, 70
Rogue River: 64
routes to the coast, auto: 47–49

S

Saddle Mountain: 181
safety: 42–43
salamander, Pacific giant: 13
sales tax, lack of: 40–41
salmon: 14–15, 25
salt marshes: 8–9
Samuel Boardman State Park: 51
Samuel H. Boardman State Scenic Corridor: 55–56
Sand Beach Campground: 160
sandcastle-building: 80, 150, 181

sand dunes: *see* dunes
Sand Lake: 160
Sandpines Golf Course: 107
sand verbena, pink: 8
Scandinavian Midsummer Festival: 207
scenic drives: Hunter's Creek Road 64; Otter Crest Loop 138–140; Samuel H. Boardman State Scenic Corridor 54–55; Three Capes Scenic Loop 153, 157–163; Twenty Miracle Miles 137
seabirds: 10
sea caves: 96
seafood: 38
Sea Lion Caves: 96, 105
sea lions: 11, 105
Seal Rock State Recreation Site: 120
seals, Pacific: 11
sea otters: 11
Seaside: 187–195; accommodations 192–193; food 193–194; map 188; recreation 190–192; sights 188–190
seismic activity: 2, 44
Shanghaied in Astoria: 208
Shark: 177
shipwrecks: Coos Bay 86; *Glenesslin* 173; *Peter Iredale* 205; *Shark* 177
shoes, beachcombing for: 189
shopping: 33–34
Shore Acres State Park: 87–88
Siletz Bay: 143
Siletz Reservation: 18
Siletz tribes: 18
Siltcoos Lake: 107
Siltcoos River: 107
Silver Falls: 90
silver salmon: 14
Siskiyou National Forest: 51
Sitka Center for Art and Ecology: 157
Sitka spruce: general discussion 8; Octopus Tree 163; scientific study of 155; world's tallest 179
Siuslaw River Bridge: 104
slugs: 13
sneaker waves: 44
snowy plover, western: 11
South Coast: 50–95; general discussion 50–51; Bandon 75–83; Bay Area 84–95; Brookings-Harbor 51–61; Gold Beach 62–70; maps 52–53; Port Orford 70–75
South Slough Estuarine Research Reserve: 89
spotted owls: 120

spruce: 7, 155; *see also* Sitka spruce
steelhead trout: 14–15
Steller sea lions: 11
Sunset Bay State Park: 87
surfing: Cove, the 191; gear 191; Indian Beach 180; Robert Straub State Park 159; Smuggler's Cove 175; Sunset Bay State Park 87
swimming risks: 42, 43
Sylvia Beach Hotel: 132

T
tectonics: 2
telephone services: 42
terrain, dangerous: 44
Thomas Creek Bridge: 55
Three Arch Rocks Wildlife Refuge: 161–162
Three Capes Scenic Loop: 157–163; general discussion 153; Cape Kiwanda 157–158; Cape Lookout 160–161; Cape Meares 161; map 158; Pacific City 158–160
Three Rocks Road: 156
Tichenor, William: 70
tide charts: 22
tidepools: Buena Vista State Park 63; Cape Arago State Park 89; Haystack Rock 179; Hug Point State Park 178; inhabitants 9–10; Lincoln City beach 143; Marine Gardens 140; Myers Beach 63; Nesika Beach 63–64; Seal Rock State Recreation Site 120; Shore Acres State Park 88; Smelt Sands State Recreation Site 114; wheelchair-accessible 128
Tillamook: 164–169; accommodations 168; cheese 153–154; climate 5; food 168–169; recreation 167–168; sights 165–167
Tillamook Air Museum: 166
Tillamook Burn: 164
Tillamook Cheese Factory: 165–166
Tillamook County Creamery Association: 164
Tillamook County Pioneer Museum: 167
Tillamook Rock Lighthouse: 179
tipping: 38
Toledo: 130
Tolovana Beach: 178
tours: bicycling 23; Oregon Connection 90; seaplane 107–108; Tillamook Cheese Factory 165; walking 199
trains: 167, 174
train travel: 45–47
transcontinental railroad: 90

transportation: 45–49
travel times, recommended: 6
treasure, pirate: 175
trees: 7–8
tsunamis: 2, 44–45
Twilight Creek Eagle Sanctuary: 202

UV
U.S. 101 (Highway 101): 48–49
U.S. Navy blimp hangar: 164
Umpqua Discovery Center: 97–98
Umpqua Lighthouse State Park: 98
United Nations Biosphere Reserves: 155
Uppertown Firefighters Museum: 201
vacation rentals: 35
visitors centers: 40–41
volcanic activity: 3
Vulcan Lake: 57

WXYZ
Waldport: 120–123
waterfalls: Golden and Silver Falls State Park 90; Munson Creek Falls 167; Tillamook State Forest 168
water-skiing: 73
waves, sneaker: 44
weather: 4–6
Wedderburn: 62
West Coast Game Park: 78
western snowy plover: 11
Westin Salishan Golf Links: 145
wetlands, freshwater: 8
Whale Cove: 138, 139
whale-watching: Betty Kay Charters 91; by land 22–23; Newport area 130; by sea 23; Seal Rock State Recreation Site 120; Whale Watching Spoken Here 22
Whale Watching Spoken Here: 120
wheelchair-accessible tidepools: 128
Wheeler: 171–172
Whiskey Run Beach: 89–90
white settlers: 17–18
wildflowers: 8
wildlife: 9–15
Willamette Valley formation: 3
Winchester Bay: 97–103; accommodations 100–102; food 103; recreation 99; sights 97–98
windsurfing: Bullards Beach State Park 73–74; Floras Lake 73; Nehalem Bay State Park 174;

Pistol River State Park 63; Pistol River Wave Basin National Windsurfing Competition 66
wineries: Flying Dutchman Winery 140; Nehalem Bay Winery 174; Shallon Tasting Room 214
World War II sentry towers: 55
Yachats: 113–119; accommodations 116–118; Cape Perpetua 113–114; food 118–119
Yaquina Bay State Park: 127
Yaquina Head Outstanding Natural Area: 128–129
Young's River: 195

Acknowledgments

This first edition of *Moon Handbooks Coastal Oregon* would not have been possible were it not for *Moon Handbooks Oregon,* penned by Stuart Warren and Ted Long Ishikawa. The thoroughly engaging coast chapter formed the solid foundation and inspiration for this guidebook.

The bulk of the information in this book was first fact-checked with the help of every chamber of commerce and visitors center from Astoria to Brookings, whose volunteers and employees are some of the most passionate experts on the coast.

The following Avalon folks were especially helpful during editing and production: Mia Lipman, Naomi Dancis, Mike Morgenfeld, and Deb Dutcher. They can now attest to the fact that old Moondogs can learn new tricks.

For assistance with photos and illustrations, thanks go to Mark Simon of Image Perfect & Design, Lynsey Turek of Windsor Nature Discovery, Bob Ward of the Drake in Oregon Society, Jane Kirby of the Salem Public Library, Karen Stevens of Independence National Historical Park, Tim Backer of the Oregon State Archives, and Christine Campbell of the British Library.

And while they're too young to read this now, we also want to thank our children (Eamon and Fiona) for learning to be patient. Thanks, too, to our loyal babysitters: Grandma Suzie, Grandpa Clark, Jamie Benedict, and Julie Davis.

And we have to thank McKinley, for bringing lime soda and tofu dip at just the right time.

U.S.~Metric Conversion

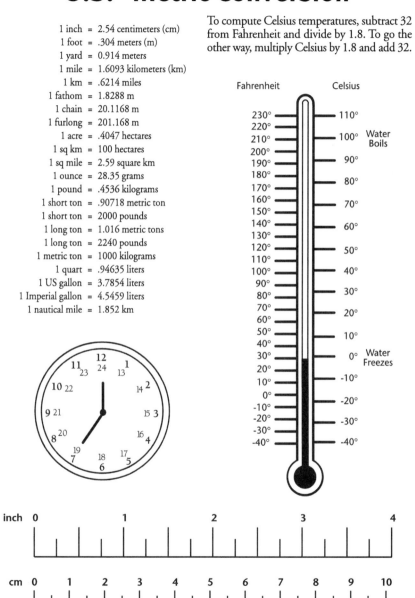

1 inch	=	2.54 centimeters (cm)
1 foot	=	.304 meters (m)
1 yard	=	0.914 meters
1 mile	=	1.6093 kilometers (km)
1 km	=	.6214 miles
1 fathom	=	1.8288 m
1 chain	=	20.1168 m
1 furlong	=	201.168 m
1 acre	=	.4047 hectares
1 sq km	=	100 hectares
1 sq mile	=	2.59 square km
1 ounce	=	28.35 grams
1 pound	=	.4536 kilograms
1 short ton	=	.90718 metric ton
1 short ton	=	2000 pounds
1 long ton	=	1.016 metric tons
1 long ton	=	2240 pounds
1 metric ton	=	1000 kilograms
1 quart	=	.94635 liters
1 US gallon	=	3.7854 liters
1 Imperial gallon	=	4.5459 liters
1 nautical mile	=	1.852 km

To compute Celsius temperatures, subtract 32 from Fahrenheit and divide by 1.8. To go the other way, multiply Celsius by 1.8 and add 32.

Fahrenheit   Celsius

Water Boils

Water Freezes

inch
cm

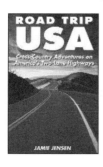

Keeping Current

Although we strive to produce the most up-to-date guidebook humanly possible, change is unavoidable. Between the time this book goes to print and the moment you read it, a handful of the businesses noted in these pages will undoubtedly change prices, move, or even close their doors forever. Other worthy attractions will open for the first time. If you have a favorite gem you'd like to see included in the next edition, or see anything that needs updating, clarification, or correction, please drop us a line. Send your comments via email to atpfeedback@avalonpub.com, or use the address below.

Moon Handbooks Coastal Oregon
Avalon Travel Publishing
1400 65th Street, Suite 250
Emeryville, CA 94608, USA
www.moon.com

Editor: Mia Lipman
Series Manager: Kevin McLain
Copy Editor: Ginjer Clarke
Graphics Coordinator: Deb Dutcher
Production Coordinator: Jacob Goolkasian
Cover Designer: Kari Gim
Interior Designers: Amber Pirker,
    Alvaro Villanueva, and Kelly Pendragon
Map Editor: Naomi Adler Dancis
Cartographers: Kat Kalamaras and
    Mike Morgenfeld
Proofreader: Erika Howsare
Indexer: Rachel Kuhn

ISBN: 1-56691-658-5
ISSN: 1546-136X

Printing History
1st Edition—March 2004
5 4 3 2 1

Text © 2004 by Elizabeth and Mark Morris
Maps © 2004 by Avalon Travel Publishing, Inc.
All rights reserved.

Avalon Travel Publishing is a division of Avalon Publishing Group, Inc.

Some photos and illustrations are used by permission and are the property of the original copyright owners.

Front cover photo: Coastline, Bandon © Frazier/Folio, Inc.
Table of Contents photos: © Mark Morris

Printed in the USA by Malloy